NEURAL NETWORKS FOR VISION, SPEECH AND NATURAL LANGUAGE

BT Telecommunications Series

The BT Telecommunications Series covers the broad spectrum of telecommunications technology. Volumes are the result of research and development carried out, or funded by, BT, and represent the latest advances in the field.

The series includes volumes on underlying technologies as well as telecommunications. These books will be essential reading for those in research and development in telecommunications, in electronics and in computer science.

1. *Neural Networks for Vision, Speech and Natural Language*
   Edited by R Linggard, D J Myers and C Nightingale.
2. *Audiovisual Telecommunications*
   Edited by N Kenyon and C Nightingale
3. *Telecommunications Local Networks*
   Edited by W R Ritchie and J Stern
4. *Digital Signal Processing in Telecommunications*
   Edited by F Westall and A Ip

NEURAL NETWORKS FOR VISION, SPEECH AND NATURAL LANGUAGE

Edited by

R Linggard

*Formerly BT Laboratories;
currently Professor, School of Information Systems,
University of East Anglia, Norwich, UK*

D J Myers

BT Laboratories, Martlesham Heath, UK

and

C Nightingale

BT Laboratories, Martlesham Heath, UK

CHAPMAN & HALL
London · New York · Tokyo · Melbourne · Madras

Published by Chapman & Hall, 2-6 Boundary Row, London SE1 8HN, UK

Chapman & Hall, 2-6 Boundary Row, London SE1 8HN, UK

Blackie Academic & Professional, Wester Cleddens Road, Bishopbriggs, Glasgow G64 2NZ, UK

Chapman & Hall Inc., One Penn Plaza, 41st Floor, New York NY 10119, USA

Chapman & Hall Japan, Thomson Publishing Japan, Hirakawacho Nemoto Building, 6F, 1-7-11 Hirakawa-cho, Chiyoda-ku, Tokyo 102, Japan

Chapman & Hall Australia, Thomas Nelson Australia, 102 Dodds Street, South Melbourne, Victoria 3205, Australia

Chapman & Hall India, R. Seshadri, 32 Second Main Road, CIT East, Madras 600 035, India

First edition 1992
Reprinted 1994

© 1992 British Telecommunications plc

Printed in Great Britain at the University Press, Cambridge.

ISBN   0   412   43000 2   0 442 31579 1 (USA)

Apart from any fair dealing for the purposes of research or private study, or criticism or review, as permitted under the UK Copyright Designs and Patents Act, 1988, this publication may not be reproduced, stored, or transmitted, in any form or by any means, without the prior permission in writing of the publishers, or in the case of reprographic reproduction only in accordance with the terms of the licences issued by the Copyright Licensing Agency in the UK, or in accordance with the terms of licences issued by the appropriate Reproduction Rights Organization outside the UK. Enquiries concerning reproduction outside the terms stated here should be sent to the publishers at the London address printed on this page.

The publisher makes no representation, express or implied, with regard to the accuracy of the information contained in this book and cannot accept any legal responsibility or liability for any errors or omissions that may be made.

A catalogue record for this book is available from the British Library

Library of Congress Cataloging-in-Publication Data available

Contents

Contributors ix
Preface xi

**Introduction: neural networks for vision, speech
and natural language** 1
C Nightingale, D J Myers and R Linggard

PART 1 VISION

Neural networks for vision: an introduction 5
C Nightingale

1 **Image feature location in multi-resolution images using a
   hierarchy of multilayer perceptrons** 13
   J M Vincent, D J Myers and R A Hutchinson

2 **Training multilayer perceptrons for facial feature location:
   a case study** 30
   J B Waite

3 **The detection of eyes in facial images using radial
   basis functions** 50
   R M Debenham and S C J Garth

4 **A neural network feature detector using a
   multi-resolution pyramid** 65
   C C Hand, M R Evans and S W Ellacott

5 **Training and testing of neural net window
   operators on spatiotemporal image sequences** 93
   M J Wright

6 **Image classification using Gabor representations with
   a neural net** 112
   P J G Lisboa

PART 2 SPEECH

Neural networks for speech processing: an introduction 129
R Linggard

7 **Spoken alphabet recognition using multilayer perceptrons** 135
P C Woodland

8 **Speaker independent vowel recognition** 148
L S Smith and C Tang

9 **Dissection of perceptron structures in speech and speaker recognition** 160
J S Mason and E C J Andrews

10 **Segmental sub-word unit classification using a multilayer perceptron** 177
S G Smyth

PART 3 NATURAL LANGUAGE

Connectionist natural language processing: an introduction 193
P J Wyard

11 **A single layer higher order neural net and its applications to context free grammar recognition** 203
P J Wyard and C Nightingale

12 **Functional compositionality and soft preference rules** 235
N E Sharkey

13 **Applications of multilayer perceptrons in text-to-speech synthesis systems** 256
W A Ainsworth and N P Warren

PART 4 IMPLEMENTATION

Hardware implementation of neural networks: an introduction 289
D J Myers

14 **Finite wordlength, integer arithmetic multilayer perceptron modelling for hardware realization** 293
J M Vincent

15	**A VSLI architecture for implementing neural networks with on-chip backpropagation learning** D J Myers, J M Vincent and D A Orrey	312
16	**An opto-electronic neural network processor** N Barnes, P Healey, P McKee, A W O'Neill, M A Z Rejman-Greene, E G Scott, R P Webb and D C Wood	330

PART 5   ARCHITECTURES

	Architectures: an introduction C Nightingale	**349**
17	**A dynamic topology net** C Nightingale	353
18	**The stochastic search network** J M Bishop and P Torr	370
19	**Node sequence networks** R Linggard	388
20	**Some dynamical properties of neural networks** S Olafsson	410
	Index	439

Contributors

W A Ainsworth	Department of Communication and Neuroscience, University of Keele
E C J Andrews	Department of Electrical and Electronic Engineering, University College, Swansea
N Barnes	Network Research, BT Laboratories
J M Bishop	Department of Cybernetics, University of Reading
R M Debenham	Department of Engineering, University of Cambridge
S W Ellacott	Information Technology Research Institute, Brighton Polytechnic
M R Evans	Information Technology Research Institute, Brighton Polytechnic
S C J Garth	Department of Engineering, University of Cambridge
C C Hand	Information Technology Research Institute, Brighton Polytechnic
P Healey	Network Research, BT Laboratories
R A Hutchinson	Broadband and Visual Networks, BT Laboratories
R Linggard	School of Information Systems, University of East Anglia
P J G Lisboa	Department of Electrical Engineering, University of Liverpool
P McKee	Network Research, BT Laboratories
J S Mason	Department of Electrical and Electronic Engineering, University College, Swansea
D J Myers	Broadband and Visual Networks, BT Laboratories
C Nightingale	Broadband and Visual Networks, BT Laboratories
S Olafsson	Advanced Concepts Unit, BT Laboratories

CONTRIBUTORS

A W O'Neill	Network Research, BT Laboratories
D A Orrey	Speech Applications, BT Laboratories
M A Z Rejman-Greene	Network Research, BT Laboratories
E G Scott	Network Research, BT Laboratories
N E Sharkey	Department of Computer Science, University of Exeter
L S Smith	Centre for Cognitive and Computational Neuroscience, University of Stirling
S G Smyth	Speech Applications, BT Laboratories
C Tang	Centre for Cognitive and Computational Neuroscience, University of Stirling
P Torr	Department of Cybernetics, University of Reading
J M Vincent	Broadband and Visual Networks, BT Laboratories
J B Waite	Broadband and Visual Networks, BT Laboratories
N P Warren	Formerly Department of Communication and Neuroscience, University of Keele; currently Speech Applications, BT Laboratories
R P Webb	Network Research, BT Laboratories
D C Wood	Network Research, BT Laboratories
P C Woodland	Department of Engineering, University of Cambridge
M J Wright	Department of Human Sciences, Brunel, The University of West London
P J Wyard	Speech Applications, BT Laboratories

Preface

This book is a collection of chapters describing work carried out as part of a large project at BT Laboratories to study the application of connectionist methods to problems in vision, speech and natural language processing. Also, since the theoretical formulation and the hardware realization of neural networks are significant tasks in themselves, these problems too were addressed. The book, therefore, is divided into five Parts, reporting results in vision, speech, natural language, hardware implementation and network architectures.

The three editors of this book have, at one time or another, been involved in planning and running the connectionist project. From the outset, we were concerned to involve the academic community as widely as possible, and consequently, in its first year, over thirty university research groups were funded for small scale studies on the various topics. Co-ordinating such a widely spread project was no small task, and in order to concentrate minds and resources, sets of test problems were devised which were typical of the application areas and were difficult enough to be worthy of study. These are described in the text, and constitute one of the successes of the project.

Research in a commercial environment carries with it obligations of confidentiality; we are grateful, therefore, to BT research managers, not only for permission to publish this book, but also for their active encouragement to do so. In particular, we would like to thank Ian Corbett, Manager of the Connectionist project. We also wish to express our thanks to Peter Wyard for his contribution to the part on natural language, and to Jon Waite for his reviews of the more mathematical chapters. Special thanks are due to David Clough, of BT Laboratories' Design and Production Services, who, with limitless patience, co-ordinated the production of the book. Thanks too, to Ellen Taylor, Computer Science Editor of Chapman & Hall, for calmness in the storm and gentle pressure when our sails flagged. But our final, and most fulsome, thanks must go to the authors themselves, who laboured long and late in pursuing the research objectives and in preparing manuscripts for this book.

Of the chapters in the book, ten originated in universities and ten in BT Laboratories. Of the authors, two who worked on the project at BT are now in universities, and one from a university is now with BT Laboratories. We think that this is a fair indication of the co-operation and interaction which has taken place between academia and BT. The material in the chapters was chosen to represent the main activities in the five research areas; naturally, the opinions expressed in them are those of the authors themselves and do not represent official BT policy.

R Linggard, D J Myers and C Nightingale
BT Laboratories
Martlesham Heath
Suffolk, England

Introduction

NEURAL NETWORKS FOR VISION, SPEECH AND NATURAL LANGUAGE

C Nightingale, D J Myers and R Linggard*
BT Laboratories and
*School of Information Systems, University of East Anglia

The field of artificial neural nets (ANNs), sometimes called connectionism, has risen to some prominence over the last few years. Regular conferences, for example the international joint conference on neural networks, draw several thousand attendees, and a society — The International Neural Network Society — and several new journals, e.g. 'Neural Networks', IEEE Trans on Neural Networks and 'Connection Science' devoted exclusively to the study of ANNs have come into existence in the last four years. In addition many new books on the subject are appearing. Increased knowledge of the physiology of the brain, and the advances made in many aspects of computational science and engineering have been important in inspiring work in this burgeoning field.

Of course our present understanding of the brain is not sufficient to enable any attempt at building a realistic model of a brain, animal or human. Indeed the modelling of even a single neuron could not be confidently essayed with current knowledge, even though advances in this area are being made. Even if the knowledge did exist it is doubtful whether the technology to implement the knowledge is sufficiently advanced.

It is thus not particularly easy to give a definition of what is meant by a neural net. If they are regarded as general algorithms, and the weights seen as parameters in an optimisation process it is difficult to see why they arouse

2 GENERAL INTRODUCTION

so much interest. It is probably better to regard them as biologically inspired devices whose ultimate development would be engineered brains, but whose intermediate stages of development may provide solutions to difficult problems. Studies being made in the field at present concentrate on sets of simple processors, highly interconnected with weighted connections, and operating in parallel, whose behaviour loosely relates to the brain's operation. They are usually capable of self-organisation either by learning in a supervised mode, in which particular responses are learned by example, or in an unsupervised mode in which regularities inherent in the data may be reflected in the final organisation of the connection weights of the network.

Whilst the theory of these ANNs is of importance, one of the main reasons for the current level of activity as mentioned above, is in the hopes vested in them for solving a number of difficult problems. This underlying motivation for the study of ANNs is the consciousness that the brain, both human and animal, seems capable of easily performing many tasks which are either difficult, or impossible for conventional serial computers (Von Neumann machines). Examples include the recognition and understanding of speech in humans, the interpretation of natural scenes and the sophisticated methods of control which allow animals ubiquitous movement.

Since the field is firmly rooted in these expectations of practical success, it is appropriate to report on the results of a coherent study of ANNs made from the point of view of solving practical problems in telecommunications using them. The problems mentioned above, in relation to speech and natural language are likely to be of crucial importance in the near future for allowing automated services over telephone networks. Slightly further into the future many requirements for image analysis are likely to arise in connection with automated database search, surveillance and image data compression. These human computer interface problems of advanced telecommunications are the critical areas for ANNs. They have proved more or less intractable for conventional computational techniques, and offer a significant challenge for the neural computing approach.

One difficulty with the plethora of literature reporting on ANNs is in determining which are the most promising methods for addressing the problems at hand. Reports on a variety of paradigms and training methods rarely do other than compare a new neural technique with a conventional technique, using data which is either of a very simple nature, such as the well known XOR problem, or which is unique to the experiments described. In such a case it is not possible to judge whether significant advances have really been made, or whether the new method would justify adoption for a practical problem.

This book attempts to make up for this weakness in the literature by describing a programme of work in which some thought and effort was given to the necessity for applying various techniques to some specially developed test problems with standard data. The program of work arose through the initiation of a connectionist project at BT Laboratories (BTL) whose objective was to evaluate neural nets for solving problems in the areas of speech, vision and natural language. Work in connectionism had been going on at BTL for a number of years, in particular in collaboration with the University of East Anglia and through participation in the Research Initiative in Pattern Recognition (RIPR). Interest began to increase in 1986 and 1987 principally in the Speech division and the Visual Telecommunication division, and an informal group was formed to exchange ideas and determine a way forward. In addition to the interest in the speech and visual areas, representatives from optical computing, natural language and human factors divisions became involved, and a project was eventually launched in 1988.

From the earliest days the principle of standard test problems and data was embraced, and a lot of early project effort went into preparing the necessary data. Of course there are many reasons why even with such standard test materials it is impractical to arrange a series of experiments in which completely reliable comparisons between different neural paradigms can be made. In the first place in some problems it is not easy to make an exact statement about the objective. It is not completely clear what is meant by locating an image feature whose shape is fairly amorphous. Of course the data could be manually tagged with target points, but this requires a lot of effort, and even humans cannot perform this task with great reliability. It is also not easy to compare certain types of paradigm with others — unsupervised nets with supervised ones, for example. Even so, the use of similar test data throughout several sections of the book introduces an element of comparability which is very useful.

One important aspect of the project was an intention to collaborate with as many university groups as possible, and here the existence of the test problems and data was invaluable. Such data was attractive to the academic partners since it saved them considerable time and effort, and enabled them to compare their own results with those of other groups. In addition it had the advantage of being related to real-world tasks whose solution was of value to BT. From the BT point of view it enabled them to quickly spot work which was showing promise.

The book is an account of the more successful studies that were carried out under the project; it is largely a set of case studies, in many cases linked by the commonality of test data and objectives. The original intention, for both the in-house BTL work, and the university collaborations was to apply as many different neural paradigms to the selected test problems as possible; in practice certain paradigms, particularly the multi-layer-perceptron (MLP) have tended to dominate. The reason for this is that for practical problems, where more emphasis is placed upon error percentages than on the biological plausibility of the nets, this paradigm has proved the most successful. Even so, the book does include a number of chapters describing experiments with other architectures some of which claim to be inspired by biological models to a greater or lesser extent. In addition, because some of the potential applications areas covered will require real-time operation, the problem of implementation is addressed, using both conventional VLSI techniques and novel opto-electronic realisations.

Part 1 — Vision

NEURAL NETWORKS FOR VISION: AN INTRODUCTION

C Nightingale
BT Laboratories

1. IMAGE PROCESSING

Image processing and pattern recognition have been an important area of application of neural nets since early days. Neurally inspired machines, like WISARD [1] have already been used in commercial applications, and complex multilayered neural architectures like the Neocognitron [2] have made advances in important areas of potential application. It is not possible to do full justice to the many contributions to this fertile area of research in a book of this size. One difficulty arises with the very varied nature of both the types of net and the applications, in that it is very rare to be able to compare like with like when examining the work of different authors. A feature of the research program described in this book is the concentration of developments on a restricted problem area. The recognition and location of features in a face has strong motivation in visual telecommunications, for improving the quality of videotelephony images. It is appropriate to have concentrated on this problem because of its relevance, and to allow comparison of different neural network techniques. There are of course visual telecommunications applications for neural nets other than feature extraction. Noise reduction and image compression are also areas where work has been done, and these topics are briefly discussed. The nature of the test data that forms the basis of the experiments reported in the chapters of this section is described.

1.1 Image coding

Image compression and coding has been an important theoretical and practical field since the possibility of digital transmission of images became feasible. Coding algorithms and techniques are well advanced, and it is likely that they already achieve near optimal performance, if techniques in which no higher level knowledge of the picture content is employed. For this reason, although interesting work has been done in conventional image compression using neural nets, it has not been a central theme of neural computation. The work on conventional coding that has been done has used various neural approaches. The hidden layers of a multilayer perceptron (MLP) [3] can be used to store an internal representation of an image block, as in the work of Cotrell [4]. Another approach is to use the associative memory aspects of neural nets to achieve compression, by associating a smaller transmitted vector with each input vector. This effectively emulates a well known image compression technique called vector quantisation, in which a codebook of vectors is searched to yield a representative vector for each block in an image. In a recent study performed at BT Laboratories [5] a number of neural techniques and a conventional technique were tested on an image compression problem. The conventional technique used was the Linde, Buzo and Gray (LBG) vector quantisation algorithm, [6], which was compared to an MLP, a modified Kohonen net [7], and some related nets. In the case of the MLP, training was performed by autoassociating 4×4 blocks of an image, in training, and using the hidden layer, which consisted of either four or two elements, to encode the information. The hidden unit data can then be transmitted, and the layer of weights succeeding the hidden layer can decode the incoming hidden layer information to produce an image block. The process of training the MLP is more computationally intensive than the LBG process for designing a vector quantiser, but the encoding process for an MLP is much less intensive. As far as decoding goes the LBG decoding process is merely a look up table, and it is therefore simpler than that of the MLP. In the case of the Kohonen net the normal unsupervised process can be used to train a neural net to cluster set of blocks in an image. The best representative for the cluster can be calculated using an averaging process weighted by the frequency with which particular input patterns are encountered. When the net is in use as a coder, the unit which fires in the Kohonen layer indicates the codebook code to be transmitted, and the representative block may be displayed. The computational requirement in all phases of the Kohonen net is similar to that of the LBG algorithm. The Kohonen net performed better than the conventional LBG coder, both as a stand alone coder, and as a building block for an adaptive transform coding system — which was superior to all the other techniques. The back-propagation algorithms gave inferior performance to both the Kohonen net and the LBG algorithm, but there was evidence to suggest that the performance could have been improved by more optimisation of parameters. Considering the small amount of effort that was expended in this area results have been promising, however in view of the importance of emerging world standards in this area the work was not pursued.

1.2 Image enhancement

An important class of image processing operations is that of image enhancement. Images may be impaired by the addition of various forms of noise. The noise can arise from the original source, or from the processes of transmission and encoding and decoding. One problem with attempting to transmit only changed information in an image sequence, is that of distinguishing between pixels which have changed from one frame to the next because of these typical random fluctuations associated with electronic imaging and those due to real changes in the transmitted scene. If noise is transmitted, not only does it constitute an impairment in itself, but it wastes transmission capacity, and therefore either increases the cost or reduces the quality of the transmitted pictures. This problem also arises with still pictures.

Neural nets have been proposed as a possible means of improving noise reduction in images. In particular MLPs can be used to filter images; training sets can consist of impaired images as the input set, with noise-free images as output. In one approach the input data consists of a moving sequence with added noise and the output data consists of the original sequence without the addition of the noise. The net then requires two input arrays, each corresponding to the same part of the image but in successive frames. Training can consist of scanning the two input frames over successive frames of a moving sequence, and the required output array over the second of the two corresponding frames of the uncorrupted sequence. After a sufficient training period the net may then be tested on a different part of the same sequence and its performance determined using mean square error criteria in addition to subjective criteria. In Chapter 5 Wright has performed some experiments in which neural net operators trained on natural images and sequences of images learned spatial or spatiotemporal filter functions.

1.2 Image analysis

The ability to perform reliable automatic image analysis enables a great number of potential applications. There are obvious military requirements for methods whereby targets can be automatically recognised and tracked. The presence of significant features on large satellite images could ideally be automatically recorded. Civil applications also abound. Methods whereby medical images can be analysed for tumours or other pathological manifestations can aid in diagnosis. Industrial robots can benefit from the ability to identify and locate important aspects of their environment. Quality inspection of certain types of product could be automated using visual information, either by itself or in combination with other techniques. There are also applications in visual telecommunications. Surveillance could benefit from intelligent interpretation of scenes. Model based videophone coding requires that heads can be identified and located, and that the features of a face can be identified and their positions tracked. Automatic face recognition requires similar capability. And in the long term if images of all kinds could be automatically characterised, new opportunities in classifying and relating the huge explosion of electronically stored images would arise.

From the above we see that image analysis is a large and potentially fruitful area of study. Many great minds have addressed themselves to the problems of vision in the past, including many famous scientists and philosophers — Isaac Newton and Ludwig Wittgenstein being two examples. In their day though, the capability of testing hypotheses did not yet exist. Today there is a very large international research effort in this and related areas — see for example [8]. Pattern recognition, computer vision and image feature extraction have been the objects of intense and thorough study. Yet in spite of the depth of knowledge, the complexity and ingenuity of image analysis systems, and the very powerful processing capability currently available it is doubtful whether anyone either inside or outside the field would claim that generally speaking the problems of image analysis are near to being solved. There are even suggestions that work in the area of machine vision has to some extent failed — see [9] for an example. The lack of standard test problems has led to difficulties in assessing the true worth of some techniques. Ad hoc solutions to certain restricted problems do exist, but these methods are seldom robust and the general problem of finding even fairly simple shapes and features in many images remains unsolved. Although there are many things that can be done with a computer that are quite beyond the powers of the human brain to solve directly, as far as vision is concerned the human brain and most animal brains are still immeasurably superior to computers.

Some reasons for the failure of many computer algorithms are simple. Although we recognise certain features in images which are self-evidently important for understanding them — boundaries of objects for example — their existence is often not deducible from simple measurements, such as edge detectors. Similarly many features that are not important for understanding images — irrelevant shadows for example — constantly give false responses to any measuring scheme designed to detect useful and relevant features. Variations in lighting and tone are constantly mistaken for evidence of non-existent objects, or lead to the suppression of features which would help to identify objects. It is not the purpose of this section to exhaustively examine the reasons for the failures of many image analysis programs, but a good example can save a lot of explanation. If someone were asked how to recognise an eye, he or she would be likely to give a good pictorial description of an eye: A petal-shaped region surrounding a lighter background in which a blue, grey, green, brown or even violet disc representing the iris seems to float. In the centre of the disc is another concentric disc, black this time, representing the pupil. And above the eye a dark horizontal streak representing an eyebrow. Yet if the same person is then shown a snapshot of a family group on the beach, in which each head may be only a half-square centimeter in area he or she will unerringly point to the eyes in the image, even though in all probability none of the features previously suggested as characteristics will be visible in the tiny speck-like eyes. And if the image were to be searched for shapes which resemble these specks by any reasonable measure of similarity, there is little doubt that dozens would appear in the shingle or other inappropriate part of the image. It immediately appears that the eyes are only spotted by their positions in the faces. Yet any algorithm designed to find the faces in such an image would almost certainly involve some way of using the eyes as feature characteristics, and we are led to the conclusion that the operation of eye finding involves unravelling a high degree of complex and variable interrelationships between high and low level processes.

Because of the poor performance of many rule-based algorithms, and because of the apparent excellence of biological vision systems it has been very natural to look to the brain as an inspiration for more successful methods for analysing images. Biological vision systems are being studied both from the neurophysical and psychological viewpoints and computational models of the human vision system have been proposed, see [10] for an example. Such models are often complex with several levels of processing and with different representations at different scales. Some of these models have been essentially neural in nature, and there is a very strong relationship between computational models of vision and neural nets. In Chapter 6 in this section Lisboa looks at preprocesses which are based on biological evidence from the early vision system. Other computational approaches to practical image interpetation may be strongly rule based, but it is often true, as in the case of eye-location mentioned above, that the rules become extremely complex and require the simultaneous use of different scales if good recognition is to be obtained. The difficulty of discovering the rules that govern such an intuitive and unconscious human capability inevitably draws research in the direction of learning implicit rules by example. Taken as a whole these considerations mean that vision and image analysis have been an early and very significant application for neural nets. Indeed neural approaches in this field are at least as numerous, and possibly more numerous than in any other field, and it is beyond the scope of this book to review them all. It may be of greater value to compare different neural approaches to a limited problem, to try to obtain some measure of success — the more so since lack of standard experimentation has been cited as one of the causes of the limited progress so far attained in the field of machine vision [9].

1.4 Image processing test problems

The subject matter for connectionist approaches to image analysis is potentially very diverse, and in order to achieve some unity of effort the application of neural nets to vision problems discussed in this book concentrates on the solution to some particular problems.

Probably the most important aspect of image processing in telecommunications is the possibility of improving methods for compression of image data. Uncompressed digitised television pictures may require a transmission channel with a capacity of as much as 216 Mbit/s, which would require thousands of ordinary telephone channels to sustain, which is prohibitively expensive. Consequently there has been a continuing drive towards techniques which reduce the amount of data which must be transmitted, whilst retaining as high a quality as possible. Noise reduction, as described in a previous section, plays an important role in the process of image compression. In addition powerful redundancy removal methods are needed, which must be applied in the space domain for still images, and in both the space and time domain in moving images. Good results have been obtained using algorithms based on the particular statistical characteristic of images as data. International standards for the transmission of still pictures, as well as moving images, at particular bitrates have been established — at 64 kbit/s for example. In the case of moving pictures the recognition of moving areas of the picture, and the prediction and interpolation of frames from existing frames have been an essential part of achieving so much compression whilst retaining adequate image quality. At the present time for rates as low as 64 kbit/s it is usual to transmit a reduced number of frames so that pictures can appear jerky. It is also usual to reduce the requirement for data to be transmitted by using the current frame with some motion estimation to predict the next frame, and transmit only the error between the prediction and the true frame. A method using a synthetic model head whose rotations, translations and mouth movements can be transmitted as simple instructions can form the basis of a very low-bitrate videotelephone [11]. It can also enable better approximations to a true frame to be used to insert missing frames, reducing jerkiness, and to make more accurate predictions so reducing the transmission rate — or improving quality.

If such a model is to be used, it is essential to both locate and track features in a human face, so that correct movements of the face and features can be transmitted to the receiver. A set of about 60 head and shoulders images were digitised at a number of resolutions and formed a common set of data for the experiments on facial feature location described by Vincent in Chapter 1, Waite in Chapter 2, Debenham in Chapter 3 and Hand in Chapter 4. Some experiments on similar data are also described in in the chapter by Bishop and Torr in Part 5 of the book, on architectures.

REFERENCES

1. Aleksander I, Thomas W V and Bowden P A: 'Wisard: a radical step forward in image recognition', Sensor Review, pp 120—124 July (1984).

2. Fukushima K, Miyake S and Ito T: 'Neocognitron: A neural network model for a mechanism of visual pattern recognition' IEEE Trans Systems, Man and Cybernetics, SMC-13, No 5, Sept/Oct (1983).

3. Rumelhart D E, Hinton G E and Williams R J: 'Learning internal representations by error propagation' in 'Parallel distributed processing' 1, in Rumelhart D E and McClelland J L eds, MIT Press, Cambridge, Mass (1986).

4. Cotrell G W, Munro P and Zipser D: 'Learning internal representations for grayscale maps: an example of extensional programming.' pp 461—473, Proceedings of 9th Annual Conf of Cognitive Science, Seattle, Washington.

5. Kaouri H: 'A comparison of the LBG algorithm and neural network based techniques for image vector quantisation' Report on work carried out as a short-term research fellow at BT Laboratories, (July-September 1989).

6. Linde Y, Buzo A and Gray R: 'An algorithm for vector quantiser design', IEE Trans Comm, COM28, No 1, (Jan 1980).

7. Kohonen T: 'Self organisation and associative memory', Springer-Verlag, Berlin, (1984).

8. Fischler M A and Firschein O: 'Readings in computer vision: Issues, problems, principles and paradigms', Morgan Kaufmann, Los Altos, (1987).

9. Jain R C and Binford Thomas O: 'Ignorance, myopia and naivete in computer vision systems', CVGIP: Image Understanding, 53, No 1, pp 112—117, (Jan 1991).

10. Marr D: 'Vision', Freeman, New York, (1982).

11. Welsh W J: 'Model-based image coding', BT Technol J, 8, No 3 (July 1990).

1

IMAGE FEATURE LOCATION IN MULTI-RESOLUTION IMAGES USING A HIERARCHY OF MULTILAYER PERCEPTRONS

J M Vincent, D J Myers, R A Hutchinson
BT Laboratories

1. INTRODUCTION

This chapter describes work undertaken at BT Laboratories to produce a system, based on the use of neural network feature detectors, to robustly locate and track features in digital image sequences. We have concentrated on the location of eyes and mouths in human head-and-shoulders images, as described by Nightingale in the introduction to this part of the book. However the techniques described should be applicable to determining the position of localised features in general images.

In section 2 of this chapter initial experiments are described, which were performed to assess the feasibility of using neural networks as feature detectors in grey scale images, and the results of these experiments, which lead to the formulation of the hierarchical perceptron feature locator (HPFL) architecture, are discussed. Section 3 describes the components of the HPFL system at its present stage of evolution. Conclusions and avenues for further development are discussed in section 4.

2. FIRST EXPERIMENTS

Initially, a number of experiments were performed to assess the feasibility of using neural networks as feature detectors in grey scale images. The MLP, trained using the backpropagation algorithm [1] was chosen as the neural net paradigm to be investigated, although some experiments were conducted using Kohonen self-organising nets [2,3]. Experiments on other networks are described in other chapters (Chapter 18: Stochastic nets, Chapter 3: Radial Basis Functions, and Chapter 4).

Most experiments were performed on data taken from a set consisting of 60 human head-and-shoulder grey scale images, 30 male subjects and 30 female, facing the camera and at approximately the same scale. The images were available at a number of resolutions, including 256×256, 128×128, 32×32 and 16×16 pixel images, each pixel consisting of 8 bits. The lower resolution images were formed by pixel averaging and sub-sampling the 256×256 pixel image. All the images used had associated with them data defining the location of the eye, as determined by a human operator.

The experiments concentrated on locating one eye in the case of higher resolution images, or both eyes in the case of lower resolution images. The form of all the experiments was similar; a $j \times k$ pixel window, which constitutes the input to the MLP, was raster scanned a pixel at a time across the $n \times n$ image. The arrangement is shown schematically in Fig. 1. The MLP had $j \times k$ inputs and a single output node, and was trained to output a high value (1.0) when the input window is centred on the eye, the response tailing

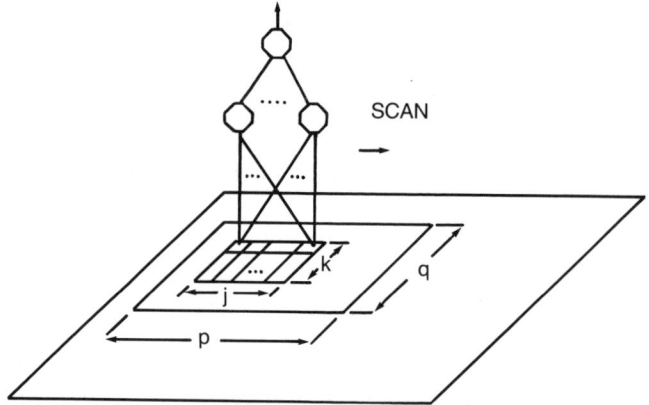

Fig. 1   Method used to input image data to the MLP.

off over a few pixels to produce a low value (0.0) when the window is displaced from the centre of the eye. The values of j,k and number of hidden nodes were varied in different experiments. In all experiments MLPs with at most one hidden layer were used.

In the case of higher resolution images a $p \times q$ search window ($j<p<n, k<q<n$) was used to restrict the search window to the vicinity of the feature of interest. In this case, the number of candidate eye points was reduced to $(p-j) \times (q-k)$. This was done in order to reduce training times, and to increase the frequency of presentation of eye data to the MLP, early experiments having quickly shown that training the MLP by raster scanning across the whole image produces very poor results. This is due to the infrequency of presentation of eye data to the net. In other experiments on lower resolution images the frequency of presentation of eye data was increased by alternately presenting raster scan data and eye data to the net. Alternatively a small number of 'representative' input vectors was chosen, including the windows centred on the eye. These three approaches to emphasising the significance of the eye data represent three examples of a wide range of 'probability of presentation' distribution functions that could be envisaged.

A number of experiments were carried out, the more significant of which are described below.

2.1 Lower resolution feature detection

Preliminary work focused on eye location in lower resolution images [4]. For 32×32 pixel images an input window size of 7×5 ($j=7$, $k=5$) was estimated to be an appropriate size to adequately cover the eye. An MLP with no hidden nodes was used (i.e. a single layer perceptron). In the first instance 10 training vectors were chosen from a single image, including the two vectors centred on the eyes. The net was successfully trained using this training data set, with expected values of 1.0 for eye vectors and 0.0 for non-eye vectors. Convergence was defined as being when every pattern in the training set produces a network output within 0.15 of the expected value.

When tested by scanning across the image from which the training set had been selected, the net successfully located the eyes. However, although positions of the input window corresponding to eyes resulted in the largest net output values, spurious large values were also generated in other parts of the image. When scanned across an image that was not in the training set the net generally gave a significant response at the locations of the eyes, although these were not in general the highest responses that the net produced.

In an experiment on image sequences the 'Miss America' sequence was sub-sampled to form a sequence of 116 16×16 images. The eye positions

16   IMAGE FEATURE LOCATION

were manually located and the first five frames were then used to train an MLP with a 5 × 5 input and no hidden nodes. Training was performed with expected values as for the experiment on 32 × 32 pixel images described above, but in this case the images were raster scanned in turn to provide input data. The net trained successfully (which is perhaps surprising in view of the fact that only 1 input vector in 60 represented an eye). The trained net was then used to detect eye locations in all the frames. The net proved to be effective in locating eye positions in the sequence, although they were not always located and spurious high outputs did occur, most notably in the mouth and hairline areas. Figure 2 shows a frame from the original high resolution sequence with the MLP output superimposed (white squares).

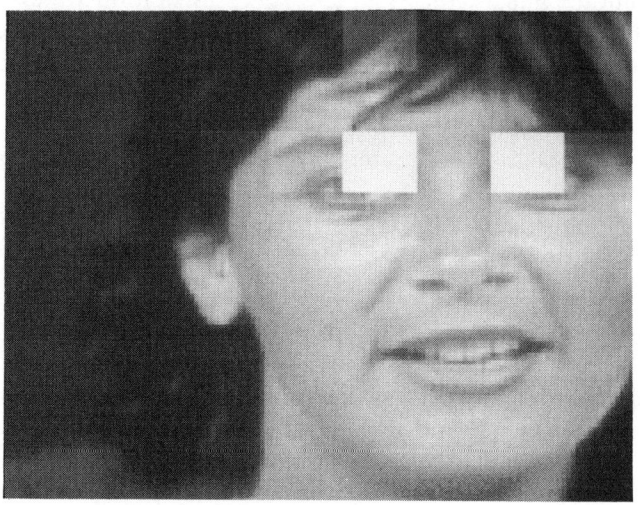

Fig. 2   MLP output superimposed on 'Miss America'.

2.2   Higher resolution feature detection

For 128 × 128 pixel images experiments have been performed using MLPs and, for comparison, template matching techniques [3]. Kohonen self-organising maps were also investigated but are not described here, see [3] for details. In all experiments 16 images (8 male, 8 female) selected from the data set of 60 images were used to form a training set, and the remaining 44 images were used as a test set. An eye was considered to have been successfully located if the position determined by the technique was within 2 pixels of the manually determined position.

Template matching

For template matching an input window of 16 × 16 was used. The template was considered to be over the eye when the pixel to the upper left of the middle of the template was centred on the eye. Two approaches were used to form the templates. In the first approach 16 different templates were used, based on 16 × 16 ($j,k = 16$) windows centred on the left eye of the training set (in all discussions of image data, left and right refer to positions in the image as seen by the observer). Each of the templates was scanned over a 32 × 32 search window centred on the eye ($p,q = 32$) in each of the images from the test set. At each position the sum of squared differences between the pixel values in the template and the image was evaluated. For each image the template position with the lowest sum of squared differences, for all the templates, is considered to be the location of the eye.

In the second approach, a composite template was created by taking the average of the pixel values at each pixel position. This was used in a similar manner to the previous template method.

The 'best of 16' approach successfully located eyes in 29 of the 44 images in the test set, a success rate of about 66%. Using the composite template resulted in the location of eyes in 36 of the test set images, a score of about 82%. However the composite template was only successful in locating 7 of the 16 eyes in the training set, leaving its apparently good performance on the test set open to question.

Multilayer perceptron

In the MLP experiments an input window size of 16 × 16 ($j,k = 16$) was used. Hidden layers of two different sizes were tried; 16 neurons and 32 neurons. The MLP was trained by scanning it across a 32 × 32 ($p,q = 32$) window centred on the left eye of each of the images in the training set. When the input to the net was centred on the eye the net was trained to output a high value (1.0). The expected value decreased linearly to zero (0.0) at a distance of 6 pixels from the eye centre. Thus near-eye vectors were expected to give a non-zero response. The net was deemed to have converged when all actual values were within 0.1 of the expected values (this was a fairly severe training criterion, as is discussed by Waite in Chapter 2).

The network was first trained on 4 images of the training set, until it performed eye recognition satisfactorily on these images (although it did not attain the convergence criterion). It was then trained further on 8 images including the initial 4, and finally on all 16 images. This was repeated for MLPs with 16 and 32 hidden nodes. The best results obtained for the MLP with 16 hidden nodes were a recognition of 38 of the 44 test images, a success rate of about 86%. The MLP with 32 hidden nodes located the left eye in

39 of the 44 test images, a success rate of about 89%. Results for all the approaches to eye location in 128 × 128 pixel images are summarised in Fig. 3.

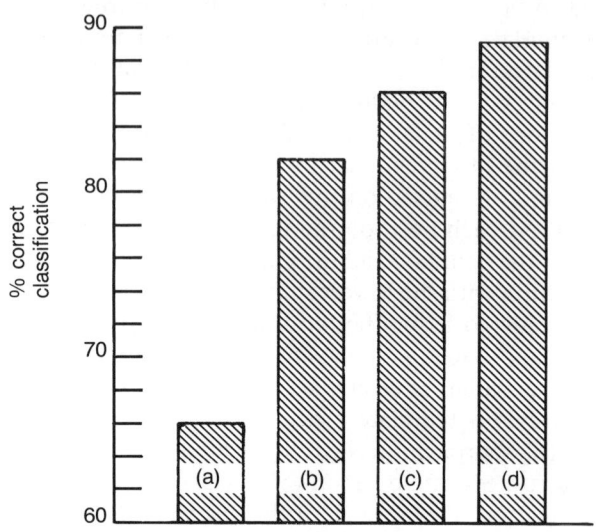

Fig. 3 Scores for eye location within 2 pixels on a 128 × 128 image; (a) best of multiple templates, (b) average template, (c) MLP with 16 hidden nodes, (d) MLP with 32 hidden nodes.

Experiments have been performed on 256 × 256 pixel images [5]. In these experiments an input window of 30 × 16 ($j=30, k=16$) was used, with a hidden layer of 32 neurons, and a search window of 46 × 32 ($p=46, q=32$). The expected output values were similar to those for the 128 × 128 pixel experiments, but scaled to the larger image size. Also, an eye was considered to have been successfully located if the maximum response of the net was within 4 pixels of the manually determined eye centre. It must be pointed out that this criterion for success is much less demanding than that in the case of the 128 × 128 pixel experiments; in that case the selection of a random point in the search space would have yielded a correct classification score of 6.25%, as compared with 25% for the 256 × 256 pixel experiments. Bearing this caveat in mind, the MLP achieved successful classification of 40 of the 44 test images, a success rate of about 91%, which is higher than for any of the 128 × 128 experiments.

Further experiments, which involved pre-processing the images in a variety of ways (see [5] for details), training up MLPs on the preprocessed images, and averaging the output from several MLPs when applied to the test set, resulted in a highest classification rate of about 98%, or 43 of the 44 test images. This approach is similar to the use of neural net ensembles [6], in which several nets are trained from different initial conditions. During training they explore different areas of the error surface, potentially converging at different points in weights space, and therefore having different generalisation properties. The outputs of the MLPs are combined by averaging or voting. This should result in higher performance with fewer spurious errors.

2.3 Discussion of the single resolution approach

Although they show promise when compared to conventional techniques such as template matching, single resolution MLP feature classifiers in all cases achieved detection rates of less than 100% on the relatively small test set used. In order to modestly improve performances, significantly increased resources (e.g. neural net ensembles) are required. The law of diminishing returns is at work, and it seems unrealistic to strive to produce a system capable of 100% recognition rates by this approach.

In the higher resolution work, the nets were confined to a relatively small search window in the locality of the feature to be detected (the left eye) during both training and testing. If a trained net is scanned across the whole of a higher resolution image, spurious detections, which were referred to in the context of the lower resolution work, become a problem.

In addition, the computation required to scan an MLP over images of the size used in the highest resolution experiments equates to about 500 million multiply/add operations. Thus an eventual implementation capable of real-time feature location in sequences of many frames per second would require much expensive high-speed hardware.

3. THE MULTI-RESOLUTION APPROACH

In order to overcome some of the limitations of single resolution MLP feature detection described in Section 2.3, a multi-resolution approach can be adopted. In this approach, shown schematically in Fig. 4, a low resolution version of the image to be searched is generated by filtering and subsampling. MLP feature locators are scanned across the low resolution image to generate candidate search areas for each type of feature. The address of a pixel in the low resolution image flagged as being a candidate feature location is passed to a search supervisor, where it translates into an area of pixels in the high resolution image. This high resolution search area can be scanned by an MLP feature detector to determine if the feature is in fact present, and to find its precise location.

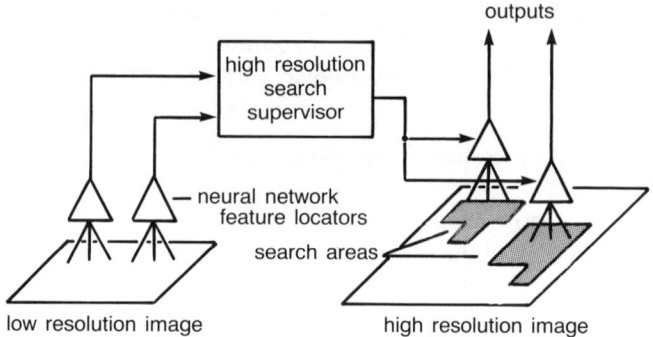

Fig. 4 Multi-resolution approach to feature location.

Provided that the number of candidate search areas is small, this scheme requires much less computation than scanning the entire high resolution image. However, as it stands it will still be prone to the location of spurious features, and fail to locate features that are present. These problems are ameliorated by higher level processing using two techniques, both of which exploit knowledge about the source image. In the first, intra-frame knowledge about the relative positions of features is used. The image is assumed to be a single human head and shoulders image, therefore simple rules such as 'left eye is to the left of right eye' and 'mouth is below eyes' can be used to select likely triples of candidate feature points. The second technique to improve performance is to use inter-frame knowledge. Constraints can be put on the extent of allowable motion between frames, and if a feature is not detected in a particular frame, its position can be extrapolated or predicted from data obtained from previous frames. If the probability of locating a feature in each frame is 0.9, then in a sequence of 3 frames the probability of locating the feature in at least one of these frames is 0.999, assuming that the probabilities are independent (an assumption which may well be questioned!).

A prototype multi-resolution system has been developed for tracking features (left eye, right eye, mouth) in sequences of human head-and-shoulders images. It embodies higher level processing exploiting knowledge about the source image and is known as the hierarchical perceptron feature locator (HPFL). It operates on source images of resolution 256 × 256 pixels, creating a 16 × 16 low resolution image by pixel averaging and sub-sampling. The component parts of the HPFL, shown schematically in Fig. 5, are now described.

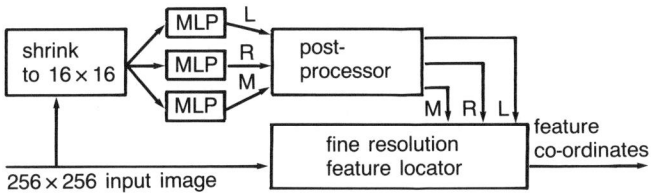

Fig. 5 Block diagram of a hierarchical perceptron feature locator incorporating post-processing of search areas generated at coarse resolution. Images containing search areas for left eyes, right eyes and mouths are labelled L, R and M respectively.

3.1 Obtaining candidate feature points in the low resolution image

The feature detectors required in the low resolution stage of the HPFL are required to perform a subtly different function to the feature detectors described in Section 2, or those required in the high resolution stage. The purpose of the low resolution feature detectors is to locate candidate feature points, therefore the detection of a point which is not a feature point (a false positive) is much less serious than the failure to detect a point which is a feature point (a false negative). False positives can be pruned out by various methods at a later stage, but false negatives cannot easily be recovered. This conditions the way the detectors are trained, as will be described.

The use of a single layer perceptron to detect eye positions in 16×16 pixel images has shown some promise (see Section 2.1). Its performance is perhaps surprising in view of the fact that its decision surface is a single hyperplane in 25 dimensional pattern space. In order to produce more complex decision surfaces, an MLP with a number of hidden nodes should be used. However there is a trade-off between number of hidden nodes and ability to generalise. In order to achieve a balance between ability to generalise, and ability to form more complex decision surfaces, '2nd degree' neurons have been used.

The output of a 2nd degree neuron (a 2nd degree neuron with two inputs is shown schematically in Fig. 6(a)) is given by

$$y_j = f(w_0 + \sum_i w_{ij} \cdot x_i + \sum_i v_{ij} \cdot x_i^2) \qquad \dots (1)$$

where v_{ij} are the weights associated with squared inputs. The simple linear neuron function can be obtained by setting these weights to zero. The 2nd degree neuron is a small step in the direction of higher order neural nets (HONNs) [7], and can form a much richer set of decision surfaces than the linear neuron. A single 2nd order neuron can form a closed decision surface (a hyper-ellipsoid) independent of the dimensionality of the pattern space,

22 IMAGE FEATURE LOCATION

whereas it requires a 2 layer MLP with a minimum of $N+1$ hidden linear neurons to form a closed decision surface in N dimensional pattern space. Assuming an infinite pattern space, a closed decision surface is one that encloses a finite region of pattern space. An open decision surface encloses an infinite region of pattern space. Figures 6(b)-(d) show three possible forms of decision surface ((b) simple open, (c) closed and (d) disjoint open) that a single 2nd order neuron can form.

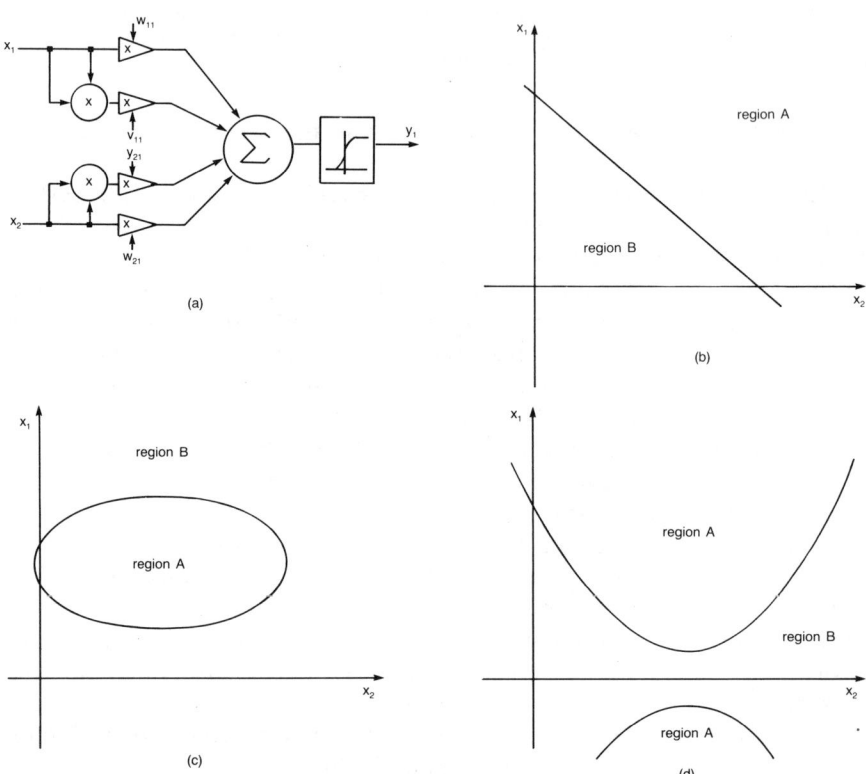

Fig. 6 (a) 2 input 2nd degree neuron. (b) Simple decision boundary. (c) Closed elliptical decision boundary. (d) Disjoint open decision boundary.

Because the squared terms can be generated by pre-processing the input pattern vector, nets with 2nd degree neurons in the first layer can be trained using the conventional backpropagation algorithm.

MLPs with a 5×5 input window, two hidden 2nd degree neurons and a single linear output neuron have been used as detectors to perform candidate feature point classification for the HPFL. Each detector is scanned across the 16×16 pixel image, and its thresholded output is used to create a 16×16

binary image known as the search area image. Unlike the earlier low resolution experiments, separate detectors are used for left and right eyes. There are therefore three search area images, one each for the left eye, right eye and mouth. After further processing (to be described later) these are passed to the high resolution stage, where they are used to define search areas for the feature detectors in the high resolution image.

As the MLP is scanned across the source image there is one occasion when the scanning window is closest to the desired feature. When this occurs the expected output of the MLP is a high value (1.0), and the pattern vector on its input will be referred to as a feature vector. In all other positions the MLP output is expected to be low (0.0). The pattern vectors that form the input to the MLP on these occasions will be referred to as background vectors.

The MLPs were trained on 30 images selected from the set of 60 images used in the experiments described in Section 2. For each low resolution image there are 144 MLP input window positions, corresponding to 143 background vectors and 1 feature vector. If each vector is presented only once during a training epoch then the contribution to weight updating made by the feature vector is swamped by the effects of the background vectors; failure to detect the feature vector means that only 1 in 144 pattern vectors are misclassified, a success rate of 99.3%! This problem is avoided by presenting the two classes of pattern vector in a 1:1 ratio; each time a background vector is presented to the MLP it is followed by the feature vector from the same image.

Because of the need to ensure that all feature vectors are detected, whilst minimising the number of background vectors that result in false positives, a selective training procedure was used. In this procedure a pattern vector is used only if the MLP's current response to it is considered unacceptable. In the selective training procedure the feature vectors are presented to the net at the end of a training epoch. If any feature is misclassified, backpropagation is applied for that vector. This is repeated until all feature vectors are correctly classified. If all feature vectors are correctly classified then in the next epoch all pattern vectors are presented to the net, but backpropagation is only applied for those that are misclassified. Misclassification is deemed to have occurred if the net gives an output <0.5 for an expected output of 1.0, or if the output is >0.5 for an expected value of 0.0.

The results of testing the three feature detectors on the 30 images of the training set and on 32 frames of a head and shoulders sequence of a subject not in the test set are shown in Table 1. The number of rejections (failure to detect a feature vector) must be read in conjunction with the figure for mean search area, which is a measure of the number of false positives. For good net performance both of these figures should be low; it is perfectly possible to have no rejections with a search area of 100%, but this is obviously undesirable.

	Raw Outputs				After Spatial Pruning				After Temporal Pruning				After Pel Extension			
	Train		Test		Train		Test		Train		Test		Train		Test	
	REJ	A,%	REJ	A,%	REJ	A,%	REJ	A,%	REJ	A,%	REJ	A,%	REJ	A,%	REJ	A,%
LEFT EYES	0/30	4.45	0/32	2.19	0/30	1.09	2/32	0.62	---	---	2/32	0.60	---	---	0/32	4.08
RIGHT EYES	0/30	0.74	3/32	0.54	0/30	0.61	3/32	0.48	---	---	3/32	0.44	---	---	0/32	3.59
MOUTHS	0/30	1.54	19/32	2.16	0/30	0.90	19/32	0.99	---	---	19/32	0.76	---	---	0/32	4.00

Table 1 Test results for HPFL low resolution stage (REJ = number of rejected features, A,% = percentage of search area retained).

3.2 Exploiting knowledge to prune the search space

As stated earlier, for the low resolution stage to perform well, it is necessary to eliminate false negatives whilst keeping the number of false positives low. The function of the low resolution stage post-processor is to reduce the number of false positives, whilst retaining the true feature points. It has three consecutive stages; spatial pruning, temporal pruning and pixel expansion.

Spatial pruning

Spatial pruning is an intra-frame process that exploits geometric constraints imposed by facial structure on eye and mouth feature locations.

Consider a triple combination of candidate feature points, one point being taken from each of the search area images generated from a single frame. The pixels have co-ordinates r_L, r_R, r_M for candidate left eye, right eye and mouth positions respectively, as shown in Fig. 7. Some combinations are clearly not feasible, because they would imply, for instance, that the viewpoint is behind the head. This would happen if the candidate left eye position is to the right of the candidate right eye position. Other combinations might imply an unnaturally distended face. A set of geometric feasibility criteria can be established, and each possible triple that can be generated from the search area image can be tested to establish whether it satisfies these criteria. If not, that triple is rejected; this is the basis of the spatial pruning algorithm.

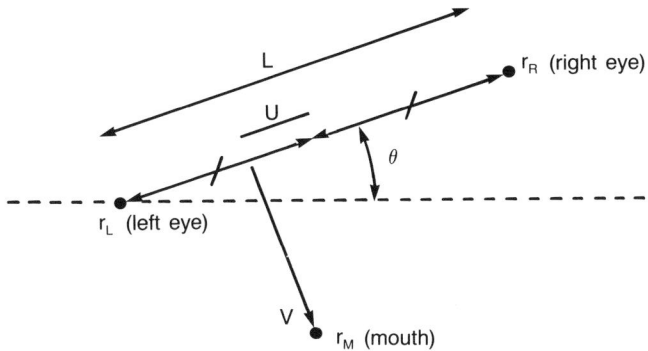

Fig. 7 A configuration of candidate eye and mouth points in a coarse image, showing the parameters involved in hypothesis testing by the spatial pruning algorithm (L, θ, U, V).

The parameters used in the HPFL low resolution stage post-processor to establish a set of criteria are shown in Fig. 7. L is the spacing between the candidate eye points and θ is the angle that L makes with the horizontal. (U, V) are the co-ordinates of the candidate mouth point with respect to a frame of reference that has as its principal axes the line L, and an orthogonal line intersecting it at its midpoint. The following inequalities are tested:

$$L_{min} <= L <= L_{max} .$$

This implies that all images are at approximately the same scale, and restricts head rotation.

$$|\theta| <= \theta_{max} .$$

This restricts the range of orientations in the image plane.

$$(U/L) <= (U/L)_{max} .$$

This restricts the mouth position to lie approximately on the perpendicular axis through the midpoint between the eyes.

$$(V/L)_{min} <= (V/L) <= (V/L)_{max} .$$

This rejects unnaturally compressed or distended face shapes.

The maximum and minimum allowed values are calculated from the training set of images, and relaxed to allow for greater variability in test images. Pixels in the search area image that do not belong to at least one triple that satisfies the above criteria are considered to be false positives, and are deleted.

The spatial pruning algorithm was applied to the images in the training and test sets. If all triples in a particular image failed to meet the pruning criteria then pruning was de-activated for that image. When pruning was not deactivated, the retained pixels in all cases included all the candidate feature points corresponding to correct location of the feature. The average reduction in search area over each data set was over 40%. The results are included in Table 1.

Temporal pruning

The occurrence of images containing no valid triples indicates the presence of one or more false rejections. The spatial pruning algorithm can therefore be used as a method of detecting false negatives. When false negatives are detected in one frame of a sequence, data from previous frames can be used to estimate the position of rejected feature points, and to allow some 'spatio-temporal' pruning.

The above scheme has not yet been implemented in the HPFL. Currently the only form of temporal pruning implemented is an inter-frame process that imposes motion constraints on candidate feature points. By comparing locations of candidate feature points in adjacent frames, false positives can be rejected. Candidate feature points are constrained to move by no more than one pixel position per frame in any direction. For a 25 frame/sec sequence this corresponds to about 1.5 image widths per second, which is not very restrictive.

Temporal pruning is applied after spatial pruning. Search area images of the same type are compared for adjacent frames of a sequence. All candidate feature pixels in the current frame that are more than one pixel away from a candidate feature pixel in the previous frame are deleted. This has the effect of reducing the search areas by removing spurious false positives which occur randomly.

The effects of temporal pruning are shown in Table 1 for the test set data (temporal pruning cannot, of course, be applied to the still images of the training set).

Pixel expansion

In the final post-processing stage, pixel expansion, the remaining candidate feature points are expanded from single pixels to an array of 3×3 pixels. Although this actually increases search areas, it is necessary because the generation of a coarsely sub-sampled image can give rise to sampling problems, where the desired feature in the high resolution image lies across the boundary of two or more low resolution pixels. In such cases a false negative may occur at the feature point, with a false positive in an adjacent pixel location. The false positive survives the spatial and temporal pruning processes, being close to the location of the feature point.

Pixel expansion ensures that the true feature point is brought within the search area, at the cost of increasing that search area. Table 1 shows the effect of pixel expansion on false negatives and mean search area, for the 32 frames of the test set.

3.3 Testing the low resolution stage

As described above, the low resolution stage of the HPFL has been tested using a 32 frame sequence of a female subject. The subject in the sequence did not appear in the 60 still images used to train the feature detectors. Figure 8(a) shows the initial search area images produced by the MLP feature detectors, superimposed on an example frame from the sequence. Figure 8(b) shows the results of spatial pruning; this has reduced the number of candidate triples, and hence the area that has eventually to be searched at the high

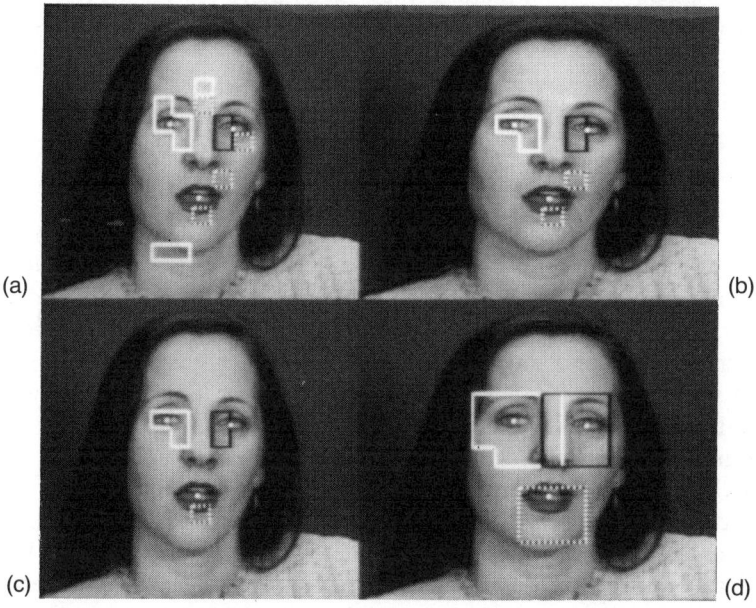

Fig. 8 Search area generation for eyes and mouth in an example frame at different stages of processing: (a) before post-processing, (b) after spatial pruning, (c) after temporal pruning and (d) after expansion. Boundaries of search areas are white for the left eye, black for the right eye and hatched for the mouth. Exact locations of features are shown as white dots.

resolution stage, from 56 to 12. Temporal pruning, shown in Fig. 8(c) reduces the number still further, to 6. The search areas after pixel expansion are shown in Fig. 8(d). This shows the feature point corresponding to the mouth, which was adjacent to a candidate feature point prior to expansion, being absorbed into the search area.

3.4 Feature location in the high resolution image

After pixel expansion, the search area images are passed to the supervisor of the high resolution stage of the HPFL (see Fig. 6). Each pixel in a search area image corresponds to a 16×16 block in the high resolution image. The high resolution feature detectors are only scanned across areas of the high resolution image corresponding to a candidate feature pixel in the search area image.

Currently, only a left eye detector has been implemented for the high resolution stage. This is based on the work of Waite, described in Chapter 2. There is scope for post-processing of the detector outputs at the high resolution stage, to perform both intra-frame and inter-frame verification. This has not yet been implemented. Nevertheless, when the high resolution detector was run on the output of the low resolution stage for the test sequence described in Section 3.3, all left eyes were located to within 2 high resolution pixels.

4. CONCLUSIONS

The hierarchical perceptron feature locator described in this chapter is a method of locating features in human head-and-shoulders image sequences that should prove to be relatively robust. It needs extension to include error recovery in the post-processors, high resolution right eye and mouth detectors, and perhaps intra and inter-frame verification at high resolution.

The system currently has most difficulty with people who are wearing glasses. In retrospect we would perhaps be justified in excising these examples from our data set, in much the same way that data of poor subjective quality is sometimes removed from speech data sets. The problem of people with glasses could be dealt with by specific 'glasses' recogniser systems.

The underlying principles of the HPFL system mean that it could be used to perform feature location and tracking on a range of sequences of restricted scenes, by customising its various modules. There are a number of ways in which the system could be evolved further. At present it deals with images at an approximately fixed scale, and assumes that there is only one head and shoulders in the image. Possible extensions include allowing the system to operate over a range of scales (possibly by using a multi-resolution pyramid), and allowing images that have a number of subjects in them. Spatial and temporal pruning, which are currently knowledge based, could be implemented by neural techniques. This is currently under investigation.

The ultimate aim of the work is to produce a real-time demonstrator system, using the VLSI chip described by Myers, Vincent and Orrey in Chapter 16.

ACKNOWLEDGEMENTS

A number of people have contributed to the work described here. We would like to acknowledge the contribution of Bill Welsh, who performed some of the early work which lead to the development of the HPFL system, and Charley Nightingale and Jon Waite for their valuable comments and advice.

REFERENCES

1. Rumelhart D E, and McClelland J L: 'Parallel Distributed Processing; Volume 1: Foundations', The MIT Press, Cambridge Ma (1987).
2. Kohonen T: 'Self Organisation and Associative Memory' 2nd Edition, Springer Verlang.
3. Hutchinson R A and Welsh W J: 'Comparison of Neural Networks and Conventional Techniques for Feature Location in Facial Images' Proc. 1st IEE Int. Conf. on Artificial Neural Networks. London, UK (October 1989).
4. Hines E and Hutchinson R A: 'Application of Multi-layer Perceptrons to Facial Feature Location' Proc. 3rd IEE Int. Conf. on Image Processing and its Applications, Warwick UK, (July 1989).
5. Hutchinson R A: 'Development of an MLP Feature Location Technique Using Preprocessed Images' Proc. INNC'90 International Neural Network Conference, $\underline{1}$, Kluwer Academic Publishers (July 1990).
6. Hansen L K and Salamon P: 'Neural Network Ensembles' IEEE Trans. on Pattern Analysis and Machine Intelligence, $\underline{12}$, No 10 (October 1990).
7. Maxwell T et al: 'Transformation Invariance Using High Order Correlations in Neural Net Architectures' IEEE Int. Conf. on Systems Man and Cybernetics, Atlanta, Georgia, USA (October 1986).

2

TRAINING MULTILAYER PERCEPTRONS FOR FACIAL FEATURE LOCATION: A CASE STUDY

J B Waite
BT Laboratories

1. INTRODUCTION

A general property of the MLP is that as the classification task grows in complexity then so does the size of network required to perform the classification. An unfortunate consequence of this is that the training time for complex tasks can increase to prohibitive levels making software simulations slow. In the case of feature location in high resolution images Hutchinson [1] reports using an MLP with an input layer containing 480 units and a hidden layer of 32 units. Typically the network took one to two days[1] to train when searching for the features in a restricted domain of each of sixteen images. When trained on complete 256 by 256 images the training time is measured in weeks.

In this chapter we extend the work of Hutchinson and describe two different approaches to reducing MLP training times in visual pattern matching problems. The first method is based on representing the image vector presented to the net in a principal component co-ordinate system constructed from a collection of facial features. The basic idea here is to

---

[1]Calculations were performed on an Apollo DN 10000 computer with a vector processor.

RHsimply compress the length of the input vector and thus reduce the size of network required, but without a loss in discriminatory power. The second method is based on the adoption of a weaker training criterion than that used by Hutchinson and allows the net to train faster without a loss of discriminatory capability. When considered alone each method provides a significant decrease in training time and when used together they provide an even greater reduction.

2. PROBLEM DESCRIPTION

The problem that we will consider is the eye location problem [1], although the techniques to be described are applicable to other two-class visual pattern matching tasks. Briefly, the problem is to locate centres of the eyes in a facial image by scanning a small image window over the image and recognising when the window is over an eye (Fig. 1). In this instance the centre of the eye is defined to be the centre of the eye pupil. The precise classification problem is to mark the pixel at the centre of the image window as being either an eye or a non-eye point depending on whether an eye is centred in the window. This is accomplished by mapping the grey levels from the image window to a corresponding window vector which is in turn presented to an MLP. A window size of 17×29 (height $\times$ width) pixels was adopted in the experiments which generated input vectors to the MLP of length 493. When the window is centred on an eye a single output node MLP is trained to produce a unit response. When the centre of the window is distant from the eye centre the network is trained to produce a response that decays from unity to zero as the distance from the eye increases.

We can consider each input vector to represent a point in $\Re^N$. This space is referred to as pattern space. Because of the visual similarity between eyes in different facial images we would expect those points representing eyes to form a single cluster in pattern space (visually similar objects should occupy similar positions in pattern space). However, as the non-eye data points do not represent any feature in particular we would not expect those points to form a single cluster but to be widely distributed in pattern space. Their distribution may of course take the form of a scatter of clusters with each cluster representing similar parts of the image (e.g. a cluster representing the mouth). We thus adopt a simple model of the pattern space which consists of a cluster of points representing eyes submerged in a sea of clusters and distributed single points representing non-eyes (Fig. 2).

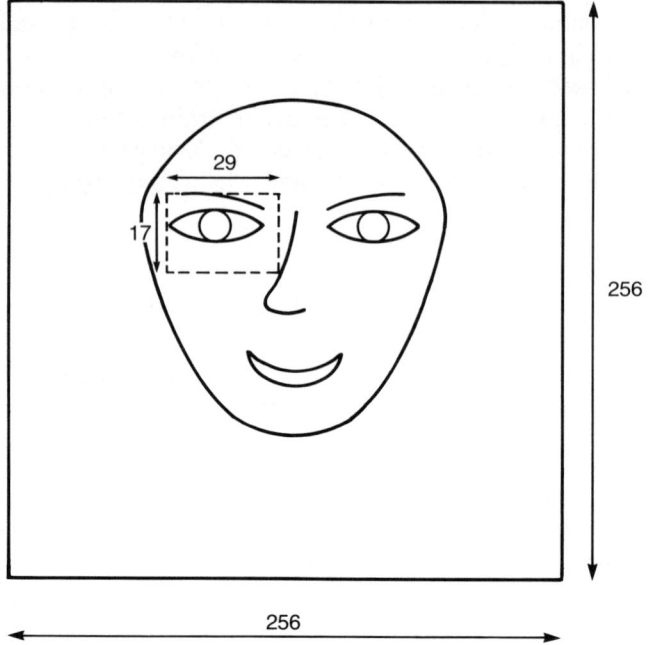

Fig. 1 MLP window scanned over image.

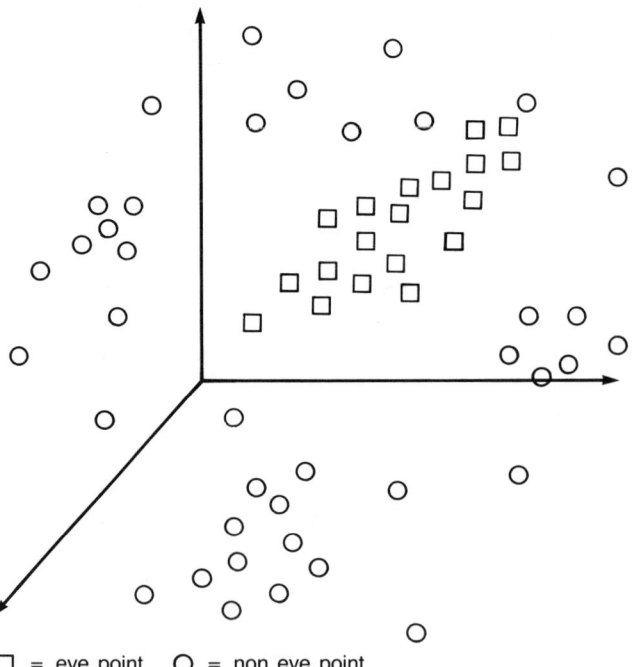

□ = eye point   O = non eye point

Fig. 2 Idealised model of pattern space.

3. DIMENSION REDUCTION

It is natural to ask what is the true dimensionality of the eye data, for if it is less than the dimension of the pattern space it may be possible to perform our classification process in a lower dimensional space and so reduce the computational overhead. For a set of experimentally gathered discrete data points it is in general difficult to define what is meant by the dimensionality of the data. However, by adopting a continuum model of an eye the task is made somewhat easier. If in general the position $\underline{x} \in \Re^N$ of an eye in pattern space were representable by a relationship of the form $\underline{x} = \underline{x}(\underline{u})$, where $\underline{u}$ is a point in $\Re^M$, then the data is said to be at most M-dimensional. If M is the smallest integer such that a relationship of this type holds then the data is said to be M-dimensional. Generally we restrict the transformation $\underline{x}:\Re^M \to \Re^N$ to be continuously differentiable which allows the equivalent view that the eyes lie on an M-dimensional smooth surface or manifold in N-dimensional pattern space. In practice we would not expect the eye data to exactly lie on such a surface as the data is noisy and the features that make an eye look like an eye are very complex. It may however be reasonable to expect the eye data to approximately lie on such a surface. That is, we may be able to find a smooth surface in pattern space such that each of the eye data points lies on the surface or is a short distance from the surface. If the surface can be represented by M independent parameters then we say that the data is approximately M-dimensional. The data can then effectively be compressed by taking each data point and representing it by its orthogonal projection onto the surface. Thus we have a transformation $T:\Re^N \to \Re^M$ of our data onto the surface and the classification process is performed on the projection of the points onto the (lower dimensional) surface. Clearly such a transformation may not be invertible as information can be lost in the projection process (distinct data points can be projected onto the same point on the surface) and thus discriminatory features may be lost.

The simplest surface that we can consider is a hyperplane. In this case we want to find a hyperplane that passes close to all the eye data points but at the same time the dimension M of the hyperplane should be small so that the projection of the eye points into the hyperplane is represented by a small number of components. If the data is such that a hyperplane can be found that is close to all the eye data points then the eye cluster information will be preserved. It was noted above however that information may be lost as the transformation T is not generally invertible. Specifically, the information loss will manifest itself as a projection of non-eye points into the eye-cluster in the plane and so result in a decrease in discriminatory capacity. The basic question therefore lies in the compromise that is to be made between the performance gain when training (in terms of training time) and the performance loss during testing (in terms of classification accuracy). In particular, can the input data be compressed in such a way that a significant decrease in training can be accomplished without a significant reduction in classification performance?

4. HYPERPLANE FITTING

A suitable way in which to fit a hyperplane through the eye data is to use a least squares criterion. That is, we choose a dimension M for the surface and construct a hyperplane so that the sum of the squared distances of the eye points from the hyperplane is minimised. A computationally efficient and hierarchical method of constructing the best least squares fit is to use a principal component decomposition of the eye data. The method is described fully in the appendices but we give a brief outline here. The basic idea is to construct a new co-ordinate system with the origin at the centroid of the eye data (the hyperplane always passes through the centroid) and co-ordinate directions chosen so that they represent the directions in which the variance of the data is maximised. By this we mean that the first co-ordinate direction is chosen so that it is in the direction of maximum variance of the data, the second co-ordinate direction is chosen from among those orthogonal to the first direction and such that the variance of the data in that direction is maximised, the third co-ordinate direction is chosen from among those orthogonal to the first two and such that the variance of the data in that direction is maximised, and so on. These directions are known as principal directions or principal components of the data and are the eigenvectors of the mean centred covariance matrix.

If the data is clustered in such a way that in some directions the variance is large but in others small then the data can be well represented by just those co-ordinates in which the data is varying most. To construct a suitable approximating hyperplane the principal directions, represented by the set of vectors $\{\underline{u}_1, \underline{u}_2, \ldots, \underline{u}_N\}$, are listed in an order corresponding to a descending order of the variances in those directions. It is shown in the appendices that the space spanned by the first M vectors then represents the best least squares M-dimensional hyperplane approximation to the data. By choosing different values for M, hyperplanes of varying goodness of fit can be constructed.

To see how this representation of the data can help reduce the training time of an MLP consider Fig. 3. Here we have for clarity just a two dimensional distribution of data. The data in the original xy co-ordinate system is represented in the new XY co-ordinate system which has been constructed from the two principal components OX and OY of the data. Because of its distribution it can be seen that the data is well represented by just a single principal component in the OX direction. The one dimensional hyperplane through OX is the best straight line fit to the data in the least squares sense. Thus for each data point (x,y) represented in the original co-ordinate system we have a mapping $P:\Re^2 \to \Re$, $X = P(x,y)$, that projects the points onto the hyperplane (straight line). The set of X's on the hyperplane will form a cluster that the MLP will be able to identify and use for pattern recognition but the data is now represented by just a single co-ordinate X instead of two co-ordinates (x,y). In the general case we would construct a projection of the data $P:\Re^N \to \Re^M$ onto an M-dimensional hyperplane.

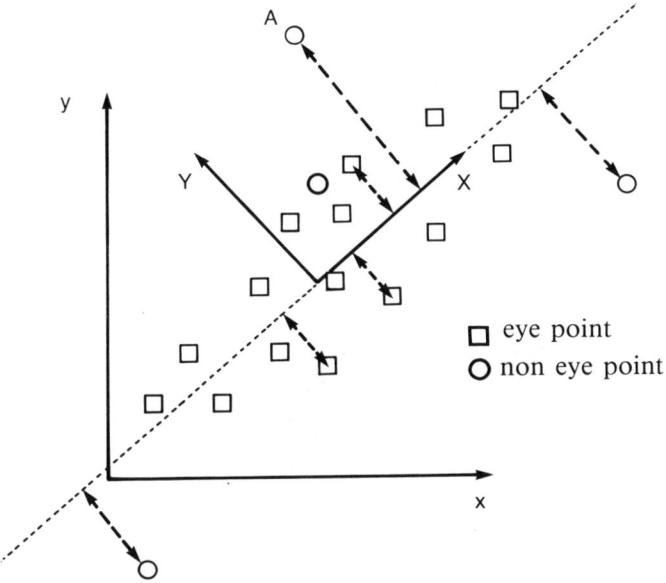

Fig. 3 Projection of eye data onto the best least squares line.

It is clear from Fig. 3 that a difficulty can arise with this approach. If we take the non-eye point A then it is projected into the eye cluster on the hyperplane and we thus have no way of distinguishing between it and the true eye-points in the cluster. We can however partially recover some of this lost information by appending the distance of the point from the hyperplane to the co-ordinate description. Thus each data point is represented by $M+1$ co-ordinates $(X_1, X_2, ..., X_M, D)$ consisting of the co-ordinates of the projection of the point in the hyperplane $(X_1, X_2, ..., X_M)$ and the distance of the point D from the hyperplane. In our two dimensional example this would simply mean representing the points by the co-ordinates (X, Y) and so no computational advantage is achieved in this case. However, in the general case a considerable dimensional reduction can result.

5. DIMENSION REDUCTION EXPERIMENTS

The data for the experiments consisted of a database of 60 monochrome test images of resolution 256×256 with each image a different subject in a frontal head and shoulders pose and each approximately the same scale (Fig. 4).

Fig. 4 Face database.

The first experiment tested the hypothesis that the eye data from a 29×17 window approximately lie in a hyperplane. Note that as we have only 60 images and we are working in 493-dimensional space it follows that all of the points in the space corresponding to eye centres necessarily lie in a 59-dimensional hyperplane. However, as we are interested in dimension reduction we want to determine if the eye points lie on a hyperplane of much lower dimension than this. The simplest way to do this is to choose a dimension and construct the best least squares hyperplane of that dimension to the eye data and calculate the resulting approximation errors (distances of the eye points to the hyperplane). As the best M-dimensional least squares hyperplane is generated by the space spanned by the first M eigenvectors of the covariance matrix (see appendix 1) of the eye data and the corresponding eigenvalues represent the variances of the data in the direction of the eigenvectors it follows that an examination of the spectrum of the matrix allows us to choose a suitable dimension for the hyperplane.

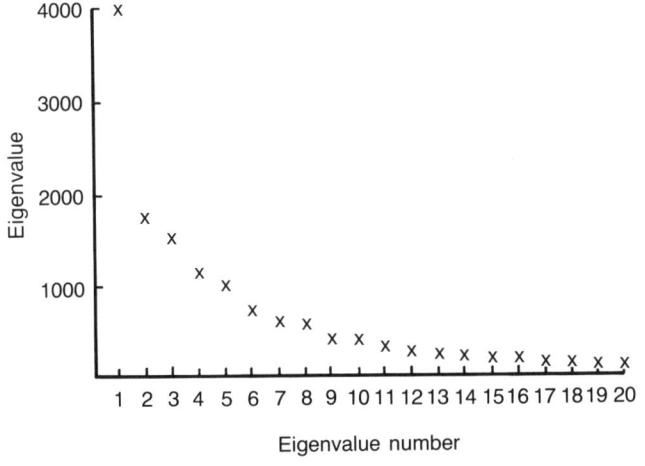

Fig. 5   First twenty eigenvalues of the data covariance matrix in order of decreasing magnitude.

From a 29×17 window centred on the right eye in each of the 60 test images the corresponding covariance matrix was constructed and the eigenvalues and eigenvectors calculated. It can be seen from Fig. 5 that the spread of the eye points is much larger in some directions than in others. On this basis it was decided that the hyperplane generated by just the first 15 eigenvectors would provide a good approximation to the eye data. For each of the test images a window of size 29×17 was scanned over the entire image and the Euclidian distance of the window vector (a point in $\mathcal{R}^{493}$) from the 15-dimensional hyperplane was calculated for each window position. This enabled a secondary inverse error image to be constructed that consisted of the reciprocal of the distance (linearly scaled in the range 0 to 255) of each window vector from the hyperplane. That is, the intensity of the pixel at location (i,j) in the inverse error image is the reciprocal of the distance of the window vector centred on (i,j) to the hyperplane. Figures 6d, 6e and 6f show examples of inverse error images constructed from the original images 6a, 6b and 6c respectively using 15 eigenvectors and are typical of the general results obtained. The most prominent feature of the error image is the sharp bright peak that occurs at the centre of the subject's right eye showing that the eye points are closer to the approximating hyperplane than most non-eye points. Occasionally a bright response on the shoulders, neck or hairline of the subject is present but generally the error images substantiate the hypotheses that the eye points are well represented by the hyperplane in comparison to the non-eye points.[2] Note that the choice of dimension for the hyperplane is important; if it is too low then the eye-points will not be well represented, if it is too high then non-eye points may be well represented. Further experiments showed that good representations are obtainable for values of the dimension between 5 and 20.

The second experiment followed the work of Hutchinson and scanned a 29×17 window over a search area of size 43×31 pixels centred on the eye. The set of 60 images were divided into the first 16 for training an MLP and the remaining 44 for testing the MLP. The image vector constructed from the scan window was represented in the principal component co-ordinate system using only the 15 components corresponding to the non-zero eigenvalues of the covariance matrix of the 16 eye points. An MLP with 15 hidden nodes, a single output node and a learning rate of 0.5 was trained on the sequence of 15 component vectors generated by scanning the window over the search areas within the 16 training images. The precise training strategy is described in section 7. The network was then tested on the 44 images in the test set. A net is judged to have correctly located an eye, during both training and testing, if the position identified by the neural net is within two pixels of the correct position. Table 1 shows the results of both the training and the testing process for ten runs with random initial weight starts drawn from a uniform distribution in $[-0.125, +0.125]$.

The third experiment is similar to the second except that the vectors presented as input to the MLP have an additional component. We have noted previously that information may be lost when projecting points onto the hyperplane and that in particular non-eye points may be projected into the eye cluster. We have also noted from the first experiment that the distance of a point from the hyperplane is a good measure of whether the point is an eye-point, as eye points are always close to the plane. Thus appending the distance of a point from the hyperplane to the fifteen principal components provides additional discriminatory information. Table 2 shows the results of training an MLP on the principal component vector appended with the distance from the hyperplane.

---

[2] A second experiment used just the first 16 images in the test set to construct a 15 dimension hyperplane approximation to the eye points. The resulting inverse error images for the remaining 44 images in the test set, when suitably filtered, proved to be a reliable eye detector without any further post processing.

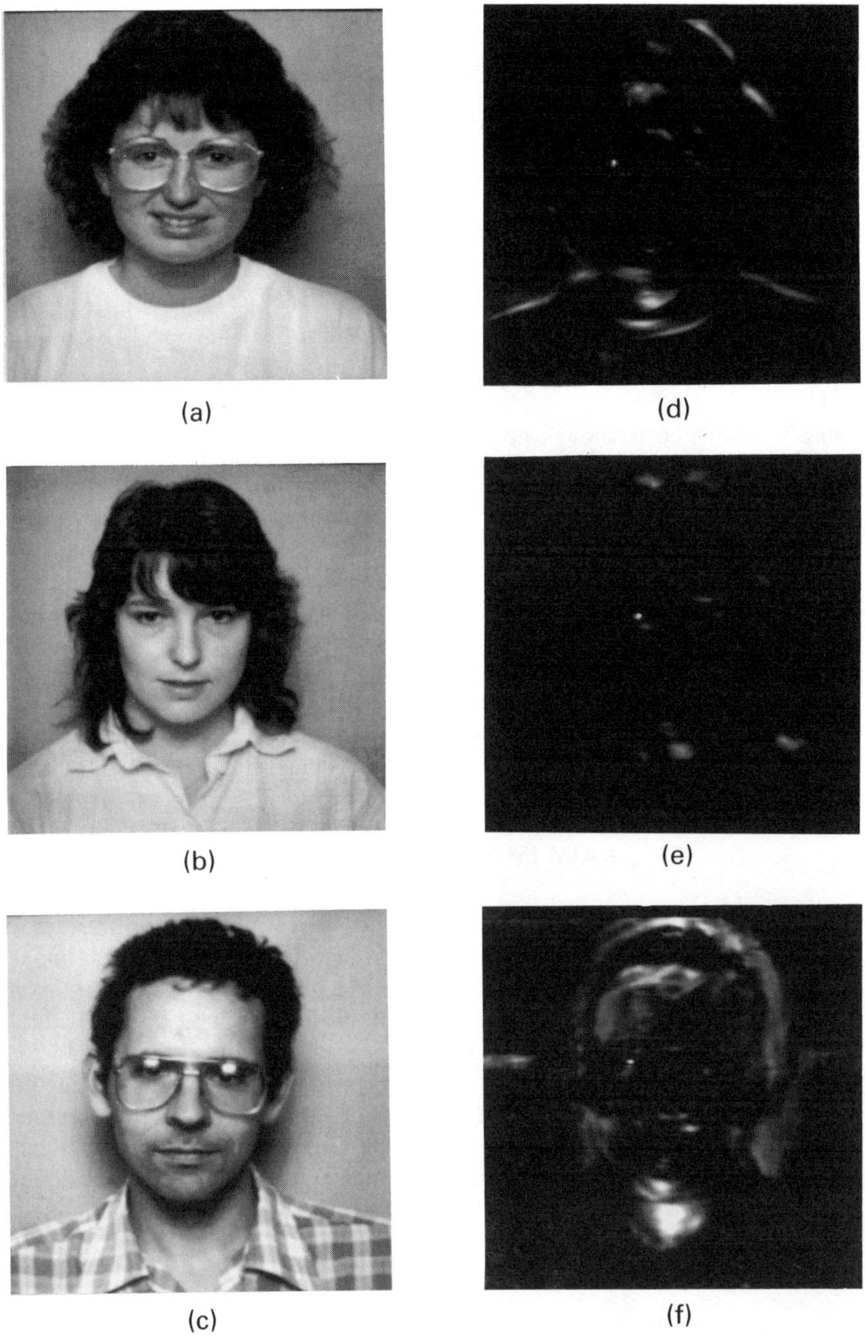

Fig. 6 Originals and inverse error images.

Table 1   Result of 10 runs training an MLP on images represented in the 15 dimensional principal component co-ordinate system
(learning rate = 0.5, 15 input nodes, 15 hidden nodes)

Epochs to Train	Training Results	Test Results
22	16/16	38/44
13	16/16	38/44
15	16/16	40/44
19	16/16	39/44
16	16/16	38/44
24	16/16	39/44
19	16/16	40/44
16	16/16	39/44
17	16/16	38/44
14	16/16	39/44

Table 2   Result of 10 runs training an MLP on images represented in the 15 dimensional principal component co-ordinate system appended with the distance from the hyperplane
(learning rate = 0.5, 16 input nodes, 15 hidden nodes)

Epochs to Train	Training Results	Test Results
14	16/16	39/44
17	16/16	41/44
17	16/16	40/44
15	16/16	40/44
17	16/16	40/44
15	16/16	41/44
16	16/16	40/44
22	16/16	39/44
24	16/16	38/44
18	16/16	39/44

6. RAW IMAGE MLP EXPERIMENTS

To provide a comparison with the principal component results some experiments were conducted on training MLPs on intrinsically raw image data. The experiments essentially follow [1] except that an alternative training strategy has been adopted in the work reported here which significantly reduces the training time. Again the images are divided into the first 16 for training and the remaining 44 for testing. Using the same input image and search window sizes as the reduced dimension experiments of the previous section an MLP was trained on image data normalised so that luminance within the image window had zero mean and unit variance. The results of 10 experiments with random initial weight starts are shown in Table 3.

Table 3 Result of 10 runs training an MLP on raw umages (learning rate = 0.5, 493 input nodes, 15 hidden nodes)

Epochs to Train	Training Results	Test Results
7	16/16	36/44
6	16/16	35/44
25	16/16	42/44
16	16/16	39/44
19	16/16	40/44
12	16/16	40/44
35	16/16	39/44
9	16/16	38/44
5	16/16	38/44
15	16/16	38/44

7. AN ALTERNATIVE TRAINING STRATEGY

The strategy adopted by [1] was to train an MLP to output 1 if the input image is centred on an eye and to output 0 if the input image is 6 or more pixels distance from the eye. When the input image is between 0 and 6 pixels distant from the centre of the eye the MLP is trained to output the linear interpolant between 0 and 1. Thus the output of the MLP is spatially a cone response as the input window is scanned over the image. Furthermore, a very strict convergence criterion was adopted which assumed that the net has trained only when the output of the net differs from the target output by less than 0.1 for all training images. We can think of this as teaching the MLP a precise spatial response to the features sought.

In this work an alternative training strategy has been adopted. The output from a MLP with the usual sigmoid activation function is continuous and differentiable function of its input. It would therefore seem appropriate to teach the MLP functions that are both continuous and differentiable. It is well known that it is difficult for an MLP to learn parity because the target output of the net differs greatly with small changes to the input vector. Similarly, training the MLP to respond as a pseudo delta function when training on the eye data is also difficult. These are both examples of functions that are discontinuous, however it is conjectured that the MLP will more readily learn continuous functions that are smooth. Thus it was decided to train the MLP on the target response $\exp(-0.128x^2)$ where x is the distance in pixels from the centre of the eye. This coefficient 0.128 was chosen so that the function is a good approximation to the Hutchinson cone function. Training with this target response and using the severe stopping criterion of Hutchinson resulted in the network training with an average of approximately 750 epochs over three repeats of the experiment from random initial weight starts. This compares with 1500 epochs elapsing, without the net having met the stopping criterion, as reported in [1].

The precise spatial response of the MLP as it is scanned over the image is in some sense arbitrary. What is required in practice is that the net responds with its highest output when the input window is centred on the eye, responds with a low output when the input window is distant from the eye and that the response generally decays with distance from the eye. The precise nature of the decay is not important, all that matters is that there is a decay. It would therefore appear unnecessary to train the MLP to closely match any given response function.

The procedure adopted here was to initially train the net, with the target response above, on the first image in the training set until its maximum response occurred within two pixels of the centre of the eye. This is a very weak criterion but all that was required of this first part of the training schedule was that the net gain just an approximate impression of what constitutes an eye (there is no point in over training the net on the first eye as this would be undone during subsequent training). Because this training takes place on just a single eye the net learns very rapidly, usually within 5 to 10 epochs. Furthermore, it was found that once this has been done the net was able to locate most of the eyes in the remainder of the training set within two or three pixels. The net was now presented with the first two images in the training set and training was stopped when the maximum response of the net for each image was within two pixels of the corresponding eye centres. This process was continued, doubling the number of images presented to the net from the training set each time. Typically intermediate parts of the training schedule took one or two epochs.

The basic philosophy of the training schedule is two fold. Firstly, only teach the net what it needs to know to perform the classification task at hand. This is achieved by using a stopping criterion which is similar to the criterion that is used during testing to judge whether the net has successfully located the eye. In this way the net learns the bare minimum that is required. Secondly, train the net incrementally, initially with a weak training criterion so that it learns rapidly but does not have to unlearn too much of what was learnt during earlier training. A comparison of Tables 3 and 4 with the results in [1] shows that this approach to training has resulted in a reduction in the number of epochs required by approximately two orders of magnitude but with similar test results to those of the previous training method.

8. DISCUSSION OF THE RESULTS

Table 4 summarises the results of Tables 1,2 and 3 showing the average results over the ten runs.

Table 4
Summary: average results over 10 runs

Method (see key below)	Epochs to Train	Training Results	Test Results
MLP + PC	17.5	16/16	38.8/44
MLP + PC + DFP	17.5	16/16	39.7/44
MLP + [0,1]	14.9	16/16	38.5/44

Key to Table 4:
MLP + PC = MLP trained on the 15 component principal component representation, MLP + PC + DFS = MLP trained on 15 principal component representation augmented with the distance from the hyperplane, MLP + [0,1] = MLP trained on [0,1] normalised data.

The main point to note from Table 4 is that reducing the dimension of the eye data before presenting it to the MLP results in test performances that are similar to MLPs trained on raw image data. In each of the experiments the number of epochs required to train the MLP is similar but for the reduced dimension experiments each epoch requires approximately 30 times less computing time than in the raw image experiments as the network has only 15 input nodes. In terms of overall training time a reduction by a factor of 30 can be achieved if all the input vectors are stored in their reduced format. It is interesting to note that a small increase in the test performance was obtained by the use of the augmented input vector.

A comparison of Table 4 with the results in [1] shows that adoption of the new training strategy has resulted in a reduction in the number of epochs required to train by approximately two orders of magnitude. When both the reduced dimension and the new training strategy are used together training times of one to two minutes are typical.

Unfortunately, for the reduced dimension experiments with the input vector augmented by the distance from the hyperplane, the MLP was trained on the same set of images that were used to construct the principal component co-ordinate system. This may be a poor choice as the component in the input vector to the MLP corresponding to the distance from the hyperplane is always zero for eye points in the training set. Thus during training the MLP does not see examples of input vectors that should be classified as eyes but which have a non-zero distance from the principal component subspace, yet during testing such vectors will arise.

9. CONCLUSIONS

Summarising the results and discussion of the previous sections the following conclusions can been drawn.

- The eye data, at least for the set of test images available, approximately lie in a low dimensional hyperplane. Projection of the data into the hyperplane compresses the image data in the eye location problem without a significant loss of information. This results in approximately an order of magnitude reduction in time to train an MLP on compressed data when compared to the uncompressed data with similar test results in both cases.

- Appending the distance from the hyperplane to the principal component representation of the data has resulted in a slightly better test score than just training on the principal component representation alone. Further tests on a larger set of images is required to show that the technique is generally beneficial. In particular, future work should ensure that the images used to construct the principal component co-ordinate system should be different from the set on which the MLP is trained.

- By adopting a less severe training strategy the number of epochs required to train can be reduced by two orders of magnitude without a reduction in test performance. Combining the training strategy with a principal component preconditioning of the input data results in a further order of magnitude reduction in training time.

It became clear during the MLP based experiments that many of the images in the training set were presenting little independent information to the net. For example, it was observed that the net would often correctly locate 10 or more of the eyes in the training set after having been trained on just a single eye. Most of the effort during training was expended in gaining an initial impression of an eye from the first image of the training set and then subsequently on learning one or two rogue eyes in the remainder of the set that presented different features to the rest of the eyes (e.g. a low fringe partially obscuring and casting a shadow on the eye). During testing it was found that all of the methods tended to fail on the same images, and in all cases they were images in which the subjects were wearing glasses. This indicates that the test results are to some extent independent of the particular classification method and must therefore be a strong function of training data. Thus it appears that an appropriate selection of the training data is crucial to obtaining good results. It is suggested that all the methods described here would do better if presented with a more representative training set. The problem of the lack of independent information highlighted during incremental training also suggests that a selective training strategy be adopted and initial work in this area has shown promising results. Here, the current training set is selected from a pool of potential training images with images from the pool being admitted to the training set only if they are misclassified by the network. This process continues until all images in the training pool are correctly classified by the network.

REFERENCES

1. Hutchinson R and Welsh W: 'Comparison of Neural Networks and Conventional Techniques for Feature Location in Facial Images', Proc First IEE International Conference on Artificial Neural Networks, Conference publication 313, pp 201—205, (Oct 1987).
2. Nering E D: 'Linear Algebra and Matrix theory', second edition, John Wiley & Sons, (1970).
3. Lloyd E: 'Handbook of Applicable Mathematics, Volume IV: Statistics Part B', John Wiley & Sons, (1984).

APPENDIX 1: LEAST SQUARES FITTING

For completeness we shall show that the first M principal component vectors $\{\underline{u}_j\}_{j=1}^{M}$ of the eye data are an orthonormal spanning set for the best M-dimensional least squares hyperplane through the data. We assume that there are P data points $\{\underline{x}_i\}_{i=1}^{P}$, $\underline{x}_i \in \mathcal{R}^N$, and that the set of unit vectors $\{\underline{v}_i\}_{i=1}^{M}$ form an orthogonal co-ordinate system, origin $\underline{O}$, that are a basis for the least squares hyperplane. Thus the problem is to find the origin $\underline{O}$ and show that the vectors $\{\underline{v}_i\}_{i=1}^{M}$ are a linear combination of the principal component vectors $\{\underline{u}_i\}_{i=1}^{M}$.

The approximation error $\underline{e}_i$ in fitting the hyperplane to the ith data point is just the difference in the position of the point and its projection onto the hyperplane:

$$\underline{e}_i = (\underline{x}_i - \underline{O}) - \sum_{j=1}^{M} \{(\underline{x}_i - \underline{O})^T \underline{v}_j\} \underline{v}_j \quad 1 \leq i \leq N \ldots \ldots (A1.1)$$

As the vectors $\{\underline{v}_i\}_{i=1}^{M}$ are orthonormal the magnitude of the error is given by

$$\|\underline{e}_i\|^2 = \underline{e}_i^T \underline{e}_i = (\underline{x}_i - \underline{O})^T (\underline{x}_i - \underline{O}) - 2 \sum_{j=1}^{M} \{(\underline{x}_i - \underline{O})^T \underline{v}_j\}^2$$
$$+ \sum_{j=1}^{M} \{(\underline{x}_i - \underline{O})^T \underline{v}_j\}^2 \underline{v}_j^T \underline{v}_j$$

46   FACIAL FEATURE LOCATION

The origin is to be chosen so that the mean squared error is a minimum[3] and so we set

$$\frac{1}{P} \sum_{i=1}^{P} \frac{\partial}{\partial o_k} \|\underline{e}_i\|^2 = 0 \quad 1 \leq k \leq N$$

where o_k is the kth component of the origin. Noting that this holds for all choices of the spanning set yields, after a simple calculation,

$$\underline{O} = \frac{1}{P} \sum_{i=1}^{P} \underline{x}_i .$$

Hence the origin is at the centroid of the data which we denote by $\underline{\mu}$. We can define matrices E, X and V by

$$E = \begin{pmatrix} \underline{e}_1 \\ \underline{e}_2 \\ \cdot \\ \underline{e}_P \end{pmatrix}, \quad X = \begin{pmatrix} \underline{x}_1 - \underline{\mu} \\ \underline{x}_2 - \underline{\mu} \\ \cdot \\ \underline{x}_P - \underline{\mu} \end{pmatrix}, \quad V = (\underline{v}_1, \underline{v}_2, .. \underline{v}_M)$$

then (equation A1.1) can be rewritten in matrix form as $E = X(I-VV^T)$. The mean squared error is now given by

$$\frac{1}{P} Tr(EE^T) = \frac{1}{P} Tr(X(I-VV^T)(1-VV^T)^T X^T)$$

$$= \frac{1}{P} Tr(X(I - 2VV^T + VV^T VV^T)X^T)$$

$$= \frac{1}{P} Tr(X(I - VV^T)X^T) \qquad \ldots(A1.2)$$

where Tr is the trace operator. Here the last line follows because the matrix V satisfies $V^T V = I$. Thus we want to minimise the last expression in equation A1.2 which is equivalent to maximising

$$\frac{1}{P} Tr(XHH^T X^T) = \frac{1}{P} Tr(H^T X^T XH).$$

The symmetric matrix $C = \frac{1}{P} X^T X$ is the covariance matrix of the data which we can decompose [2] into $C = UDU^T$ where $D = diag(\lambda_1, \ldots, \lambda_N)$ is the matrix with diagonal the eigenvalues of C and U is the $N \times N$ modal

---
[3] Note that we are guaranteed a minimum as (A1.2) is in general a non-negative semi-defined quadratic form in the origin components.

matrix whose columns are the eigenvectors (principal components) of C. Note that as C is symmetric then U is orthogonal [2]. It follows that we now want to maximise

$$Tr(V^TCV) = Tr(V^TUDU^TV) = Tr(G^TDG)$$
$$= \sum_{i=1}^{P} \lambda_i(g_{i1}^2 + g_{i2}^2 + \ldots g_{iN}^2) \qquad \ldots(A1.3)$$

where $G = \{g_{ij}\} = U^TV$. Because U is orthogonal and V has orthonormal columns it follows that G also has orthonormal columns. If we write [3] $f_i = g_{i1}^2 + g_{i2}^2 + \ldots g_{iN}^2$ then because of the orthonormality of the columns of G we have

$$0 \le f_i \le 1 \text{ and } \sum_{i=1}^{N} f_i = M. \qquad \ldots(A1.4)$$

Hence, from equation A1.3, we want to minimise $\sum_{i=1}^{N}\lambda_i f_i$ subject to the constraints of equation A1.4. This is a linear programming problem and so the solution occurs when M of the f_i's are one and the remaining $N-M$ are zero. For a maximum those f_i's corresponding to the largest eigenvalues must be non-zero. Those rows of G that correspond to zero values of f_i are necessarily identically zero and so G has the form

$$G = \begin{pmatrix} G_M \\ O \end{pmatrix}.$$

From the definition of G and the orthogonality of U we have that $V = UG$ and so the spanning set $\{v_{-i}\}_{i=1}^{M}$ is a linear combination of the first M eigenvectors $\{u_{-i}\}_{i=1}^{M}$ of the covariance matrix.

When represented with respect to the principal component co-ordinate system the covariance matrix is diagonal with the eigenvalues in the diagonal. Thus it is seen that the eigenvalues are the variances of the data along the principal component co-ordinate directions. Notice that with this interpretation it is easily seen that if there are less data points P than the dimension of the space N then at least $N-P$ of the eigenvalues will be zero. In addition, because the data has been spatially shifted so that the centroid lies at the origin of the space the mean centred data is necessarily linearly dependent (it sums to the zero vector) and so at least $N-P+1$ of the eigenvalues will be zero.

APPENDIX 2: EFFICIENT EIGENVECTOR CALCULATION

For the eye location problem the pattern space is of dimension 493 and consequently the mean centred covariance matrix is of order 493 and fully populated. Calculation of all the eigenvalues and eigenvectors is therefore not a trivial task. However, when the number of eye points P is less than the dimension of the space N there will be at most $P-1$ non-zero eigenvalues and we require a method of calculating them directly without the overhead of having to calculate eigenvectors corresponding to zero eigenvalues.

If we denote the centroid of the eye data by $\underline{\mu} = \frac{1}{P} \sum_{k=1}^{P} \underline{x}_k$ and put $\underline{\hat{x}}_i = \underline{x}_i - \underline{\mu}$, $1 \leq i \leq P$, then as shown in appendix 1 we need to find the eigenvectors and eigenvalues of the mean centred covariance matrix:

$$C = \frac{1}{P} \sum_{k=1}^{P} (\underline{x}_k - \underline{\mu})(\underline{x}_k - \underline{\mu})^T = \frac{1}{P} \sum_{k=1}^{P} \underline{\hat{x}}_k \underline{\hat{x}}_k^T .$$

We assume that the eye data $\{\underline{x}_i\}_{i=1}^{P}$ is linearly independent[4] and then it follows that the mean centred data $\{\underline{\hat{x}}_i\}_{i=1}^{P}$ is linearly dependent as it sums to the zero vector. However, a simple calculation shows that if we remove any of the mean centred vectors from the set then the resulting set is linearly independent. That is, the set of vectors $\{\underline{\hat{x}}_1,...,\underline{\hat{x}}_{k-1},\underline{\hat{x}}_{k+1},...,\underline{\hat{x}}_P\}$ is linearly independent for any $1 \leq k \leq P$.

The eigenvectors $\{\underline{\phi}^{(n)}\}_{n=1}^{P-1}$ corresponding to the non-zero eigenvalues $\{\lambda^{(n)}\}_{n=1}^{P-1}$ of the mean centred covariance matrix satisfy

$$\left(\frac{1}{P} \sum_{k=1}^{P} \underline{\hat{x}}_k \underline{\hat{x}}_k^T \right) \underline{\phi}^{(n)} = \lambda^{(n)} \underline{\phi}^{(n)} \quad for\ n=1,2,...,P-1. \quad ...(A2.1)$$

When the dimension of the best least squares hyperplane is $P-1$ the hyperplane actually interpolates the data. Hence the space spanned by the first $P-1$ eigenvectors is the same as the space spanned by any $P-1$ of the mean centred eye points. Hence we can write

$$\underline{\phi}^{(n)} = \sum_{j=0}^{P-1} \alpha_j^{(n)} \underline{\hat{x}}_j \quad for\ n=1,2,...,P-1 \quad ...(A2.2)$$

for some set of scalars $\alpha_j^{(n)}$ to be found. Substituting this expression in equation A2.1 we find

---

[4] In practice this will almost certainly be true.

APPENDIX 2

$$\left(\frac{1}{P}\sum_{k=1}^{P}\underline{\hat{x}}_k\underline{\hat{x}}_k^T\right)\sum_{j=1}^{P-1}\alpha_j^{(n)}\underline{\hat{x}}_j = \lambda^{(n)}\sum_{i=1}^{P-1}\alpha_i^{(n)}\underline{\hat{x}}_i \quad \text{for } n=1,2,\ldots,P-1$$

$$\Rightarrow \frac{1}{P}\sum_{k=1}^{P}\underline{\hat{x}}_k\left(\sum_{j=1}^{P-1}\alpha_j^{(n)}\underline{\hat{x}}_k^T\underline{\hat{x}}_j\right) = \lambda^{(n)}\sum_{i=1}^{P-1}\alpha_i^{(n)}\underline{\hat{x}}_i \quad \text{for } n=1,2,\ldots,P-1$$

Putting $l_{kj} = \frac{1}{P}\underline{\hat{x}}_k^T\underline{\hat{x}}_j$ gives

$$\sum_{k=1}^{P}\left(\sum_{j=1}^{P-1}\alpha_j^{(n)} l_{kj}\right)\underline{\hat{x}}_k = \lambda^{(n)}\sum_{i=1}^{P-1}\alpha_i^{(n)}\underline{\hat{x}}_i \quad \text{for } n=1,2,\ldots,P-1$$

and using the fact that $\underline{\hat{x}}_P = -\sum_{i=1}^{P-1}\underline{\hat{x}}_i$ we obtain

$$\sum_{k=1}^{P-1}\left(\sum_{j=1}^{P-1}\alpha_j^{(n)}(l_{kj}-l_{Pj})\right)\underline{\hat{x}}_k = \lambda^{(n)}\sum_{i=1}^{P-1}\alpha_i^{(n)}\underline{\hat{x}}_i \quad \text{for } n=1,2,\ldots,P-1$$

As they are linearly independent we can equate the coefficients of the $\underline{\hat{x}}_i$, $1 \leq i \leq P-1$, yielding

$$\sum_{j=1}^{P-1}(l_{kj}-l_{Pj})\alpha_j^{(n)} = \lambda^{(n)}\alpha_k^{(n)} \quad \text{for } n=1,2,\ldots,P-1 \quad \ldots(A2.4)$$

And finally putting $L = \{l_{kj}-l_{Pj}\}$ and $\underline{\alpha}^{(n)} = \{\alpha_i^{(n)}\}$ we can rewrite equation A2.4 in matrix form as

$$L\underline{\alpha}^{(n)} = \lambda^{(n)}\underline{\alpha}^{(n)} \quad \text{for } n=1,2,\ldots,P-1. \quad \ldots(A2.5)$$

Here equation A2.5 is an $P-1$ dimensional eigenvalue problem which for $(P-1) < N$ is computationally less expensive to solve than equation A2.1. Furthermore, the solutions to equation A2.1 corresponding to non-zero eigenvalues can be reconstructed from the solutions to equation A2.5 via equation A2.2.

3

THE DETECTION OF EYES IN FACIAL IMAGES USING RADIAL BASIS FUNCTIONS

R M Debenham and S C J Garth
Department of Engineering, University of Cambridge

1. INTRODUCTION

This chapter describes work done by the authors on the problem of locating eyes in human head and shoulders images, as described in the Introduction to Part 1 of this book, and in Chapters 1 and 2.

2. RADIAL BASIS FUNCTIONS

Most existing neural network models use neurons which calculate an output as a function of the weighted sum of their inputs. We will refer to these as linearly weighted input (LWI) neurons. Examples of neural networks which use LWI neurons are backpropagation MLP networks [1], Hopfield networks [2] and Boltzmann machines [3]. If the n inputs to a neuron are thought of as defining a point in an n dimensional hyperspace, then the LWI neuron's output is a function of the distance from that point to a plane defined by the weights on the inputs and the bias of the neuron. If we define S_j to be the output of the jth neuron, then

$$S_j = f(X_j)$$

where

$$X_j = \sum_{i=0}^{N_i} S_i W_{ij} + \theta_j$$

In this equation the W_{ij} terms represent the weights on the neuron's inputs from other neurons, and the θ_j term is the bias of the neuron. The W_{ij} terms are often referred to as synaptic weights. The synaptic weights define the angle of the hyperplane mentioned above, while the bias determines its exact position. Typical functions $f(x)$, known as **activation functions** are simple step functions or sigmoid functions. These functions are illustrated in Fig. 1.

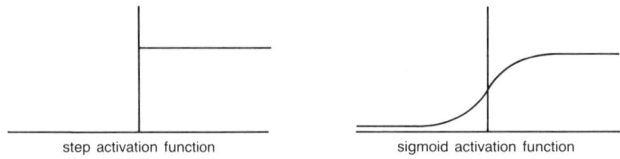

Fig. 1 Typical activation functions for LWI neurons.

Radial basis functions (RBFs) on the other hand are used by comparatively few current models. Examples of those that do include Kohonen self-organizing feature maps [4] and restricted coulomb energy (RCE) networks [5]. Other research into RBFs has been carried out by Broomhead and Lowe [6], and Robinson, Niranjan and Fallside [7] generalise the back propagation algorithm to include such neurons. Neurons that use RBFs compute their outputs not from the weighted sum of their inputs, but by regarding the input weights as defining a point in the input space. The output is then computed as a function of the distance from this point to the point defined by the inputs. This can be compared to the way in which LWIs compute their output from the distance to a plane. Mathematically, this can be written

$$S_j = g(X_j)$$

where

$$X_j = \sqrt{\sum_{i=0}^{N_i} \left(\frac{S-W_{ij}}{r_j}\right)^2}$$

Here, the W_{ij} terms represent the **centre** of the RBF, and the r_j is a **radius** term. These are analogous to the synaptic weights and bias of the LWI neuron. Typical forms for $g(x)$ are Gaussians, 'Mexican hat' functions or step functions. These are illustrated in Fig. 2. It should be noted that, in general, RBF activation functions tend to 0 as x tends to infinity, whereas LWI activation functions tend to a finite non-zero value, usually 1, as x tends to infinity.

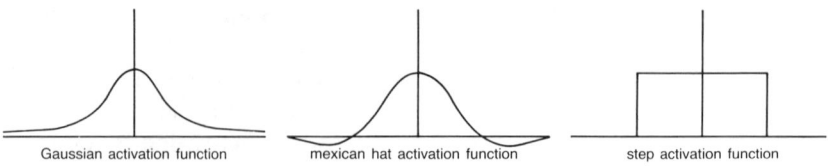

Fig. 2 Typical activation functions for RBF neurons.

Having noted these general characteristics of LWI and RBF neurons, we now turn our attention to the implications for their use in neural networks. Most neural network problems are pattern classification problems. A pattern is presented on the input neurons, and the output neuron activations are used to assign a label to the pattern. An example of this is character recognition — some representation of the character to be recognised is presented on the inputs, and the output labels this representation as being an 'A', 'B', 'C' etc. This sort of task is often expressed as being a labelling of regions of the multidimensional input space formed by the inputs to the first layer of neurons. Each pattern is thought of as occupying one or more regions of the space (see Fig. 3). This input space is exactly the same as the multidimensional space that was mentioned in the discussion of the differences between types of neurons. The question of which type of neuron to use then becomes one of which type of neuron is better at defining a region of space. In order to define an arbitrary, possibly finite, possibly convex region of space in an understandable manner, three layers of LWI neurons are necessary [8], although it can be shown that an arbitrary mapping is possible with just two layers [9]. Using similar arguments to Lippmann, however, it is clear that just two layers of neurons are necessary if the first layer consists of RBF neurons. This is because RBF neurons encode a finite region of space, whereas LWI neurons encode an infinite region of space.

Most of the current neural network algorithms suffer from a number of drawbacks. These include the fact that the size of the network must be fixed at the start of the simulations; a lack of incremental learning, that is the ability to learn a new set of mappings without forgetting any mappings previously learned; poor generalisation from testing data to training data; and a tendency for 'overtraining' whereby extra training actually reduces the system's ability to generalise. These were among the problems that we wished to address.

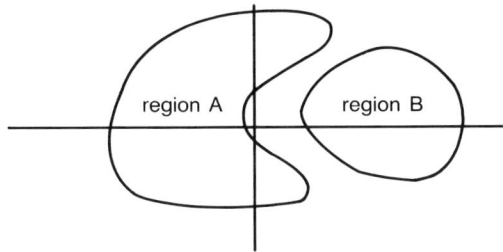

Fig. 3 Labelling regions of the input space.

3. THE RESTRICTED COULOMB ENERGY ALGORITHM

We decided to start our work from the RCE algorithm of Nestor Inc [5]. Our two main reasons for starting from this algorithm were that it avoids the problem of sizing the network beforehand, and that it has the ability to learn new mappings incrementally.

The algorithm defines a two layer network. In the first layer are RBF neurons, which are connected to the network inputs. In the second layer are LWI neurons which form the network's outputs. Each output represents a possible class to which the input could belong, that is it provides a label to a region of hyperspace as described above. This architecture is shown in Fig. 4. The network starts with no neurons in the first layer and then grows or 'spawns' them as they are required.

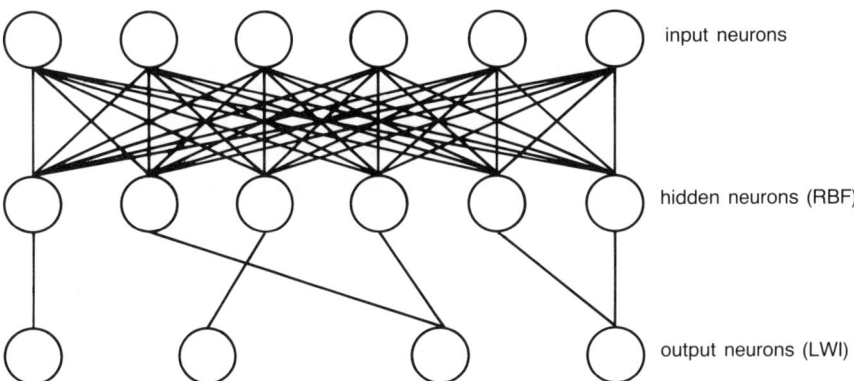

Fig. 4 The architecture of the RBF network.

All of the inputs are connected to each RBF neuron. The RBF neurons have a step activation function with $g(x)$ being 1 for $x < 1$ and 0 for $x > 1$. The neuron therefore turns 'on', with $S_j = 1$ if the input falls within a distance r of the RBF centre. Each RBF neuron is connected to one LWI unit only, with a weight W_{jk} of 1. The output neurons have step activations functions and a bias θ_k of -0.5. An output turns 'on', therefore, if any of the RBF neurons to which it is connected turn 'on'. The learning algorithm is outlined below.

The RCE algorithm
1. Apply a pattern on the inputs and calculate outputs based on this pattern.
2. For each output.
   If 'on' and should be 'on' do nothing.
   If 'off' and should be 'off' do nothing.
   If 'on' and should be 'off':
      shrink the radius of all 'on' RBF neurons connected to this output just to touch the input point.
   If 'off' and should be 'on':
      'spawn' a new RBF neuron centred on this input point.
3. Go to 1.

This algorithm has been proven in such applications as character recognition (Nestor publicity material), but there are a number of areas in which we feel that it can be improved. These are set out in the next section.

4. PROBLEMS WITH RCE

While the RCE algorithm has advantages, notably an ability to learn new mappings incrementally, no need to fix the size of the network, simplicity and rapid training, it does have a number of drawbacks and features that could be improved. These are detailed below.

- There is no way for the radii of the RBF neurons to increase; they can only decrease. If a new input point lies just outside the boundary of an RBF neuron's 'sphere of influence' then it may be much more efficient to increase the radius slightly in order to incorporate the new point in an existing neuron than to spawn an entirely new one. In this latter case it may well be that the new neuron's radius would have to be repeatedly reduced as it overlapped regions of space representing other outputs. This problem would be particularly acute if it were required to encode a cluster of points of roughly hyperspherical shape whose radius was slightly bigger than the default starting radius of the network. In this case the existing algorithm would require that new neurons be spawned all around the base hypersphere.

- There is no way for the centres of the RBF neurons to move once they have been spawned. This problem is related to the first one. It may be much more efficient to move the centre of an RBF neuron slightly in order to cover a new point than to spawn a new one. This would be particularly true in the case where it is required to encode a cluster of points, but the first example point from this cluster is situated towards one edge. In this case the existing RCE algorithm would be forced to spawn a new neuron where in fact it would be simpler to move the existing one so that its centre coincided with that of the cluster of points.

- There is no way of knowing how much information about the problem is encoded in a given neuron. An RBF neuron may exist where it does as the result of the cumulative action of a large number of example points or as the result of just a single point. In the existing algorithm these two cases are indistinguishable and are treated in exactly the same way, whereas the former obviously encodes more information about the input space than the latter and should accordingly be more fixed in the input space. One isolated example may represent noise and so its influence should be limited. If some form of 'synaptic ageing' is introduced, whereby it is more difficult to change the parameters of an RBF neuron that has been activated by many examples this can be achieved, both by reducing the influence of a single point upon old neurons, and by making it easy to reduce the radius of those single points that do represent noise.

- For an output to turn 'on' in the RCE algorithm one of the RBF neurons must turn completely 'on' — there is no grey area at the edge of the sphere of influence. If a point lies close to the boundaries of several RBF neurons that encode the same output then it may well be appropriate to turn on that output even though none of the neurons in the RBF layer have turned 'on'. The RCE algorithm provides no method for doing this. One way is to use activation functions $g(x)$ that are not sharp step functions but have a tail off at the edge. By using a bias θ of between -1 and 0 on the outputs and varying the sharpness of the tail off the size of the grey area could be controlled.

We have incorporated all of the above changes into a new algorithm — the extended restricted coulomb energy algorithm (ERCE).

5. THE EXTENDED RESTRICTED COULOMB ENERGY ALGORITHM

The ERCE algorithm's system architecture is identical to that of the RCE algorithm, with one layer of RBF neurons and one of LWI neurons. The activation function $g(x)$ used for the RBF neurons is different, however, as are the learning rule and the bias of the LWI neurons. For the RBF neurons the ERCE algorithm uses a 'step + linear' activation function of the form shown in Fig. 5.

The bias for the output neurons is between -1 and 0, typically -0.8. The algorithm is outlined below.

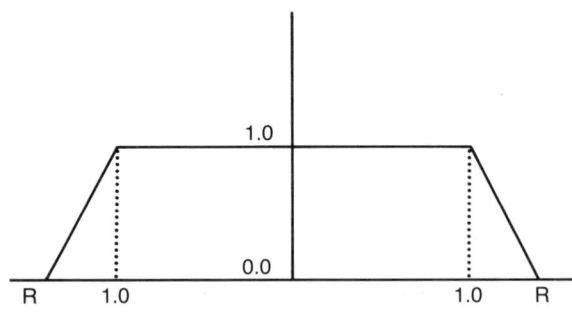

Fig. 5 The 'step + linear' activation function of ERCE.

The ERCE algorithm
1. Apply a pattern on the inputs and calculate outputs based on this pattern.
2. For each output.
   If 'on' and should be 'on':
   update the age of all 'on' RBF neurons connected to this output.
   If 'off' and should be 'off': do nothing.
   If 'on' and should be 'off':
   attempt to adjust all 'on' RBF neurons connected to this output so that the net input to the output neuron $= -\theta$. The maximum adjustment for each RBF neuron is determined by the age of that neuron.
   If 'off' and should be 'on':
   attempt to adjust the nearest RBF neuron connected to this output so that the net input to the output neuron $= -\theta$. If this adjustment exceeds the maximum adjustment allowed by that neuron's age, then spawn a new neuron.
3. Go to 1.

Adjustments to the parameters of the RBF neurons are made both by moving the centres of the functions and by increasing or decreasing the radii. A 'learning ratio', L, is defined in terms of the relative movement in each of these quantities. If $L=1$ then the system learns solely by changing the radii, and if $L=0$ then the system learns solely by moving the RBF centres. L is a parameter that must be supplied to the system at the start of simulations in much the same way that a learning rate η must be supplied to MLP systems.

6. APPLICATION TO THE PROBLEM

Description of the problem

The problem to be solved is that of eye location as described in the introduction to Part 1. The exact formulation of the problem was to 'locate the positions of the eyes. Position is defined as the centre point of the line joining the corners of the eye'. There were 60 images on which to test the performance of the algorithm, and each image was 256×256 pixels in size with 256 grey levels.

Network to solve the problem

In order to solve the problem we used a network with 64 inputs and 64 outputs. The inputs were taken from an 8×8 template which was then moved over the image one pixel at a time. We did not test the network on the entire image, but in order to reduce processing times we used a 64×64 pixel subimage in the region of the right eye. For each image, therefore, $(64-7) \times (64-7) = 3249$ sets of data were presented to the network. Each of the outputs corresponded to one of the inputs. The network was trained so that when the centre of the eye, as defined in the problem, was coincident with one of the inputs, the corresponding output was to turn 'on'. All outputs apart from this were to turn 'off'. As the template moves across the image a record is kept for each point of how many times an output has turned 'on' while corresponding to that point, and when the image has been fully processed a cluster of points appears corresponding to the position of the eye. Of course a few other points appear but these are simply noise and not part of the main cluster. The architecture of this network is shown in Fig. 6.

58 DETECTION OF EYES

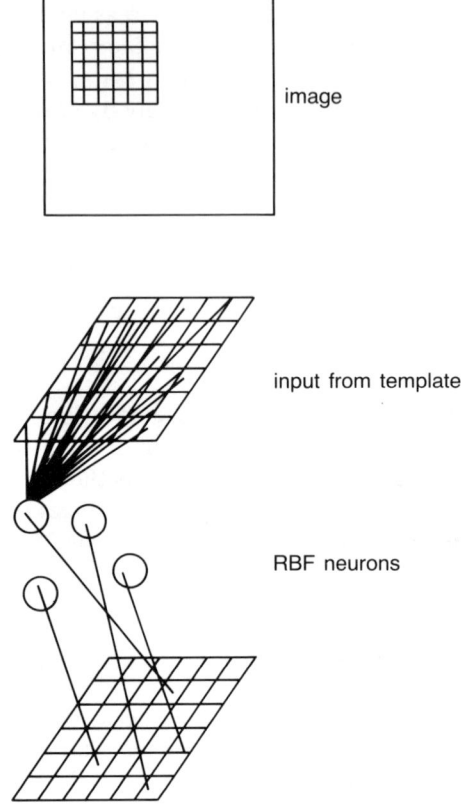

Fig. 6 The image processing system architecture.

The images were divided into two sets of 30. One of these sets of images was used to train the system and the other set of 30 was used to test the system. The network was trained using some or all of the training data set and tested using the entire testing data set. The only network parameter that was varied was the initial radius that the RBF neurons were given, r_0. The other parameters of the system, that is the rate of synaptic ageing K_3, the learning ratio L and the rate of fall off of $g(x)$ R remained constant throughout the simulations.

The position taken as indicating the centre of the eye was the 'median' of the points indicated by the system. In two dimensions the meaning of the term 'median' is somewhat ambiguous. The way that we defined it was first to ignore the y co-ordinates of all the points given and simply calculate the median of the points in the x direction, and then to repeat this with the axes reversed. This method was found to give good results. We also tried calculating the mean of the points, but this was found to give poor results as it tended to be unduly influenced by false positives some distance from the actual eye. If the median is used then a false positive close to the eye has the same effect as a false positive some distance from the eye, whereas the latter has a greater effect on the mean than the former.

First results

The network was first trained using unprocessed images and an initial RBF radius (r_0) of 100 with a single pass through the training data. At first just the first 10 images of the data were used in order to reduce the time taken for images to be processed. As more images are used in the training set more RBF neurons are spawned which results in an increased processing time. The processing time is almost linear with the number of RBF neurons in the network. This initial system correctly classified only 11 of the 30 eyes in the testing set. Training the system in the above way was found to be unsatisfactory for two main reasons. The first was that an initial radius of 100 was found to be too small to produce sufficient generalisation from training data to test data. An unseen eye has to look too much like an eye that has already been seen for enough RBF neurons to fire. The second and seemingly opposite effect was that RBF neurons spawned as a result of the last images in the training set had radii that had not been 'moderated' by training on other images and which were therefore too large. These large radius RBFs tended to cause spurious points to be indicated in the test images that were not near the actual position of the eye. This resulted in a large number of eyes failing to be correctly classified as a result of too few points being indicated in the actual region of the eye (true positives) and too many points being indicated away from the eye (false positives). 10 images was also found to be too few to cause sufficient generalisation, with too many images having no points at all indicated by the network.

To combat all of these effects the network was then trained on all 30 images in the training set with 3 passes through the set and an initial RBF radius of 1000. When trained in this way the network correctly classified 14 of the eyes in the test set. While this was an improvement on the previous result it is still unacceptably low. To improve the rate to an acceptable level it was found necessary to make some changes to the way in which the network was trained.

Modifications to the network

One effect that was apparent when examining the results from the network described in the previous section was that when the network was classifying eyes correctly it tended to place quite a small number of points (5—10) exactly in the centre of the eye but none in its general area. This was in contrast to the cluster of points around the centre of the eye that we had expected. The reason for this was also one of the reasons for the low classification rate of the network so far. During training, if the network indicated that a point was close to the centre of the eye but not exactly coincident with it, the training algorithm would treat it as giving an incorrect answer and shrink the radius of the firing RBF neurons accordingly. This resulted in insufficient generalisation with only those eyes that were very similar to those in the training set being recognised by the network. In order to overcome this problem, the training algorithm for the network was modified. A 'dead zone' was defined in the region of each eye in the following way. If the network indicated that a point lying within a 5×5 square centred on the centre of the eye was in fact the position of the centre then this was taken as being a correct answer and the radii of the corresponding RBF neurons were not shrunk. Thus the network would ignore false positives as long as they were not 'very' false.

When the network was trained with this modification using three passes through all 30 images in the training set and an initial RBF radius of 1000 the system correctly classified 28 of the eyes in the testing set. This was a major improvement, resulting in a satisfactory level of correct classification. This system took about 5 minutes to process one image on the TMS320C30 DSP accelerator card that we were using. In order to speed up the network's processing time we tried training the system using three passes through just the first 10 images in the training set. This yielded a system that could correctly classify 22 of the training images but did so in 1.5—2 minutes. There was therefore a trade-off to be had between processing time and accuracy of classification.

Preprocessing of image data

In an attempt to increase the success rate of the network still further the images were first processed using a conventional spatial filter. The first attempt in this direction was to process the image using a simple averaging filter. This had the effect of blurring the details in the image, the idea being that this would enable the network to learn using just the large scale features of the image and without being affected by small details which could be regarded as noise. The filter coefficients used are shown below in Fig. 7.

1	1	1
1	1	1
1	1	1

Fig. 7 Averaging filter coefficients.

Use of this filter was not successful, however, as the eyes tended to merge too much into the surrounding areas and not stand out enough. This resulted in a large drop in the successful classification rate. This problem was particularly acute for those images where the person was wearing glasses, particularly tinted ones. In these cases the eyes merged completely into the background and were indistinguishable from it. A second filter was therefore tried with the opposite effect of the previous filter, that of enhancing the edges in the network. The filter used was the 'unsharp mask' filter, the coefficients for which are shown in Fig. 8.

0	−1	0
−1	5	−1
0	−1	0

Fig. 8   Unsharp mask filter coefficients.

This filter is actually the result of subtracting the Laplacian of the image from the original. This had the effect of making the eyes appear to stand out much more from their surroundings. When the network was trained and tested on images that had undergone this preprocessing the classification rate for the testing set improved to 29 of the 30 images. This preprocessing was therefore a success.

We now had a network that could successfully recognise the positions of the eyes in facial images, but it still took about 5 minutes to process each image. In an effort to speed up this processing we decided to reduce the area of the image that the network searched, thus reducing the number of presentations of data to the inputs. The first approach that we took was to observe that the eyes were almost always darker than the surrounding area. It seems reasonable, therefore, to restrict the search to those areas where there is a change in the intensity of the pixels. We constructed a search map of the image in the following way. First, a grey scale histogram of the image is formed, and the grey level of the first quartile calculated. The image is then thresholded at this grey level, with all pixels greater than this grey level being assigned the value 1 and all pixels less than this grey level the value 0. An edge map of this new image is then calculated in which each pixel is assigned the value 1 if any of its four immediate neighbours has a different value, and 0 otherwise. This edge map forms the search map for the image. At each template position the network is run using the template values if the edge map contains a 1 in any of the template positions; if not the template moves on to the next position. This technique was found to work better if the original image was used instead of the Laplacian filtered image as the filter magnifies noise and causes spurious edges to appear. The filtered image was still used for the values given to the network, however, and the network was still trained using the entire image. When this preprocessing was used the network still correctly classified 28 of the 30 test eyes. The time taken for each image to be processed was approximately halved, however. The actual time taken for processing varied, as the number of positions that needed to be searched was not the same for all images.

Hierarchical network

The edge detection method of reducing the search space was reasonably successful in reducing the time taken to process the images but reduced the success rate of the network in classifying the positions of the eyes. It was desirable that some way could be found to reduce the time taken still further which had no effect on the success rate of the network. Reducing the time further involved finding the rough position of the eye with greater accuracy, and also finding a technique to do this which was more immune to noise. To this end a two network system was devised. The first network was to work on groups of pixels clumped together, that is at a lower resolution than the actual image data, and give a rough indication of the position of the eye. This network was effectively to calculate the search map to be used by the second network, which was to be as before. This hierarchical arrangement of networks is shown in Fig. 9.

In order to test the feasibility of such a system we first tested a low resolution system which worked on a 64×64 pixel image calculated from the original 256×256 pixel image. Thus the pixels that were used for this image were the means of 4×4 squares of pixels in the original image. We trained this network to find just the right eyes in the images, which it did with 100% success when trained using 3 passes through all 30 of the training images and an initial radius of 1000. We therefore decided that such a system was feasible. One notable feature was that the system was very specific to the right eye. It was expected that some points might have been indicated in the region of the left eye as well as the right, as eyes appear to be symmetrical, but this did not happen. This is perhaps because the network not only uses the shape of the eye to make its classification but also the shape of the surroundings.

Having demonstrated the workability of the system we now tested it using the actual image data. Using the coarse network described above and the most accurate fine network (that trained on all 30 images with 3 passes) the system successfully identified all 30 of the eyes in the testing data set. The time taken to process the images was reduced by typically 75% over the simple system. When the fine network was trained on the first 10 images in the data set with 3 passes the success rate was 25/30, but the time taken to perform the processing was only about 20 seconds. As before the exact time varies from image to image as the reduction in search area depends on the exact

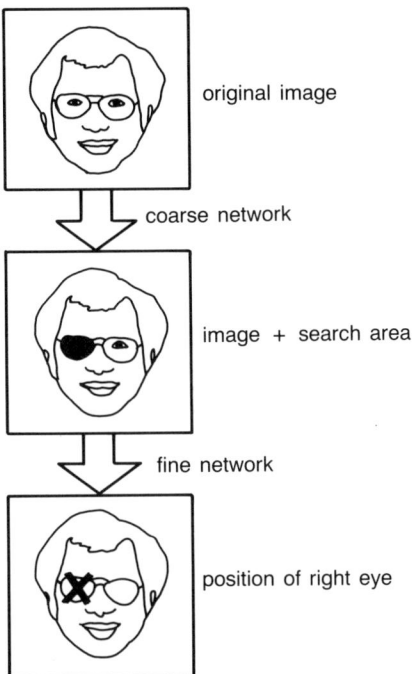

Fig. 9 The hierarchical image processing system.

image. The improvement in success rate can be attributed to the reduction in the number of false positives given by the fine network. The coarse network effectively restricts the area of search to the area immediately around the position of the eye. As a result the only points that the fine network recognises as the eye are in the correct position. This system is also much less prone to noise in the image which was a problem that affected the edge detection system. In that system noise had a tendency to create 'blips' in the edge map and so reduce the effectiveness of the reduction in search area.

7. CONCLUSIONS

The ERCE algorithm has been shown to work very well on the test problem. The algorithm learns classifications very rapidly compared to conventional algorithms such as back-propagation, and with a much smaller training set. Both of these are significant advantages. It also has the ability to learn new mappings independently of old ones which gives it the potential for great adaptability in use. The main use for the algorithm is clearly in pattern recognition and classification problems such as this one. It works particularly well for problems where the solution can be readily expressed in terms of labelling regions of space; indeed it is designed specifically with these in mind. For other problems the algorithm would not work as well, but as the majority of neural network solutions can be expressed in this way we foresee a wide potential use for the algorithm.

REFERENCES

1. Rumelhart D E & McClelland J L: 'Parallel distributed processing.' $\underline{1}$: Foundations. MIT Press, Cambridge MA (1986).
2. Hopfield J J: 'Neural networks and physical systems with emergent collective computational abilities'. Proc National Academy of Sciences, USA $\underline{79}$, pp 2554—2558 (1982).
3. Ackley D H, Hinton G E & Sejnowski T J: 'A learning algorithm for Boltzmann machines'. Cognitive Science $\underline{9}$, pp 147—169 (1985)
4. Kohonen T: 'Self-organization and associative memory'. Springer-Verlag, Berlin (1984).
5. Reilly D L, Cooper LN & Elbaum C: 'A neural model for category learning'. Biological Cybernetics, $\underline{45}$, pp 35—41 (1982).
6. Broomhead D & Lowe D: 'Multi-variable interpolation and adaptive networks'. RSRE Memo No 4148 Royal Signals and Radar Establishment, Malvern (1988).
7. Robinson A J, Niranjan M & Fallside F: 'Generalising the nodes of the error propagation network'. Cambridge University Engineering Department Technical Report No CUED/F-INFENG/TR.25 (1988).
8. Lippmann R: 'An introduction to computing with neural nets'. IEEE ASSP Magazine, $\underline{3}$, No 4, pp 4—22 (1987).
9. Minsky M & Papert S: 'Perceptrons'. MIT Press, Cambridge MA (1969).

4

A NEURAL NETWORK FEATURE DETECTOR USING A MULTI-RESOLUTION PYRAMID

C C Hand, M R Evans and S W Ellacott
Information Technology Research Institute,
Brighton Polytechnic

1. INTRODUCTION

This chapter describes a technique used to solve the problem of accurately locating the positions of eyes within a particular set of sixty images supplied by BT; half of the images could be used as training data, the other half as test data. The subjects in each image are at the same viewing distance, the faces are roughly in a vertical position, with a face in the centre of the frame looking forward with eyes open and directed at the camera.

When looking for facial features within an image, one approach would be to take a standard neural network learning algorithm, train a network on a set of images, and convolve the input units of the trained network over a set of test images. However, this is often a time consuming process. Furthermore, it ignores, to some extent, the structure of the problem. To this end a multi-resolution approach has been used, both for the image representation and for the training of the neural networks. Such an approach is desirable for a number of reasons. First, different features may have different optimal resolutions for the purpose of feature detection; this implies a hierarchical representation of the image. Second, the use of a hierarchical representation would help to cut down the search space when looking for a feature in an image. It seems plausible that if a feature could be detected at a coarse level of resolution then this could be used to guide, and limit, the search process at a higher level of resolution. The system would be able to deal with complete facial images; it would not have to be given a pre-selected small area containing an eye. It should also be of benefit in terms of search time. If an image is of a high resolution, the convolution process can take a great deal of time when using a sequential implementation. By focusing the search to those areas of interest likely to contain the significant features, the amount of time required to process an image should be reduced. Finally, a hierarchical representation allows one to investigate the relationship between the different rates of convergence of the learning algorithm with different scales of resolution for the image.

2. THE IMAGE REPRESENTATION

The images used are eight bit grey level images. No filtering operations have been applied because of the problem of selecting sensible global parameter values suitable for all of the images, and because a number of such operations (such as median filtering) introduce non-linearities which would hinder the analysis of the system's operation [1]. The main difference between this study and most other studies of neural networks in the visual domain is the use of a multi-resolution representation of the image. There exists a number of possible candidates for a hierarchical representation of the image. The grey level average pyramid (a pyramidal version of a quad tree) was chosen for its computational simplicity, the linear nature of the transformation of the image, and because information loss between layers does not appear to be large [2].

The structure of the pyramid is simple. Starting at the base, which represents the original image, each successive level is half the linear size of the level immediately below. The value of a pixel at level $n + 1$ is simply the average of the values of the four pixels directly below it at level n (see Fig. 1) [2-4].

The notation adopted for the data structure is that the base image, with a resolution of 256×256, is at pyramid level zero, or pr0. Although the representation could extend to level pr7, where the image is represented by a 2×2 array, most of the work has been conducted at levels pr0, pr1, and pr2 (with image resolutions 256×256, 128×128, and 64×64 respectively).

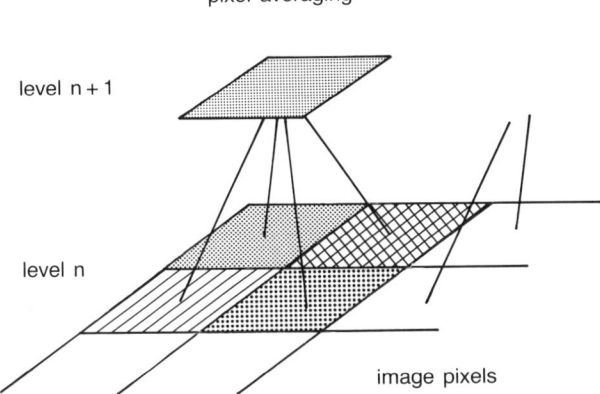

Fig. 1a Generation of a multi-resolution pyramid using grey level averaging of pixels.

Fig. 1b A multi-resolution representation of image a24 at levels pr0, pr1, and pr2.

3. TRAINING THE NETWORK AT A SINGLE LEVEL — A PILOT STUDY

A pilot study was conducted at a single level of the pyramid, pr2, to determine a suitable architecture for the network. This particular level of the pyramid was chosen because it is the coarsest level of resolution at which the centre of the pupil could be reliably located in all of the images; thus ensuring consistency between training patterns. The study concentrated upon finding the right training conditions which would enable a neural network to learn to recognise input patterns which contain instances of the left eye, as one looks at the image.

3.1 The learning rule

The learning rule used throughout is standard backpropagation, or the generalised delta rule [5,6]. This seems to achieve a good level of performance in a number of different domains; for example see [7-10].[1]

3.2 The network architecture

A common problem when designing a network using the backpropagation algorithm is determining the appropriate parameters governing the number of hidden layers, the number of units per layer, the learning rate, and so forth. This has resulted in the adoption of an empirical approach in that whatever value seems to work has been used. However, recent work [10] using back propagation to learn to play backgammon indicated that the performance of a network only improves slightly when one increases the number of hidden layers, the number of units per layer, or the size of the training set, once an adequate, minimal, size for the training data has been determined. The average improvement of the performance of the network is to the order of only a few percent. If one assumes that this is not an artifact of the problem domain then this seems to indicate that, once one has found a set of parameters conducive to learning within the network, increasing the amount of resources will not have a marked effect upon performance. (This is a common feature in approximation and data fitting problems.)

The smallest number of inputs possible was used to reduce the number of weights and to reduce training complexity. After examining the images it was found that an 8×8 window would be required to cover an eye taken from an image at pr2. The window defines the number of units required for the input level. The actual values given to the input layer are the grey levels normalised to the range of 0 to 1. Once a network has been trained an 8×8 window is convolved over the image representation to find instances of an eye in the image at pr2.

The output layer consists of a single unit whose target values for the training patterns are 1, representing the presence of an eye, and 0 for the absence of an eye.

A single hidden layer is used and the number of units in it was determined by trial and error. It was decided that the smallest number of units which demonstrated adequate learning would be used for the reasons given above. Four hidden units did demonstrate learning, with the network apparently converging to a minimum.

---

[1] The particular version of the back propagation algorithm used in the 'bp' programme from the PDP software [11].

3.3 Training data

It should be obvious that the quantity and variety of the training data is a very important factor in what the network learns. A key problem with the current study is the small number of patterns in the training set. There are only sixty images and only half of those could be used in the learning phase. Clearly one requires at least as many training patterns as degrees of freedom (i.e. weight connections) in the model otherwise the system of non-linear equations is under-determined. A 'rule of thumb' suggests that the number of training patterns should be approximately six times the number of weight connections in the network [12]. Because of the paucity of data this criterion has not been met.

3.3.1 Creating the data set

Starting with an initial training set of just thirty patterns, the number was gradually increased until it reached four hundred. The performance of the network was poor with smaller sized training sets. This pool of training patterns is split into two classes; positive and negative instances. Positive instances are patterns containing a left eye whilst negative instances are patterns taken from randomly selected areas of the images. (More structured negative instances were hand selected by taking patterns containing features such as hair, mouth, and background.)[2] With only thirty patterns containing eyes this resulted in the positive instances being 'swamped'; consequently the network's performance was poor. This problem was partially overcome by using multiple copies of the eyes in the training data; each pattern being presented six times during each epoch.

3.4 Evaluating the pilot network's performance

The performance of the pilot network was first evaluated by presenting it with patterns taken directly from the training set. The network correctly separated all of the training patterns. When positive instances were presented to the network, the response of the output unit ranged from 0.90 to 0.99. When negative instances were presented the output unit's response ranged from 0.00 to 0.15 (to two decimal places).[3] It was also tested by presenting patterns which were positive instances of eyes which had not been used in

---

[2]To some extent, this choice is *ad hoc* but it appears to produce a sensible training set.

[3]An output of 1.0 and absolute 0 can not be achieved without an infinite input as the activation function is based on a sigmoid, or logistic, function.

the training phase. Again the majority of the responses were within the 0.90 to 0.99 range. However, a few responses to positive instances were outside this range, though all were greater than 0.60.

Although these results appear to be promising, further experimentation revealed an important deficiency in the performance of the network in that it finds a large number of 'false positives' whereby it incorrectly classifies an input pattern as an eye. A typical set of results given by convolving the input window over an image is given in Fig. 2. Each white square represents a positive response from the network, i.e. a response greater than or equal the threshold (0.85). The network has correctly found the centre of the eye at $(x,y) = (23,22)$, but has also found a large number of false positives. These 'false responses' can be readily identified in the image. For example, the largest cluster at the top of the figure is the area corresponding to the hair of the subject in the image. The cluster around (23,22), where the actual eye is, is probably due to network generalisation; slight differences in position, size, shape and colour of the training patterns results in the network finding the general region where the eye is located.

Fig. 2 The result of convolving the input layer of the network over image a01, at pyramid level two, with a threshold of 0.85.

One interesting cluster is that in the area of (30,22). This corresponds to the location of the right eye in the image; the network gives a strong response even though the positive training patterns consisted only of left eyes. To some extent this is a desirable feature in that it suggests that the trained network has modelled some general features of eyes. On the other hand it may mean that overgeneralisation of response has taken place.

3.5 Improving the performance of the network

To reduce the number of false positives, a number of such patterns were fed back into the training set as negative instances. This is simply a form of negative feedback. An exception to this feedback is the set of patterns forming the clusters associated with the right eye in the various images. This is because, if the network is learning to abstract general features of both the left and right eye, then their feedback would act against the positive instances in the data. The network was retrained with the new training data and convolved over image a01 once more. The response is shown in Fig. 3. The misclassifications have decreased both in terms of number and size (though there is still similar clustering around the eye). Note that the cluster associated with the right eye has also disappeared even though such false positives were not fed back into the training set as negative instances. This suggests that the old network was overgeneralising rather than abstracting some feature description common to both classes of eye and that the improved network has picked up features specific to left eyes.

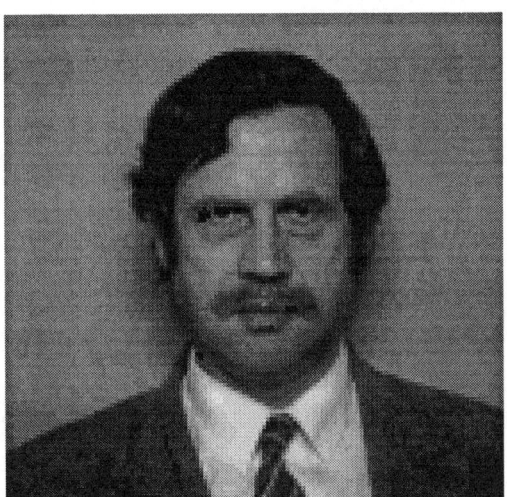

Fig. 3 Response to the convolution of the retrained network over image a01 at pr2 with a threshold of 0.85.

Although there are a few, spurious, false positives remaining this result is extremely encouraging. Because the network is operating at pr2 it should be obvious that the network is being trained on a subspace of the original image (see section 4). Therefore, the results discussed so far are attempts at determining a best approximation to the problem. In the context of coarse-fine hierarchical search these points form the areas of interest for the further examination at higher levels of resolution within the pyramid.

Similar results were obtained when the network was also convolved over a number of test images — images not in the training set. Furthermore, two new networks were trained at pr1 and pr0; again the results were essentially the same. Note that the network architecture is standardised for each level in the pyramid. Each network is of the form X-4-1 with X being dependent upon the size of the window which is in turn dependent upon the level of the pyramid, i.e. 8×8, 16×16, and 32×32 for levels pr2, pr1, and pr0 respectively.

4. WEIGHT PROJECT BETWEEN LEVELS

Training a network at pr2 is an attempt at finding a solution which is the best approximation to training a network on the original image. The input space at pr2 can be considered as a subspace of the input space for pr0. (The projection of the weights is a linear transformation, the details of which are given in appendix A.)

It was hypothesised that one could speed up the training of the networks by training a network at a lower level of resolution and projecting the resulting set of weights onto a network at a higher level of resolution. Since the projected set of weights is a subspace approximation to the problem solution, it was expected that it would speed up the rate of convergence of a higher resolution network. The projected weights would be the initial weights for the network at the higher level of resolution which could then be fine tuned by further training. In terms of the architecture of the network, the weights between the input and hidden layers are projected whilst the weights between the hidden and output layers are simply copied.

4.1 Network response with projected weights

The weights for the network trained at level pr2 were projected down to level pr1 and no further training was conducted. Figure 4 shows the effect of convolving the resulting network over pr1 with the same image representation used in Fig. 3. One can see that the cluster pattern is similar. The network has correctly located the eye at (46,44). This demonstrates that the weights can be projected from one level to another without a marked loss of accuracy in separation. As would be expected the responses are less successful when the weights are projected up to the next level of the image pyramid. This is due to the need to represent four weights by an average value — see appendix A.

Fig. 4 Response of network when projected weights, trained at pr2, are convolved over image a01 at level pr1.

The response of the network using the projected weights can be compared with the response of a network actually trained at pr1 (with feedback of misclassifications). This is shown in Fig. 5. The final error of both networks was the same (0.5), and one can see that the responses of the networks are similar.

Fig. 5 Response of a network trained at pr1 and convolved over image a01 at pyramid level one.

4.2 The effect of pyramid level upon training time

To investigate the relationship between the pyramid level and the network response with respect to training time, different networks were trained at three different levels of the image pyramid. The design of the networks followed that of the pilot study with each being fully connected and consisting of a hidden layer containing four units and an output layer with one unit (X-4-1). The same parameter values and data set, consisting of the same images at different levels of resolution, were used for all three networks in order to standardise the conditions as much as possible. The parameter defining the convergence of the network, the total sum of squares (tss), was set to 0.5 for each network. The positive instances were constructed by centring over the pupils of the eyes at the three scales of resolution.

The higher the resolution, the fewer epochs that were required for the network to converge to the specified final error. This relationship is not linear; it follows a seemingly exponential function, as shown in Fig. 6. This behaviour is probably due to the loss of information as one climbs the pyramid; there is simply less information to discriminate between the two classes.

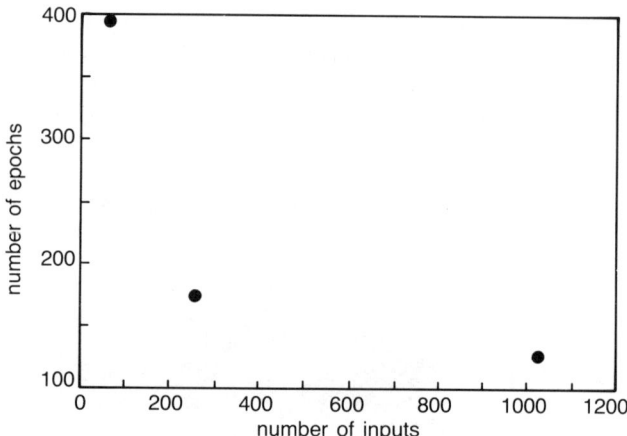

Fig. 6 A graph of the number of epochs required for each level of the pyramid averaged over 10 trials.

Although the tss was set the same for each level in the pyramid in order to standardise conditions, in retrospect this may not have been appropriate. This is because one would expect to obtain a smaller error with a finer resolution model which has more degrees of freedom. Furthermore, the learning rate may have to be decreased by a factor of four as one projects down each level of the pyramid [13]. Furthermore, Plaut & Hinton [8] suggest that there should be a different learning rate for the different layers of the network.

4.3 Projecting sets of learned weights

The pattern of results described in the previous section tends to go against the suggestion that one could decrease the training time by the projection of a set of weights trained at a coarse level of resolution with further fine-tuning at the higher level of resolution. However, the results of Fig. 6 must be discussed in two different, but interrelated, contexts. Firstly, when dealing with simulations, does the projection of weights lead to quicker training in terms of the run time? Secondly, does the projection of weights result in swifter convergence, in terms of the number of epochs required, when a set of projected weights is 'fine-tuned' at the next level?

Turning to the first question, the average run time taken for the networks to converge is simply the average number of epochs multiplied by the average time per epoch. The average number of epochs required, rounded to the nearest epoch, for each level is 394, 172, and 127 for pr2, pr1, and pr0 respectively. The average time taken for one epoch is 29.4 s, 109.6 s and 436.4 s for pr2, pr1, and pr0 respectively.[4] These give total run times for independently trained networks at the three levels of resolution of 11 583.6 s for pr2, 18 851.2 s for pr1 and 55 422.8 s for pr0. Thus, when dealing with sequential simulations, it is still quicker to train a network at pr2 than it is at either pr1 or pr0, despite the fact that the training requires many more epochs at the coarser level of resolution.

These results may be compared to the networks created by the successive projection and fine-tuning of weights from pr2 to pr1 and then from pr1 to pr0. The results, in terms of the number of epochs required for the networks to converge, are given in Fig. 7 ('Projected Weights'); the data from Fig. 6 has been superimposed for comparison ('Original Data'). Some of the projected networks failed to converge at pr0 altogether. The data in Fig. 7 presents the seven out of the 11 trials which did converge within a set training limit of 250 epochs for pr0.

In terms of the run time, the average total training times (as defined above) for the given levels, in the same order, are 11 877.6 s, 986.4 s, and 37 966.8 s. Comparing the two sets of times for levels pr1 and pr0, the projected networks converge 19.11 and 1.46 times faster than the randomised networks at the same levels respectively. These are significant increases in the convergence rates of the networks. Furthermore, if one totals the time

---

[4]These are the run times for a grey-level SUN 3/50 with a floating point co-processor.

for the entire system to be created (i.e. the time taken to train the networks at all three levels) then the times are 85 857.6 s and 50 830.8 s for the original networks and the projected networks respectively. Therefore, by projecting the weights as described above, one can decrease the training time by a factor of approximately 1.69. This represents a significant saving in run time; a reduction from approximately 23 to 14 hours. It should be stressed that this is concerned with speed efficiency in sequential simulations. Obviously a different analysis would apply in the case of a parallel implementation.

Turning to the second point, one can see that there is quicker convergence, in terms of the number of epochs, when one fine-tunes a set of projected weights. However, these results are more difficult to interpret. There is a drastic reduction in the number of epochs for pr1; approximately 9 on average as opposed to 172. Unfortunately, when the set of fine-tuned weights at pr1 is projected to pr0 the network requires far more epochs to converge; 87 epochs on average (though this is still better than training a fresh network at pr0 which takes an average of 127 epochs). Furthermore, as has already been mentioned, some of the networks failed to converge within the set number of epochs at this level.

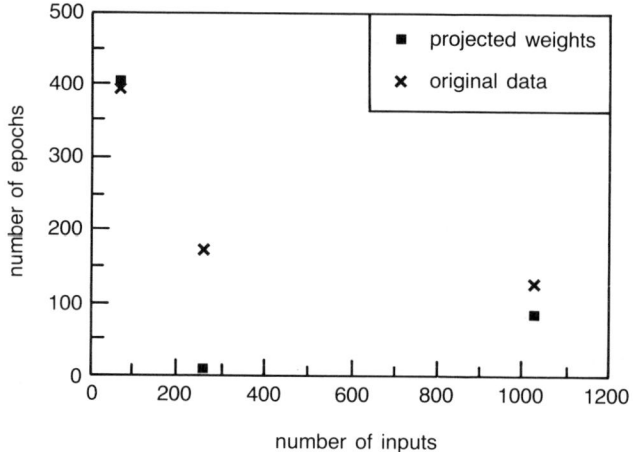

Fig. 7 A graph of the number of epochs required using projected weights between levels averaged over 7 trials.

This raises some interesting theoretical questions concerning sampling, shift variance in quad-tree image pyramids, the interaction of the learning rate and other parameters with the hierarchical representation, and the preconditioning effect of various possible filters. This will be the subject of further study.

5. USING PYRAMIDS TO CONSTRAIN THE SEARCH SPACE

In addition to affecting the training behaviour, it was previously stated that a hierarchical representation could be used to constrain the search space by initially convolving a trained network at a low level of resolution, finding areas of interest (AOIs) within it, and using such areas to confine the search at higher levels of resolution. This can be thought of as projecting an AOI to specific regions of the image at a higher of resolution, thus focusing the search on small regions that may contain an eye. These regions are examined using the finer details revealed by the higher resolution, to refine the boundaries of the AOI or to discredit and therefore eliminate the region from further investigation at the next level of resolution.

It was determined empirically that pr2 (assuming a base level of size 256×256) is the coarsest level at which an eye can reliably be detected. Therefore, networks were trained at levels pr2, pr1, and pr0; with pr2 being the level where the search is initially conducted. Thus a trained network is convolved over pr2 of the image pyramid and any responses greater than a set threshold are taken as possible locations for an eye. Responses are clustered according to simple 8-connected pixel adjacency, i.e. each pixel in a cluster is connected to at least one other pixel in the same cluster, where connectedness is defined as a pixel being adjacent to one of its eight nearest neighbours. The limits of the AOI corresponding to a cluster is simply the smallest bounding rectangle of the cluster. The limits of all of the AOIs are projected down to the next level for further processing. This process continues recursively until the base level is reached. The AOI with the largest number of responses above the threshold is taken to give the rough location of the eye. The exact location may be specified by either the point within the AOI giving the largest reponse or by finding the centroid of the pixels forming the cluster.

With sequential simulations this technique can reduce the search time considerably. In the current system the typical reduction is from about two hours to one minute; thus the multi-resolution approach is approximately 120 times faster. Furthermore, there is also a significant reduction in the number of false positives at the base level of the pyramid (see Fig. 8). This too is brought about by constraining the search process through the hierarchical use of AOIs.

78 NEURAL NETWORK FEATURE DETECTOR

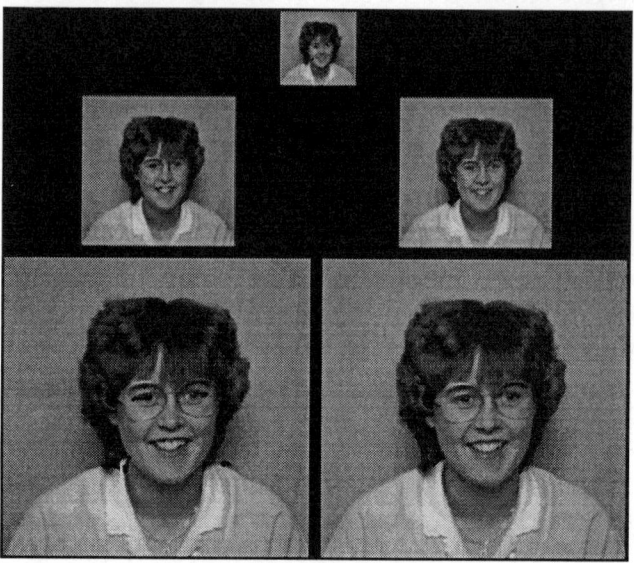

Fig. 8 Comparison of three levels of the pyramid for image a26 (left) using separate convolutions for each level, and (right) constraining the search via AOIs.

5.1 Testing the hierarchical approach

The initial results using the multi-resolution approach are summarised in the first row of Table 1; Training Set 1. The number of correct classifications from the training set is good but the generalisation properties of the networks are poor; only 38% of the test image set are correctly classified.[5] In this set there were 34 images in the training set and 26 in the test set.

Weights	% Correct			% Incorrect		
	Training Set	Test Set	Average	Training Set	Test Set	Average
Training Set 1	91	38	68	9	62	32
Training Set 2	87	80	83	13	20	17

Table 1 A summary of the results for the two different training sets (figures rounded to the nearest integer).

---

[5] A correct classification is a response within four pixels of the designated centre of the eye. This corresponds to the two pixels used by BT on an image size of 128×128 [14].

It was hypothesised that the poor generalisation of the network may be a function of the sample chosen for the training set rather than the approach adopted. The training set used so far only contained examples of 'good' eyes; these were eyes that were not closed, people not wearing glasses, and so forth. Hence it would not be expected to generalise well when the test images have people wearing glasses, people of different skin colour, squinting/closed eyes, etc. Assuming a uniform distribution for the presence of various feature types, the new training set, Training Set 2, was created by sampling the images based upon the relative frequency of the various eye types within the population of the images. Thus the mean of each feature type was used as a basis to model the central tendencies of the data. For example, if six people in the population wear glasses, then half are placed in the training set and the other half in the test set.

The results for the new training set are given in the second row of Table 1. There is a dramatic improvement in the system's response to the test set; from 38% to 80%. Furthermore, if the task of the system is made more difficult, by defining success when the response is within two pixels of the designated eye centre rather than four, then the results with the second training set are much better than the first. The average correct classification for Training Set 1 drops from 68% to 40% whilst the average correct classification for Training Set 2 drops from 83% to 80%.

A Chi-Square test was used to determine whether the difference in results between the two training sets is statistically significant. The probability of the null hypothesis being correct is $p < 0.1$ so it can be rejected; the improvement is due to the better choice of training set by closely modelling it upon the incidence of features found in the population (see Appendix B for further details).

5.1.1 Two typical examples

By examining the response of the network for specific images, one can gain an insight to how the network operates. At level 2 in test image a23, there are twenty responses which are grouped into nine clusters; the largest being the region containing the eye which is as shown in Fig. 9. A white pixel indicates a response by the network above the threshold.

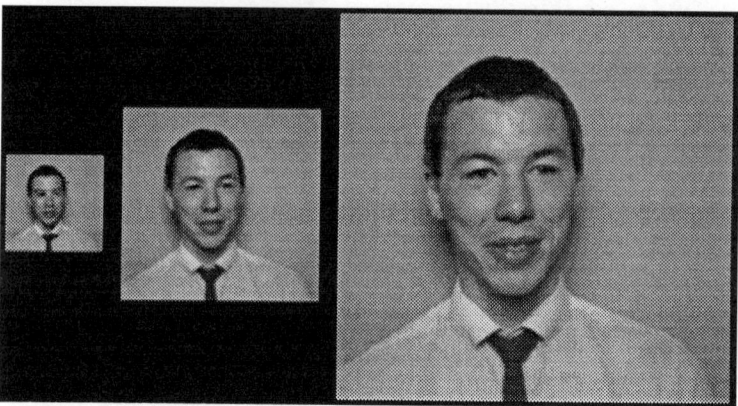

Fig. 9 The image a23 at levels pr2, pr1 and pr0 with response of network shown in white.

The cluster containing the eye has four responses, all having the same vertical co-ordinate. This was found to be a general response from the networks; there is more variation in the x-direction than the y-direction. These four responses are greater than those from other parts of the image. When all of the AOIs are projected to pr1 the non-eye clusters of pr2 disappear. That is, at the corresponding locations in pr1 there are no responses greater than the threshold except at the AOI corresponding to the cluster centred upon the eye. The finer detail at the higher level of resolution obviously enables the network to discriminate more accurately.

At pr1 there are more responses around the eye; six in the same horizontal plane. Though the overall response seems to be wider the reverse is the case as the four points from level 2 correspond to sixteen pixels at level 1. This is also the case at the base level, pr0, where there are five responses (all above 0.85). Thus the AOI from level 2 has been reduced from a 4×16 area (on the same scale as level pr0) to a 1×5 region. The final position of the centre of the eye is (93 104), compared to (93 105) selected manually.

Turning to a test image that was not classified correctly, a40, one can see the limitations of the system. With this image there are six initial clusters at pr2, one of which includes the centre of the eye (see Fig. 10). Again the responses around the eye are the highest. At pr1 the network gives two responses greater than the threshold; the first is within one pixel of the centre of the eye, the other is a false positive. When these are projected down to the base level the network fails to give an adequate response to either. The reason why the network fails to detect the eye is probably due to both the fact that the person is wearing dark glasses and that the person's head is at a slant. This highlights a failing of the current system in that the images have to be normalised; there is no way of dealing with rotation in the image plane[6]. Furthermore, the single response at pr1 is not at the exact centre of the eye; thus, when the AOI is projected, it does not align with the precise centre of the eye at the base level and fails to give a response greater than the threshold.

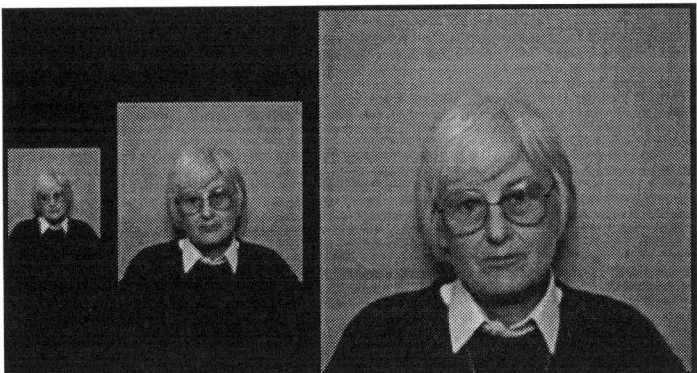

Fig. 10 The image a40 with response of network shown in white.

An analysis of those images incorrectly classified reveals that the majority of the incorrect classifications (eight out of ten) are concerned with these two sources of potential error; people with glasses and/or people whose head is at a slant within the image. The remaining two misclassifications are due to window size and quantising effects and are discussed below.

5.1.2 Improvements in network generalisation

Table 1 clearly shows a distinct improvement when the system is trained on Training Set 2 as opposed to Training Set 1. Furthermore, an improvement is also apparent when one analyses the character of the system's misclassifications. With Training Set 1 there were eleven failures to find an AOI covering the eye at pr2, three failures at pr1, and two at pr0. (Three more images did find an AOI over the eye at pr0 but could be counted as failures in that they did not give the largest response i.e. other AOIs were found at the base level, which did not include the eye, yet gave a greater reponse.) With Training Set 2 there were only three failures at pr2, five at pr1, and one at pr0. (Again, there was one image whereby an AOI at pr0 containing an eye was found but which was not chosen as the best response.) Thus the majority of the failures with the Training Set 1 are at pr2 whilst the majority with the second set are at pr1.

---

[6]Uniform scaling is a different matter. Because a hierarchical approach has been taken the problems of scaling should naturally 'drop out' as the different levels of the pyramid pick up information at different scales of resolution. However, this has yet to be tested.

The pattern of failures shows how under-constrained the problem is, even when one models the training set on the underlying population. The results show it is possible to produce a network with satisfactory generalisation at pr2, but not at levels pr1 and pr0 (or at least, not as good). This is supported by the fact that at pr2 over 600 training patterns were used, less than half the normally suggested number [8,12,15]. For the other levels, only a small number of the required training patterns could be generated, hence the inadequate generalisation.

Finally, it should be noted that not all of the failures are because of the lack of constraints due to inadequate data. Some of the failures in the second system were due to quantising effects between levels. Though the network might find the centre of the eye, the projection of the AOI could be off centre due to image quantisation. Thus the restricted search at the next level will be improperly aligned, with a consequent failure of the system. This is particularly true if the image is difficult, i.e. it contains glasses, or has a face at a slant, etc.. One method to overcome this could be to slightly increase the projection area covered by an AOI. Unfortunately, such an approach is essentially *ad hoc* and introduces yet more parameters which would have to be fine-tuned, bringing with it all of the problems associated with such tweaking.

6. WEIGHT ANALYSIS

An intuitive understanding of the network's internal representation can be gained by examining the weights.[7] Figure 11 shows a typical set of weights for the hidden units, and their connections to the output unit, for a network trained on Training Set 2 at pr2. Each 8×8 block represents the weights from the input units to a hidden unit. The 4×1 block (hidden weights) represents the weights between the hidden units to the output unit. A black background indicates a negative value and white a positive one; all weight values and biases are scaled by a factor of 100.

The behaviour of the trained network can be described by the behaviour of the output unit and the factors influencing its performance. Notice from Fig. 11 that the bias for the output unit is large and positive (4.86). Thus, given the logistic (sigmoid) activation function, this unit tends to be on, with an output value of approximately 0.99, when no input is received. The weights from the hidden units to the output unit are negative, thus any input received by the output unit must be either negative or zero. (Again this is due to the logistic activation function; the range of permissible output values for any unit is [0, 1].) Thus the effect of the hidden units on the output unit is either

---

[7]A brief description of the training parameters used in the complete system is given in Appendix C.

to do nothing or to inhibit it. These two types of behaviour are illustrated in Fig. 12. Therefore, the tendency of the output unit is to be strongly active unless the hidden units are also active. One can think of this as the output unit always assuming that an eye is present. Similarly, the hidden units should 'lie dormant' in the presence of an eye but react strongly in its absence.

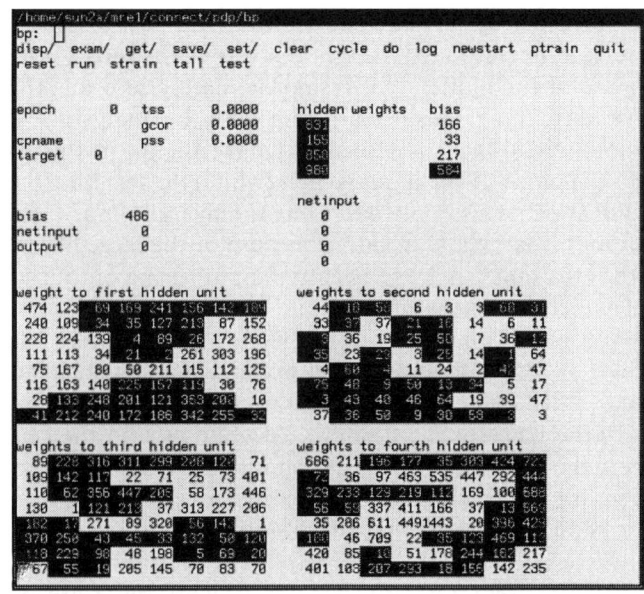

Fig. 11 Weights for the network at pr2.

$$f(x) = \frac{1}{[1 + e^{-(\Sigma w_i o_i + \theta)}]}$$

x_1 : the level of activation of the output unit is due to the bias when there is little input from the hidden units

x_2 : the activation of the output unit as the input from the hidden units is increased.

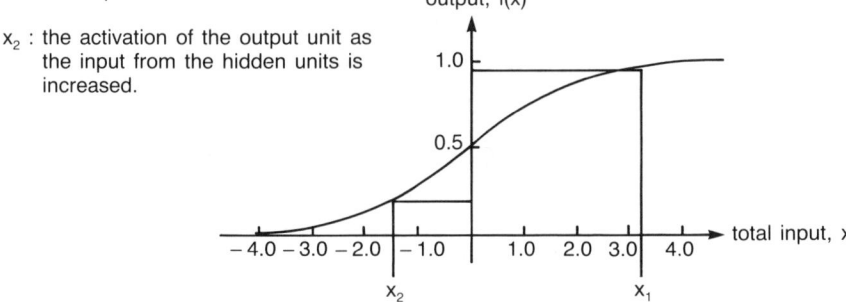

Fig. 12 Graph of the output unit's response to different inputs.

It is more problematic to determine what the hidden units' weight patterns reveal about the types of image structures to which they strongly react. In the absence of a more rigourous analysis it is tentatively suggested that one significant structure is the pupil. This should appear in the centre of the window, which corresponds to the central four weights of each of the weight blocks. Examining the central weights of the fourth hidden unit (the bottom right weight block in Fig. 11) one can see that with a low (dark) input[8] to this central region the output of the unit tends towards zero. (With no input the natural state of the hidden unit is approximately zero due to the unit's large negative bias term.) This is consistent with the analysis of the output unit's behaviour mentioned previously. A dark region in this case would correspond to the pupil. If the input is high (white) the resulting output from the hidden unit is large and positive. Thus the overall input from this unit to the output unit is large and negative because of the large negative weight connecting the two units. A large negative input to the output unit results in an output which is almost zero.

To study this effect, the four central pixels of an eye were converted to white (grey level of 255) with all the other pixels remaining unchanged. When this corrupted pattern was applied to the network of Fig. 11 the response was to classify the pattern as a non-eye. A white area in the centre of the window, where the dark pupil of the eye should be, would seem to be a very significant feature in determining the presence of an eye.

Finally, it should be noted that the situation is not so clear in the case of the other three hidden units. Whilst the first and third units do have a central region with predominantly positive weights there are one or two significantly sized negative weights. Furthermore, the second hidden unit seems to be redundant; its weights are small and distributed about zero. Similarly, the weight connecting this unit to the output unit is small, reinforcing the probability that it has little effect on the decision process of the network. Experiments have been conducted with networks with less than four hidden units and the networks have successfully learned to discriminate between eyes and non-eyes [1]. However, it is usually better to give the network more units than are actually required so as to ensure adequate resources for the learning process. Once a solution has been found one could remove any excess units to improve the network's efficiency in terms of resource usage. Any degradation of the network's performance due to this pruning could probably be overcome by a small amount of training as the fundamental structures would be preserved in the other units.

---

[8]A dark input would be low value in the grey scale range 0 to 255, white being 255.

7. SUMMARY

The multi-resolution approach to training neural networks has a number of benefits. First, one can achieve a speed up in training time by using a coarse to fine projection of weights. This is despite the fact that networks take longer to train, in terms of the number of epochs, at coarser levels of resolution. The mathematical model of the projection of the weights may also be useful in understanding the network's behaviour. This is currently under investigation. Second, there is a dramatic speed increase in the run time of a fully trained system using coarse to fine constraints in the search process. In the current implementation this increase is by a factor of 120, with the system taking approximately one minute to find a solution. Furthermore, the coarse to fine search operation leads to a significant reduction in the number of false positives at the finest level of resolution thus leading to improved accuracy in locating the eye. Third, the problem is underconstrained due to the lack of an adequate amount of training data. This can be improved, to some extent, by the feedback of false positives and by modelling the training sample closely on the underlying population. However, multi-resolution training also helps as a network trained at a coarse level is working on a subspace approximation of the original problem which may prove acceptable as an initial 'best guess'.

APPENDIX A

A theoretical framework for hierarchical training of neural nets

When dealing with a multi-resolution representation one needs to know both how the representation at one level is related to the representation at another level, and the properties of the underlying transformational operator. This will obviously have an effect upon the input to a neural network and will affect both its training and its response at different levels of resolution. Furthermore, since it is intended to prune the search space at the finest level of resolution by looking for areas of interest at lower levels of resolution, one needs to know how to move through the levels of the pyramid. This is true both for searching for an eye once the complete system has been trained, and in training the different networks at each level of resolution.

Suppose a neural net with (input) weight matrix W takes an input vector x in $\Re^n$, and output vector in $\Re^k$. (For example, using an 8×8 pixel block of an image, $n = 64$.) We wish to make use of a shrinking operator

$$s: \Re^n \rightarrow \Re^m \quad \text{where } m < n.$$

86 NEURAL NETWORK FEATURE DETECTOR

Provided s is linear (as it will be if it is an averaging or other simple filter) we can represent this operation by a matrix S:

$$x^* = s(x) = Sx.$$

For example, consider the reduction of a 4×4 image to 2×2 in Fig. 13; thus $n = 16$, and $m = 4$. Number the 4×4 and 2×2 images as shown (the reason for this numbering will soon become apparent) and assume non-overlapping windows.

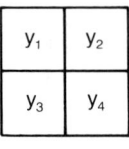

Fig. 13   Pixel correspondence between adjacent levels of a quad tree.

Denote the mask coefficients by s_1, s_2, s_3, s_4: i.e.

$$y_1 = s_1 x_1 + s_2 x_5 + s_3 x_9 + s_4 x_{13}$$
$$y_2 = s_1 x_2 + s_2 x_6 + s_3 x_{10} + s_4 x_{14}$$
$$y_3 = s_1 x_3 + s_2 x_7 + s_3 x_{11} + s_4 x_{15}$$
$$y_4 = s_1 x_4 + s_2 x_8 + s_3 x_{12} + s_4 x_{16}$$

(For the simple Quad Tree of §2, $s_1 = s_2 = s_1 = s_1, = 0.25$).

Thus

$$S = \begin{bmatrix} s_1 & 0 & 0 & 0 & s_2 & 0 & 0 & 0 & s_3 & 0 & 0 & 0 & s_4 & 0 & 0 & 0 \\ 0 & s_1 & 0 & 0 & 0 & s_2 & 0 & 0 & 0 & s_3 & 0 & 0 & 0 & s_4 & 0 & 0 \\ 0 & 0 & s_1 & 0 & 0 & 0 & s_2 & 0 & 0 & 0 & s_3 & 0 & 0 & 0 & s_4 & 0 \\ 0 & 0 & 0 & s_1 & 0 & 0 & 0 & s_2 & 0 & 0 & 0 & s_3 & 0 & 0 & 0 & s_4 \end{bmatrix}$$

$$= \begin{bmatrix} s_1 I & : & s_2 I & : & s_3 I & : & s_4 I \end{bmatrix}$$

A.1 Moving down the pyramid

The idea is initially to train a smaller net taking x^* as input, say with weight matrix V, and then distribute these weights to the full net W, for final training. How do we perform this extension? The most obvious criterion is that Wx should produce the same output as VSx, i.e.

$$Wx = VSx \quad \text{for all } x, \qquad \ldots\ldots (1)$$

whence

$$W = VS.$$

Note, this gives $\text{rank}(W) \leq \text{rank}(V) \leq m$. It follows that

$$W = VS$$
$$= \begin{pmatrix} s_1 V & : & s_2 V & : & s_3 V & : & s_4 V \end{pmatrix}$$

The mask coefficients s_n are as described above.

This ordering of the pixels illustrates the simple nature of the weight distribution operation; it is not particularly convenient for practical use, and for the implementation described in §2 the standard Quad Tree sampling has been used.

A.2 Moving up the pyramid

Suppose we have a net that works on the $\sqrt{n} \times \sqrt{n}$ grid. Can we have a reduced net that works as well as possible on the $\sqrt{m} \times \sqrt{m}$ grid? This could have a number of possible uses such as returning an initial region of interest for a more detailed search, or as a basis for a multigrid technique. Mathematically, this problem is more difficult than that of §A.1. We want (ideally) to choose V such that

$$Vx^* = Wx$$

or

$$VSx = Wx \quad \text{for all } x.$$

(Of course, if we could achieve this, there would be no point in using the larger net at all!) In general, this is impossible since rank(V) < rank(W). Instead we must set up an approximation problem, for instance, to choose V such that

$$\max_{||x||=1} ||(VS-W)x||$$

is minimised, where $||\ ||$ denotes a suitable vector norm. By definition, this is equivalent to minimising

$$||VS-W|| \quad\quad\quad\quad \ldots\ldots (2)$$

for the equivalent matrix norm (see Isaacson & Keller [16], pp 2—11). In practice the two most useful norms are the ∞ and 2 norms; the latter seems more natural in this context since the corresponding vector norm is simply the Euclidean distance. However, ∞ leads to a simpler approximation problem.

It is well known (Isaacson & Keller [16], p 10) that for any matrix A,

$$||A||_2 = \sqrt{\rho(A^T A)}$$

where ρ denotes the spectral radius, i.e. the absolute value of the largest eigenvalue, and [16], p 9)

$$||A||_\infty = \max_j \Sigma_i |a_{ij}| \quad \text{('The maximum absolute row sum.')}$$

A.2.1 The structure of the approximation problem

The problem (§A.2) is an example of a well known class of problems known as 'best linear approximation', albeit with unusual norms. It is instructive to make explicit the basis of the vector space of approximating functions. Recall that W is to be approximated, S is fixed and the elements of V are to be determined.

The jth row of VS is formed from

$$v_{j1} \times (\text{1st row of } S) + \ldots + v_{jm} \times (m\text{th row of } S).$$

This has to approximate the jth row of W. In a sense, each row approximation problem occurs separately: they are only linked by the norm. Thus the approximation space for the problem (2) is the Cartesian product taken k times of the row space of S.

Since the only link between rows of W is through the norm, the ∞ norm case, in which the error is given by the maximum absolute row sum, decomposes completely into separate row approximation problems. In the special case of disjoint windows discussed in Fig. 1 above, it is often possible to give an explicit solution. The jth absolute row sum error is given by

$$\sum_{i=1}^{m}|w_{j,i}-s_1 v_{ji}| + \sum_{i=1}^{m}|w_{j,m+i}-s_2 v_{ji}| + \sum_{i=1}^{m}|w_{j,2m+i}-s_3 v_{ji}| + \sum_{i=1}^{m}|w_{j,3m+i}-s_4 v_{ji}| \quad \ldots (3)$$

so the problem decomposes into a family of very simple conventional l_1 problems. Actually, the ∞ error is determined only by the member of this family which has the worst error, hence the problem (2), at least with the ∞ norm, does not have a unique solution. However examination of the derivation of the expression for the ∞ matrix norm in [16] shows that it is worth minimising each problem in (3) individually, as this will minimise the maximum error for the jth component of the output vector.

As stated above, the set of solutions to (3) can sometimes be given explicitly. For instance, if all the s_j are equal, we simply sort the $w_{j,tm+i}$ $t = 0,1,2,3$ into increasing order and then choose v_{ji} to be any number between the middle two. An obvious choice is the median. This would give some heuristic justification for using the $||\ ||_\infty$, since use of the median will demonstrate similar 'discontinuity preservation' as median smoothing in the geometric domain.

For the case of overlapping windows, the ∞ problem is not quite so simple, but it still decomposes into a family of l_1 problems for each row of W, which could be solved by linear programming. (For example, see Barrodale and Roberts [17]).

The problem of approximating each row of W in the least squares sense is solved by

$$V = WT$$

where T is the Moore-Penrose pseudoinverse of S (see for example, Gill et al [18], p 40 ff). Algorithms for pseudoinverses are readily available. However it is not clear if this actually solves the 2 matrix norm problem; a detailed analysis using the singular value decomposition will be required. For the experimental results described in §3, the $||\ ||_\infty$ with the approximation process described above has been used.

Of course, the theoretical model does not tell us whether or not the approximation process is 'sensible' in the sense of producing small errors in output vectors. It only tells us that we are doing the best possible with this type of pyramid and shrinking matrix. In order to understand the inner structure of the approximation problem one needs to investigate the correspondence of information, as represented in the networks' weight matrices, between various levels of the pyramid.

APPENDIX B

Statistical analysis of the two training sets

The Chi-square test was used due to the nominal nature of the results; a correct or incorrect classification. This has the disadvantage in that the Chi-square ignores the fact that the same images are used in both sets.

It is not possible to use non-parametric tests such as the Mann-Witney, as they require actual output, and it was not possible to combine whether the image was correctly classified, the distance from the exact centre and the output response. There is also no way to indicate if an image was contained in the training set or not.

The independent variable is the weights and the dependent variable is the network response. The two conditions are the different training sets; Training Set 1 and Training Set 2. The contingency table for the network classifications is given below in Table 2:

	Correct		*Incorrect*		*Total*
Weights from Training Set 1	41		19		60
		E = 45.5		E = 14.5	
Weights from Population Training Set	50		10		60
		E = 45.5		E = 14.5	
Total	91		29		120

Table 2 Contingency table for networks classification of the 60 images using two different training sets.

Using the values of χ^2 calculated from the table and the degrees of freedom, the level of significance can be found from tables. This value reflects the size of the difference between the expected and observed frequencies, thus indicating the extent to which the observed frequencies depart from the NULL hypothesis. For the results above the significance is 0.1 indicating that the differences are due to the different conditions.

APPENDIX C

The learning parameters for the hierarchical recognition system

A number of different training sets and architectures have been investigated. However, the ability of the network to converge seems to be dependent upon the learning rate which is in turn dependent upon the number of weights (the number of weights being a function of the level of resolution.) [1]. If the learning rate is too large the network oscillates around the initial value of tss; never descending to a minimum in the error surface. Conversely, if the learning rate is too small, the tss of the network decreases slowly.

Once an optimum learning rate was determined (0.1, 0.05 and 0.01 for pr2, pr1 and pr0 respectively) the network would quickly descend to a small value relative to the starting tss. From this point it would slowly reduce to the final tss. On a few occasions the network would get stuck at this point and remain fixed unless the learning rate was reduced. One reason could be that the system is stuck in a limit cycle if the learning rate was set too large (Ellacott, [13]). Alternatively, it could be due to the system being stuck in a local minimum. Furthermore, the larger number of patterns in the training data the smaller the learning rate had to be (though this has less of an effect than the general value for the learning rate). In addition, the momentum was constant (0.9) for most of the training sets.

It is not suggested that this technique or the choice of parameters is the optimal one for training such networks. They were chosen to allow comparison between neural networks trained at different levels of the pyramid.

REFERENCES

1. Ellacott S W, Evans M & Hand C C: 'Training Neural Networks Using a Multi-Resolution Pyramid — an Interim Report', Research Report for British Telecom's Connectionist Project (1989).

2. Schalkoff R J: 'Digital Image Processing and Computer Vision', John Wiley & Sons, Inc (1989).

3. Levine M D: 'Region Analysis Using a Pyramid Data Structure'. In Tanimoto S & Klinger A (Eds), Structured Computer Vision, New York, Academic Press (1980).

4. Tanimoto S: 'Image Data Structures'. In Tanimoto S & Klinger A (Eds) Structured Computer Vision, New York, Academic Press (1980).

5. Rumelhart D E, Hinton G E & Williams R J: 'Learning Representations by Back-Propagating Errors', Nature, $\underline{323}$, pp 533—536 (1986a).

6. Rumelhart D E, Hinton G E & Williams R J: 'Learning Internal Representations by Error Propagation'. In Rumelhart D E & McClelland, J L, 'Parallel Distributed Processing: Explorations in the microstructure of cognition', $\underline{1}$, Cambridge Mass, MIT Press (1986b).

7. Sejnowski T J & Rosenberg C R: 'NETtalk: A Parallel Network that Learns to Read Aloud'. In Anderson A & Rosenfeld E, 'Neurocomputing: foundations of research', Cambridge Mass, MIT Press (1986).

8. Plaut D C & Hinton G E: 'Learning Sets of Filters Using Back-Propagation', Computer Speech and Language, $\underline{2}$, pp 35—61 (1987).

9. Gorman R P & Sejnowski T J: 'Analysis of Hidden Units in a Layered Network Trained to Classify Sonar Targets', Neural Networks, $\underline{1}$, pp 75—89 (1988).

10. Tesauro G & Sejnowski T J: 'A Parallel Network that Learns to Play Backgammon', Artificial Intelligence, $\underline{39}$, pp 357—390 (1989).

11. McClelland J L & Rumelhart D E: 'Explorations in Parallel Distributed Processing: A Handbook of Models, Programs, and Exercises', Cambridge Mass, MIT Press (1988).

12. Barrow H: 'Neural Networks Tutorial' AISB 89 Conference, Sussex University (18th April 1989).

13. Ellacott S W: 'An Analysis of the Delta Rule', INNC-90, Int Neural Network Conf, $\underline{2}$, Paris, pp 956—959 (July 9-13 1990).

14. Hutchinson R A & Welsh W J: 'Comparison of Neural Networks and Conventional Techniques for Feature Location in Facial Images', Proc First IEE Int Conf on Artificial Neural Networks, London (1989).

15. Lang K J & Witbrock M J: 'Learning to Tell Two Spirals Apart', In Proceedings of the 1988 Connectionist Models Summer School, Morgan Kaufman, California (1989).

16. Isaacson E & Keller H B: 'Analysis of Numerical Methods', (chapter 1), John Wiley & Sons, New York (1966).

17. Barrodale I & Roberts F D K: 'An Improved Algorithm for Discrete 1_1 Linear Approximation', SIAM J Numerical Analysis, $\underline{10}$, pp 839—848 (1973).

18. Gill P E, Murray W & Wright M H: 'Practical Optimization', New York, Academic Press (1981).

5

TRAINING AND TESTING OF NEURAL NET WINDOW OPERATORS ON SPATIOTEMPORAL IMAGE SEQUENCES

M J Wright
Department of Human Sciences, Brunel,
The University of West London

1. INTRODUCTION

The purpose of the investigation was, first, to analyse the ability of single layer neural network algorithms to learn aspects of the local image structure from image sequence data, and second, to test trained networks for their image processing and noise suppression capabilities.

The starting point was the problem of removal of Gaussian noise from a sequence of images by neural net techniques [2]. The data base consisted of 20 successive frames of the head and shoulders of 'Miss America' talking to camera (MISSA sequence) which was supplied in uncontaminated original and with three levels of added noise (SD = 2, 4 or 8 grey levels).

It will be shown that single-layer associative nets and unsupervised, competitive learning nets are capable of learning spatial or spatiotemporal filter functions which depend upon the statistics of the training image. The use of spatiotemporal filters in image smoothing and noise suppression is well known, both for static images [3] and image sequences [4,5].

Experiments on backpropagation [6] suggest that more complex, nonlinear operators can also be learned, and the properties of trained networks may be understood in terms of receptive and projective fields of hidden units. A fully-developed image restoration technique based on Hopfield nets has been described by Zhou et al [7]. However techniques depending upon hidden units were not considered in the present study, which is based on processes with low computational costs.

For a general application, such as teleconferencing, it is assumed that a wide range of time-varying images will be encountered, and that noise removal will be required whatever the detailed content of the image, so that the relevant image statistics will be local. The problem differs from a recognition or scene analysis problem where global or relational image properties are important, and it might be necessary to provide a neural network with parallel input from the whole image. It will be appropriate for learning the local statistics of images to train the neural nets on spatiotemporal windows of various sizes which scan the image sequence.

1.1 Preliminary analysis: what kind of regularities are there to be learned in the image?

1.1.1 Spatial regularities

Many natural images have a characteristic spatial frequency content in which the log power (root mean square contrast) declines in proportion to log spatial frequency. The slope of this function is a measure of the 'roughness' (fractal dimension) of the surfaces in the image [8]. A log power/log spatial frequency function was measured for the test image data and it shows the expected predominance of low spatial frequencies and a monotonic slope with no marked spatial frequency peaks and troughs (Fig. 1). This implies that to capture this image structure a multi-resolution analysis is necessary [9]. All the training operations in the present study were replicated at a range of spatial scales using a Gaussian or Laplacian pyramid [10].

Many natural images differ from random noise in that they contain extended boundaries which have a range of orientations. The prominence of the main object boundaries at certain spatial bandwidths of face images has been noted previously [11,12]. To demonstrate this oriented structure in a selective way, face image test data were bandpass-filtered with a difference of Gaussians (DOG) operator, at 20 cycles/face width, then thresholded to produce a binary image. A frequency histogram of bit patterns in a 3×3 window scanned across the image showed a preponderance of bars and edges, demonstrating regularities in the orientation domain (Fig. 2).

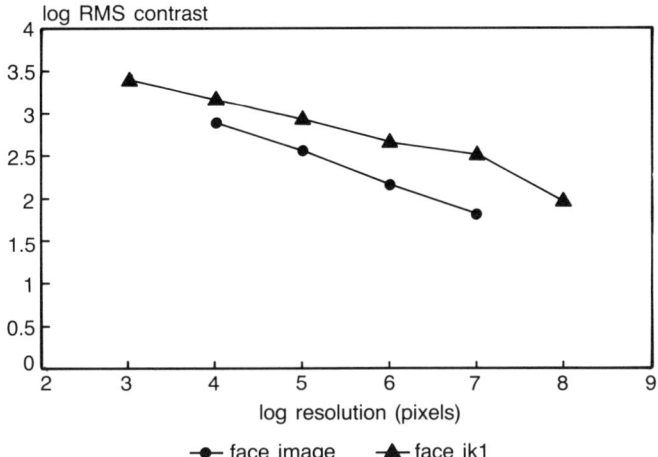

Fig. 1 Log RMS contrast (ordinate) in sub-images of a Laplacian pyramid (log resolution refers to the number of pixels in x and y dimensions). Data from two original face images are shown.

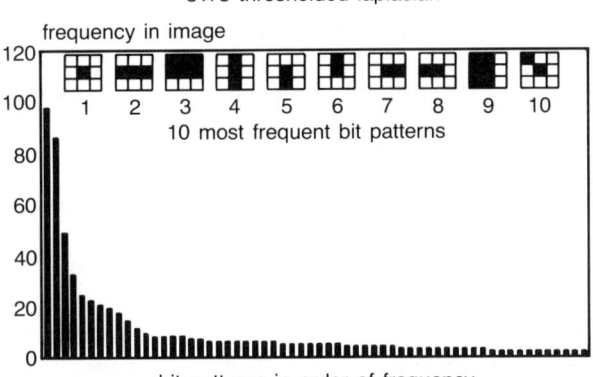

Fig. 2 The most common pixel patterns appearing in a 3 × 3 window scanning a face image which has been bandpass-filtered with a centre frequency of 20 cycles/face width, then thresholded to produce a 'cartoon' image [11].

1.1.2 Spatiotemporal regularities

There are several possible mathematical analyses of the temporal variations of image functions caused by moving objects [13]; one of the simplest is to consider the degrees of self-correlation within the image sequence

[14]. There are regularities similar to those already noted for the spatial domain. Adjacent pixels in both spatial and temporal domains tend to have highly correlated grey values (first-order correlation). Dots or stippled surfaces which are stationary or move generate oriented lines of correlated grey values (second-order correlation) in the spatiotemporal domain, and stationary or moving boundaries and edges generate oriented planes or slabs in the spatiotemporal domain (third order correlation). There are also higher-order correlations such as those due to periodic textures.

The human visual system contains filter mechanisms sensitive to the kinds of self-correlation produced by moving objects, and the filter functions can likewise be thought of as being oriented in space-time [15]. Neural net systems have recently been developed as a model of visual motion analysis [16,17]. One characteristic of these models is that the determination of motion vectors in the image is preceded by a decomposition into oriented spatio-temporal components. Such an analysis may also be of value in noise removal in image sequences in the same way as spatial filtering for single images [18].

2. TRAINING SPATIOTEMPORAL FILTERS USING A DELTA-RULE

The stratagem adopted was to start with the simplest network architectures and learning rules and to assess their capabilities, moving on to more complex networks and architectures at a later stage. The initial stage looked at single-layer nets and a delta-rule training algorithm. The second stage used a single-layer net and an unsupervised learning rule [1].

2.1 Associative: two-dimensional version

2.1.1 Methods

The absolute value of the difference in grey level between the centre pixel of a window and each of the surround pixels can be taken as an error term in a delta-rule algorithm for training a single layer network. Each window pixel cell in the network was connected to the centre pixel cell so that the window pixels' grey values can be compared with the centre pixel's grey value (Fig. 3). Link weights were incremented when the window pixel and centre pixel had a similar grey level and decremented when they had a dissimilar grey level.

In the autoassociative version of this net a link connects the centre pixel cell to itself as well as to the other pixels in the window. In the heteroassociative version this self link was disconnected.

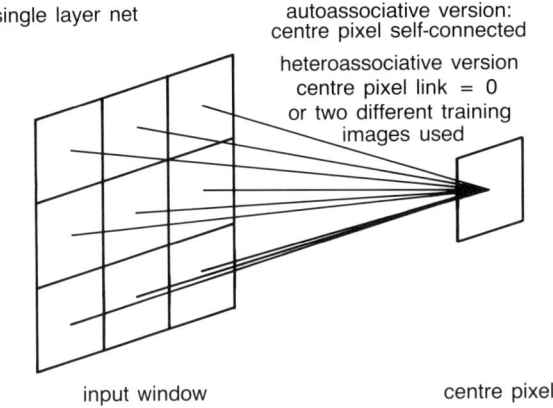

Fig. 3 In the autoassociative net, all the cells of the input window are connected via modifiable links to the cell representing the centre pixel of the input window. In the heteroassociative net, the self-connected link of the centre pixel is omitted.

Link modification proceeded by the following delta-rule

$$\text{Delta } W_{ij} = -k.abs(X_i - A_j) + \Sigma_{ij} \, m.abs(X_i - A_j)/N \qquad \ldots (1)$$

where X_i = activation of window pixel cell,
A_j = activation of centre pixel cell
W_{ij} = weight of connection between window and centre pixel
k and m are constants
N = number of links.

Associative nets of this type were trained on images of the MISSA sequence. The input window scanning area was concentrated on the face region of the image. Network and training parameters were varied systematically.

2.1.2 Results

Single-layer delta-rule nets learned a link weight distribution over the window (receptive field) which was positive peaked (Fig. 4). In the autoassociative versions a strong positive weight accumulated to the centre pixel, and the minimum weight (negative) was found at the window extreme (usually a corner). In the heteroassociative version (Fig. 5) the centre pixel weight was unmodifiable and set to zero. In the trained net it was surrounded by positive weights. Again, the minimum weight was found at the window boundary.

The learning rule ensured that when $k = m$ the learned link weights were distributed symmetrically so that the sum of the negative weights was minus the sum of the positive weights (Laplacian-type). The trained windows resembled centre-surround receptive fields and trained operators were bandpass filters.

When a constant was added to the filter weights to set the lowest link weight at the window edge to zero, a smoothing filter (low pass) was produced. The trained windows differed from mammalian centre-surround receptive fields in that there was a monotonic weight gradient from the centre to the edge of the window.

In the heteroassociative net, weights of the surround links were no longer driven downwards by the predominance of the centre pixel self link, and the detailed topography of the weight landscape in the surround was unmasked. Trained filters deviated from circular symmetry and there was evidence of strong oriented structure. This anisotropy was entirely due to the training image since when the image was rotated by 90° the trained weights also rotated by 90°.

Note that the second expression on the right-hand side of equation (1) is a measure of the variation of grey values within a given window sample. The trained link weights thus reflect the first-order correlation of grey values in the image. Each trained link weight can be taken as a predictor of the centre pixels value given a sample pixel in the window. The closer to the centre pixel, the better a predictor it is of the centre pixel's value.

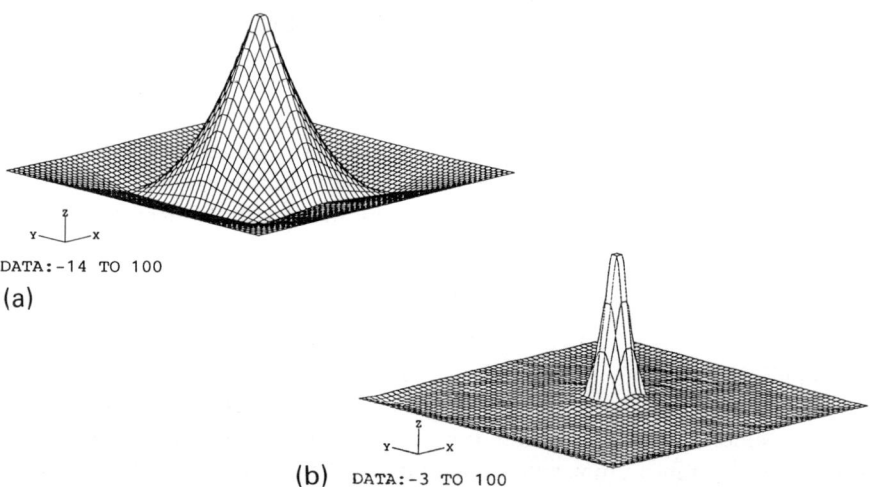

Fig. 4 Weight function (receptive field) learned by autoassociative delta rule net connected to scanning windows of two sizes, after training on frame 1 of the MISSA sequence. A continuous surface is interpolated between the discrete weight values.
  a 3×3 pixel window   b 13×13 pixel window. The axes are normalised.

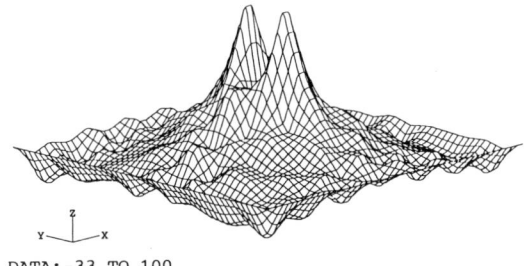

DATA:-33 TO 100

Fig. 5 Weight function (receptive field) learned by heteroassociative delta rule net connected to a 9×9 scanning window. The axes are normalised.

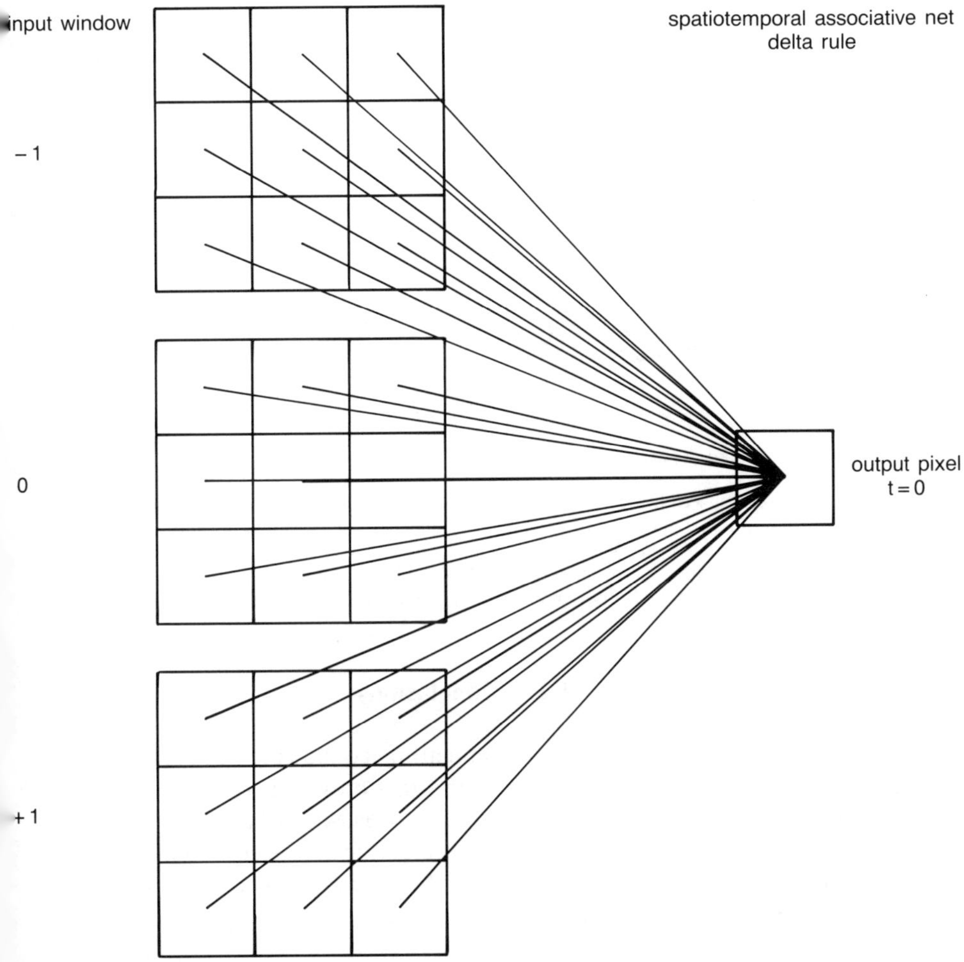

Fig. 6 In a spatiotemporal autoassociative net, pixel cells representing a spatiotemporal input window, x,y,t are connected via modifiable links to the centre pixel cell of the input window.

2.2 Associative net, three-dimensional version

2.2.1 Method

The foregoing method for training spatial filters was extended into the spatiotemporal domain by using a three-dimensional (x,y,t) window to scan a sequence of frames. The learning rule was identical to that for two-dimensional nets. A $3 \times 3 \times 3$ window was used (Fig. 6).

2.2.2 Results

The same rule applied to a $3 \times 3 \times 3$ spatiotemporal window reveals an asymmetry in the spatial and temporal domain. The learned weights (and by implication the correlation in grey levels) for corresponding pixels in adjoining frames were stronger than for adjacent pixels in the same frame. The three-dimensional receptive field has the form of a spatiotemporal centre peaked operator (Fig. 7).

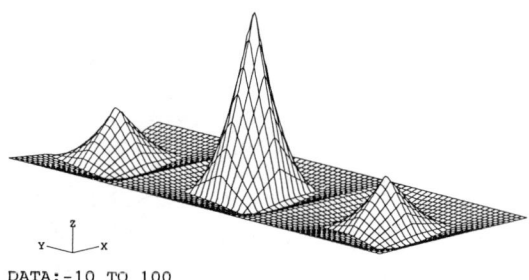

Fig. 7 Pattern of weights learned by a $3 \times 3 \times 3$ pixel (x,y,t) spatiotemporal window scanning three successive frames of the MISSA sequence. The spatiotemporal filter is displayed as three displaced spatial filters. The centre peak represents the autoassociative link to the window centre pixel ($t=0$). The flanking peaks represent the weights on the heteroassociative links from the centre pixel at $t = +1$ and $t = -1$ to the centre pixel at $t = 0$.

2.3 Conclusions

Single layer associative nets implementing a delta rule will learn a centre-peaked bandpass or low pass weighting function when trained by scanning a natural image with a window. In trained autoassociative nets the bandpass was broad because of the high positive weighting of the self-connected link. Various anisotropies were prominent in heteroassociative net filters, which reflect anisotropies of the image training set.

In spatiotemporal associative nets the correlation of grey values between adjacent frames was higher than that of adjoining pixels in the same frame, so the shape of the operator was different in spatial and temporal domains. This property is likely to be of value in removing noise from images since the between-frame correlation of noise is low.

3. TRAINING ORIENTED SPATIAL FILTERS USING COMPETITIVE LEARNING

It was shown that regularities in orientation as well as in spatial frequency exist in natural images. To pick up feature regularities from the image a richer representation is needed. Two possible neural net approaches were considered: supervised and unsupervised learning. An unsupervised approach was chosen in order to assess the capabilities of the simpler learning algorithms. A simple Kohonen net was used [1].

3.1.1 Method

The input to the net was a window of $N = P \times P$ pixels, which was fully connected to the output layer. The output layer was a one- or two-dimensional array of M neural elements (feature array). Each training trial consisted of input from a scan position of the window. The scan position was incremented consecutively by one pixel until scanning of the selected area of the image was complete. At the commencement of training the weight vectors are initialised with random values. Training proceeds by taking an input vector consisting of grey values (normalised between 0 and 1) from the initial position of the window in the training image.

The output O_j of the jth neuron is given by:

$$O_j = \Sigma_i (X_i . W_{ij}) \qquad \ldots (2)$$

where X_i = input window vector

W_{ij} = weight vector.

The connectivity of the net in the training phase is shown in Fig. 8. Learning is competitive, with modification of links to the most excited output cell, plus cells in an excitatory neighbourhood.

The learning rule was,

where w = winner,

for $k = w$ to $w + n$,

$$W_{ik} = W_{ik} + \alpha_k (X_i - W_{ik}) \qquad \ldots (3)$$

α_k = learning rate

An alternative rule gave similar results:

$$W_{ik} = W_{ik} + \alpha_k (X_i - \Sigma_i X_i/N) \qquad \ldots (4)$$

Those are variants of Kohonen's training algorithms [1]. Because the size of the feature array was small (dictated by the need for convergence from the input layer) the excitatory neighbourhood was confined to adjacent cells in the array. Instead of shrinking the neighbourhood, the learning rates in the excitatory neighbourhood were decreased as learning progressed to provide focusing of the emerging feature topology. Training was carried out by scanning single image frames. It was replicated (with a new feature array) on sub-images at multiple spatial resolutions, derived from a Gaussian pyramid.

In the test phase, the trained features were convolved with the original image (with or without noise) (Fig. 9). For each scan position, an output window is computed from the activations of the feature cells (equation 5) by 're-playing' them through the learned weights (equation 6).

$$O_j(n) = \Sigma_i G_i . W_{ij} . X_i(n) \qquad \ldots (5)$$

$$Y_k(n) = \Sigma_j W_{jk} . O_j(n) \qquad \ldots (6)$$

$$Z_n = \Sigma_n Y_k(n). \qquad \ldots (7)$$

$W_{ij} = W_{jk}$ = trained weights of feature cells

O_j = outputs of feature cells

G_i = quantised Gaussian mask

Y_k = output window

Z_n = output image

The output image is formed by summing the overlapping window outputs for every scan position (Equation 7). More descriptively, each feature cell 'prints down' its receptive field to form the output image. The strength of the 'print' is the strength of the feature cell's activation. The output image is the sum of the overlapping 'receptive field prints' of all the feature cells for every position in the image.

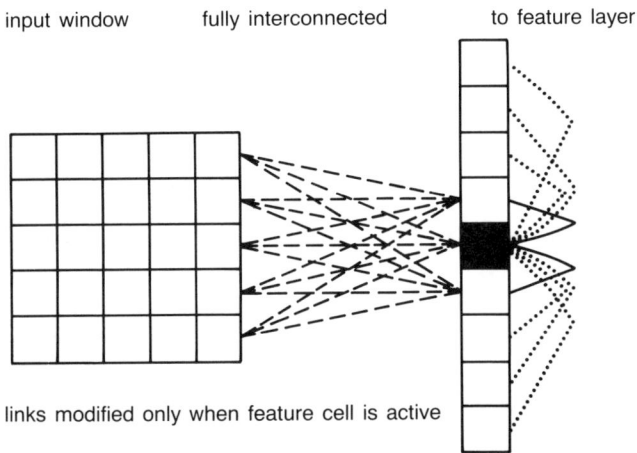

Fig. 8 Connectivity of 5×5 input window to competitive feature array in competitive network in training phase. The filled cell in the feature layer represents the most strongly activated cell (winner) on a single learning trial. It is connected to its neighbouring cells by excitatory links (solid lines) and to the other cells by inhibitory links (dotted lines). The only connections which are modified are those from the input window to the most strongly activated cell and its excitatory neighbourhood (dashed lines).

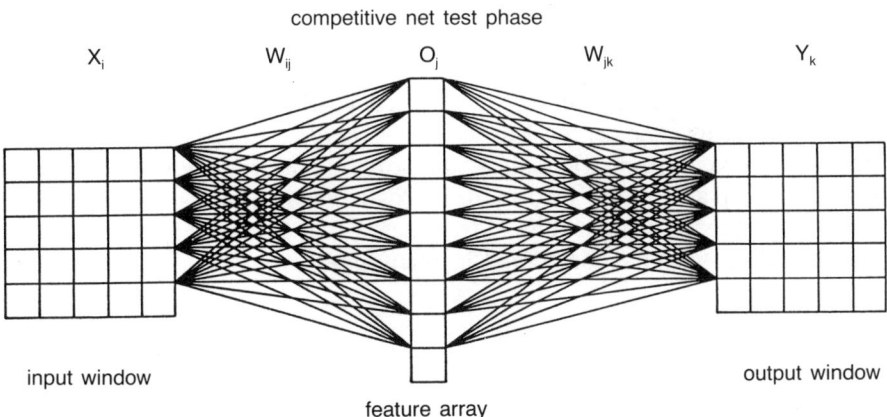

Fig. 9 Connectivity of competitive net in output phase.

3.1.2 Results

Feature cells trained on unprocessed face images develop as oriented edge detectors. In the raw state these filter functions were well approximated by tilted planes,

$$\text{so, for } x = 1 \text{ to } P, y = 1 \text{ to } P$$
$$W_{xy} = ax + by + c \qquad \ldots (8)$$

Multiplying the raw weights by a Gaussian mask, or using a Gaussian input window during training gives filters of the form

$$W_{xy} = G_{xy}(ax + by + c) \qquad \ldots (9)$$

These filters resemble Hubel and Wiesel [19] simple cells (Fig. 10). A full range of different orientations was learned, with neighbouring feature cells in the feature array representing similar orientations, and distant cells dissimilar orientations. Topographic ordering was found both in one- and two-dimensional feature arrays. Edge-detectors rather than bar-detectors were produced, unless the input image was pre-filtered to remove spatial frequencies lower than the centre frequency of the window.

Training on an isotropic texture did not give rise to oriented cells (Fig. 11), even at high learning rates. In this respect the Kohonen net appears to differ from the net described by Linsker [20] which develops oriented features from a non-oriented input. Results with one- and two-dimensional feature arrays were similar. Bar detectors were not developed from training on raw images, but they were found after training on band-pass-filtered images. Training on images containing contrast edges at a single orientation results in edge feature filters tuned to those edges (Fig 12).

The images reconstructed from the test phase show some distortion from the original, whereas an ideal set of Gabor-function filters at multiple spatial scales gives full regeneration of the original [14,21]. The distortion is not surprising because the net has learned filters representing the odd-symmetric but not the even-symmetric Gabor functions; therefore they must transmit incomplete spatial phase information. Also, normalisation across spatial scales is required. The possibility of training the output links (Fig. 9) to correct the distortion must be considered in this context.

Fig. 10 In the top right corner is shown an array of 25 oriented edge-sensitive features developed by a Kohonen net trained by scanning an input window of 5×5 pixels over a low resolution (128×128) face image. The image shown is the output image produced by convolving the input image with this set of features. The output image emphasises low-frequency edges.

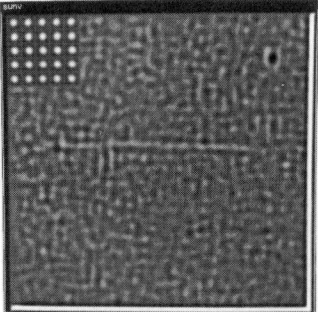

Fig. 11 In the top right corner is shown an array of 25 features developed by a Kohonen net trained on a textured surround. The features were non-oriented and similar even at higher learning rates. The output image is similar to the input image.

Fig. 12 In the top right corner is shown an array of 25 features developed by a Kohonen net trained on a vertical low spatial frequency square-wave grating. The features were sensitive to the edges of the stripes. Note a spurious line down the centre of each stripe of the output image due to the limited spatial bandwidth of the input window.

3.2 Conclusions

Competitive nets can learn the orientation structure of natural images and develop a set of feature detectors similar to those found in mammalian visual systems. The ability of a trained network to reconstruct an image was worse than that of a set of Gabor function filters [14,21]. Without image preprocessing the network will learn only the predominant features in the image and in natural images low spatial frequency content predominates. Pre-filtering in a Laplacian pyramid may provide a solution. The approach could be extended to time-varying images; the main practical difficulty was very extended training times required.

4. TESTING SPATIOTEMPORAL FILTERS FOR NOISE REMOVAL

The purpose of the testing phase of the investigation was to determine whether spatio-temporal filters of the type developed by neural network training algorithms are of value for removing noise from face image sequences.

4.1.1 Methods

The HIPS picture processing software [22] was used as an environment to assess the noise-removal capacities of filters of the type developed by neural nets. The trained filters from the first (delta-rule) algorithm resembled a set of difference-of-Gaussian operators in the space domain with different weighting in different time-slices of the image. The centre peak of the weight distribution did not move over time. The trained filters of the second (Kohonen) algorithm could be compared with Gabor functions in the space domain. For simplicity, testing was done on idealised filters.

Noise removal was assessed by four methods:

- visual inspection of filtered images,

- examination of Fourier transforms,

- the 'sigmaspat' operation of HIPS which estimates the standard deviation of noise: used on originals and difference images (noisy filtered minus original),

- grey value histograms.

Spatial and temporal filter methods were compared with various standard noise-removal algorithms from the HIPS package [23].

4.1.2 Results

The results of various filtering operations on the first MISSA image with 8 dB noise were shown in Table 1.

Table 1

A. Standard deviation of noise in difference image (SD of noisy filtered image minus clean image).		
B. Degree of blur of image.		
	A.	B.
Original noisy	5.0	No blur
Optimum multi-filter algorithm	2.6	Low blur
Smoothed Laplacian pyramid base	1.9	High blur
Temporal smoothing	12.3	High blur
Gated filter	4.6	No blur

- Spatial filtering. Analysis of FFT's for clean and noisy images indicates that noise will be most visible at high spatial frequencies. Neural nets can learn approximations to Laplacian or Gaussian operators, and using a range of training resolutions, could generate a Laplacian pyramid. It was found that smoothing and replacing the base of the Laplacian pyramid was more effective in noise removal than smoothing the raw image with standard algorithms. Smoothing the pyramid base (low-pass spatial filtering) is a trade-off between noise suppression and loss of resolution; thus results which were good in terms of the reduction of RMS noise were subjectively poor in terms of reduced image sharpness. In this respect spatial filtering was worse than standard algorithms such as the multi-filter algorithm ('mfs' of the HIPS package: Table 1). This selects the best filter for smoothing each pixel on the basis of local gradient measurements and minimises blur.

- Spatiotemporal filtering. The neural net simulations proved that there was a higher correlation between the grey levels of pixels (with the same spatial co-ordinates) in adjacent frames than for adjacent pixels in the same frame. Applying a spatiotemporal low pass filter of the type learned by a delta-rule net reduced pixel noise. However, images reconstructed from spatio-temporal sequences showed unacceptable levels of blur due to motion. Motion blur contributed to the measured SD of noise in the difference image.

- Gated filtering. The best all-round performance obtained by spatial filters used a technique of gated filtering which is applicable to face images. A delta-rule net trained on an original image (as opposed to an image pyramid) will develop as a broad-bandwidth centre-surround operator. Such an operator will give a 'broad brush' response to object boundaries and may be thresholded to give a 'cartoon' type of binary image [11,12]. The most obtrusive image noise falls, not at face or feature boundaries, but in flat luminance areas of the face image, such as the cheeks. The gated filtering approach uses the 'cartoon' image as a mask. Pixel smoothing was applied to the non-boundary areas of the image, and the boundary areas were allowed through unmodified. The result was that boundaries remain sharp, even in moving images, and the more noticeable, non-boundary noise, is removed. The most effective of the standard noise reduction algorithms (multi-filter algorithm) relies on a similar principle in that the most effective filter is selected on the basis of local image contrasts.

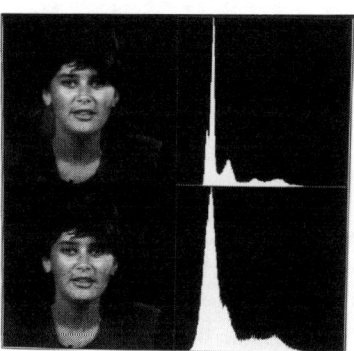

Fig. 13 Top left: clean original image from MISSA sequence.
Top right: histogram of frequencies of grey values from clean image.
Bottom left: MISSA image with added noise, SD = 8 grey levels.
Bottom right: histogram of frequencies of grey values from noisy image.

How might the 'gated-filter' be implemented in a neural net? It is possible to hand-craft such a filter from nodes of the type generated by the first (delta rule) or second (Kohonen) training algorithm. A typical circuit would contain at least one 'hidden unit' to mediate inhibitory (XOR) interactions between boundary-detecting and smoothing filters. A plausible training algorithm for a net connected to a scanning window might be backpropagation, if an appropriate error signal could be found. Because the requirement is jointly to minimise noise, motion blur, and blur due to low-pass filtering, then both noisy and blurred images would be required for the input training set, and the corresponding clean image used to provide error feedback.

Fig. 14 Top left: negative boundary mask (thresholded DOG filter) applied to noisy MISSA image.
Bottom left: positive boundary mask.
Top right: boundary-masked image which is the product of negative boundary mask and smoothed noisy MISSA image.
Bottom right: boundary-unmasked image which is the product of positive boundary mask and unsmoothed noisy MISSA image.

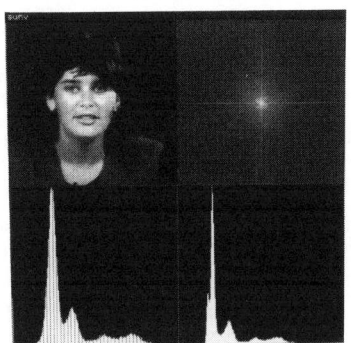

Fig. 15 Top right, gate filtered image formed by ANDing the complementary boundary-masked and boundary-unmasked images of Fig. 14.
Top left, FFT of gate filtered image.
Bottom left, grey value histogram of filtered image.
Bottom right, grey value histogram of clean image.

5. CONCLUSION

Autoassociative, heteroassociative and Kohonen nets trained to windows scanning natural images at multiple spatial resolutions can learn the regularities in the image. Essentially the trained nets were sets of spatiotemporal filters, and the three different algorithms each yield characteristic types of filters. The general value and limitations of spatiotemporal filtering for noise removal are already well known, so the possible value of a neural net approach comes from the ability to match a filter to a particular image set. The topography of weights was sensitive to the overall image statistics. A technique of gated filtering was demonstrated. This is likely to require hidden units for an efficient neural net implementation.

ACKNOWLEDGEMENTS

The software for the delta-rule nets was written by Patrick Brady.

REFERENCES

1. Kohonen T: 'Self-organisation and associative memory'. Springer-Verlag, Berlin (1984).
2. Nightingale C and Hutchinson R A: 'Artificial neural nets and their application to image processing'. Br Telecom Technol J 8, 81—93 (1990).
3. Niblack W: 'An introduction to digital image processing'. Prentice-Hall (1986).
4. Huang T S and Hsu Y P: 'Image sequence enhancement'. In Huang T S (ed) Image Sequence Analysis. Springer-Verlag, Berlin (1981).
5. Cano D and Benard M: '3-D Kalman filtering of image sequences'. In 'Image sequence processing and dynamic scene analysis'. Huang T S (ed), Springer-Verlag, Berlin (1983).
6. Lehky S and Sejnowski T: 'Neural network model of visual cortex for determining surface curvature from images of shaded surfaces'. Proc Roy Soc Lond B 240, 251—278 (1990).
7. Zhou Y-T, Chellappa R, Vaid A and Jenkins B K: 'Image restoration using a neural network'. IEEE Trans Acoustics Speech and Signal Processing, 36, 1141—1151 (1988).
8. Pentland A P: 'Fractal-based description of natural scenes'. IEEE Trans Pattern Recognition and Machine Intelligence $PAMI-6$, 661—674 (1986).
9. Braddick O J: 'Vision in humans and computers'. Nature, 323, 201 (1986).
10. Burt D and Adelson: 'The Laplacian pyramid as a compact image code'. IEEE Trans Commun $COM-31$, 532—540 (1984).
11. Pearson D E and Robinson J A: 'Visual communication at very low data rates'. Proc IEEE 73, 795—812 (1985).
12. Wright M J, Pinnington A and Yazdanfar M: 'Perception', 18, 33A (1989).
13. Nagel H H: 'Image sequence analysis: what can we learn from applications?' in Huang T S (ed): 'Image sequence analysis', Springer-Verlag, Berlin (1981).
14. Daugman J G: 'Complete discrete 2-D Gabor transforms by neural networks for image analysis'. IEEE Trans Acoustics, Speech and Signal Processing 36, (1988).

15. Burr D C, Ross J and Morrone M C: 'Seeing objects in motion'. Proc Roy Soc Lond B 227, 249-265 (1986).

16. Grzywacz N and Yuille A L: 'A model for the estimate of local image velocity in the visual cortex'. Proc Roy Soc Lond B 239, 129-161 (1990).

17. Gurney K N and Wright M J: 'Perception', in press (1990).

18. Gonzalez R C and Wintz P: 'Digital Image Processing', 2nd ed Addison-Wesley (1987).

19. Hubel D H and Wiesel T N: 'Receptive fields, binocular interaction and functional architecture in the cat's visual cortex'. J Physiol, 160, 106—154 (1962).

20. Linsker R: 'Self-organisation in a perceptual network'. Computer, 21, March 1988.

21. Porat M and Zeevi Y Y: 'The generalised Gabor scheme of image representation in biological and machine vision'. IEEE Trans Pattern Recognition and Machine Intelligence, PAMI-10, 452—467 (1988).

22. Landy M S, Cohen Y and Sperling G: 'HIPS: a UNIX-based image-processing system'. Computer Vision, Graphics and Image Processing, 25, 221—245 (1984).

23. Neville-Neil R: 'Testing spatiotemporal filters'. MSc Dissertation. Brunel University, Department of Electrical Engineering (1990).

6

IMAGE CLASSIFICATION USING GABOR REPRESENTATIONS WITH A NEURAL NET

P J G Lisboa
Department of Electrical Engineering, University of Liverpool

1. INTRODUCTION

Computer vision is a complex process which starts with a direct physical representation of an image, consisting of luminance and colour information from an array of transducers, and aims to modify this representation to provide an interpretation of the image at a higher level. This process is carried out in several stages, each concerned with a different level of image definition, ranging from local representations involving only a few neighbouring pixels to global representations which culminate in some form of scene analysis [2,3].

This chapter addresses the first two stages in this process, namely feature extraction and image classification. There is, as yet, no canonical formalism for feature extraction in low level vision. Each problem uses a different pre-processor which is assembled ad hoc from the multitude of available filters [4-8].

The situation with regard to classifiers is no clearer. Hand-crafted classifiers still rate among the most successful, particularly in the area of artificial neural networks [9,10]. Although there is growing interest in some of the long-standing biologically inspired networks, arguably the most commonly used connectionist architecture, which is the multi-layered perceptron, is trained simply by gradient descent [11-12]. However, it is a versatile and effective general purpose classification algorithm, which has been widely applied [13-17], performing well in comparisons with fuzzy logic and traditional statistical classifiers [15-16]. Therefore, it was adopted as the standard classifier for image classification tests.

This chapter is concerned primarily with the choice of pre-processor and how it may be used to improve neural network performance in image classification. The formalism and biological background for the use of Gabor functions [1] is reviewed first. This formalism is then applied to generation of image representations, which are tested in classification tasks. All images have 16×16 grey levels, and only luminance information is used.

2. GABOR FUNCTIONS

One of the most fundamental limitations in computer vision arises from the conflicting requirement of good spatial resolution allied to accurate pattern identification. Visual features are naturally spatially extended objects and, consequently, in order to identify them accurately some degree of spatial resolution may have to be sacrificed.

Texture segmentation has traditionally been carried out using one of two fundamental approaches. One approach using templates of visual primitives defined in the spatial domain, and the other using characteristic signatures in the frequency domain. A compromise between perfect resolution in either domain separately can be obtained by working out explicitly which functions provide optimal sampling in the joint spatial-frequency domain [1].

2.1 Optimality argument

The effective spatial extent of an arbitrary 2-dimensional function $f(x,y)$, and the effective frequency bandwidth of its associated Fourier transformation $F(u,v)$, can be defined in terms of the signal variance in each domain, namely

$$(\Delta x)^2 = \frac{\int_{-\infty}^{\infty} \int_{-\infty}^{\infty} (x-x_0)^2 f(x,y) f^*(x,y) \, dx \, dy}{\int_{-\infty}^{\infty} \int_{-\infty}^{\infty} f(x,y) f^*(x,y) \, dx \, dy} \qquad \ldots (1)$$

$$(\Delta u)^2 = \frac{\int_{-\infty}^{\infty}\int_{-\infty}^{\infty} (u-u_0)^2\, F(u,v)\, F^*(u,v)\, du\, dv}{\int_{-\infty}^{\infty}\int_{-\infty}^{\infty} F(u,v)\, F^*(u,v)\, du\, dv} \qquad \ldots (2)$$

Here, '*' denotes complex conjugate. Similar expressions apply for the remaining dimensions. The variances are referred to 'centres of expansion' respectively at (x_0, y_0) and (u_0, v_0).

Translating the expansion centres to the origin, note that for the one-dimensional Fourier transform

$$\Psi(x) = \int_{-\infty}^{\infty} \Phi(u)\, e^{2\pi i(u.x)}\, du \qquad \ldots (3)$$

$$\Phi(u) = \int_{-\infty}^{\infty} \Psi(x)\, e^{-2\pi i(u.x)}\, dx, \qquad \ldots (4)$$

therefore, the following identity applies

$$\frac{1}{2\pi i} \cdot \frac{d}{dx} \Psi(x) = \int_{-\infty}^{\infty} u.\Phi(u)\, du \ . \qquad \ldots (5)$$

It is readily shown that the bandwidths in either domain are related, i.e.

$$\frac{1}{4\pi^2} \int_{-\infty}^{\infty} \frac{d}{dx}\Psi(x) \frac{d}{dx}\Psi^*(x)\, dx = \int_{-\infty}^{\infty} u^2\, \Phi(u)\, du, \qquad \ldots (6)$$

The inequality

$$\int \left| f - g\, \frac{\int fg^* dx}{\int |g|^2 dx} \right|^2 dx \geq 0, \qquad \ldots (7)$$

which leads to

$$\int |f|^2 dx \cdot \int |g|^2 dx \geq |\int f^* g\, dx|^2, \qquad \ldots (8)$$

can be written as follows

$$\int_{-\infty}^{\infty} |\Psi|^2 dx \cdot \int_{-\infty}^{\infty} \left| x \cdot \frac{d}{dx}\Psi \right|^2 dx \geq \left| \int_{-\infty}^{\infty} \Psi^* x \cdot \frac{d}{dx} \Psi \, dx \right|^2 \quad \ldots (9)$$

with suitable substitutions for f and g. The right hand side of this equation can be simplified further by expressing it as a sum of odd and even combinations of the operators x and d/dx, each combination weighted by a factor of $1/2$. The former yields a constant, half of the unity operator, while the latter is equivalent to $d/dx(x|\Psi|^2)$. Since this is a perfect derivative, it is generally assumed to vanish for suitable integration boundary conditions [18]. To conclude, equation (9) now states that under suitable restrictions on $\Psi(x)$,

$$(\Delta x)^2 \cdot (\Delta u)^2 \geq \frac{1}{4} \cdot \frac{1}{4\pi^2} . \quad \ldots (10)$$

Using the separability of the 2-dimensional Fourier kernel it can be shown that the same relation holds in two dimensions [19], regardless of the direction of the principal axes. The resulting inequality expresses the following fundamental uncertainty in resolution in the conjoint spatial-frequency domain, written in terms of the image bandwidths

$$(\Delta x).(\Delta y).(\Delta u).(\Delta v) \geq \frac{1}{16\pi^2} . \quad \ldots (11)$$

In its simplest interpretation, this inequality arises because a function and its derivative cannot simultaneously be made arbitrarily small.

This elementary 'quantum' of visual information represents the smallest area that can be resolved in 'phase space', which consists of both spatial co-ordinates and both frequency co-ordinates. Although stated generally, this is an approximation valid strictly only for continuum images.

It is natural to enquire about the particular class of elementary functions which assume the minimum area in phase space, since they represent the finest sampling that can be achieved simultaneously in both domains. These functions consist of sinusoids with a quadratic Gaussian envelope, and are known as Gabor functions after his seminal work in 1946. The formalism has since been extended into two spatial dimensions and studied there from the viewpoints of signal processing [20,21] and biology [22,23].

Gabor functions are generally parameterized using two constants, α and β, together with variable expansion centres in space (x_o, y_o) and in the frequency domain (u_o, v_o), according to the following equations:

$$G(x,y) = e^{-\pi[(x-x_o)^2 \cdot \alpha^2 + (y-y_o)^2 \cdot \beta^2]} \cdot e^{-2\pi i[u_o(x-x_o) + v_o(y-y_o)]} \quad \ldots (12)$$

$$F(u,v) = e^{-\pi[(u-u_o)^2/\alpha^2 + (v-v_o)^2/\beta^2]} \cdot e^{-2\pi i[x_o(u-u_o) + y_o(v-v_o)]} \quad \ldots (13)$$

The form of these functions is suggested by the fact that the Gaussian is the only mathematical form that exhibits self-similarity under Fourier transformations.

The parameters α and β span a continuum which includes a pure pixel representation at one extreme ($\alpha,\beta \to \infty$) and a pure Fourier representation at the other ($\alpha,\beta \to 0$). They achieve this always with the minimum area product, as the shape of the cell is deformed from a delta function along the spatial axes to one along the frequency axes.

These functions are frequency and orientation selective, which is apparent from the illustration of their 2-D kernels shown in Fig. 1. Different orientations and filter sizes, as well as varying aspect ratios, are easily achieved.

In the next section, a scheme to select a near complete array of Gabor filters is developed, with reference to biological data.

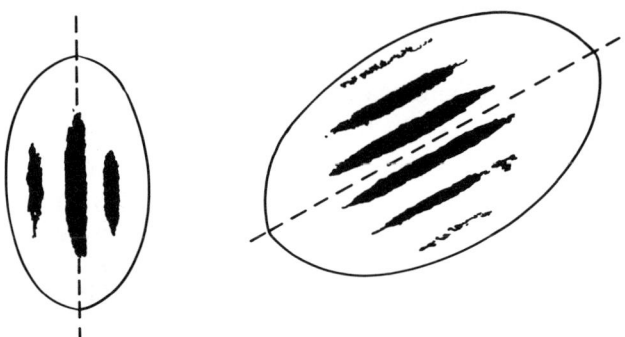

Fig. 1 Representation of the real and imaginary part of Gabor filters.

2.2 Neurobiological consideration

The visual nervous system continually processes vast amounts of information. It must select and extract the information which it needs among large amounts of redundant data, in effect performing several classification tasks rapidly and in parallel in different areas of the visual field. Given the importance of visual classification and the ease with which it is executed by biological systems, it is natural to use insights gained from the natural world in the construction of artificial classification schemes.

In order to prevent simplistic analogies leading to 'flight by the flapping of wings' an attempt has to be made to understand the theoretical foundations behind information processing in the cortex. This is part of the original motivation for the study of connectionist architectures, but the same issue can be addressed from a different angle if the visual nervous system is viewed as a signal processing network. Regarded in this way, the natural visual system comprises physical transducers, pre-processors and associative memories, in the same way as artificial image classification systems.

Among the accepted classification of neuronal cells in the mammalian visual cortex there are some with linear response functions. They are called simple cells [24] and are generally regarded as constituting edge or bar detectors. Their receptive fields are highly localised (sometimes tuned to less than 1 deg^2 out of 30 000 deg^2 in the visual field [25]) with elongated excitatory and inhibitory zones. These characteristics of individual cells were first related to 1-dimensional Gabor functions by Marcelja, who studied the response profiles along a cut normal to the direction of preferred orientation of the cell [26]. This work was further quantified still in 1-dimension [27] and finally extended into 2-dimensions [19].

In an attempt to verify this interpretation of the characteristics of simple cells and correlate the responses of different cells of this type, a number of systematic studies was carried out involving measurements the receptive fields of 36 simple cells in the cortex of 14 cats [28-30]. This included both the spatial and spectral responses of 25 cells, obtained using regular arrays of light sources, and spatial frequency gratings, respectively. The results were statistically consistent with a linear response accurately fitted by 2-dimensional Gabor functions.

These results also provided a foundation for a tessellation of the 2-dimensional frequency domain, by means of what was called a 'wavelet scheme' [23,31]. This scheme postulates a log-polar radial distribution of Gabor basis functions, in multiple tiers and with quantised orientation selectivities, as shown in Fig. 2.

Computationally, the log-polar distribution allows a reasonable tiling of the frequency domain to be achieved using a relatively small number of basis functions. Arrays of similar filters are generated, and translated across the image at the corners of a rectangular array of spatial expansion centres. This is the Gabor function scheme used in the remaining sections.

118 IMAGE CLASSIFICATION USING GABOR REPRESENTATIONS

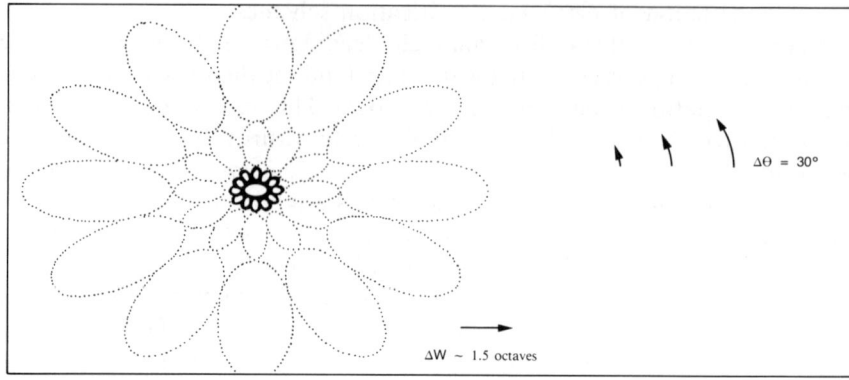

Fig. 2 Map of the characteristic iso-half-amplitude contours of a family of Gabor basis functions in the frequency domain — see equation (13). The outer layer has index m = 1 with the index increasing towards the centre. Layers m = 1-4 only are shown.

3. IMAGE REPRESENTATIONS

In this section the parameters used to define the basis functions are discussed in detail, together with the techniques used in the numerical calculation of the expansion coefficients.

3.1 Basis functions

There are several requirements to be met in the design of Gabor filters, even within a set scheme such as the one illustrated in Fig. 2. The iso-half-amplitude contours of each function, in the frequency domain, consist of a pair of ellipses which form a convenient characterisation of its frequency and orientation selectivity properties.

The first requirement concerns the trade-offs between the required frequency and orientation bandwidths, and the aspect ratio of the filter. These quantities are related by the following equations.

$$\frac{1 - \Delta w}{1 + \Delta w} = \frac{ar.\tan\Theta_{1/2}}{(1 + ar^2.\tan^2\Theta_{1/2})^{1/2}} \quad \ldots (14)$$

Here, $bw \equiv f/f_o$ represents the frequency bandwidth as described by the labels in Fig. 2, $\Delta\Theta_{1/2}$ is the orientation half-bandwidth, and the aspect ratio is $ar \equiv \alpha/\beta$. In the software, these parameters assume the following values:

$$ar = 2 : 1$$
$$\Delta\Theta_{\frac{1}{2}} = 15° \text{ or } 30° \qquad \ldots (15)$$
$$\text{and consequently } \Delta w = 1.5 \text{ or } 3 \text{ octaves.}$$

The second requirement is to set limits for the maximum and minimum frequencies. The maximum is set by the sampling theorem at 0.5 cycles/pel [3]. The lower limit of the frequency modulus was taken to be a circle of radius equal to a half cycle over the distance between the spatial centres of expansion. This is to avoid aliasing among the coefficients at neighbouring expansion centres.

Once the centre frequencies have been chosen, the parameters α and β in equations (12) and (13) are related to the center frequency R_o, indicated in Fig. 2, the aspect ratio and the orientation bandwidth, as follows:

$$\frac{\alpha}{R_o} = \left(\frac{\pi}{\ln 2}\right)^{\frac{1}{2}} \frac{ar.\tan\Delta\Theta_{\frac{1}{2}}}{(1 + ar^2.\tan^2\Delta\Theta_{\frac{1}{2}})^{\frac{1}{2}}} \qquad \ldots (16)$$

$$\frac{\beta}{R_o} = \alpha/ar .$$

Given the aspect ratio of 2:1 and orientation quantization in steps of 30° and 60°, α takes the values $\sim R_o$ and $\sim 1.6 R_o$, respectively. For reference, the attenuation of the Gaussian envelopes at half the grid spacing, d, along the principal axis is $\exp(-\pi\alpha^2 d^2/4)$ and the number of full cycles is $R_o d/2$.

It remains, as the third requirement, to specify how the complete set of basis functions can be generated from a single template. This done using the following transformations [23,31]:

$$G_{pqm\Theta}(x,y) = 2^{-m}.G(x',y') \qquad \ldots (17)$$

$$x' = 2^{-m}.((x-p)\cos\Theta + (y-q)\sin\Theta)$$

$$y' = 2^{-m}.(-(x-p)\sin\Theta + (y-q)\cos\Theta) ,$$

where p and q denote the x- and y- co-ordinates of a spatial expansion centre in multiples of the grid spacing, m is also an integer and it labels the tiers radially starting with $m=0$ at the outer ring of ellipses, and I represents the preferred orientation in the frequency domain in multiples of the full bandwidth $2\Delta\Theta_{\frac{1}{2}}$. Note that the directions in the spatial and frequency domains are orthogonal, as seen by inspection of equations (12) and (13).

Apart from overall normalisation factors, these relations generate layers of filters with centre frequencies in octave multiples. Since the frequency bandwidths are generally bigger than one octave, as indicated in equation (15), this results in an over-sampling along the radial dimension. In addition, the Gabor basis functions are not mutually orthogonal, although their overlap in either the spatial or frequency domain is small, hence the term 'pseudo-orthogonal' which is often applied to them.

In order to provide complete flexibility in the choice of basis functions a numerical method was chosen for the calculation of the Gabor expansion.

3.2 Expansion techniques

Although there are analytical techniques for the evaluation of Gabor coefficients when sampling using a rectangular lattice in the frequency domain [6], these techniques are computationally expensive and no longer apply for log-polar sampling. In this case, a simple relaxation algorithm for least squares minimisation can be used [23].

Denoting the Gabor basis functions by $G_i(x,y)$ and the coefficients by a_i, where the index i represents the 4-tuple (p,q,m,Θ) introduced in the previous section, the expansion of the image reads

$$G(x,y) = \sum_i a_i \cdot G_i(x,y) . \qquad \ldots (18)$$

If the original image $I(x,y)$ is not exactly recovered in that expansion, a quadratic error can be defined.

$$\Delta \alpha_i = - \frac{\partial}{\partial a_i} (\frac{1}{2}(I(x,y) - G(x,y))^2) . \qquad \ldots (19)$$

Defining the projection

$$\sum_{x,y} I(x,y) G_i(x,y) \equiv < I \mid G_i > . \qquad \ldots (20)$$

then the algorithm for updating the expansion coefficients may be written in the form

$$\Delta a_i = < I\text{-}G \mid G_i > . \qquad \ldots (21)$$

The convergence is measured in terms of the percentage error in pixel luminance in the reconstruction of the original image relative to the root mean square pixel luminance of the original picture. The calculation ended when this value was in the range 5-10%. Although it does not follow that this value should be exactly minimised for optimal performance in image classification, in these preliminary tests the errors were chosen to ensure an adequate representation of the image.

4. TEST RESULTS

The coefficients in the Gabor expansion of an image represent the relative strengths of the presence of the component basis functions. Consequently, the relaxation network described in section 3 defines a pre-processor which extracts the presence of Gabor functions, regarded here as primitive features.

Image classification was subsequently performed by a multi-layer perceptron which receives at its input nodes the values of coefficients of suitable Gabor expansions. In order to make the coefficient values compatible with the constraints of the perceptron they have to be scaled to span the full range from zero to one. This was done separately for each image. Other forms of scaling are possible, but they are not discussed here.

In addition, classification tasks involving the multi-layer perceptron may be expedited using a binary representation of the input data. This is related to the reduction in the number of linearly separable regions by sampling only at the corners of the hypercube of possible input configurations. In image processing this corresponds to applying a threshold filter to label each image primitive as present or absent. This approach was used in both tests, using median filtering applied to the coefficients of the Gabor expansion.

The ability of the neural network to classify or interpret images is measured ultimately by its success in generalising from the samples in the training set to new images, although an indication that a good image representation has been achieved is the speed of training in the first place. Both of these quantities are the measures used in the discussion of the results.

4.1 Eye detection

This problem consists of identifying images of eyes from a set of arbitrary images containing 16 examples of eyes and 48 non-eyes. Both the training set and the test set have the pictures of eyes normalised and centred in the same way.

The 16×16 pixel images were expanded using a set of Gabor functions centred spatially at the origin, with an outer centre frequency nominally of one cycle/pel but using only the layers with indices m:1-6 (see Fig. 2). The orientation bandwidth used in this case was 30°. The total number of coefficients used for representing one image is therefore 72, counting the real and imaginary parts of the basis functions separately. The schedule for processing each group of 64 images was to perform 16 iterations of the relaxation algorithm in equation (21), resulting in a r.m.s. reconstruction error of 10% of the error after the first iteration.

Two classification experiments were carried out, both sharing the same set of Gabor coefficients and using the same neural network architecture, comprising 72 input nodes, 8 hidden nodes and a single output node. The required excitation at the output was unity for eyes, and zero for non-eyes. The difference between the two experiments lies in using real values of the coefficients in the first case, with three digit accuracy, and binary values in the other case, using a median filter as described earlier.

The results of the first test (real valued inputs) are described in the histograms in Fig. 3. Here the horizontal axis represents the response from a single output node MLP, and the vertical axis represents the number of eyes/non eyes producing that response. The numbers above the histograms indicate the pattern numbers of those that were misclassified. The multi-layered perceptron is trained to a maximum output error of less than 0.1 in 800 cycles.

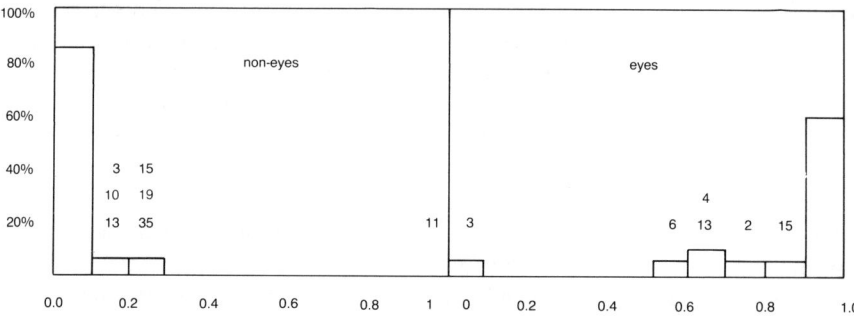

Fig. 3 Histogram of the results for the classification of eyes v non-eyes with real valued Gabor coefficients. The figures are pattern numbers for the output response values shown.

These results are qualitatively similar to those obtained directly from the pixel luminances, representing the image by a pixel map. The main difference between the two approaches is the degree of compactification achieved by reducing the 16 × 16 pixels to 72 Gabor coefficients.

The second classification test involved median filtering to convert the expansion coefficients into a binary form. This time the network trained in only 19 cycles, which represents a very substantial speed up of the training process. The generalisation to test patterns still was not perfect (see Fig. 4).

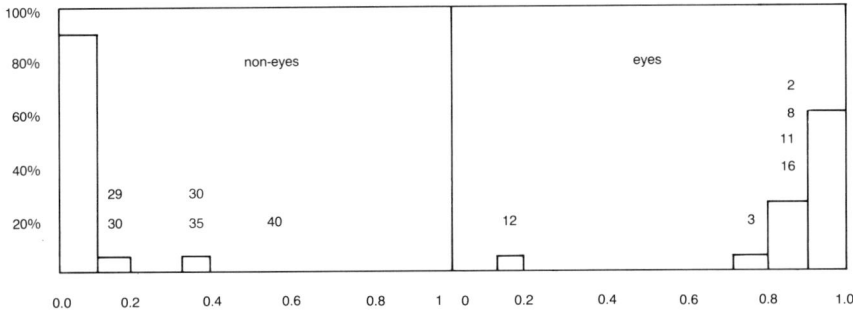

Fig. 4 Results for the classification of eyes v non-eyes using a binary representation of the Gabor coefficients. The data are labelled in the same way as in Fig. 3.

In spite of the considerable reduction in the training time, this network performs in much the same way as the ones mentioned earlier. There are odd severe misclassifications which require further attention, since the reasons for their occurrence is by no means apparent by visual inspection of the offending images.

The main advantages of the Gabor representation over using the luminance values directly are data reduction and faster convergence of the multi-layer perceptron.

4.2 Eye location

The task is to identify the correctly centred image of an eye from a set of 16×16 masked images of the same eye, translated horizontally and vertically by one pixel at a time. A moving mask of size 16×16 operates on an image with 32×32 pels. During training a single output value is nominated for each image according to the displacement of the centre of the mask from the centre of the original image. The maximum output is unity when both coincide, reducing to zero when the boundaries of the moving mask and the original picture overlap.

The classification test is judged to be successful when the maximum output for the test image lies within 2 pixels in either direction from the nominated centre located at the pixel with co-ordinates 7-7.

Since this test requires good spatial accuracy, the 16×16 mask was divided into 16 windows of size 4×4 pels. Some amount of orientation selectivity is preserved by using Gabor functions with 60° orientation bandwidths. The nominal centre frequencies for the outer layer in Fig. 2 was 1.4 cycles/pel and four layers were used, with indices m:1-4.

Using such a large grid results in 384 expansion coefficients to represent each image. These coefficients were median filtered, as described earlier.

A perceptron with 384 input units, 8 hidden units and a single output was used to perform the required classification of the masked images. The results of this test are shown in the top half of the table in the next page, followed by the results from a similar test training the perceptron directly from the pixel luminances, again with 8 hidden units. In the second case only the results on the test set are shown.

The subjects are identified according to whether or not they wear glasses, as this can affect the results. The network is attempting to generalise from a small training set, therefore its performance in this task was considered encouraging (see Table 1). The main difference between the two sets of results described in Table 1 is the nature of the misclassification that occur. The Gabor representation failed on one of the eyes but still retained a high excitation at the correct centre of the image. The failure is due to a high, albeit isolated, peak near the top left-hand corner of the picture. This is probably due to specular reflection from the glasses, which was not eliminated from the original images, and it is likely training on a larger set of images would remove this spurious effect. This was not the case for the way where the bit map representation failed, since there the excitation at 7-7 is minimal.

In fact, the failure to correctly identify the centre of this particular image using only the luminance values persists even after extensive training.

Table 1 Classification results for eye location.

	Gabor representation					
	Name	*Max O/P*	*Location*	*Success*	*O/P @ 7-7*	*Glasses*
Training set	A	0.99	7-7	yes	0.99	no
	B	0.99	7-7	yes	0.99	no
	C	0.98	7-7	yes	0.98	no
	D	0.99	7-7	yes	0.99	yes
Test set	E	0.96	7-6	yes	0.79	no
	F	0.72	8-8	yes	0.62	yes
	G	0.98	7-7	yes	0.98	no
	H	0.96	0-1	no	0.82	yes
	Bit map representation					
Test set	E	0.94	7-7	yes	0.94	no
	F	0.97	4-0	no	0.01	yes
	G	0.96	6-8	yes	0.91	no
	H	0.90	8-8	yes	0.90	yes

5. CONCLUSION

The application of Gabor functions to image representation and their performance in image classification were demonstrated with reference to the problems of eye detection and eye location.

It was shown that Gabor functions allow the sampling of images using intermediate representations, along a continuum ranging from pure pixel representations at the one extreme, to Fourier transformations at the other. It is a characteristic of Gabor functions that they achieve the theoretical maximum resolution in the conjoint spatial-frequency domain throughout.

By combining localized basis functions with particular frequency and orientation selectivities, the resulting set of expansion coefficients can be used to represent the image in ways that enhance the training speed and generalisation ability if neural network classifiers. This was demonstrated for a particular type of natural images.

REFERENCES

1. Gabor D: 'Theory of communication'. J. IEE Lon., 93, 429—457 (1946).

2. Simon J C: Introduction to: 'From Pixels to Features'. North-Holland, Amsterdam (1989).

3. Duda R O and Hart P E: 'Pattern classification and scene analysis'. Wiley, New York (1973).

4. Marr D and Hildreth E: 'Theory of Edge Detection'. Proc. R. Soc. B 207, 187—217 (1980).

5. Bertero M, Poggio T A and Torre V: 'Ill-Posed Problems in Early Vision'. Proc. IEEE, 76, 8, 869—889 (1988).

6. Porat M and Zeevi Y Y: 'The Generalized Gabor Scheme of Image Representation in Biological and Machine Vision'. IEEE PAMI-10, 4, 452—468 (1988).

7. Gidas B: 'A Renormalized Group Approach to Image Processing Problems'. IEEE PAMI-11, 2, 164—180 (1989).

8. Papathomas T V and Julez B: 'Lie Differential Operators in Animal and Machine Vision', in 'From Pixels to Features', J C Simon ed., North-Holland, Amsterdam. 115—126 (1989).

9. Fukushima K, Meiyake S and Ito T: 'Neocognitron : A Neural Network Model for a Mechanism of Visual Pattern Recognition'. IEEE SMC-13, 5, 826—834 (1983).

10. Fukushima K: 'A Neural Network for Visual Pattern Recognition'. IEEE Computer, 21, 3, 65—75 (1988).

11. Le Cun Y: 'A learning scheme for assymetric threshold network'. Cognitiva, 600—604 (1985).

12. Rumelhart D E, Hinton G E and McClelland J L: 'Learning representations by back-propagating errors'. Nature 323 , 533—536 (1986).

13. Sejnowski T J and Rosenberg C M: 'Parallel networks that learn to pronounce English text'. Complex Systems 1, 1 , 145—168 (1987).

14. Gorman R P and Sejnowski T J: 'Analysis of Hidden Units in a Layered Network Trained to Classify Sonar Targets'. Neural Networks 1, 1 , 75—89 (1988).

15. Bounds D G, Lloyd P J, Mathew B and Waddell G: 'A Multi Layer Perceptron Network for the Diagnosis of Low Back Pain'. IEEE Int. Conf. Neural Networks, San Diego, Vol. II, 481—489 (1988).

16. Shea P M and Lin V: 'Detection of Explosives in Checked Airline Baggage Using an Artificial Neural System'. IEEE Int. Conf. Neural Networks, Washington DC, Vol. II, 31—34 (1989).

17. Waibel A, Hanazawa T, Hinton G, Shikano K and Lang K: 'Phoneme Recognition Using Time-Delay Neural Networks'. IEEE ASSP-37, 3 , 328—339 (1989).

18. Schiff L I: 'Quantum mechanics'. McGraw-Hill Kogakusha, Tokyo (1968).

19. Daugman J G: 'Uncertainty relation for resolution in space, spatial frequency, and orientation optimized by two-dimensional visual cortical filters'. J. Opt. Soc. Am. A-2, 7 , 1160—1169 (1985a).

20. Wilson R and Granlund G H: 'The Uncertainty Principle in Image Processing'. IEEE PAMI-6, 6 , 758—767 (1984).

21. Wilson R and Knutsson H: 'Uncertainty and Inference in the Visual System'. IEEE SMC-18, 2 , 305—312 (1988).

22. Daugman J G: 'Six formal properties of two-dimensional anisotropic visual filters : structural principles and frequency/orientation selectivity'. IEEE SMC-13, 3 , 882—886 (1983).

23. Daugman J G: 'Complete Discrete 2-D Gabor Transforms by Neural Networks for Image Analysis and Compression'. IEEE ASSP-36, 7 , 1169—1179 (1988).

24. Hubel D H and Wiesel T N: 'Receptive fields and functional architecture in the monkey striate cortex'. J.Physiol, 195 , 215—243 (1968).

25. Daugman J G: 'Representational issues and local filter models of two-dimensional spatial visual encoding', in Models of the Visual Cortex, eds. D Rose and V G Dobson. Wiley, New York, 96—107 (1985b).

26. Marcelja S: 'Mathematical description of the responses of simple cortical cells'. J. Opt. Soc. Am. 70, 11 , 1297—1300 (1980).

27. Pollen D A and Ronner S F: 'Visual Cortical Neurons as Localized Spatial Frequency Filters'. IEEE SMC-13, 5 , 907—916 (1983).

28. Jones J P and Palmer L A: 'The Two-Dimensional Spatial Structure of Simple Receptive Fields in Cat Striate Cortex'. J. Neurophysiol., 58, 6, 1187—1211 (1987a).

29. Jones J P and Palmer L A: 'The Two-Dimensional Spectral Structure of Simple Receptive Fields in Cat Striate Cortex'. J. Neurophysiol., 58, 6, 1211—1232 (1987b).

30. Jones J P and Palmer L A: 'An Evaluation of the Two-Dimensional Gabor Filter Model of Simple Receptive Fields in Cat Striate Cortex'. J. Neurophysiol., 58, 6, 1233—1258 (1987c).

31. Daugman J G: 'Entropy Reduction and Decorrelation in Visual Coding by Oriented Neural Receptive Fields'. IEEE BE-36, 1, 107—114 (1989).

Part 2: Speech

NEURAL NETWORKS FOR SPEECH PROCESSING: AN INTRODUCTION

R Linggard
School of Information Systems, University of East Anglia

1. SPEECH PROCESSING

The field of speech processing can be divided into three main areas, coding, synthesis and recognition. Each area has its own problems and they provide unique and interesting tasks for neural networks.

1.1 Coding

Almost all speech coders are based on the idea that speech is linearly separable into a system function and a source of excitation. Dudley's original channel vocoder (1938) used ten, fixed-frequency, band-pass filters to define the spectral shape of the system function. This can be reduced to only four filters (if the centre frequencies are allowed to vary), each representing one the four formats known to exist in telephone bandwidth speech. However, in the 'formant vocoder' (1964), the task of separating the excitation signal from the system function is extremely difficult.

Work on formant vocoders was curtailed in the early 1970s by the invention of linear predictive coding (LPC). This enables speech to be encoded by an analytic method of source/system separation, whereby the signal can be reconstructed within an arbitrary error. LPC makes it possible to represent the system function parsimoniously using transforms of the LPC coefficients. However, since the excitation signal has the same bandwidth as the original speech, reducing its bandwidth is still quite difficult. Almost all the variation within modern speech coders is in the way the excitation signal is approximated and reduced in bit-rate. By various means, the bit-rate of LPC-based speech coders has been reduced from 16 kB/s in the early 1970s, to about 4 kB/s in the late 1980s.

All the power of modern speech processing has been brought to bear on squeezing out the last drops of redundancy from the LPC residual, but there is still a belief that more could be done with non-linear methods. This is where neural networks may have some application.

1.2 Synthesis

As early in 1964, Holmes showed that a synthesiser, developed as part of a formant vocoder, could be used to generate speech from phonetic input. The speech quality was not good, but it was usually intelligible. The idea behind this scheme, (and of the others which rapidly followed), was that individual phonemes of phonetic text could be realised as sounds via a formant synthesiser driven by 'target' formant values, and an algorithm to compute the transitions (or coarticulation). The target values for each phoneme were stored in 'drive tables' together with other information on duration and voicing. Since that time, many different synthesis schemes have been devised, using a variety of formant synthesisers, target scheme and coarticulation algorithms. This activity has become known as synthesis-by-rule, or text-to-speech synthesis.

The motivation for the original synthesis-by-rule research was the realisation of a phonetic vocoder for communications; since then, the wider commercial use of digital computers has provided a more important focus — speech output from machines. Today, many of the application areas for text-to-speech systems have become commercially viable — even though synthesis is by no means perfect. The main problem now, is not the intelligibility of the synthetic speech, but the voice quality, which stubbornly resists efforts to improve it. One major problem is the difficulty with which text is converted to a convenient phonetic representation — that is, a string of symbols. Another is the problem of finding adequate rules for converting such symbols into speech. The ability of neural networks to learn arbitrary mappings makes them ideal candidates for these tasks.

1.3 Recognition

The earliest speech recognition schemes were heavily influenced by naive idea about phonetics and a fascination with analogue electronics. Many early attempts to recognise phonemes used ingenious analogue circuitry to detect phonetic features and simple logic to effect classification. Some of these systems worked surprisingly well on carefully pronounced speech. However, repeatability and reliability were poor and, as digital computers became more widely available, digital signal processing gradually took over. The availability of the FFT and the invention of LPC took the mysticism out of feature extraction which had become somewhat of a 'black art'. Spectral measures based on over-lapped and windowed frames of about 10 mS duration soon became standard. The task then reduced to that of recognising patterns sequences of such frames. The discovery of dynamic time warping (DTW) solved the problem of variable duration, and by the late 1970s small-vocabulary recognition algorithms were in commercial use. These were most reliable for a single speaker using isolated words, but performance was still useful with connected words and multiple speakers. The advent of hidden Markov modelling (HMM), in the early 1980s, has since enabled recognition systems to become speaker-independent — even over telephone lines. The more difficult task of recognising continuous, fluent speech has been tackled in the 1980s by returning to the ideas of phoneme recognition, this time via unspecified acoustic elements called, 'sub-word units'. In the years since the 1970s, it has been realised that phonemes do not exist as acoustic events in the way that early recognition researchers imagined. However, it is thought that some acoustic structures do exist which correspond to 'phonemes-in-context', and 'triphones' (phonemes triples) have become useful as sub-word units. Though there are, potentially, many thousands of these units, a set of about 2000 can give good recognition.

In the test problems described below, the utterances are isolated words, thus the amount of input data to the neural network varies in proportion to the duration of the word. However, the input data is finite, and by time-normalisation or other techniques, it can be fitted to the dimensions of the neural network input field. This is not the case with continuous speech, in which the flow of parameterised data is not limited and simple neural network like MLPs will not suffice. Given the success of the neural networks with isolated words, it seems likely that they could readily take on the more several problems of continuous speech. Indeed, the current literature in this field reports several attempts to do this.

2. THE SPEECH PROCESSING TEST PROBLEMS

The following test problems, devised as being typical for speech processing, are part of the BTL neural networks initiative.

2.1 Test problem 1

Recognition of spoken letters of the alphabet. The alphabet has been used as a bench-mark in speech recognition for many years and conventional algorithms perform less well on this task than on smaller, more specialised vocabularies. Machine recognition of the names of the letters of the alphabet is known to be difficult — much harder than digit recognition for example. This is because many letter-names are distinguished only by their initial consonant, sharing the final open vowel with several others. The two instances of this are the 'E-set' which consists of the letters B, C, D, E, G, P T and V, and the 'A-set' which consists of A, J and K. Both sets are very confusable — even for human listeners.

Three repetitions of the names of the letters of the alphabet were recorded in a silence cabinet from each of 104 speakers, 54 males and 50 females, using a wideband telephone handset. The signal was appropriately filtered then sampled and recorded digitally at 20 000 samples per second and 16 bits per sample. This data was then end-pointed manually, only incorrect utterances being discarded. The resulting database contains a total of 7977 word tokens each stored in a separate file. Since this data cannot be applied directly to neural network without considerable pre-processing for data reduction, the data was also made available in processed form. The processed version of each file is the original data converted as follows. The signal is blocked in frames of 25.6 mSec duration, overlapped 50%, Hamming windowed, and then reduced to 8 MFCCs (Mel frequency cepstral coefficients). The network is trained on half of the speaker set and tested on the other half. In multi-speaker mode the network is trained and tested on all the whole speaker set using different versions of the each utterance for training and testing.

2.2 Test problem 2

LPC coefficients are effectively filter parameters which will reproduce the original speech signal when fed with the LPC residual. Conceptually, therefore, the residual is the result of passing the speech signal through an inverse of the LPC filter. However, the actual residual signal is usually computed as part of the LPC processing which is carried out on blocks of samples of fixed duration.

It is conventional to remove obvious correlations in the residual due to pitch by using of a further stage of prediction. The final residual is thus a noise like signal sampled at the original rate, (in this case 8000 samples per second) with the original quantisation (16 bits per sample). For good speech coding this signal must be reduced to as few bits as possible.

The test problem data consists of the LPC residual processed from 615 seconds of speech from 14 different speakers. The original signal was in the form of speech passages of average duration 45 seconds. The LPC was 16th order performed over a frame of samples equivalent to 30 mS, overlapped to give 50 frames per second. The pitch predictor produces new coefficients every 4 mS. The original speech data together with the residual is stored in single files 16 bits per sample integer format. The corresponding LPC parameters and pitch prediction coefficients are stored as real numbers in ASCII format. The task is to use neural networks to encode and regenerate the residual. The degree of success is to be measured by the degree of compression achieved in the encoding process, and by the signal/quantisation-noise ratio of the reconstructed residual.

2.3 Test problem 3 — Yes/no recognition using simple features

A major application area for speech technology is the simple recognition of the words YES and NO when spoken over the telephone network. A data base of these two words spoken by a large number of people over telephones was processed to provide the data for this problem. The processing was designed to give a small, fixed number of parameters per word, ideal for input to a neural network.

The original speech data consists of YES/NO utterances collected over long-distance, dialled-up telephone lines within the UK. Each speaker in the database made only a single call and gave one token of each of the utterances YES and NO. This signal was then band-pass filtered between 170 Hz and 3400 Hz, sampled at 8000 samples per second and stored digitally. These files were manually end-pointed and automatically segmented into five sections on an energy basis. Finally, each section was processed, using a low order LPC algorithm, to provide two alternative representations, with 15 and 25 parameters per word, respectively.

The processed data is divided into training and test sets, the latter consists of 381 YESes and 417 NOs, the former consisting of 301 YESes and 319 NOs. The task for the neural network is to act as a speaker-independent recogniser. Since the original speech is of low band-width and considerably noisy and has been reduced to relatively few parameters, this is not an easy problem.

3. THE SPEECH CHAPTERS IN THIS BOOK

As part of the BTL connectionism project, attempts were made to solve the speech test problems outlined above, and one also concerned with speech synthesis which is reported in the section on natural language processing. These attempts have met with greater and lesser degrees of success. The least successful was the LPC residual compression problem; the results on this task were so poor, that they have not been included here. However, the other two problems, both on speech recognition, were tackled with some success and the two chapters below report this work.

Speech recognition is the main topic of the chapters in this section and the task which has been addressed is that of classifying utterances using spectral information. The extraction of spectral parameters from the raw speech signal has been performed by conventional methods; it is the classification using these parameters that forms the original contribution to the field of speech recognition.

7

SPOKEN ALPHABET RECOGNITION USING MULTILAYER PERCEPTRONS

P C Woodland
Engineering Department, University of Cambridge
(formerly of BT Laboratories)

1. INTRODUCTION

The recognition of spoken letters of the alphabet by machine has been long accepted as a challenging and important problem, and has been viewed as a benchmark for automatic speech recognition [1]. The alphabet vocabulary contains several highly confusable subsets such as the 'E-set' ('b', 'c', 'd', 'e', 'g', 'p', 't' 'v'), the 'A-set' ('a', 'j', 'k'), and the pair 'm' and 'n'. Not surprisingly, most of the recognition errors occur due to the misidentification of one of the members of these subsets. It is clear that an effective algorithm for alphabet recognition must exploit all the available discriminatory information present in the speech signal.

Most speech recognition systems use some form of similarity measure between the input speech of unknown identity and stored reference patterns. In the case of DTW pattern matching, the templates are previously recorded (possibly averaged) parameterised utterances of the word in question and the similarity measure is a distance between optimally time aligned reference and unknown patterns. Hidden Markov models (HMMs) use a stochastic model of individual word production. In this case, the similarity measure is the probability that a word model produced the observed speech. Neither method accounts for the specific discriminations that are required in a recognition system that employs a particular vocabulary since the standard training algorithms for these techniques only employ within class information. Hence, it might be expected that these systems would not perform particularly well on highly confusable vocabularies such as the alphabet, especially in audio conditions that produce a large range of (irrelevant) differences between different utterances of the same word.

The recogniser in this chapter uses a recently developed multi-layer neural network (connectionist) model — the MLP [2] — in place of a more traditional recognition algorithm. When used as a classifier, this type of network is explicitly trained to perform discriminations between classes of inputs. It is therefore hoped that this type of approach will have advantages over similarity measures for difficult speech recognition tasks that exhibit real world variability between examples of the same class. A number of studies on typically very small vocabularies have shown that this can indeed be the case (e.g. [3]).

As well as acting as a good benchmark of recognition performance, alphabet recognition is also important for directory access applications. In this type of application, a database, of telephone numbers for example, can be interrogated using speech input. It is a requirement of such an application to be able to enter name information. Speech recognition techniques have not advanced to the stage where names can be entered without spelling (it might be noted that operators for telephone directory enquiries often require a name to be spelt for confirmation or clarification), and therefore high performance spoken letter recognition is required to form the basis of a viable service. However, as well as giving a low error rate, the recogniser must also be speaker independent, and operate under the non-ideal audio conditions encountered over a telephone link (i.e. it must be robust). Further, it is important that the algorithm can be implemented efficiently. The approach described in this chapter is accurate, robust and computationally efficient. To demonstrate its capability in the context of directory access, a simple directory enquiries system is described that uses a standard PC and digital signal processor.

2. MULTILAYER PERCEPTRONS

A MLP is a feedforward neural network whose nodes are arranged in layers. Input data to the network is presented at the input nodes, which simply pass their input to their output. Each input node is connected to all the nodes in the second layer (the hidden layer) via weighted links. The input to each hidden node j, x_j is formed as $\Sigma\, y_i w_{ji}$, where node i is a node in the input layer, and w_{ji} is the link weight between nodes i and j. Node j computes its output y_j as

$$y_j = F(x_j + \theta_j)$$

where θ_j is the bias (effectively another weight) associated with node j, and F is a non-linear function known as the activation function. The fact that each node computes a non-linear function of its input allows the complete network to perform non-linear vector transforms. The non-linear function used here is the ubiquitous logistic function:

$$F(x) = \frac{1}{1+e^{-x}} \quad \ldots\ldots (1)$$

This function can be viewed as a smoothed step function whose value varies from zero to unity. The next layer of weighted links and nodes, the output layer, receives its input from the hidden layer nodes and performs computations identical to those at the hidden layer nodes.

The network is trained to perform a particular mapping from a certain set of input patterns to patterns on the output nodes. If the network is performing a classification task (as it is here) then it is usual to use one output node for each of the classes to be recognised (a '1-in-N' coding). When a particular class is present on the inputs, the output node corresponding to the input class should respond with a high output value, while all the other nodes should respond with a low value. The network learns to respond in a certain way to input data by adjusting all the weight and bias values in the network. To do this successfully, a large labelled database of examples of class members is required along with a training algorithm to set the weight values.

It should be appreciated that the MLP described above takes a fixed dimensional input vector and maps it to a fixed dimensional output vector. Since speech utterances vary in overall length, and also have non-linear internal timing variations, some sort of pre-processing needs to occur before feeding speech data to the network.

3. TRAINING MULTILAYER PERCEPTRONS

MLPs are trained to minimise some function of the error between the desired output values for each node, that here represents class identity, and the actual value obtained when the input pattern is presented. This is done by using a gradient descent algorithm, with the necessary partial derivatives calculated by a process known as error backpropagation [2].

Here a sum squared objective function is defined so that

$$E = \frac{1}{2} \sum_n \sum_j (y_{j,n} - d_{j,n})^2 \qquad \ldots (2)$$

where n is an index over input-output patterns in the training set; j is an index over output nodes; y_j represents the actual output of node j and d_j represents the ideal, desired output from the node. During training, the object is to minimise E by adjusting the network weights.

Firstly, consider a particular training utterance (value of n), and differentiating (equation 2) gives

$$\frac{\partial E}{\partial y_j} = y_j - d_j$$

The chain rule is used to calculate the differential of E with respect to the input of node j, x_j as

$$\frac{\partial E}{\partial x_j} = \frac{\partial E}{\partial y_j} \frac{dy_j}{dx_j}$$

Now, using differential of the activation function (equation 1) the relation

$$\frac{\partial E}{\partial x_j} = \frac{\partial E}{\partial y_j} y_j(1-y_j)$$

is obtained. Now, the differential of E with respect to a weight w_{ji} from hidden node i to output node j can be expressed as

$$\frac{\partial E}{\partial w_{ji}} = \frac{\partial E}{\partial x_j} y_i$$

This gives a method of calculating the required partial derivatives for the hidden to output layer weights. For a hidden layer node i connected to output nodes j

$$\frac{\partial E}{\partial y_i} = \sum_j \frac{\partial E}{\partial x_j} w_{ji}$$

Proceeding as above then allows calculation of the error derivative for the input to hidden layer weights. If there is more than one hidden layer, the same approach could be used to calculate the error derivatives for the weights in the other layers. The derivative of the error with respect to the node biases θ_j is calculated by viewing the bias as a weight connected to a node with a constant output value of unity. The total error derivative for all patterns can be calculated simply by summing the contribution from each pattern.

The MLP is trained by presenting each pattern, using a forward pass through the network to calculate the node output values, and then a backward pass to calculate the error derivatives. The network weights are then updated so as to reduce the error E. Representing the vector of error derivatives (in the weight space) at time t as $\nabla E(t)$ and the update to the vector of network weights W as $\Delta W(t)$ then the standard update rule [2] is

$$\Delta W(t) = \eta \nabla E(t) + \alpha \Delta W(t-1) \qquad \ldots (3)$$

where η is a constant called as the learning rate, and α is the momentum.

It is known that the update rule (equation 3) is very inefficient and tens of thousands of complete learning iterations may be needed for E to be reduced to an acceptable value. If this is coupled with a large number of training patterns then the MLP training procedure can become prohibitively costly. Further, the values of the constants in (equation 3) need to be carefully chosen. If η is too small then learning will proceed very slowly. If it is too large, then the training procedure may become unstable. In fact, as training proceeds the magnitude of ∇E usually decreases. Hence, if η is small enough not to cause initial instability then this implies that learning will be very slow in the later stages. Therefore in this work the update rule adaptively selects the values of the learning rate and momentum.

The adaptive parameter update rule dynamically adjusts the value of α and η in (equation 3) at each iteration (to α_t and η_t) in order to keep the total update magnitude approximately constant. The relation used is

$$\eta_t |\nabla E(t)| + \alpha_t |\Delta W(t-1)| = S$$

where S is called the total step size. Also the ratio of the relative contribution from the instantaneous gradient and the momentum is set such that

$$\frac{\alpha_t |\Delta W(t-1)|}{\eta_t |\nabla E(t)|} = |\sin(\gamma)|$$

where γ is the angle between $E(t)$ and $\Delta W(t-1)$. These two equations are solved to give values for η_t and α_t.

The method ensures that large gradients do not cause excessive steps in weight space, and allow reasonable steps with small gradient magnitudes. The amount of momentum smoothing increases to a maximum when the angle between the previous update vector and the current gradient vector is 90°. Although the algorithm has been used as presented above, for the experiments reported here, the value of S is reduced if the value of $E(t) - E(t-1)$ exceeds a threshold. The initial value of S has been set by a formula that involves the number of weights in the network.

The adaptive parameter update algorithm has been found to be successful in reducing training time by several orders of magnitude on the problem addressed here. The same parameters have been found to be effective for a number of problems and it is insensitive to training set size. Further it produces only a small computational overhead. However, it does require weight updates to be made after all the patterns have been presented (after each epoch). The method was found to give better performance than that offered by the algorithm described by Chan & Fallside [4].

4. DATABASE

The database used in this work was collected by BT for investigating the performance of neural network models in speech recognition tasks. The database contains three utterances of each of the letters of the British English alphabet from each of 104 talkers. It was collected in a silence cabinet, using a wideband telephone handset, the speech was filtered between 170 Hz and 8 kHz, sampled at 20 kHz and stored on disk. All utterances were automatically endpointed, the endpointing being manually checked, and if necessary corrected. After removal of any incorrect utterances (e.g. utterances of the wrong word) or truncated utterances, 7976 utterances were available for speech recognition experiments. The database was partitioned in two ways so that either speaker independent or multiple speaker experiments could be performed. The speaker independent set was split so that 52 speakers would be available for training (3999 utterances) and 52 speakers for testing (3977 utterances). For multiple speaker work the first two utterances from every speaker were used for training (5302 utterances) and the third for testing (2974 utterances).

The speech waveform was converted into Mel frequency cepstral coefficients (MFCCs) by taking 25.6 ms frames of speech at 12.8 ms intervals. Each frame was Hamming windowed, a 512 point FFT performed and the resulting log magnitude spectrum split into twenty-six channels that were linearly spaced on a Mel frequency scale. The first eight coefficients of a discrete cosine transform were taken as the MFCC feature vector to describe each frame. This type of representation is widely used in speech recognition work.

To convert a variable number of MFCC vectors to a fixed dimensional representation, a simple linear interpolation scheme was used to reduce each utterance to just 15 frames (actual utterance lengths varied between 17 and 82 frames). The first and last frame of the utterance are taken along with frames generated (by linear interpolation) at 13 linearly spaced points throughout the utterance. The data was presented to the networks in two alternate forms. The first form, designated RAW, was simply scaled so that the range of the largest coefficient was approximately from -1 to 1. In the second form, designated NORM, each coefficient was scaled separately to have zero mean and a standard deviation of one third.

5. RECOGNITION EXPERIMENTS AND RESULTS

A number of MLPs were trained on both the speaker independent and multiple speaker datasets. All MLPs had 120 input nodes (15 frames of eight coefficients each), a variable number of hidden nodes and 26 output nodes. During testing, the output unit with the highest activation level was taken as the recognised class. The network architecture used is illustrated in Fig. 1.

During training, the target value for the node representing the class of the current input pattern was set to 0.9, with the target for all other nodes set to 0.1. These values are preferable to (0,1) targets since they can be reached without an infinite value as the input to the output node. In turn this means that weight values are less likely to become large and that generalisation performance (i.e. the performance on unseen data) tends to improve. Previous work [5] had shown that generalisation performance can be improved still further if the absolute magnitude of the weights in the network is limited during training. This causes the network to have less flexibility and prevents the network from learning the fine features of the training set in too much detail. For natural data, much of this fine detail is in effect 'noise', and therefore test set performance improves at the expense of training set accuracy when the weights are limited. Further, the weight range limiting technique increases the network robustness to weight quantisation — this is especially important for practical implementations that may use fairly coarsely quantised weights.

All networks were trained with 1500 presentations of the complete training set, by which time a local minimum of the mean squared error had been found. The adaptive parameter update algorithm was used and was found to be essential to train networks with this amount of data. For the multiple speaker data, the training run on a single processor of an Apollo DSP10040

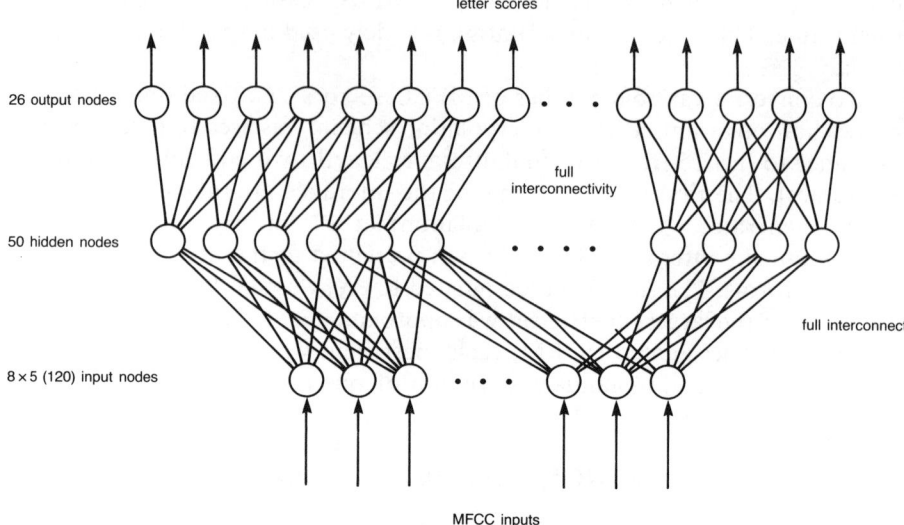

Fig. 1 MLP architecture for recognising spoken letters.

takes about 33 hours, while testing the resultant network on the 2974 multiple speaker test utterances takes only 20 seconds.

Table 1 lists the results for the multiple speaker data. It can be seen that in all cases for the same network configuration the NORM data outperforms the RAW data on the training set, while on the testing set the results are similar. The effect of weight limiting can be clearly seen. As the weight limit is reduced, the training set accuracy is reduced, but in general, the difference between training set and test set accuracy is also reduced (i.e. generalisation improves). The best multiple speaker test set performance of 91.0 comes with the RAW data, 75 hidden nodes and a weight limit of 1.5.

Table 2 gives the results for the speaker independent data. Here it is clear that while the NORM data is superior on the training data, the reverse is true for the test data. Comparing these values to the corresponding results in Table 1, it can be seen that the training set accuracy is higher for the speaker independent data, but the test set accuracy is lower. This is because with fewer training speakers in the speaker independent set there is less variability, and hence the data can be more completely characterised by a fixed size network. Conversely, the multiple speaker test data bears greater resemblance to training material and hence the generalisation is better and the test set accuracy for the multiple speaker data higher. Again weight limiting improves the test set accuracy and the best test set performance of 88.3 comes with the RAW data, 75 hidden nodes and a weight limit of 1.5.

Table 1 Recognition results for multiple speaker data.

Data type	Number of hidden nodes	Maximum weight value	Training set accuracy %	Test set accuracy %
RAW	25	no limit	95.6	84.4
RAW	50	no limit	98.9	87.3
RAW	50	2.0	97.2	89.8
RAW	50	1.5	94.7	90.3
RAW	50	1.0	93.7	89.4
RAW	75	1.5	94.7	91.0
NORM	25	no limit	96.6	83.3
NORM	50	no limit	99.3	86.7
NORM	50	2.0	97.3	90.1
NORM	50	1.5	98.2	89.8
NORM	50	1.0	96.6	89.4
NORM	75	1.5	96.8	90.8

Table 2 Recognition results for speaker independent data.

Data type	Number of hidden nodes	Maximum weight value	Training set accuracy %	Test set accuracy %
RAW	25	no limit	97.8	80.9
RAW	50	no limit	99.3	85.5
RAW	50	2.0	97.4	87.4
RAW	50	1.5	96.5	87.6
RAW	50	1.0	94.6	87.4
RAW	75	1.5	97.4	88.3
RAW	75	1.0	96.8	88.2
NORM	25	no limit	98.2	80.7
NORM	50	no limit	99.7	82.7
NORM	50	2.0	99.3	86.2
NORM	50	1.5	98.6	86.1
NORM	50	1.0	96.9	86.1
NORM	75	1.5	99.9	87.3
NORM	75	1.0	99.6	86.5

A dynamic time warping (DTW) system was trained and tested on the original MFCC files. The DTW system used a clustering algorithm to generate 12 clustered templates for each word making a total of 312 averaged templates. During testing, an unknown utterance is compared to each of the templates and the 'distance' from each calculated. A k-nearest neighbour decision rule was then used to choose the class with the lowest average distance taken over the best k templates from each class. The best test set results for the DTW system ($k = 3$) along with the best MLP results are collected together in Table 3. It should be noted that, on the basis of the statistical test discussed in [6], the MLP results are superior with more than 99% confidence for both the speaker independent and the multiple speaker datasets.

Table 3 Comparison of DTW and MLP performance.

Data set	Best DTW accuracy %	Best MLP accuracy %
Multiple speaker	85.8	91.0
Speaker independent	86.0	88.3

6. DISCUSSION

It is clear from these results that the MLP recogniser (with weight range limiting) is more accurate than the DTW system. Further, once trained it is frugal in terms of computational and storage requirements. The simulations showed that compared to the DTW system, the MLP uses about 10% of the storage and 0.1% of the computation. It should be noted that the computation of the MLP outputs cannot begin until the utterance has been endpointed (unlike DTW). Using the adaptive parameter training algorithm, MLP training times are about an order of magnitude greater than those required for DTW.

Further exact comparisons with published results on different data are impossible, but the method appears to be at least comparable to the benchmark results [4] published for an advanced HMM system for an alpha-digits database. Such a database would be expected to give higher recognition rates than an alphabet only database. Their most accurate HMM system achieved 89.5% in multiple speaker mode on the 100 talker database used.

It is interesting to note that the MLP achieves this good performance in spite of the crude nature of the input representation. An alternative form of time alignment before interpolating was briefly investigated. This segmented the utterance uniformly along the 'trace' [7] of the utterance. This means that parts of the utterance in which the spectrum is changing rapidly are sampled more often (in time) and at the expense of relatively steady state portions. Unfortunately, the algorithm reduces robustness, and the test set recognition results offered no improvement over the simple linear time normalisation scheme used here.

7. DSP IMPLEMENTATION FOR A DIRECTORY ACCESS DEMONSTRATOR

Due to the modest computational requirements and good weight quantisation properties of the MLP system described above, it is a fairly straightforward task to implement a complete recognition system on a digital signal processor.

The system as described above has been implemented using a Motorola 56001 DSP mounted on a development board in a BT PC, as shown in Fig. 2. Pre-trained network weights values are downloaded to the board. The audio input is from a wideband telephone handset, and the board performs the necessary A/D conversion, endpointing, calculation of MFCCs and finally linearly normalises the utterance to 15 frames. The DSP calculates the 26 MLP output values that can be thought of as pseudo-probabilities of each letter having been uttered[1].

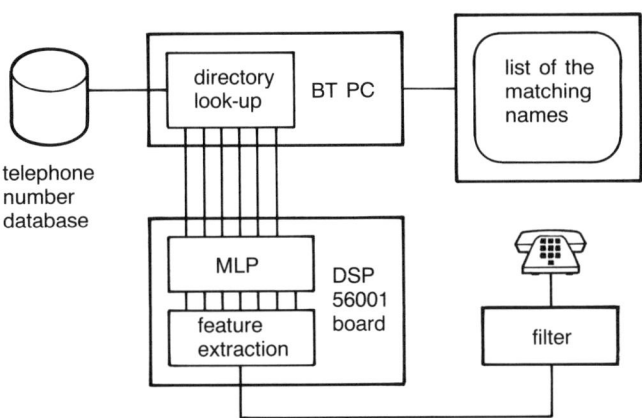

Fig. 2 Block diagram of the directory access demonstrator.

The network architecture used in the DSP implementation had 50 hidden nodes and weight limits of 1.5. There are a total of $120 \times 50 + 50 + 50 \times 26 + 26 = 7376$ weights and biases in the system. The value of the non-linear logistic function is calculated by table look-up. Since the DSP is optimised to performing the type of operations required to calculate the MLP output (mainly multiply-adds) the whole procedure only requires about 8000 cycles. With a processor cycle time of 97.5 ns, 8000 cycles requires 780 μs. Allowing for length normalisation and other overheads, the time taken for recognition after endpointing is complete is still less than 1 ms. The storage requirements are in total less than 1 k for MFCC and MLP programs, about 7.5 k for weight storage and about 1 k all told for the FFT sine, logistic sigmoid, DCT and Mel scale look-up tables.

---

[1] Strictly speaking, the output values should not be treated as probabilities unless they have been first normalised and the network trained using an objective function such as cross-entropy [3]. However, in practice, the use of the network outputs as probabilities seems to be effective.

A directory access program on the PC prompts the user for the first five letters of the required person's surname (or initials as well if the surname has less than five letters). The MLP system then supplies a set of 26×5 output scores. These are used to retrieve the most probable entry from a directory of some 3000 names. If the directory contains multiple entries for the same surname (e.g. 'Smith') that cannot be disambiguated on the basis of five letters entered, then the system will not be able to produce a single unique answer. If a single answer is found, the directory entry is then displayed by the PC. In a remote access situation it would be a simple task to replace the current system of prompting and reporting information to use text-to-speech synthesis.

Although the demonstrator has not, as yet, undergone any formal evaluation, the system has been tried by many people and has been shown to be remarkably accurate. It successfully operates under a range of background noise conditions and seems very resilient to using an automatic endpointing algorithm. This clearly points to the robust nature of the technique used. It has been noted that when a recognition error for an individual letter occurs, the correct class is invariably within the top few nodes. This fact, combined with the constraints inherent in the name directory, give rise to very high name accuracy from a recogniser with a first choice error rate of about 10%.

8. CONCLUSIONS

A speaker independent speech recognition system for recognising the difficult alphabet vocabulary has been developed using a multi-layer perceptron based recogniser. It has been shown that the recogniser is robust, computationally simple and highly accurate — out-performing standard recognition algorithms if a weight range limiting technique is used.

Successful recognition of an alphabet vocabulary is needed in many directory access applications. A demonstration of the current technique's applicability to such tasks was given by a real-time implementation on a standard DSP that can rapidly and reliably access information from a 3000 name directory.

ACKNOWLEDGEMENTS

Thanks to Dave Coleman, Simon Ringland and Gavin Smyth, all of BTL, for their contributions toward the work reported here.

REFERENCES

1. Rabiner L R and Wilpon J G: 'Some performance benchmarks for isolated word speech recognition systems'. Computer Speech and Language, 2, 343—357 (1987).

2. Rumelhart D E, Hinton G E, Williams R J: 'Learning internal representations by error propagation'. In Rumelhart D E and McClelland J L (eds). Parallel Distributed Processing: Explorations in the Microstructure of Cognition. 1: Foundations. MIT Press, Cambridge, MA (1986).

3. Woodland P C and Millar W: 'Fixed dimensional classifiers for speech recognition'. In Wheddon C and Linggard R (eds.) Speech and Language Processing, Chapman and Hall, London (1990).

4. Chan L W and Fallside F: 'An adaptive training algorithm for back propagation networks'. Computer Speech and Language, 2, 205—218 (1987).

5. Woodland P C: 'Weight limiting, weight quantisation and generalisation in multilayer perceptrons'. Proc IEE Int Conf on Artificial Neural Networks (1989).

6. Gillick L R and Cox S J: 'Some statistical issues in the comparison of speech recognition algorithms'. Proc ICASSP-89 Glasgow, Scotland (1989).

7. Pieraccini R and Billi R: 'Experimental comparison among data compression techniques in isolated word recognition'. Proc ICASSP-83 Boston, USA (1983).

8. Hinton G E: 'Connectionist learning procedures'. Tech Report CMU-CS-87-115, Carnegie Mellon University (1987).

8

SPEAKER INDEPENDENT VOWEL RECOGNITION

L S Smith and C Tang
Centre for Cognitive and Computational Neuroscience,
University of Stirling

1. INTRODUCTION

In designing artificial devices to perform human perceptual functions which map the initial sensory stimuli to their corresponding responses, there are at least three aspects to be considered: the representation of sensory input, the representation of the output or response, and the mechanism which maps the input to desired output. Since Dudley first invented his vocoder more than four decades ago, many vocoders have been designed to develop a representation of speech in an efficient way such that the representation contains all the information necessary for separating signals and at the same time has minimum redundancy [2]. Within the backprop learning connectionist framework, researchers have tried different network architectures — varying the number of layers of the network, and varying the connectivity, such as Harrison's experiment with single and multilayer perceptrons, and his use of zonal units instead of making the network fully connected between layers [3]. On the output level, McCulloch and Ainsworth tried two types of output representation in their attempt to recognize steady state vowels [2]. One is local representation in which each unit represents a vowel; the other is based on the vowel quadrilateral in which each vowel is represented by a pair of real numbers indicating the first two formant frequencies. The vowel quadrilateral is illustrated in Fig. 1. The vowel quadrilateral is motivated partly by following the position of the tongue hump in the mouth: in that sense, it is physiologically motivated representation.

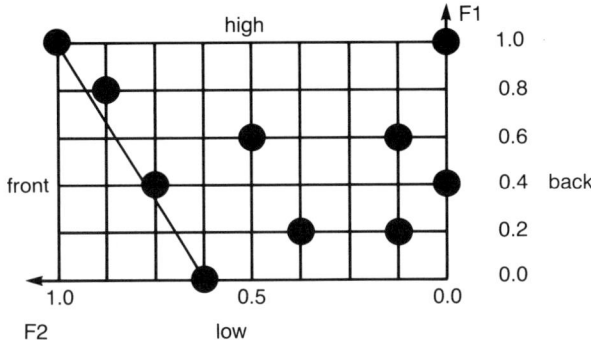

Fig. 1 The vowel quadrilateral.

The particular problem we tackle and the data we used are exactly as in the McCulloch and Ainsworth experiments. 30 speakers of RP English were recorded saying the words: heed, hid, head, had, hard, hod, hoard, hood, who'd, Hudd, heard. These words contain the 11 steady-state vowels in RP English. The speech was processed by digitisation at 44.1 kHz, followed by a 54 channel filter bank analysis. The output frame rate was 100 Hz. We used the data supplied to us by McCulloch, in which he had hand-extracted the steady-state portion, and averaged over the number of frames to give a single spectral cross-section for each vowel. The data was normalised to have a mean of 0 and a standard deviation of 1. Three sets of training and test files were constructed from the dataset: mixed data, from 8 males and 8 females in the training set, and 7 of each in the test set; female data, with 8 speakers in the training set and 7 in the test set, and male data, again with 8 and 7 speakers respectively.

From [1] we note that purely local representation of the vowel output performed much better that the vowel quadrilateral representation: this was unexpected in that one might expect that using a representation which followed an aspect of sound production would help identify vowel output. We considered that this might be because of the way in which the vowel quadrilateral was coded. Thus our work described here has its emphasis on output representation. Our task is to recognize 11 steady state vowels with an MLP using the backpropagation learning algorithm. Three sets of experiments were conducted to test:

- how encoding the vowel quadrilateral using a number of output units (i.e. using a more distributed representation) could affect network performance,

150 SPEAKER INDEPENDENT VOWEL RECOGNITION

- how a two-layer readout network could be used to measure network performances,

- whether learning could be transferred among training procedures based on mixed, female and male data.

Throughout this chapter, an *n*-layer network has *n* layers of units, including the input units.

2. ENCODING THE VOWEL QUADRILATERAL

The coding used in McCulloch and Ainsworth's work for the vowel quadrilateral was a simple pair of cartesian co-ordinates, with one output unit representing position on each co-ordinate. Based on [4] we considered that better performance could be obtained using a coarse coded system. In our coding, each output unit represents some elliptical area of the vowel quadrilateral (Fig. 2). On training, the desired activation level of a unit in response to a given vowel is determined by its distance from that vowel in the vowel quadrilateral. Each unit has a circular or elliptic receptive field, and each vowel is represented by the activation across all the coding units.

z, the activation level of a coding unit with centre (μ_x, μ_y) in response to vowel (x,y), is a function of the position of the vowel in the quadrilateral (x,y), and the position of the coding unit, (μ_x, μ_y):

$$z = \exp^{-(x-\mu_x)^2/2\sigma_x^2} \cdot \exp^{-(y-\mu_y)^2/2\sigma_y^2}$$

The standard deviation along the x axis, σ_x defines the width of the receptive field in the x dimension; along the y axis, σ_y defines the width in the y dimension. The receptive field is circular when σ_x is equal to σ_y. The effect is that if μ_x equals x and μ_y equals y, the unit has output 1. Otherwise, the unit's output falls off in a Gaussian fashion, dependent on the distance from (x,y) and on the constants σ_x and σ_y.

Notice that the vertical and horizontal distances between any two vowels in the quadrilateral are always multiples of a grid value, .125 along the x axis, .2 along the y axis. We made $\sigma_x = 0.125N$, and $\sigma_y = 0.2N$ ($N = 2,3$) in order that each unit has equal sensitivity to a vowel in both x and y dimensions. N is chosen such that the receptive field is neither so small that many units have a response of almost zero, nor so big that all the units have very similar responses.

The result of this form of coding is that there will be a great many more output units than in McCulloch's work, and thus more weights from the hidden layer of the net to the output layer. The output units form a coarse coded layer. Such units have been found useful in coding data for arithmetic problems [4].

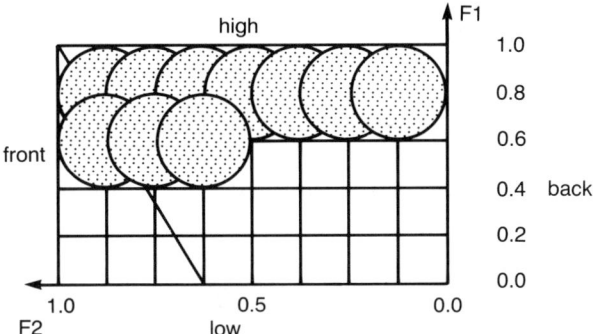

Fig. 2 Receptive fields of encoding units.
Only some of the receptive fields are shown, for clarity.
In this case, $N=1$, and there are 28 encoding units.

3. EXPERIMENT TECHNIQUE

The networks have 3 layers: an input layer with 54 units, each corresponding to one of the 54 energy channels; a hidden layer; an output layer, whose number of units corresponds to the number of coding units in the previous section. Throughout, a learning rate of 0.1, and a momentum term of 0.1 were used.

There are three variables involved in the experiment:

- the number of units by which the positions of 11 vowels in the vowel quadrilateral (two real numbers) are encoded (9, 16 and 28). It is also the number of output units in the networks,

- the size of receptive field of each unit σ_x, σ_y ($N=1,2,3$),

- the number of hidden units in the network (11, 15 and 20).

In each experiment, many simulations were run. The best results are reported, although we always checked that these were not simply freak results.

3.1 Experiment one

For this experiment, the performance measure is based on the Euclidean distance between the actual output vector and its desired vowel vector. If this distance is the smallest one among the distances between the actual output vector and all the possible vowel vectors (there are 11 of them corresponding to the 11 vowels), then the output is counted as a 'hit'; otherwise, a 'miss'.

As we expected the performance of the networks on mixed, female and male data all improved considerably. Table 1 summarizes the best performance and makes a comparison with McCulloch's result.

Table 1 Performance of 3-layer nets with encoded vowel quadrilateral. (Best results).

	Experiment 1	*McCulloch's Results*
Mixed	75.3%	64.5%
Female	66.2%	57%
Male	75.3%	58.5%

Notes: The results from Experiment 1 used $N=2$, and 16 output units. For mixed and female networks, 20 hidden units were found best, and for male 11 hidden units. The results from McCulloch's paper are the averaged best results from different runs.

3.2 Experiment two

Instead of using nearest Euclidean distance measure, we used a two layer network to measure the network performance. A two layer network to map the 11 vowel vectors with real values (from the receptive field output units illustrated in Fig. 2) to 11 vowel vectors with discrete (1 or 0) values was trained. This net maps the coarse coded values into a local coding. When measuring the performance, we fed the outputs of the three layer network trained in experiment one into the two layer network as inputs, and let the two layer network determine whether an output is a 'hit' or a 'miss'. In order to do so, the number of input units in the two layer network has to be the same with the number of output units in the three layer network; the number of output units is 11, each representing one of the 11 vowels.

By using a secondary network to read out the performance of the three layer network, we found that the number of 'hits' is, for some networks, increased, and others decreased. Most importantly the two layer network seemed to be able to take advantage of the potential of a network whose performance was mediocre in terms of experiment one, and read out up to 8 more 'hits' from it than the nearest neighbour method. It thus outperformed all the networks trained in experiment one. Table 2 summarizes the best result obtained with the aid of the two layer network.

Table 2 Performance measured using the readout network.

	Experiment 2 (Readout net)	Experiment 1 (Euclidean distance measure)
Mixed	79.9%	74.0%
Female	68.8%	63.6%
Male	79.2%	72.7%

Notes: The best performance was again achieved using $N=2$, and 16 coding units. However this time, the best male system used 15 hidden units.

3.3 Experiment three

It is a traditional approach to study a speech recognition problem by running experiments with mixed speech data, female speech data, and male speech data separately, and then testing the recognition device on mixed, female and male data correspondingly. In the McCulloch study, networks trained on mixed data were tested on mixed data, female on female data, and male on male data. Though the power spectrum of male and female speech data look quite different, there is undoubtedly a great deal of similarity between the male and female pronounciation of a given vowel. Thus, we hope that by studying how much learning can be transferred between training on female and male data, we might find a way to improve network performance on female and male data.

We fed mixed, female and male speech data to the trained networks across groups, e.g. fed female data into a network trained on mixed data or male data. First of all, networks trained on data from one sex recognized a considerable amount of input data from the opposite sex (compared with networks with random weights) although they did not recognize as much as those trained on data from the same sex (Table 3). Secondly, the networks trained on mixed data performed better on male or female data than those trained on single sex data (Table 4) (comparison made among the best networks trained on mixed, female and male data). The first result showed that a considerable amount of learning was transferred between learning on male and female data. The second result, furthermore, showed that training with extra data from the male speakers improved a network performance on female data, and vice versa although the improvement on male data is very small. Table 5 is a qualitative summary on the interaction among different learning or training procedures. Table 6 gives the final performance in comparison with McCulloch's results.

Table 3 Transferred learning.

Net trained on	Net tested on	
	Female data	Male data
Female	—	53.9%
Male	52.7%	—

Notes: 20 hidden units and 16 coding units, with receptive field size $N=2$, were used.

Table 4 Improved performance as a result of transferred learning

Training data	Performance on Female data	
Mixed:	79.2%	(1)
Female:	68.8%	(2)
Training data	Performance on Male data	
Mixed:	80.5%	(3)
Male:	79.2%	(4)

Notes: These best results were produced using
  (1) 20 hidden units, 16 coding units, $N=2$
  (2) 20 hidden units, 9 coding units, $N=2$
  (3) 20 hidden units, 16 coding units, $N=2$
  (4) 16 hidden units, 16 coding units, $N=2$

Table 5 Summary performance using different training procedures.

Training Data	Test Data		
	Mixed	Female	Male
Mixed	same	improved	improved
Female	worsened	same	worsened
Male	worsened	worsened	same

Table 6 Final best performance comparison.

	Best Performance	McCulloch's
Mixed	79.9%	64.5%
Female	79.2%	57%
Male	80.5%	58.5%

Notes: The best performance was achieved using 20 hidden units, and 16 coding units, with $N=2$.

4. DISCUSSION AND CONCLUSIONS

4.1 The appropriateness of using the vowel quadrilateral as output

Although improved performance was achieved by using a coarse coded vowel quadrilateral, we were still unable to bring it up to the level of performance of the simple MLP classifier with local representation (we also trained networks with local representation for the purpose of comparison, see Table 7). The explanation might lie in the use of the vowel quadrilateral as output.

Table 7 Results using local representation vs distributed representation based on vowel quadrilateral.

	Performance			No of Hidden Units		
	Mixed	Female	Male	Mixed	Female	Male
Our local representation	85%	87%	83.1%	13	13	13
McCulloch's local representation	80.5%	77%	81%	50	50	50
Our distributed representation based on vowel quadrilateral	75.3%	66%	75.3%	20	20	11

Though as McCulloch and Ainsworth pointed out that there is a correlation between the vowel positions on the vowel quadrilateral and the positions of the tongue during speech production, and that the tongue position is a relatively speaker independent feature, it remains controversial whether the vowel quadrilateral should be used as a general classifier of vowels [5]. For an individual speaker, different vowels are well separated on the vowel quadrilateral. However, when we increase the number of speakers, when we introduce speakers from different sex, age and geographic groups, considerable overlap among different vowels was observed [6]. In this case, according to the vowel quadrilateral, different vowels from different age or sex groups might be classified as the same; while the same vowels from different age or sex group might be classified as different. With our speech data, the sample size is still quite small (15 male and 15 female speakers), and all the speakers speak the same dialect. Therefore, even with the positions of vowels in the vowel quadrilateral as output, we still obtained quite good results. However, the weakness of using the vowel quadrilateral in classification might well explain why a network with local representation as its output gave a slightly better performance.

Nonetheless, a very significant improvement was achieved by using a better coding for the vowel quadrilateral. Since the aim of the work was to demonstrate the effectiveness of appropriate coding, we consider the project to have been worthwhile.

4.2 Discussion on experiment one

The encoded vowel quadrilateral representation does improve performance in comparison with a network using only two real numbers. The difference cannot be considered as simply a result of a greater number of weights used in the network since our best network was obtained using 16 encoding units and a receptive field of $N=2$, rather than using 28 units and larger sizes of receptive field. Clearly, using a greater number of weights does not necessarily lead to a better performance.

It is interesting to note the effect that a slight error in programming the coding units had: the centres of these units were offset from the correct values of μ_x and μ_y, and this resulted in a slight improvement in performance. We believe that this occurred because the desired vowels were now at locations where the receptive fields of the coding units had non-zero gradient, thus making them more sensitive to small differences near desired outputs. Certainly, it suggests that there are subtleties in coding location in a 2-dimensional space.

4.3 Discussion on experiment two

The justification for using a readout net to determine the interpretation of the output layer is that the Euclidean distance used in experiment 1 is inappropriatcly giving cqual wcight to all the units. By training the readout net, we provide a data-driven classifier: alternatively, we could have attempted to derive mathematically a more appropriate distance function. Since we could be fairly sure that the coded data space can be mapped to the vowel outputs by a straightforward delta rule net, the readout net was the simpler option. The results show the benefits of the technique.

Another way of looking at this is to consider that we have decided on an internal representation for the network to use, and then trained up a 4 layer net in two parts: 3 layer and 2 layer networks. Since the nets which give best performance in experiments 1 and 2 differ, we suspect that even better performance would be achieved if we directly used the readout net to generate errors during back propagated training of the 3 layer network. The way to do this is to first train the 2 layer network which is later incorporated into the 4 layer network, and then to train the 4 layer network whilst freezing the weights of the readout net itself. Unfortunately, the simulation tools to hand do not permit this option. We believe that this inconsistent form of training was also responsible for the readout net sometimes resulting in poorer performance.

4.4 Discussion on experiment three

It is not surprising that when we fed female or male data into a network trained on mixed data, the performance could be improved because the extra examples contained in the mixed data from the other sex group provided a certain amount of transferable learning. The networks might have received more information on features of the vowels and have been prevented from learning those features that are sex specific.

However, we cannot generalize that for any three networks trained on mixed, female and male data, the one trained on mixed data will perform better on female or male data than the networks trained on female or male data only. With the back propagation learning algorithm, the choice of learning rate, momentum, the timing of the change of those parameters, and the input data themselves can be very crucial to the position of the network in the error space. With a certain combination of the above parameters, the network might get trapped in a local minimum and never learn very well; while with a slightly different combination, the network might end up being in a much better position with much lower error rate. It might still be a useful heuristic that if you have tried to train networks on mixed data and then pick the best one, this one is very likely to perform better or at least as well as the networks trained only on female or male data using the same method. If this heuristic could be confirmed by further research using larger data sets and run on more independent networks, the consequence would be that one does not need to train networks using mixed, female and male data separately, but simply find the best network by training on mixed data.

5. CONCLUSION

The primary conclusion from experiments 1 and 2 is that careful coding of the vowel quadrilateral and the introduction of a data-driven output measuring mechanism can lead to very significant improvements in performance. From experiment 3, we conclude that there is enough similarity (though in some undefined sense) between male and female steady-state vowels to make transference of learning possible. Thus, training networks on mixed data is very likely to give us better performance then training on single sex data.

Further work really needs a larger database. With the limited database it will be difficult to tell significant improvements from those due purely to particularities of the data itself. Given the availability of more data (and this could be achieved by direct collaboration with the laboratories involved in its production: namely RSRE and Cambridge), we should certainly like to investigate the extension to experiment 2, i.e., using a readout network to measure the performance during both training and testing.

Hand selecting vowels from sampled data, and considering that the vowel sound is well represented by one power-spectrum vector can be criticised both on the grounds of artificiality, and of throwing away possibly useful contextual information. It would be interesting to try out the system on continuous speech data. One would hope that the network would pick out the steady-state vowels from the data directly. It would also be interesting to compare, again using continuous speech, the performance of the 3 layer network using encoded quadrilateral representation with that using local representation and that using a readout network.

Since the network is feedforward, and the units have no history-preserving state, it is entirely insensitive to context. Extensions of backprop which are sensitive to context (and can therefore process time-varying input) do exist (e.g. [8], [7]). The question of what is an appropriate representation arises again, this time with even wider choices. As here, one can use a static localised, or static distributed representation; however, one can also use a dynamic representation, perhaps representing the movement of the tongue in articulation. Again, this could be represented in a localised or a distributed way. Certainly, whatever the representation used, one needs to use the nature of the variation in the input directly in the coding and this must have a direct influence on the way the net works. This is an area of current research at the Centre for Cognitive and Computational Neuroscience (CCCN) in Stirling.

So far as generating input representations is concerned (as opposed to specifying them in backprop and backprop type nets) research at Stirling is looking at extensions to Kohonen's self-organising nets ([9]). We are interested in systems in which different types of synapse have a range of operating speeds.

ACKNOWLEDGEMENTS

BT funded Ms Can Tang on this project. The equipment used was funded by the UK SERC, and by the Department of Computing Science, Stirling University. The original data was from the Oxford Alvey Vowel Database, provided by the Phonetics Department at Oxford University, and it was processed by the Speech Research Unit at RSRE, Malvern. The data used in the experiments was provided by Neil McCulloch, seconded to the Research Initiative in Pattern Recognition, also at RSRE. Many thanks are due to

Peter Hancock at the CCCN, Stirling University; Neil McCulloch at the Research Initiative in Pattern Recognition, RSRE; Ian Watson at Phonetics Laboratory, Oxford University; Richard Rowher at the Centre for Speech Technology Research, Edinburgh University. Special thanks for the technical support from Sam Nelson and Graham Cochrane at the Department of Computing Science, Stirling University.

REFERENCES

1. McCulloch N and Ainsworth W A: 'Speaker Independent Vowel Recognition Using a Multi-Layer Perceptron', Technical report, Research Initiative in Pattern Recognition, RSRE (1988).

2. Flanagan J L: 'Speech Analysis, Synthesis and Perception', 2nd edition Springer-Verlag, Berlin (1972).

3. Harrison T D: 'A Connectionist Framework for Continuous Speech Recognition dissertation', Sidney Sussex College, Cambridge University (1988).

4. Hancock P J: 'Data Representation in Neural Nets: an Empirical Study', Proceedings of the Connectionist Summer School at Carnegie Mellan University (1988).

5. Watson I: Personal Communication, Oxford University (1989).

6. Peterson G E and Barney H L: 'Control Methods Used in a Study of the Vowels Journal of the Acoustical Society of America, 24, 175—184 (1952).

7. Pearlmutter P: 'Learning State-space Trajectories in Recurrent Nets Neural Computing', 1, 2, (Summer 1989).

8. Waibel A: 'Modular Construction of Time-Delay Neural Networks for Speech Recognition Neural Computing', 1, 1, (Spring 1989).

9. Kohonen T: 'Self-Organization and Associative Memory', Springer-Verlag, Berlin (1984).

9

DISSECTION OF PERCEPTRON STRUCTURES IN SPEECH AND SPEAKER RECOGNITION

J S Mason and E C J Andrews
Department of Electrical and Electronic Engineering,
University College, Swansea

1. INTRODUCTION

Classification decisions in speech and speaker recognition systems are based upon the processing of sets of feature vectors that are derived from the original speech signal, each vector spanning typically 20 or 30 ms. The decision on any given utterance is based upon the statistical distribution of the features of that utterance, together with any information on the ordering, or time sequence, of the features.

The MLP may be configured in a variety of structures but in its basic form it has no memory. The output vector is calculated using only the information contained in the current input vector and it is necessary to design special structures if the time dependency of events is deemed important to the decision process.

Presenting speech features to the network serially, one vector at a time, leads to the MLP structure shown in Fig. 1(a). With this structure the output vectors form a sequence corresponding to the input and this can be averaged across a word or phrase to make the final decision. Since each vector is calculated from a single frame of speech with no knowledge of previous frames, no time sequence information is available and the final decision is based solely on the distribution of the features.

INTRODUCTION

Perhaps the best known structure with some internal memory or storage within the MLP is the time delay neural network, or TDNN, developed by Waibel et al [1]. This structure, while retaining the frame-by-frame input of the serial network, aims to improve performance by providing a representation of the context of each frame of speech as well as an insensitivity to the absolute temporal position of the input features.

In considering the problem of isolated word recognition, we have used an alternative system that has no internal memory to address the problem of short term context: an entire word is presented to the network as a single parallel input as suggested by Woodland and Millar [2], see Fig. 1(b). This obviates the need for internal storage, and the total output is calculated in a single pass of calculations through the network. As the whole word is available to the net it may make use of any time sequence information through examination of the ordering of the feature vectors, but does not possess memory as such. This makes training a much simpler task.

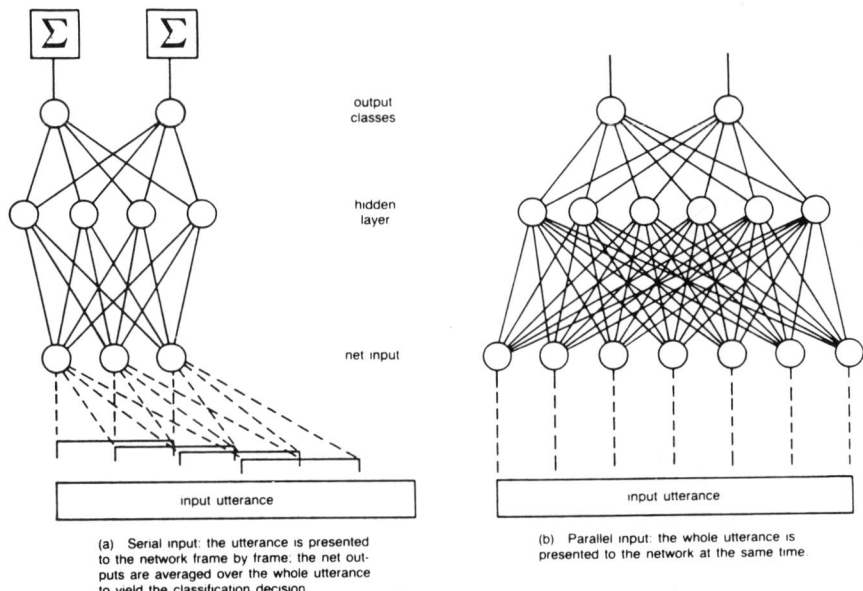

(a) Serial input: the utterance is presented to the network frame by frame; the net outputs are averaged over the whole utterance to yield the classification decision.

(b) Parallel input: the whole utterance is presented to the network at the same time.

Fig. 1 Two possible MLP structures for recognising a speech utterance.

This chapter compares the serial and parallel MLP structures to investigate the importance of the time sequence information. To illustrate its obvious importance consider the problem of recognising isolated words from the English alphabet, 'a', 'b',..., 'z', and in particular the items 'd' and 'z'. The English pronunciation of the word 'z' [zed] contains an initial [z] sound that is unique within the vocabulary, and a trailing [d] sound that is also present at the beginning of the letter 'd'. If only short term information is available, as with serially presented feature vectors, then only the first half of the word 'z' is useful for its recognition, the [d] sound being present in both 'd' and 'z' utterances. If knowledge of the time sequencing of the feature set is available to the net then this confusability is reduced since a [d] sound is present only at the start of 'd' and at the end of 'z'.

In a larger vocabulary speech recogniser it can be advantageous to divide the vocabulary into subsets containing easily confused items and then apply a more specialised, small vocabulary discriminator to the final classification [1,3]. Within the English alphabet the E-set is an obvious candidate. Knowledge of the time sequence of these utterances gives any classifier the potential to discard the trailing [e] and make decisions based solely on the useful initial transient.

We examine the ability of an MLP to make use of this important time series information without any external supervision[1]. The examination here focuses on the relative weighting associated with each input feature coefficient as a function of time, demonstrating how the time series information is used in the E-set problem.

2. STRUCTURING OF THE SYSTEM

This section examines the configuration of an MLP classifier that is to perform **speech** or **speaker** recognition. The input to the MLP is some form of feature or feature sequence extracted from the raw speech signal. We use a perceptually based linear prediction, known as PLP [7], to derive our input features. These features are chosen because of their good performance with relatively low order, particularly for speech recognition [8].

Once the features have been calculated they must be presented to the MLP in a form that causes a minimum loss of information. For speech recognition in particular the time sequence of the features provides valuable information. In this context structures such as Waibel et al's TDNNs are particularly appropriate for continuous, connected speech recognition since they allow the speech to be presented frame-by-frame whilst retaining the local contextual information in an internal representation of previous frames. In the case of isolated words it is possible to use the strategy of concatenating all the feature vectors of one word and entering these into the MLP in parallel as one large input vector. We compare this strategy with the serial case to assess the importance of the time sequence information.

---

[1]It is possible for example to 'hand craft' classifiers for particular problems. For example in the E-set problem Bedworth et al [4] tie the final states of the HMM together to achieve the best results, whilst Zhang [5,6] adds a restriction on which speech frames may map to each state; these are two different techniques that acknowledge the overlap of the 'e' sound.

Finally we consider the likely characteristics of various sizes of network, varying from those with two few parameters to accurately model the speech, to those with redundant parameters.

2.1 Perceptually based LP, PLP

Many researchers have demonstrated the benefits of incorporating knowledge of some physiological effects in the speech feature extraction process. One such approach is Hermansky's perceptually based linear prediction, PLP [7]. We have used PLP cepstral features in preference to the standard LP cepstra due to the lower feature order needed to give equivalent recognition performance.

PLP is an all pole spectral representation of the speech incorporating the effects of:

- critical bands,
- masking,
- variation in the equal loudness level with frequency, and
- intensity law.

These are represented by the following transformations:

- $\omega = B(f)$,
- $P_2(\omega) = \int_0^\pi C_k(\omega).P_1(\omega).d\omega$,
- $P_3(\omega) = E(\omega_k).P_2(\omega)$ and
- $Q_k(\omega) = P_3^{1/r}$.

The overall mapping may be written as

$$Q_k = (E(\omega_k) \int_0^\pi C_k(\omega).P(\omega).d\omega)^{1/r}$$

where $B(f)$ is a critical band warping function, $P(\omega)$ is the power spectrum of the speech, $C_k(\omega)$ is a set of critical band weighting functions, $E(\omega_k)$ is an equal loudness (pre-emphasis) curve, and $1/r$ is the intensity loudness conversion.

Hermansky [9] and Gu [10] have shown that it is the lower order coefficients, such as PLP-5, that contain the information most useful for speaker independent speech recognition, whereas for a speaker-dependent system orders such as PLP-8 or higher are better. This implies that it is the higher order coefficients that contain speaker specific information and that low order PLP would perform relatively poorly for speaker recognition; this hypothesis is confirmed by Xu et al in their speaker identification experiments [8].

2.2 Serial and parallel input structures

There are two distinct ways in which the feature vectors from a word may be presented to the network. The manner of their presentation has a major influence on the type of information that is available for the recognition decision.

The first format we consider is that of **serial** input, shown in Fig. 1(a). Each feature vector is presented to the network in isolation and the output vectors are averaged to yield a single decision vector; the highest average activation level signifies the network's decision. As the input to this structure is only a single feature vector, a network with sufficient hidden nodes for a typical problem assumes a diamond shape.

Alternatively the feature vectors from a whole word may be presented to the network as a single concatenated or **parallel** input, the final decision vector being calculated in a single pass through the network rather than through the averaging process needed for serial systems. The large number of inputs required by this structure leads to a more triangular shaped network, Fig. 1(b).

The decision made by these structures is governed by the information available. Both structures have access to the statistical distribution of the speech vectors. However, the time sequence information is available only in the parallel system. Since time sequence information is likely to be very important in speech recognition (more than in **speaker** recognition), then an MLP that uses the serial input format would be expected to perform poorly except on the simplest of problems.

2.3 Size of the MLP

An MLP can theoretically perform any arbitrary mapping from its inputs to outputs, as long as sufficient free parameters are available. The free parameters are available as a series of weights connecting the inputs to the outputs via some number of 'hidden' nodes (nodes that are not directly visible at the input or output of the network).

In the standard, fully interconnected MLP structure the number of weights is determined by the number of nodes in each layer. However, the number of nodes in the input and output layers are fixed by the form of the input and the classification task, respectively.

The number of output nodes usually equals the number of classes to be distinguished since an MLP classifier indicates its decision as the most active output. Also the number of inputs must match the number of feature coefficients that are to be presented to the network in a single pass, i.e. the feature order for a serial network or the product of the feature order and the number of vectors across the utterance for a parallel network. So both the input and output dimensions are defined by the classification problem and the form of input. Only the number of nodes in the other, hidden layers may be optimised for a specific problem. In our own experiments we have found no case of an MLP with two or more hidden layers achieving better performance than a single hidden layer network, hence we restrict our results to zero and 1 hidden layer structures.

It follows that the 'free' variable in the network structure is the number of nodes in the single hidden layer. This is quite an important parameter since too few nodes may prevent the net from forming a suitably complex mapping of the problem, whereas too many hidden nodes may encourage the overlearning of training data and consequently poor performance on unseen data. Fortunately, small variations around a net deemed to have sufficient hidden nodes appear to cause only small changes to the recognition performance.

3. SPEECH RECOGNITION EXPERIMENTS

This section examines the recognition performance of an MLP on three related speaker independent speech recognition tasks. First we consider the simple problem of 'd'/'z' discrimination to determine the importance of time sequence information. Next we examine a large alphabet recognition problem to examine the scalability of the chosen network structure. Finally we investigate a recogniser restricted to the E-set vocabulary; this structure might be used as a building block in a hierarchical system for larger vocabulary speech recognition.

3.1 Dependence in speech recognition

A system which is to perform a classification task must 'know' how to make its decisions. For speech or speaker recognition there is no simple rule describing each class. The NN approach to this problem is to 'teach' a system the characteristics of each class by the presentation of examples. The system is gradually adapted to improve its recognition performance. Eventually it may be able to classify the **training** utterances perfectly. However, it is not the performance of the system on its training data that is important, but rather its ability to classify previously unseen speech.

The composition of the data in the training group should always be representative of the intended user population. The different classes of system reflect the make-up of this group; each has some distinct properties and is applicable only in certain situations.

- A **speaker dependent** system is one where the training data is provided by its one eventual user. A **cross speaker** situation is a variant on this where there are two people, one training and one testing.

- Now consider a system which is trained to be used by several speakers. If all these speakers contribute to the training data the system is defined as **multi-speaker**.

- Finally there is the **speaker independent** system, trained by several speakers, but eventually used (or tested) by speakers who have not contributed to its training. If the training data is truly representative of the eventual user population then recognition performance can be expected to approach that of multi-speaker systems.

These different types of speech recognition system are shown in Table 1.

		Test speakers same as training speakers?	
		Yes	No
Number of training speakers	one	speaker dependent	cross speaker
	many	multi-speaker	speaker independent

Table 1 Operation modes of speech recognition systems

In this chapter our experiments are performed using a number of different speakers for training and testing and we have concentrated on the speaker independent recognition performance of the system.

3.2 A simple problem: 'd'/'z' discrimination

To demonstrate the importance of time sequence information in a speech recognition system we consider the very simple problem of discriminating between the utterances 'd' and 'z'. These two utterances are phonetically distinct; the trailing [ee] sound in [dee] and the initial [z] in [zed] are unique to their respective utterances and should enable a simple statistical model of feature frequency to perform accurate discrimination. The initial transient [d] in 'd' is easily confusable with the trailing part of a 'z' utterance, but is more useful if its temporal position is known, as is the case in a parallel input MLP.

The choice of the extremely low order PLP-3 in this case is to ensure the presence of some errors and allow a comparison of the performance of the serial and parallel net structures. If for example the order is increased to PLP-8 both serial and parallel systems achieve a 100% recognition accuracy. These experiments use 2 versions of each utterance from 50 speakers for training; testing is performed using the utterances from 50 different speakers.

Table 2 shows the recognition performance of both a single layer perceptron (i.e. no hidden layers) and an MLP with one hidden layer trained to perform this discrimination task, using a serial or parallel input structure as described in Section 2.2.

Recognition error	serial	parallel
Single layer perceptron	8%	3%
MLP with 1 hidden layer	4%	2%

Table 2   Recognition errors made by a 'd'/'z' discriminator

Clearly the extra time sequence information available in a parallel input structure is useful even in a system as a simple as a 'd'/'z' discriminator. The improvement is less significant for the MLP than the single layer perceptron due to the simplicity of the problem and the greater relative increase in the number of weights in the serial structure (Table 3), allowing a far more complex mapping than that possible in the single layer structure.

Number of weights	serial	parallel
Single layer perceptron	8	121
MLP with 1 hidden layer	242	2482

Table 3   Number of weights in the 'd'/'z' discriminator

3.2.1   Net dissection

To examine the way in which the time information is used by the network we consider the workings of a single layer system. The output corresponding to class u has an activation level given by

$$\sum_{p=1}^{P} \sum_{n=1}^{N} C_{pn} \omega_{upn} + \theta_{u}$$

where P is the order of feature, N is the number of frames in the utterance, C is the feature series corresponding to the utterance, ω is the corresponding weight series and θ is the threshold value.

In a simple, single output network this activation level represents the likelihood that the test utterance is within that class. When there are two or more outputs, each represents a separate class and the classification decision is based on the most active output. Thus if we examine, for example, the difference between the two highest activations, we may observe the relative importance of each time frame and each feature component to the classification decision. We consider for illustrative purposes the simple case of a 'd'/'z' recogniser and a single layer network. There are only two outputs to consider, one for 'd' and one for 'z'. The difference between these outputs may be written as

$$D_{dz} = \sum_{p=1}^{P} \sum_{n=1}^{N} C_{pn}(\omega_{dpn} - \omega_{zpn}) + (\theta_d - \theta_z).$$

To evaluate the importance of each coefficient and temporal position, we conceptually re-order the weights and coefficients into three time sequences, the first containing the first coefficient from each of the P vectors, the second containing the second from each of the P vectors, etc. Using a 'd' utterance for the test input gives the coefficient sequences C_1, C_2 and C_3 shown in Fig. 2(a). Both the C_1 and C_2 profiles are predominantly positive whereas the C_3 profile is generally negative.

Next we examine the corresponding weight series, ω_{d1}, ω_{d2} and ω_{d3}, shown in 2(b). These profiles are much more irregular than the coefficient series, with several sign changes for both the 1st and 3rd coefficients.

However, it is not the sign of the feature coefficients or their weights in isolation that are important, but rather their **product**, shown in Fig. 2(c). Note that in these and subsequent graphs the contribution of the threshold, θ, has been divided equally between all coefficients to ensure that the decision boundary coincides with a zero net output, i.e. we calculate the activation level as

$$\sum_{n=1}^{N} \left(\sum_{p=1}^{P} C_{pn}\omega_{upn} + \frac{\theta_u}{N} \right)$$

and hence

$$D_{dz} = \sum_{n=1}^{N} \left(\sum_{p=1}^{P} C_{pn}(\omega_{dpn} - \omega_{zpn}) + \frac{(\theta_d - \theta_z)}{N} \right)$$

We are examining the product of coefficients from a 'd' utterance with 'd' weights so a high output leads to the correct decision. Figure 2(c) shows that both the 1st and 2nd coefficients give the desired positive values although the C_1 product has some erroneous values just after the midpoint of the utterance. The C_3 product totals -3.48, contributing towards a decision error. Interestingly the part of the utterance making a correct positive contribution to the decision in the C_3 profile coincides with that causing errors in the C_1 profile.

SPEECH RECOGNITION EXPERIMENTS 169

To make the final decision the **highest** output is used, so we must consider the products and differences along the time course. Figure 2(d) shows the cross-product of the same 'd' utterance with the weights corresponding to the 'z' output:

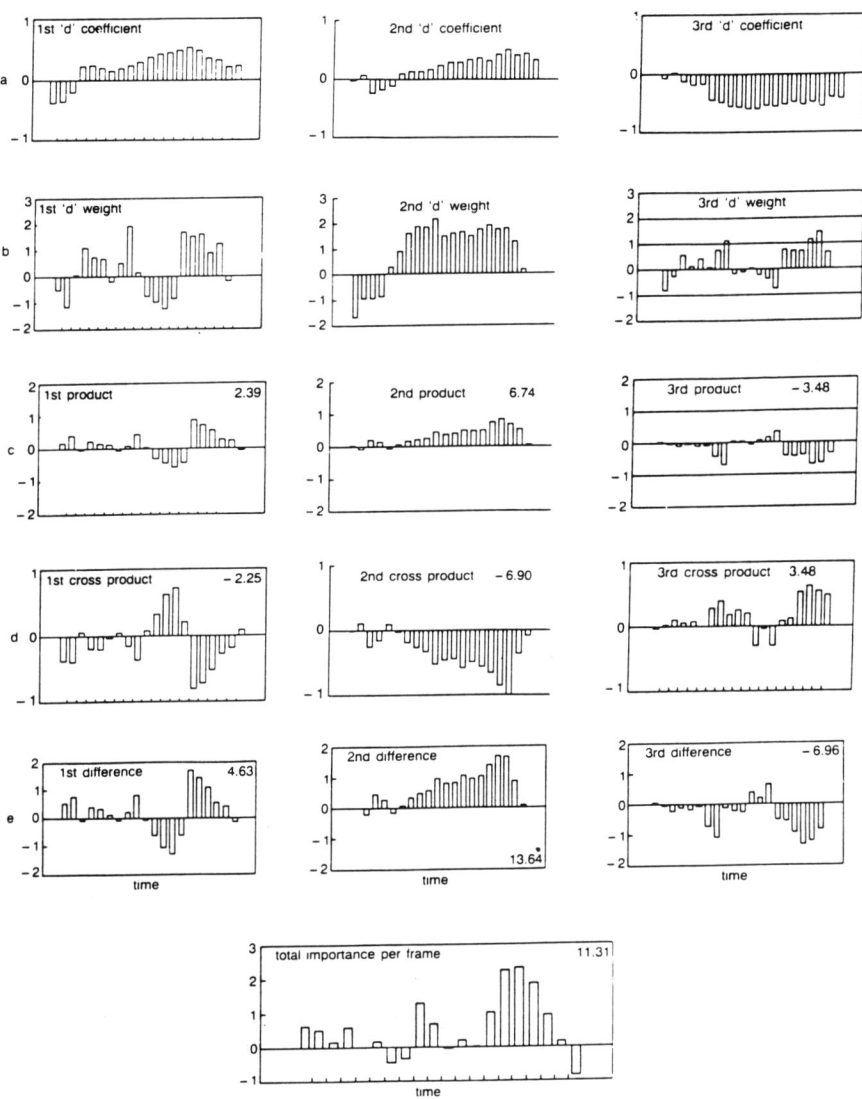

Fig. 2 Relative importance of each frame to the decision for the 'd'/'z' problem using a single layer perceptron with the whole word as input.

$$C_i \omega_{zi} + \frac{\theta_z}{N}, \quad \text{for } i = 1 \text{ to } N.$$

Figure 2(e) shows the difference between this and the straight product graphs,

$$(C_i \omega_{di} - C_i \omega_{zi}) + \frac{(\theta_d - \theta_z)}{N}, \quad \text{for } i = 1 \text{ to } N.$$

Clearly C_2 makes the dominant contribution to the decision with a total of 13.64, with very few negative frames. C_1 also aids the decision (4.63) despite an erroneous contribution corresponding to the negative weights in Fig. 2(b), whereas the C_3 difference total is -6.96, and would give a decision error if considered in isolation.

Finally we sum the differences for each utterance across all three coefficients to find the total importance per time frame. This shows that it is the last third of the utterance, the [e] sound, that most strongly identifies this as a 'd'; overall only 2 frames near the middle and one frame at the end make negative contributions to the decision.

3.3 Alphabet recognition

We now consider the much more difficult task of speaker independent alphabet recognition. During training, 26 utterances from each of 50 speakers form the training data; PLP-8 features from a complete word form the parallel input to the network.

Figure 3 shows learning curves for different net structures. At regular intervals during training the status of the network is recorded and performance measured in a speaker independent manner, using the 26 vocabulary items spoken by 50 persons not in the training set. The effect of varying the number of hidden nodes and hence the number of weights on recognition performance is shown in these profiles. The number of hidden nodes is varied from 10 to 100, leading to systems containing between 2000 and 19 000 weights. Note that the x-axis is measured in training iterations, rather than in terms of computation; the computation time required per iteration is approximately proportional to the number of hidden nodes.

As the complexity of the system and the number of nodes are increased from 10 to 40 the minimum recognition error achieved drops from 35% to 20%. The 40, 60 and 100 hidden node systems all follow the same initial learning trajectory, but the 40 and 60 hidden node systems achieve a minimum error rate of 20%, while the larger 100 node system reaches a minimum error of 15%. Only the 40 hidden node system shows the characteristic of overtraining: the error rate reaches a minimum of approximately 20% and then increases back to 25%. In contrast, the 60 hidden node profile settles at its minimum error rate of 20% with no further improvement or degradation.

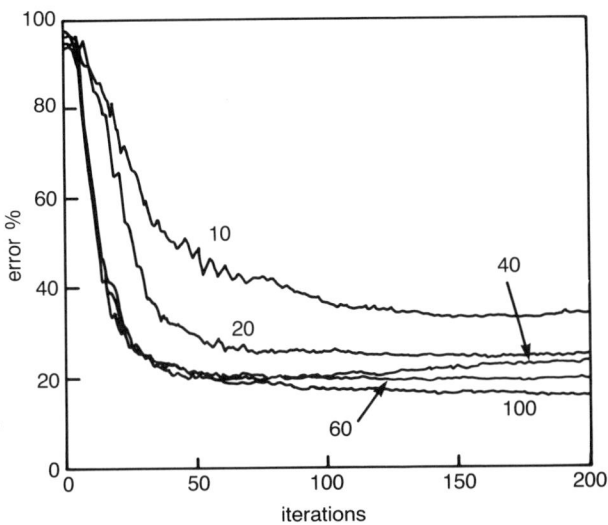

Fig. 3 Speaker independent recognition of the alphabet using a parallel input MLP with a varying number of hidden nodes.

We now examine the distribution of the recognition errors made by the alphabet classifier. Table 4 shows the classification decisions made for each utterance and allows an inspection of the confusion between different letters. The vertical axis shows the test input utterance and the horizontal axis shows the item recognised. If every utterance were correctly recognised the table would be empty except for a leading diagonal of 50s. Clearly the errors are not evenly distributed across vocabulary items. Instead, as expected, they tend to be concentrated within subsets containing easily confused items, such as the E-set or 'm' and 'n'; 24 errors from 100 tests are associated with 'm' and 'n'. The items with the least errors are 'f', 'q' and 'y' (just 2 errors each) whereas 'd' and 'v' have the most errors (17 each).

This leads to the concept of dividing a large vocabulary speech recognition problem into several distinctive subsets, followed by more accurate classification by a subsystem specialised on the appropriate subset. We now consider a small, E-set network suitable for use in the final recognition stage of an alphabet recognition system.

	Decision																									
	b	c	d	e	g	p	t	v	a	f	h	i	j	k	l	m	n	o	q	r	s	u	w	x	y	z
b	39	3	3		1				4																	
c		43				1	3						2	1												
d	6		33	4		3	2								1					1						
e	1		4	43																					2	
g	1	1		1	40	2								4		1										
p				1		35	5	4	2							2										
t		2				1	3	39	1					2					1					1		
v	4	2	5	1		2	1	33	1											1						
a				1	1			2		40		4				2										
f									48						1		1									
h						1					47							1		1						
i									4		45														1	
j		1		4	1							41	2				1									
k						1	1	1	1				3	42				1								
l												1			46	2	1									
m																41	8	1								
n												1				13	35									1
o						1										2		44	1				1	1		
q																	1		48		1					
r									1								1		1	17						
s								8			1	1		1							38			1		
u		1		1																		48				
w						1																	47	1	1	
x							2	2												2				44		
y										1							1								48	
z	1	1				1						1							1	1				1	12	

Table 4 Alphabet recognition confusion matrix (total error 15.7%).

3.4 Analysis of an E-set recogniser

Clearly there is a high degree of similarity between the utterances of the E-set. In this section we examine an MLP, and show that it makes use of the important discriminating information at the start of the utterance.

To simplify the analysis of the network's operation we restrict our input feature to PLP-5 and follow the same process as that described in Section 3.2.1. This problem has 8 possible outputs but we shall consider only two, namely those associated with the labels 'e' and 'g': the 'e' output corresponds to a correct decision and the 'g' to the next highest for the particular test utterance used. The feature vectors, feature/weight products and difference graphs for the C_2, C_5 and C_5 profiles are shown in Fig. 4; the C_1 and C_4 profiles have been omitted since their contribution to the decision is minimal in this case.

Only small changes in the values of the 3rd coefficient are evident throughout the whole utterance; all lie in the range -0.25 to -0.5. The 2nd and 5th coefficients have a clear transitional stage at the start and end of

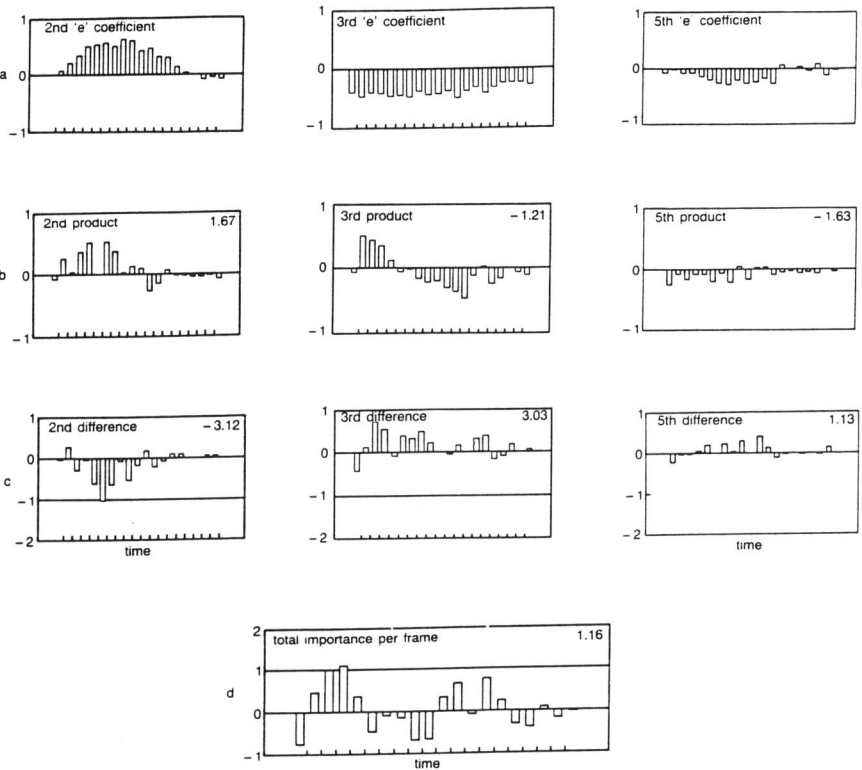

Fig. 4   Net dissection profiles from an E-set discrimination problem.

their time courses, with C_5 exhibiting a sharp negative to positive transition at the 13th frame.

An examination of the difference profiles (Fig. 4(c)) shows that the 2nd and 3rd coefficients almost cancel each other with the contribution from the 5th coefficient effectively making the decision. The contribution of the 2nd coefficient is smaller at the end of the word and totals -3.12; in contrast the 3rd and 5th coefficients have positive components throughout giving 3.03 and 1.13 to the total activation level.

The sum of all five difference profiles yields the total importance for each frame along the time course of the utterance, shown in Fig. 4(d). The first quarter of the word provides the dominating positive contribution with the middle and end of the word containing roughly equal positive and negative components.

Despite the low values of the feature coefficients at the start of the word the network 'notices' their importance and weights them correspondingly highly; this is evident by the high contribution of these early frames, seen in Fig. 4(d).

4. TIME SEQUENCE IMPORTANCE IN SPEECH AND SPEAKER RECOGNITION

We have already examined the importance of time sequence information in **speech** recognition and found it to be useful even in a problem as simple as 'd'/'z' recognition. For more realistic problems such as alphabet recognition this information is likely to be essential.

In contrast, time sequence information is likely to be far less important for speaker recognition since a model of the physical characteristics of the speaker is desired and short term variations are less important.

First we examine a system required to recognise each of eight different speakers using a single utterance of a letter from the alphabet; to ensure that the features contain a reasonable amount of speaker specific information a higher order analysis is used, namely PLP-14.

Again we use the whole-word parallel structure to construct an MLP that can make use of the time sequence information, and the serial input for a system that has access only to the feature distribution. These are similar structures to those used in the speaker recognition experiments.

The serial and parallel speaker recognition performance in a multi-text mode, (i.e. the same vocabulary is used for training and testing) is shown in Table 5.

	serial	parallel
training	8%	0%
testing	12%	23%

Table 5 Recognition errors of parallel and serial speaker recognition systems. Performance is measured on training data and on unseen, testing data.

The parallel system quickly reaches a state where there are no errors when tested with the **training** utterances. However, this is relatively unimportant; the more relevant error rate is that for unseen test data, 23%. The serial network does much better on this set with an error rate of 12%. The parallel system is exhibiting a characteristic that can be compared with overtraining, namely that the training data has been modelled accurately at the expense of a more general representation, leading to poor generalisation of the network to unseen data.

Clearly better performance is achieved when time sequence information is discarded in this case. However, it is possible that the training data is insufficient; we use only two versions of each utterance by each speaker. In the serial system the training of each of the weights in the first layer incorporates information from every frame of data, whereas in the parallel system the information is restricted to that from a single input frame; this allows the incorporation of twenty times the information in each weight modification and may force the construction of a more useful, generalised model.

To increase the information available for training we increase the number of speakers from 8 to 26. This trebles the information available for the training of each weight but retains the 20:1 input data/weight ratio between serial and parallel systems; the results are as shown in Table 6.

	serial	parallel
training	29%	2%
testing	30%	32%

Table 6 Recognition errors of parallel and serial speaker recognition systems for a 26 speaker problem.

Again the parallel system reaches a state of very low error on the training data but still has a high error rate of 32% on the test data. In contrast for the serial system the test and training recognition performances are very similar, with an error rate of around 30%.

So in this larger problem similar **speaker** recognition performance is achieved by both the serial and parallel systems and clearly the presence of time sequence information as provided by the parallel structure is of little use in this case.

This finding suggests that such speaker identification decisions are, to a large degree, dependent on longer term averages rather than temporal structure, i.e. decisions are based on feature averages reflecting discriminating physical characteristics.

The poor generalised performance of the parallel system is characterised by its rapid learning of the training data; the model formed includes utterance specific detail not useful for recognition of the **speaker**.

REFERENCES

1. Waibel A, Sawai H, and Shikano K: 'Consonant recognition by modular construction of large phonemic time-delay neural networks', ICASSP-89, 1:112—115, (1989).

2. Woodland P and Millar W: 'Fixed dimension classifiers for speech recognition', In C Wheddon and R Linggard, eds, Speech and Language Processing. Chapman and Hall, (1990).

3. Cole R A, Stern R M, Phillips M S, Brill S M, Pilant A P and Specker P: 'Feature based speaker-independent recognition of isolated English letters', ICASSP-83, 731—733, (1983).

4. Bedworth M, Bottou L, Bridle J et al: 'Comparison of neural and conventional classifiers on a speech recognition problem', Proc First IEE Inter Conf on ANNs, 86—89, London (1989).

5. Zhang X: 'A semi-hidden Markov model and its application to speech recognition', PhD Thesis, University College of Swansea, (1987).

6. Zhang X and Mason J S: 'Improved training using semi-hidden Markov models in speech recognition', ICASSP-89, 1:306—309, (May 1989).

7. Hermansky H, Hanson B A and Wakita H: 'Perceptually based linear predictive analysis of speech', ICASSP-85, 509—512, (1985).

8. Xu L, Oglesby J and Mason J S: 'The optimization of perceptually-based features for speaker identification', ICASSP-89, 1:520—523, (May 1989).

9. Hermansky H: 'An efficient speaker-independent automatic speech recognition by simulation of some properties of human auditory perception', ICASSP-87, 1159—1162, (1987).

10. Gu Y and Mason J S: 'A speaker-correlation weighted RPS distance measure for speech recognition', IEEE Symposium on Information Theory, Kobe, Japan (June 1988).

10

SEGMENTAL SUB-WORD UNIT CLASSIFICATION USING A MULTILAYER PERCEPTRON

S G Smyth
BT Laboratories

1. INTRODUCTION

Most ANN techniques do not address the problem of the varying duration of speech utterances, and of the timing of speech events within utterances. This is because the networks employed generally require fixed dimensional input. An example of fixed dimensional input is given in [1], where the recognition of whole words is achieved by capturing the word and linearly adjusting its duration to fit the ANN's input window, as illustrated in Fig. 1.

Although recognition accuracy may be quite good, the method is unsatisfactory for several reasons: the speech has to be endpointed; varying duration is treated simplistically as a linear time normalisation; but, more importantly, the method cannot be extended to connected speech. It is expected that the flexibility of the system would be improved if ANN processing were retained whilst treating the duration variability problem in a more sophisticated manner. This chapter describes such an approach.

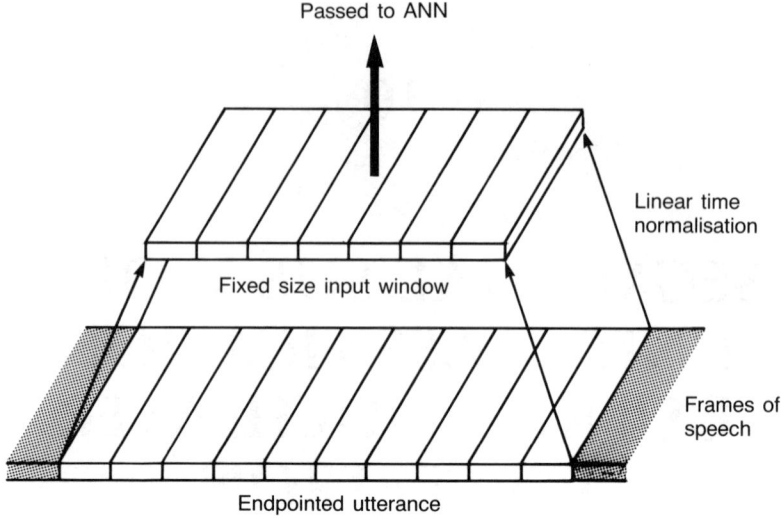

Fig. 1 Whole word recognition using an ANN.

The system discussed here uses the ANN in the form of an MLP to map fixed-size short fragments of speech data (a few frames, up to at most 90 ms) on to symbols representing sub-word units. Sequences of these symbols are then integrated using dynamic programming (DP) alignment. This segmental MLP approach is analogous to HMM techniques [2], in that the MLP provides local probability scores and the DP alignment procedure is used to find an optimal symbol sequence.

This system has been applied to the task of speaker independent, isolated word recognition. The vocabulary used was the British English alphabet data set, as described in [1] and in the Introduction to Part 2 of this book.

After being trained to perform the frame classification task, the MLP generates a set of scores for each frame which indicates its 'closeness' to each sub-word unit. DP is used to evaluate the likelihoods of strings of frames as legal sequences of sub-word units. The word recognised is that with the most likely symbol sequence. This not only gives word recognition but also the best segmentation of the word into sub-word units. Thus, given the correct recognition of a word, the DP alignment can be used to provide a more accurate segmentation for the original training data, similar to the approach in [3]. The MLP may then be retrained using the new segmentation, and by iterating this process, the recognition accuracy can be improved.

The structure of this chapter is as follows. The sub-word units are described in section 2. Section 3 explains the mapping performed by the MLP and the DP alignment procedure. The process of resegmentation is explained in section 4, and experimental results are presented in section 5, followed by a discussion and suggestions for future work in sections 6 and 7.

2. SUB-WORD UNITS

Each endpointed utterance was divided into a number of sub-word units. ('Sub-word' in this context means units smaller than a whole word, but not the conventional, phonetically based sub-word units generally used in recognition.) The data was initially segmented by dividing each word into a number of equal time units. Later, a more reasonable segmentation was implemented by automatic resegmentation and labelling. Although it might have been preferable to use a phonetically defined labelling [3], a labelled database was not available. Thus the initial segmentation was done with no assumptions other than that each word consisted of a small number of sub-word units of equal duration.

The main experiments described below were performed on the basis of three sub-word units per word. This number was chosen after earlier experiments, carried out with more units and a variable number of units per word, confirmed that a three-units-per-word system represented an optimum for the alphabet vocabulary with the given size of database.

2.1 Distinct units

Initially, each word was assumed to consist of a sequence of three, unique sub-word units: that is, a sub-word unit appearing in one word did not appear in any other word. Since there were 26 words and three symbols per word, this resulted in 78 distinct sub-word units. Obviously, a significant number of these units sound very similar; for example, the final units in the E-set and A-set (see Chapter 7) or the initial units of 'M' and 'N'. However, these 'phonetic preconceptions' were not used in the initial segmentation, and any similarities were allowed to emerge via the procedures described below.

2.2 Clustering of units

An MLP, with 78 outputs, was trained to recognise individual sub-word units. The trained MLP was then used to classify the data, and its outputs used to construct a recognition confusion matrix. From this, the most confusable sub-word units were identified and amalgamated, or tied. Several iterations of this process reduced the symbol set from 78 to 45 units, resulting in a much smaller MLP with no loss of performance.

For example, consider the word 'B' consisting of symbols 3-4-5, and 'C' of 6-7-8. The confusion matrix showed that most of the symbol 8 occurrences were recognised as symbol 5. The symbol set could then be refined, such that 'B' was 3-4-5 and 'C' became 6-7-5. In fact, one of the confusions identified in this experiment included the last symbol of all of the words in the E-set. The resulting amalgamation permitted all eight final sub-word units in the E-set to be mapped on to a single symbol.

2.3 Larger sets

Since three sub-word units per word seems a somewhat arbitrary choice, experiments were performed with different numbers of units to establish an optimum number of units per word. As many as seven units per word were tried, and symbol confusion matrices produced to cluster them down to a more manageable number. However, the results were poor (reasons for this are discussed in section 6) and the main experiments were performed using three units per word.

3. SYSTEM DESCRIPTION

This section will describe the recognition system, starting with the MLP and then covering the DP alignment.

3.1 MLP

The MLP was a three layer, fully interconnected network, as shown in Fig. 2. It was trained using error backpropagation, as described in [4], to map each input frame (and context) to a set of symbol pseudo-likelihoods. The speech data presented to the input was already in the form of vectors of features, or frames, each frame representing 25.6 ms of speech. The speech had been endpointed (that is, the valid speech portion of the signal had been identified and labelled), as will be explained in section 5.1.

The task of the MLP was to map a frame of speech (together with context frames) to the symbol of the sub-word unit containing that frame, an output unit being provided for each sub-word symbol. At the input, the current frame is accompanied by some context frames, an equal number before and after the current frame. The size of this 'context window' is an experimental variable and results for windows of 7, 5 and 1 (no context) are given.

In training, the current frame and its context frames are presented to the input of the MLP, and the correct output is set to a high value while holding all others low: a 1-in-n coding scheme. The MLP was trained using many iterations of segmented and labelled training data.

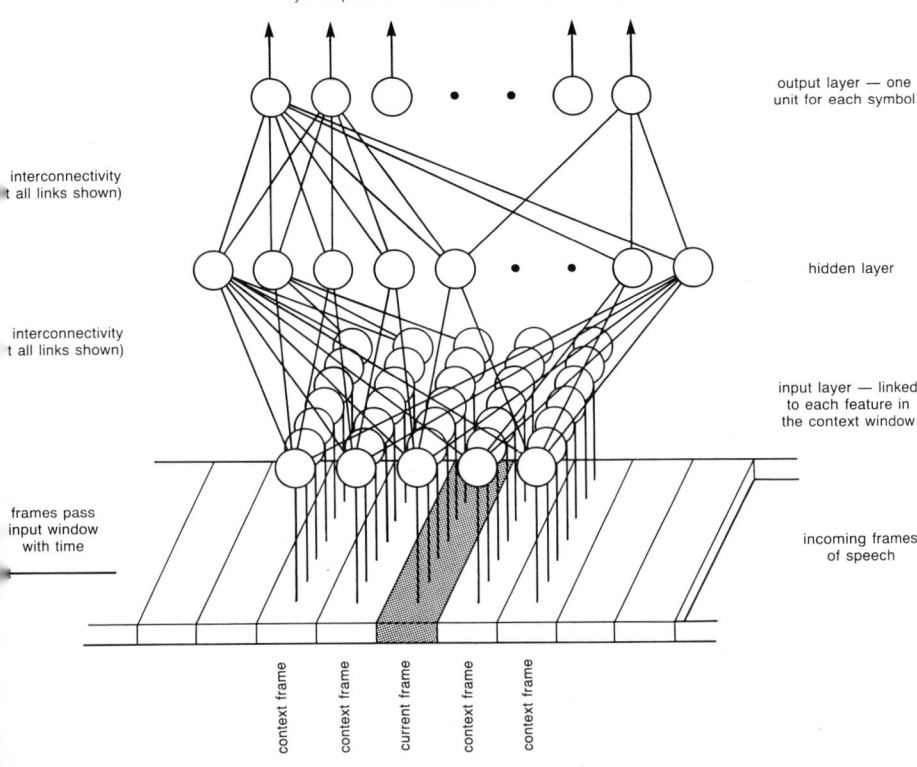

Fig. 2 The symbol processing MLP.

In operation, for the current input frame, each MLP output takes up a value between zero and one, the highest being the symbol most likely to represent the current frame. The set of values at the output is thus the set of pseudo-likelihoods of the current frame being contained in each of the sub-word units.

With the 1-in-n output coding, the MLP can be viewed as approximating an HMM local probability distribution (strictly a likelihood distribution) for the identity of the frame [5].

Naturally, this mapping process is not very precise if each frame is identified simply by choosing the symbol representing the maximum value output. This simple scheme is illustrated in Fig. 3 where the MLP is shown mapping a frame (with context) on to a sequence of symbols: the MLP has been trained to map the data on to the symbols at the top of the diagram. In the absence of any information about constraints on the sequences of symbols, the best that can be done is to choose the symbol with the highest activation at each frame — representative results are given on the bottom of the diagram. Symbol recognition rates of the order of 50% are typical for a very well trained network.

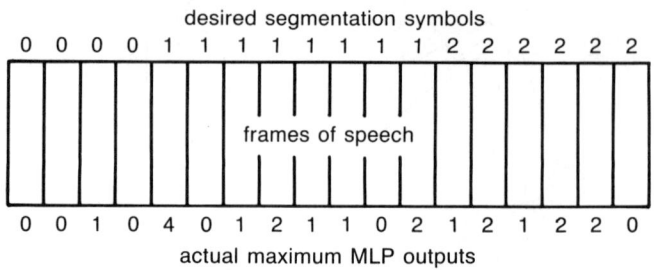

Fig. 3   The task to be performed by the MLP.

3.2   DP alignment

Since the segmentation and labelling of the speech data has been defined for each word in the vocabulary, it is known what sequences of symbols are legal. This knowledge can be used to impose constraints on the sequence of MLP outputs. For example, the MLP in Fig. 3 has symbol 4 following symbol 0, but this is not a legal sequence and has to be filtered out somehow. The way in which this is done is to use the whole vector of MLP scores for each frame (instead of the single maximum output) and choose the highest scoring legal path. These scores can be viewed as likelihoods, which are similar to probabilities, but do not necessarily sum to unity. (The output scores are not true likelihoods, but this approximation suffices for the current experiments.)

For each word in the vocabulary, there is a defined sequence of symbols: for example, 'A' might be 0-1-2. However, the transition between any two symbols can occur anywhere throughout the utterance — some example routes are shown in Fig. 4. Along each particular path, the likelihoods are combined by multiplication, giving a score for each path. (To be more exact, since the likelihoods rapidly tend towards zero, the calculation involves summing their logarithms.)

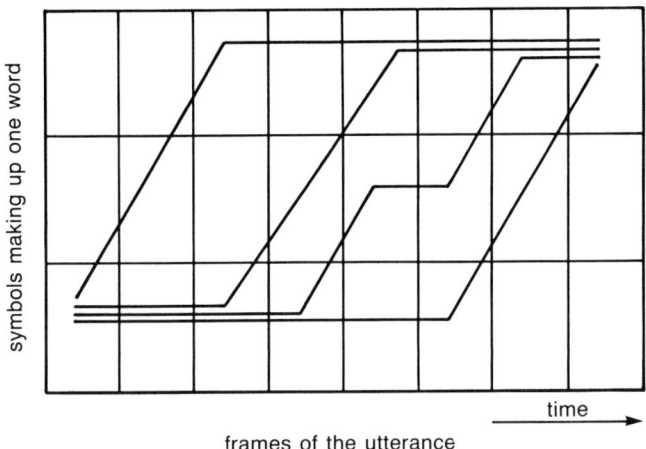

Fig. 4 Example paths through an utterance.

The symbols must occur in the specified order for each word, with transitions occurring on a frame boundary. As can be seen there is a very large number of possible paths which can be taken. In these experiments, each word had three possible symbols, so with, say, 50 frames there are over 10^{34} possible paths. The only other constraints are that the first frame of the utterance is forced to be the first symbol, and the last one is forced to be the last symbol: that is, the path in Fig. 4 must start at the bottom left and terminate at the top right. The desired path is the one with the 'best' score; that is, the total score for the symbol sequence as a whole is maximised. For recognition, this 'best-path' score is calculated for each word in the vocabulary and the word with the maximum score is the recognised identity.

Obviously, it is not economic to calculate the scores of all possible paths. Fortunately, the best path can be computed incrementally, using an algorithmic technique known as dynamic programming. The particular instance of DP used here is the Viterbi alignment algorithm, illustrated in Fig. 5.

The aim of the process is to find the path giving the highest score when the frames of input speech data are matched to the sequence of symbols for a particular word. In this context 'matching' means identifying frame-to-frame transitions consistent with the sequence of symbol labels. At each frame along the input data, the path is extended from the previous frame either by a horizontal transition (same symbol), or by a diagonal transition (next symbol), depending on which gives the higher accumulated score.

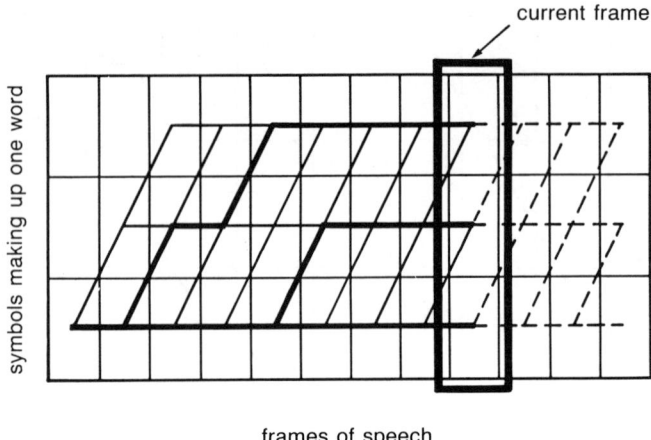

Fig. 5 Viterbi alignment process.

In the example shown in Fig. 5, the partial paths entering the current frame have been evaluated for each of the three symbols. The bold lines represent the best of the sub-paths for each symbol up to that point. After this, similar evaluation and comparison will occur for the next frame, and so on until the end of the word — the dashed lines show the future sub-paths to be considered. The search allows the model to remain in the same symbol or hop into the next symbol with equal probability. These are the only two transitions allowed in this model, though more sophisticated systems may permit a different set of transitions.

The accumulated score for each symbol in the current frame is the better of the previous scores multiplied by the likelihood of that symbol being current. At the end of the utterance, the value accumulated in the final symbol is the score for matching the given sequence of frames to that word model. The alignment process is carried out for every word in the vocabulary, resulting in a score value which represents the likelihood of each vocabulary item being the unknown utterance.

3.3 Entire system

A block diagram of the full system is presented in Fig. 6.

The signal from the microphone is filtered, sampled, digitised and blocked into 25.6 ms frames with 50% overlap. Each frame is then time-windowed and converted to a vector based on MFCCs; the data is then stored on disc in this form. The MLP maps frames of speech (MFCC vectors) to vectors of symbol likelihoods (78 of them if there are three distinct symbols per word in the alphabet vocabulary, or 45 in later experiments). These are combined by the Viterbi parser to produce a set of word likelihoods (26 for the alphabet), and the highest one is hypothesized as the spoken utterance.

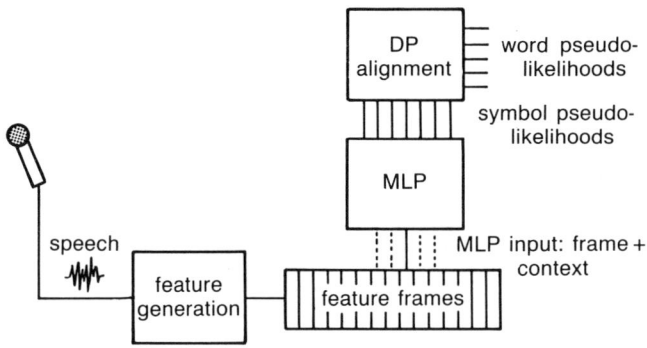

Fig. 6 Segmental MLP recognition system.

4. SEGMENTATION

4.1 Initial segmentation

For these experiments, the initial segmentation was performed linearly; that is, the first third of an utterance was labelled as the first sub-word unit, and so on. Earlier experiments tried using an HMM to segment the data; however, there was no appreciable improvement in performance. Since, in addition, this required a large amount of extra processing time, the HMM technique was abandoned in favour of the simple linear process.

4.2 Machine defined segmentation

Initially, the MLP was trained using the linearly segmented data. The data was then passed through the system to obtain a more accurate segmentation. As well as calculating the maximum likelihood, the DP process also provides a record of the best path. The symbol transition information from the best scoring path was used to relabel the data frames, as shown in Fig. 7.

The MLP was then retrained using the new segmentation data, and the whole process repeated until no further improvement in recognition accuracy was forthcoming. This is an example of segmental k-means training [6].

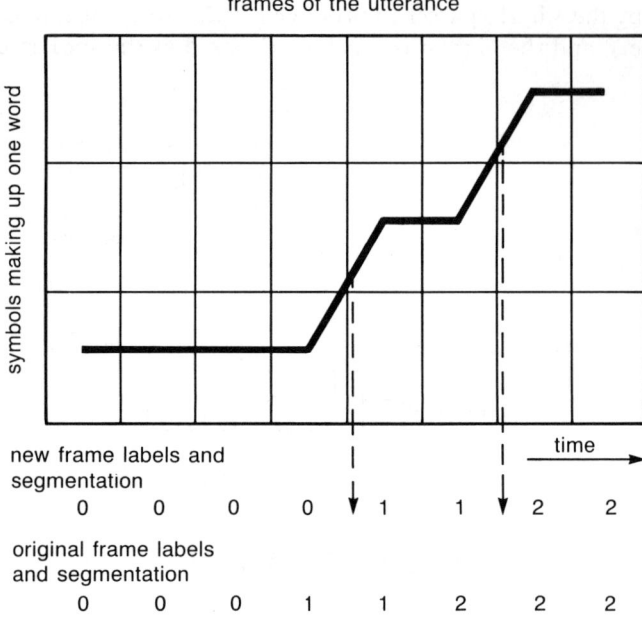

Fig. 7 Segmental k-means iteration.

5. EXPERIMENTS

5.1 Database

The data set contained three utterances of each letter of the British alphabet spoken by 104 talkers as discussed in the Introduction to Part 2. The speech was sampled at 20 kHz, endpointed and manually checked (with bad utterances removed) before further processing. The database was split into 52 speakers for training and 52 speakers for testing, balanced with respect to sex and age group, resulting in a training set of 3999 utterances and a test set of 3977 utterances.

The speech waveform of both the training and test data was converted into MFCCs. The data used as input to the MLP were the MFCC feature vectors over a window of several frames. The required output of the MLP for training was a 1-in-n vector with the high output being the desired segment identifier. In testing the MLP output was the vector of pseudo-likelihoods.

5.2 Results

An initial experiment was carried out with the MLP having only a single frame (no context information) to establish a baseline score for later comparison. In further experiments, the context window was expanded to five frames (two on each side), and seven frames (three on each side), representing a total of about 64 ms and 90 ms of speech, respectively.

From the results of the experiments with totally distinct sub-word units, symbol confusions were identified and the symbol set was clustered to 67 sub-word units. A second iteration reduced this number to 45 units. No further significant symbol confusions were discovered at this stage.

Each configuration was evaluated with several different numbers of nodes in the hidden layer of the MLP, and a number of random starts for the MLP weight values. A summary of the results obtained before resegmentation appears in Table 1.

Table 1 Results before resegmentation.

Number of sub-word units	Context window size	Number of hidden nodes	Frame accuracy		Word accuracy	
			Training	Test	Training	Test
78	1	20	18.3%	17.2%	—	—
78	5	70	31.9%	29.7%	78.2%	74.6%
78	7	70	35.3%	32.6%	83.7%	80.6%
67	7	70	42.5%	39.4%	74.6%	72.7%
45	7	70	55.9%	53.4%	84.1%	83.1%

At this stage, the training data was resegmented using the best system. This consisted of 45 sub-word units, 7 context frames, and 70 hidden nodes in the MLP. The MLP was then retrained. The results of iterating this resegmentation process are given in Table 2.

Table 2 Results after resegmentation.

Resegmentation	Frame accuracy		Word accuracy	
	Training	Test	Training	Test
Initial segmentation	55.9%	53.3%	84.1%	83.1%
First resegmentation	57.9%	55.1%	86.9%	85.4%
Second resegmentation	68.1%	65.3%	89.1%	86.5%
Third resegmentation	69.8%	67.0%	88.5%	85.9%

As can be seen, there is a marked improvement in recognition accuracy when the training data is resegmented. Resegmenting again gives a further increase in accuracy especially at the frame level. At the next resegmentation, word accuracy falls slightly even though frame accuracy increases. Since word accuracy is the more important parameter, no further resegmentations were carried out.

6. DISCUSSION AND COMPARISON WITH OTHER SYSTEMS

The results clearly show that window size is an important parameter in determining frame recognition accuracy. The maximum window size of 7 frames gave the best result, suggesting that the window size could have been increased further. However, the context would then have been a significant portion of a word duration (the average word length being about 40-50 frames).

The frames which occur between adjoining sub-word units are not good examples of either the preceding or following units. They could, perhaps, have been eliminated from the training set. However, though these transition frames form unreliable training data they do provide valid context information, so they can still appear as context frames for other data. In practice, removing them reduced the training set to such an extent that the resulting MLP did not generalise very well. A better solution would be to increase the frame rate to provide more frames, so that the transition frames would constitute a smaller proportion of frames and could be safely ignored.

The initial assumption of linear segmentation turns out to be fairly realistic since the initial accuracy, as is illustrated in Table 2, is only a few percent below optimum. The first resegmentation gives a small improvement in the frame accuracy, while the second one gives a much larger increase. Though further resegmentations give small improvements in frame accuracy, the word accuracy begins to fall off. The improvement in performance with the first resegmentation can be attributed to the system 'correcting' the clustering from the linear division. Subsequent relabelling moved the transition boundaries only very slightly, and the drop in word accuracy after the third resegmentation is probably due to corruption of the MLP's sub-word unit models by the transition frames.

Some other experiments were performed with a much larger symbol set, using seven sub-word units per word. The intention was to eventually reduce the total number of symbols by amalgamating many units whilst still retaining unique units where they were required. These experiments gave very poor results, probably due to the initial linear segmentation giving poor clustering, and there being much less training data per sub-word unit. Again, a faster frame rate would have increased the total data available for training.

One problem with the process of clustering similar sub-word units is that the confusion matrix only shows symbols which may be amalgamated, but cannot indicate which symbols contain contradictory information and ought, therefore, to be split. Single symbols being used to cover different information occurs, for example, when a word is pronounced differently by different speakers. This is where a linguistically based initial data labelling would have been useful.

Table 3 shows a comparison of the segmental MLP recogniser with other recognition systems. It is clear that the performance of the segmental MLP method is better than DTW and HMM systems. In mitigation, it should be noted that there is not really enough data to train a discrete symbol, or vector quantised (VQ), HMM. The static MLP (with linear time normalisation) [1], however, does give better accuracy than the present segmental system (with a slightly different front end representation). In addition, it must be admitted that a continuous density HMM has achieved about 90% test set accuracy on this database, but with a modified front end.

The greatest advantage of the segmental technique is that it is easily extensible to connected and continuous speech utterances. This is very important for two reasons. The first is that a connected recogniser does not need an endpointing algorithm since it can detect noise or silence as part of the speech stream. Secondly, 'whole word' recognisers do not work well on connected or continuous speech utterances because they have no way of modelling coarticulation between words.

Table 3 Comparison with other systems.

Classifier	Test set accuracy
VQ HMM	82.4%
DTW	84.3%
Segmental MLP	86.5%
Static MLP	88.3%

In HMM terms, the MLP is providing 'local probabilities' and the DP process is traversing states. The MLP makes use of context information which is unavailable to the frame level HMM processing. Other work [3] has taken the analogy further and included HMM state transition probabilities within the DP task. However, the HMM state traversal is flawed in that the state duration is restricted to an exponential distribution — this is also true of the equiprobability process implemented here. It was therefore felt that the extra work involved in modelling the state transitions more fully would not have been justified.

7. EXTENSION TO CONNECTED SPEECH

The recognition process described here has dealt with isolated utterances only. The extension to connected speech is fairly straightforward, given a suitable syntax for the utterances. In the isolated word recognition system, a word is made up from a very simple syntax. For example, the word 'A' consists of the sequence 0-1-2, as shown in Fig. 8. The utterance starts in symbol 0, and makes its way through the syntax graph via symbol 1 to symbol 2. On each frame, the utterance remains in the current symbol (effectively a self-transition which is not shown in the diagram) or moves to the next one.

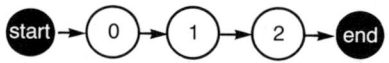

Fig. 8   Syntax for 'A'.

The same principle can be applied to sequences of connected words. Figure 9 shows the very simple syntax required to recognise the utterance 'AB:' that is, the utterance 'A' followed by 'B' without a pause. Now, the matching procedure has to find its way though the symbols for the first word followed by the symbols for the second. The parsing process (Viterbi alignment) is identical to that for a single word.

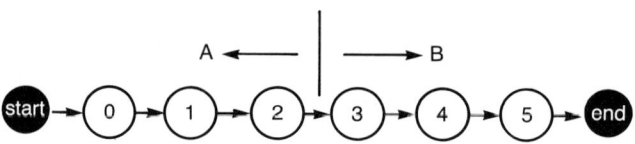

Fig. 9   Syntax for 'A'—'B'.

In order for the syntax to allow one of several words to follow 'A', the syntax graph of Fig. 10 is required. This is slightly more difficult in that the parser has to keep track of a (potentially large) number of possible paths through the graph. This can be achieved by adding just a little more information to the Viterbi process, but basically the best path through the syntax is being found, as before, by scoring all possible paths.

A more general grammar would allow any word to be followed by any word. This could be done simply as a loop. If the words were letters of the alphabet it would then be possible to spell names. In a practical system it would be necessary to include silence/noise models at the juncture between words.

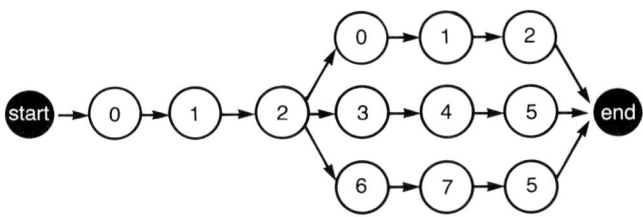

Fig. 10 Syntax for 'A' followed by 'A', 'B' or 'C'.

8. CONCLUSION

A technique for speaker independent isolated word recognition combining MLP and DP has been described, and results obtained. The MLP is used for frame recognition, and DP combines sub-word units. The performance of the recognition system is similar to that of HMMs on the same problem, and indeed, the process has much in common with the HMM method.

The technique described here does not rely on phonetic labelling of the training data, and the arbitrary initial segmentation can be improved by automatic methods. For general application it might be that some phonetic insights could be useful in segmenting the training data, since this would make the sub-word clustering more efficient.

However, the main advantage of this recognition technique is that it can be applied readily to connected or continuous speech. It can also be adapted to cope with non-endpointed speech data, simply by adding silence/noise as additional sub-word units.

REFERENCES

1. Woodland P C & Smyth S G: 'A Neural Network Speech Recogniser for Directory Access Applications', Proc Voice Systems Worldwide, p196 (1990).

2. Rabiner L R: 'A Tutorial of Hidden Markov Models and Selected Applications in Speech Recognition', Proc IEEE, 77 (2), p257 (1989).

3. Morgan N & Bourlard H: 'Continuous Speech Recognition using Multilayer Perceptron with Hidden Markov Models', Proc ICASSP-90, p413 (1990).

4. Rumelhart D E, Hinton G E & Williams R J: 'Learning internal representations by error propagation', in 'Parallel Distributed Processing: Explorations in the Microstructure of Cognition', eds Rumelhart & McClelland, MIT Press Cambridge, Ma (1986).

5. Bourlard H & Wellekens C J: 'Links between Markov Models and Multilayer Perceptrons', IEEE Trans Pattern Analysis and Machine Intelligence 12 , Part 12, p1167 (1990).

6. Rabiner L R, Wilpon J G & Juang B H: 'A segmental k- means training procedure for connected word recognition', AT&T Tech J, 65 (3), p21 (1986)

Part 3: Natural Language

CONNECTIONIST NATURAL LANGUAGE PROCESSING: AN INTRODUCTION

P J Wyard
BT Laboratories

1. A BRIEF HISTORY

Connectionist natural language processing (CNLP) dates back to near the start of the 1980s, when connectionism in general began its second life after the ascendancy of symbolic artificial intelligence in the 1970s. Hinton [1] published some seminal work on distributed semantic representations. Connectionist parsing, in the broad sense, got under way in 1982 with the localist work of Small, Cottrell and Shastri, Cottrell and Small, and the similar work of Pollack and Waltz [2-4]. These were spreading activation models whose main focus was lexical disambiguation. They typically had a number of layers of nodes, such as a lexical level, a word-sense level and a case logic level. The models were motivated by two factors: firstly the belief that disambiguation requires integrated, parallel processing of knowledge from multiple sources, and secondly the attempt to model semantic priming, which means that the activation of concept structures in the brain reduces the reaction time for subsequent judgements involving associated concepts.

Another burst of activity occurred in 1985. Pollack and Waltz [5] extended their earlier work by fronting the net with a 'symbolic' chart parser, and Cottrell [6,7] extended his work on lexical disambiguation by incorporating connectionist syntactic constraints. Two other groups of researchers produced different types of neural net systems which were aimed specifically at context-free parsing. Fanty [8] used a deterministic weight update rule, while Selman and Hirst [9,10] used a stochastic update scheme similar to the Boltzmann machine, and applied simulated annealing. Both these systems are neural nets which implement fairly explicitly a grammar which has been written in advance. However, they model parsing as constraint satisfaction (where the constraints are the grammar rules), and can cope naturally with ungrammatical sentences.

The following year saw the start of a line of research inspired by AI theories of natural language understanding, typically concerned with 'higher-level' processes such as causal schemata and script activation in simple stories (e.g. Golden; Sharkey et al., [11,12]). Of greater significance were the papers by McClelland and Kawamoto [13] on case role assignment, and Rumelhart and McClelland [14] on learning the past tense of verbs. The former paper was significant in using semantic microfeatures and a distributed representation.

Since 1986, many more CNLP papers have been published, and the field has grown steadily, particularly in the last two years, although it remains a very small subset of connectionism as a whole. It is impossible to list all the published papers here. The following is a brief selection of some of the most significant papers, dealing with the following topics: syntax and parsing (Hanson and Kegl; Benello et al, [15,16]), question answering (Allen, [17]), prepositional attachment (Sharkey; Wermter and Lehnert; St. John and McClelland, [18-20]), anaphora (Allen and Riecken, [21]), inference (Lange and Dyer, [22]), variable binding (Smolensky, [23]).

One of the reasons that CNLP remains a relatively small field is that it deals with very different tasks and subject material from the engineering and signal processing of mainstream connectionism. Natural language processing is sometimes called a 'higher-level' cognitive task, and it may be asked whether connectionism is adequate for this task. Fodor and Pylyshyn [24] provided the strongest critique of CNLP, attempting to show in fundamental terms that neural nets could not cope with certain key features of natural language, such as its productivity (and the building of recursive structures), its systematicity (the fact that our ability to produce/understand some sentences is intrinsically related to our ability to produce/understand other sentences), its compositionality, and the systematicity of inference (the fact that if we can make the inference P from P&Q&R we can also make the inference P from P&Q). Only symbolic processing systems were adequate to cope with these more or less universally agreed phenomena, according to Fodor and Pylyshyn. The result of this critique was to spur the CNLP research community into action to refute these claims, partly by theoretical arguments (e.g. Smolensky, [25]) but primarily by empirical results (e.g. van Gelder; Pollack; Smolensky, [26-28]). Although CNLP has not yet made much of a dent in traditional natural language processing (NLP), its credentials as a promising line of study are now fairly well established.

It can be difficult to track down the latest CNLP research, because the field is small and there is no journal or regular conference devoted exclusively to it. The annual conference on neural information processing systems (NIPS) in Denver usually has a handful of papers on CNLP, and the journal Connection Science has published a number of papers on CNLP. From the specifically cognitive science approach to CNLP, the annual conference of the Cognitive Science Society is a good source of material. Apart from these major sources, papers on CNLP can be found scattered through the standard neural net and AI literature.

2. WHY CONNECTIONIST NATURAL LANGUAGE PROCESSING?

If connectionism has to struggle to prove its credentials for natural language processing, why make the effort, apart from a perverse determination to do things the difficult way? Why not use neural nets for tasks like speech and image signal processing, and leave NLP to traditional symbolic methods? CNLP researchers believe that connectionism offers the hope of dealing with some long-standing problems in NLP which have beset traditional methods ever since research on them began four decades or more ago.

2.1 Brittleness in the face of new or incorrect input

Traditional systems are often not robust in the face of input which is not covered by the system's grammar, although not necessarily 'wrong' in terms of normal definitions of English. Other problems are vocabulary which is not covered, punctuation or other formatting, definite errors which a human would nevertheless easily understand, and so on. Traditional symbolic systems either crash or have to go into a recovery routine which is a bolt-on to the main system, and often does not yield a good response.

Neural nets, particularly if they use distributed representations, are able to cope with effects like these much more naturally, as long as the training data has exposed the net to something similar. Since the grammar is not contained in the net in the form of a list of rules, one does not experience disastrous brittle failure if the input requires what would be a new rule in a traditional system to parse it. In the case of vocabulary, a distributed representation (DR) allows extrapolation from words on which the net has been trained to words not in the training data (although this requires that the net has the word in its lexicon, with an associated DR). Other 'noise' in the input can be coped with in robust fashion due to the parallel distributed nature of the processing.

2.2 Pattern completion from incomplete input

Two common problems in NLP which require pattern completion are anaphora and ellipsis. An example of anaphora is:

'The bully hit the small boy and he began to cry.'
The pronoun 'he' must be identified with a preceding noun phrase, either 'the bully' or 'the small boy'.

An example of ellipsis is the following dialogue:

A: Where did you find the potatoes?
B: The third aisle.
A: The carrots?

The third sentence is incomplete, but is easily interpretable in context as an elliptical form of 'Where did you find the carrots?'

In spoken language, other forms of incomplete input are likely. For example, many sentences are left unfinished because the rest can be inferred (though often with less than 100% reliability). In the unfinished fragment 'It's very draughty. Could you shut.....?', we might infer that the door or the window should be shut, depending on context.

Traditional NLP systems have ways of dealing with these problems, but neural nets deal particularly well with the task of pattern completion, when it is cast in the form of completing a pattern vector which has some elements missing.

2.3 Coping with the irregularities and 'fuzziness' of real natural language

The task of capturing the grammar of natural language in a finite set of rules has proved extremely difficult over the years, because language has tremendous diversity and variability. No-one has yet succeeded in writing a grammar for the whole of any natural language, and many would regard the task as impossible.

Connectionists abandon the attempt to write explicit symbolic grammar rules. Instead they allow the neural net to learn an implicit grammar from the training data, which is a corpus of natural language, usually from a particular application domain.

2.4 Learning from language data

This follows on from the previous point. The ability of an NLP system to learn a language automatically would give a tremendous saving in human effort, quite apart from the potential of dealing better with the real data. The biggest and best traditional NLP systems have hundreds or thousands of rules, and have required many man-years of top-quality expertise. Much of this would have to be repeated for each new language tackled by a traditional system.

It must be clearly stated that connectionists do not yet have the ability to learn a very big fragment or a very wide range of aspects of natural language. Nevertheless, current architectures and learning algorithms have been used to give promising results in several different areas of NLP, as mentioned above in Section 1.

2.5 Sensitivity to soft regularities

This follows in a different way from Section 2.3 above. Although natural language has tremendous variability, there are of course many regularities. If it were not so, the rule-based approach would never have got off the ground. It is believed that these regularities are soft in nature, and neural nets are ideally suited to cope with this, as has been clear since Rumelhart and McClelland's [14] work on learning the past tense of verbs, at least.

2.6 Integrating multiple, graded constraints in a natural way

It is accepted that the interpretation of a single sentence, say, requires the integration of many different sorts of constraint; for example, syntactic, semantic and pragmatic. In the case of spoken language understanding, there are further constraints, such as phonological and prosodic. These constraints have to be given different relative weightings dependent on the circumstances. Traditional systems have found this integration of constraints very difficult. They often attempt to process each different set of constraints sequentially, whereas most people agree that parallel constraint satisfaction is the ideal.

An example from Marcus [29] illustrates how syntactic and semantic constraints can vary in relative strength in extremely similar sentences:

(1) Which dragon did the knight give the boy?
(2) Which boy did the knight give the dragon?
(3) Which boy did the knight give the sword?
(4) Which boy did the knight give to the sword?

The interpretation of these sentences is somewhat reader-dependent, but for most readers a weak syntactic constraint in the first two sentences makes us prefer the first noun as the patient and the noun after the verb as the recipient, in spite of a weak semantic constraint in (2) that knights don't give boys to dragons. In (3), a stronger semantic constraint overrides this syntactic constraint: swords, which are inanimate objects, cannot receive boys. Finally, in (4), a stronger syntactic constraint overrides the semantics.

Neural nets, using parallel distributed processing, are ideally suited to integrate multiple, graded constraints for language processing, particularly if powerful learning algorithms allow the relative weighting of the different constraints, and even to a certain extent the precise nature of the constraints, to be learned automatically.

2.7 Psychological modelling

The human brain is far superior to machines at the task of language processing. Therefore, even if one is not interested in psychological reality for its own sake, the way that the brain processes language may give useful clues in doing NLP by machine. In particular, it seems clear that that the brain does not carry out hundreds of logical inferences to understand a single simple sentence, but uses a much more direct, intuitive type of inference.

It is not claimed that connectionists are currently modelling human psychological processes at all exactly. However, CNLP does give the chance of breaking free from the stranglehold of rule-based processing which in most cases seems so implausible psychologically.

To summarise, seven problem areas for traditional NLP techniques have been discussed, and it has been indicated how neural nets offer the hope of making progress in these areas. This suggests that the infant field of CNLP has a viable future.

3. FUTURE DIRECTIONS FOR CONNECTIONIST NATURAL LANGUAGE PROCESSING

Section 1 indicated that a sound start has been made to the enterprise of connectionist natural language processing. But of course, there is far more still to do. Some of the major future directions for investigation that face us now are discussed over page.

1. A sustained effort is required to answer the critique of Fodor and Pylyshyn mentioned in Section 1. How neural nets can cope with recursion must be investigated, with compositional structure in their representations, with structure-sensitive operations on representations, with variable binding, and so on. Whether all these things can be done in a truly neural architecture, or whether some kind of traditional controller is required on top of the neural net, must be looked into. For some applications of CNLP, it may be possible to disregard these issues, but for many applications they are far from irrelevant theorizing.
2. The size of the applications dealt with in CNLP systems must be scaled up. If this can be done, it will go a long way to giving a practical answer to some of the issues raised in 1 above. A major limitation of many traditional NLP systems is their toy nature, and it would be a pity if CNLP went down the same route.
3. As well as bigger applications, there is a need for more realistic applications. Many, but not all, CNLP applications to date have used artificial data, but it ought to be one of the strengths of neural nets that they can cope with real data.
4. In order to meet the demands of the three points above, there is a need for more advanced architectures, which almost certainly means integrated modular architectures, rather than simply devising further variants of unitary architectures such as the MLP. The work of Lee, Flowers and Dyer [30] is a recent step in this direction.

4. AN INTRODUCTION TO THE REMAINING CHAPTERS IN THIS SECTION

The rest of this section, devoted to connectionist natural language processing, contains three chapters. Ainsworth and Warren describe a series of experiments using MLPs for text-to-speech synthesis systems. They investigate several different aspects of the problem, ranging from the choice of coding scheme to the division of the overall task into a set of sub-tasks. Their chapter represents a considerable body of useful results in this field.

Sharkey, in his chapter on functional compositionality and soft preference rules, addresses some of the issues raised in this Introduction. The experiments on prepositional phrase attachment are relatively simple, but the analysis of the learned weights and the introduction of the notion of dynamic preference values may be very fruitful for future developments.

Wyard and Nightingale describe a novel architecture, applied to context free grammar recognition. Although their net has only a single layer, it uses what they call higher order input nodes, which give it surprising power at the grammar learning task.

REFERENCES

1. Hinton G E: 'Implementing semantic networks in parallel hardware'. In G E Hinton & J A Anderson (Eds) Parallel Models of Associative Memory. Hillsdale, NJ: Lawrence Erlbaum (1981).

2. Small S L, Cottrell G W & Shastri L: 'Towards connectionist parsing'. In Proceedings of the National Conference on Artificial Intelligence, Pittsburgh, PA (1982).

3. Cottrell G W & Small S L: 'A connectionist scheme for modelling word sense disambiguation'. Cognition and Brain Theory, $\underline{6}$, 89—120 (1983).

4. Pollack J & Waltz D: 'Natural language processing using spreading activation and lateral inhibition'. In Proceedings of the Fourth Annual Conference of the Cognitive Science Society, Ann Arbor, Michigan (1982).

5. Pollack J & Waltz D: 'Massively parallel parsing: A strongly interactive model of natural language interpretation'. Cognitive Science, $\underline{9}$, 51—74 (1985).

6. Cottrell G W: 'A connectionist approach to word sense disambiguation'. Doctoral dissertation, available as Tech. Report 154, Computer Science Department, University of Rochester, NY (1985).

7. Cottrell G W: 'A connectionist approach to word sense disambiguation'. Pitman, London or Morgan Kaufmann, California (1989).

8. Fanty M: 'Context free parsing in connectionist networks'. Tech Report 174, Computer Science Department, University of Rochester, NY (1985)

9. Selman B & Hirst G: 'A rule-based connectionist parsing system'. In Proceedings of the Seventh Annual Cognitive Science Society Conference, Irvine, CA (1985).

10. Selman B: 'Rule-based processing in a connectionist system for natural language understanding'. Tech Report CSRI-168, Computer Systems Research Institute, University of Toronto (1985).

11. Golden R M: 'Representing causal schemata in connectionist systems'. Proceedings of the 8th Annual Conference of the Cognitive Science Society, pp 13—21 (1986).

12. Sharkey N E, Sutcliffe R F E & Wobcke W R: 'Mixing binary and continuous connection schemes for knowledge access'. Proceedings of the American Association for Artificial Intelligence (1986).

13. McClelland J L & Kawamoto A H: 'Mechanisms of sentence processing: assigning roles to constituents'. In J L McClelland & D E Rumelhart (Eds) Parallel Distributed Processing, $\underline{2}$, Cambridge, MA: MIT Press (1986).

14. Rumelhart D E & McClelland J L: 'On learning the past tense of verbs'. In J L McClelland & D E Rumelhard (Eds) Parallel Distributed Processing, $\underline{2}$, Cambridge, MA: MIT Press (1986).

15. Hanson S J & Kegl J: 'PARSNIP: a connectionist network that learns natural language grammar from exposure to natural language sentences'. Proceedings of the 9th Annual Conference of the Cognitive Science Society, Seattle, WA, pp 106—119 (1987).

16 Benello J, Mackie A W & Anderson J A: 'Syntactic category disambiguation with neural networks'. Computer Speech and Language, 3, 203-217 (1989).

17 Allen R B: 'Sequential connectionist networks for answering simple questions about a microworld'. In Proceedings of the 10th Annual Conference of the Cognitive Science Society, Montreal (1988).

18 Sharkey N E: 'Implementing soft preferences for structural disambiguation. KONNAI (in press) (1990).

19 Wermter S & Lehnert W G: 'Noun phrase analysis with connectionist networks'. In R Reilly & N E Sharkey (Eds) Connectionist Approaches to Natural Language Processing. Hove: Lawrence Erlbaum (in press) (1990).

20 St John M F & McClelland J L: 'Learning and applying contextual constraints in sentence comprehension'. In R Reilly & N E Sharkey (Eds) Connectionist Approaches to Natural Language Processing. Hove: Lawrence Erlbaum (in press) (1985).

21 Allen R B & Riecken M E: 'Anaphora and reference in connectionist language users'. International Computer Science Conference, Hong Kong (1988).

22 Lange T E & Dyer M G: 'High-level inferencing in a connectionist network'. Connection Science, 1, 181—217 (1989)

23 Smolensky P: 'On variable binding and the representation of symbolic structures in connectionist systems'. Tech Report CU-CS-355-87. Dept of Computer Science, University of Colorado, Boulder, CO (1987).

24 Fodor J A & Pylyshyn Z W: 'Connectionism and cognitive architecture: a critical analysis'. Cognition, 28, 2—71 (1988).

25 Smolensky P: 'On the proper treatment of connectionism'. The Behavioural and Brain Sciences, 11 (1988).

26 Gelder T van: 'Compositionality: a connectionist variation on a classical theme'. Cognitive Science, 14 (1990).

27 Pollack J: 'Recursive distributed representations', Artificial Intelligence, 46, Nos 1—2 (1990).

28 Smolensky P: 'Tensor product variable binding and the representation of symbolic structures in connectionist systems'. Artificial Intelligence, 46, Nos 1—2 (1990).

29 Marcus M P: 'A theory of syntactic recognition for natural language'. MIT Press, Cambridge, MA (1980).

30 Lee G, Flowers M & Dyer M G: 'Learning distributed representations of conceptual knowledge and their application to script-based story processing'. Connection Science, 2, No 4 (1990).

11

A SINGLE LAYER HIGHER ORDER NEURAL NET AND ITS APPLICATIONS TO CONTEXT FREE GRAMMAR RECOGNITION

P J Wyard and C Nightingale
BT Laboratories

1. INTRODUCTION

Most NLP requires attention to syntax as a basic prerequisite. Syntax involves order and constituency in the input text. A common method of coping with order is to present the words of the input text one at a time, sequentially, as in Elman [1]. If the alternative strategy of presenting complete sentences is adopted, a crude way of coping with order is to create different input nodes for a particular word at each different absolute position in a sentence. This is inefficient and fails to capture the idea of constituency (the words 'black cat' in positions 2 and 3 of a sentence would be regarded as having no relation to the same words in positions 6 and 7 of a sentence, for example).

An improvement on this strategy is to use a higher order net in which tuples of words (singletons, pairs, triples, etc.) are stored in nodes in the input layer, rather than just single words. The term 'higher order' has nothing to do with higher-order cognitive processes. Rather, it is used in the sense of Minsky and Papert [2] and a considerable body of pattern recognition work

(Giles and Maxwell; Giles, Griffin and Maxwell; Pao and Beer; Reid, Spirkovska and Ochoa [3-6]) to describe a net in which the inputs to the nodes in the first layer are formed from the product (or more complex function) of more than one pixel (picture element) value in the input image. Machado and da Rocha [7] have used the same term in the context of neural nets acting as expert systems, handling symbolic knowledge. In this chapter a higher-order input node refers simply to a node whose input is formed from the concatenation of words in the input sentence. Section 2 will discuss the reasons for this choice of net further.

A common concern in the design of neural nets is the choice of the optimum number of nodes and the best pattern of interconnections. Much early work presented nets in which the number of nodes was chosen according to rather *ad hoc* heuristics, and the nodes were then fully interconnected (between layers). More recent work (e.g. Mozer and Smolensky [8]) has explored ways of dynamically changing the architecture of a net during training. In the natural language processing domain, where the vocabulary may not be fully specified in advance, it is beneficial to have a dynamic architecture. Because the net described in this paper was designed with rather general sentence processing in mind, it has a dynamic architecture, which will be described briefly in Section 2. However, no great stress is laid on this feature in this paper, since with the parameters chosen for the particular problem tackled, a static architecture would have performed equally well.

The resulting higher order dynamic topology neural net (HODYNE) has been applied to the problem of grammaticality determination, using two fairly simple context-free grammars (CFGs), the second a little more complex than the first. Although the grammars are simple, the training and test data sets are quite large. Results on this problem will be presented, and the reasons for the surprisingly good performance will be analysed informally.

Besides the link with earlier higher-order nets, the current work is related to a number of different strands of earlier work. There is a close link with what are usually called n-grams, mostly used in large scale statistical speech recognition systems, as in the work of Bahl, Jelinek and Mercer [9]. Indeed it may be that HODYNE ultimately operates in a way very similar to these methods, the chief difference being that in the former case the statistical information is stored as a table of frequencies, while in the latter it is in the weights of the net. However, it should be noted that the weight strengths are not a direct mapping of the tuple frequencies.

As far as the grammaticality problem is concerned, several neural net parsers have appeared in the literature. These vary widely in size, in approach and in functionality. Some have the grammar built in, others allow it to be learnt. 'Parsing' does not have a universally accepted definition. It can range from grammaticality determination to construction of syntactic tree structures to case role assignment to the general interpretation of an input sentence.

Fanty's [10] context free parser is a large scale, massively parallel, purely syntactic parser, which constructs a new net for each CFG it is presented with (it does not learn the grammar). Selman and Hirst's [11] CFG parser is another non-learning parser, which uses simulated annealing to arrive at a parse instead of deterministic updating of units' activations. Cottrell [12] and Pollack and Waltz [13] both use spreading activation techniques and localist representations, with the network built to implement a grammar which is known in advance. Hanson and Kegl's [14] system is closer to a recogniser than a parser, and in contrast to the previous systems it induces a grammar from exposure to syntactically tagged sentences taken from a large corpus of natural language, using a standard MLP with backpropagation. McClelland and Kawamoto [15] take a very different approach to sentence processing. Their system assigns case roles to the words in simple sentences, using an MLP. It has a distributed representation using semantic features, and is also a learning system. St. John and McClelland [16] present further work in the same paradigm, but in this case the hidden layers learn appropriate representations, so that there is no need for hand-coded micro-features. They also use feedback in a similar way to Jordan [17] and a sequential presentation of words from the input sentence. Finally Pollack's [18] recursive auto-associative memory may be a very important new tool in connectionist parsing, since it can compress a recursive data structure to a fixed length vector representation.

Another line of research has investigated sequence recognition and prediction, which can be used for grammaticality determination. Allen [19] used a recurrent net as introduced by Jordan [17] and Elman [20]. His net learnt a grammar of a similar complexity to that presented in this paper to within 'a few percent error at a few positions in the strings'. Servan-Schreiber et al. [21] and Elman [1] describe similar work.

The rest of the paper is organised as follows. Section 2 introduces HODYNE, and describes its architecture and *modus operandi*. Section 3 describes the experimental work, with four main sections: 3.2 and 3.3 cover the experiments on the two CFGs, 3.4 presents an analysis of performance and 3.5 describes some experiments using near-miss negative strings.

2. DESCRIPTION OF THE HIGHER ORDER DYNAMIC TOPOLOGY NET (HODYNE)

2.1 Introduction

In general, the design of a neural net should be matched to the intended problem area (although some nets such as the MLP have proved to be suitable for a wide range of low-level processing tasks). The problem at which HODYNE is targeted in this chapter is the determination of the grammaticality of strings of syntactic categories (preterminals), such as det adj noun verb (det = determiner, adj = adjective, prep = preposition).

Order is crucial to grammaticality judgements. For example, det noun verb ('the cat slept') is grammatical, but noun det verb ('cat the slept') is not grammatical. It is not the absolute position of preterminals in a sentence which is usually important for grammaticality, but rather the relative ordering of preterminals and of groups of preterminals (constituents).

HODYNE captures the order information in an input sentence by forming contiguous pairs, triples, 4-tuples etc. of preterminals from the sentence and storing each of these in an input node. This is why it is called a higher order net, as explained in the previous section. Consider the two sentences noun verb prep det adj noun ('cats sleep in the hot sun') and adj noun verb prep det adj noun ('lazy cats sleep in the hot sun'). If the net is trained on the first (grammatical) sentence, it ought to be strongly inclined to judge the second sentence grammatical as well, although in some cases, of course, the addition of an extra preterminal at the start of the string will make it ungrammatical. For example, the first example sentence in the paragraph above would cause the generation of the following tuples (ignoring singletons): noun verb, verb prep, prep det, det adj, adj noun, noun verb prep, verb prep det, prep det adj, det adj noun, noun verb prep det, verb prep det adj, prep det adj noun, noun verb prep det adj, verb prep det adj noun, noun verb prep det adj noun. Not all of these would necessarily be incorporated into the net as will be explained below. The second sentence would cause all these tuples to be generated, plus adj noun, adj noun verb, adj noun verb prep, adj noun verb prep det, adj noun verb prep det adj, adj noun verb prep det adj noun. Because there is a large degree of overlap between these sets of tuples, HODYNE should have a good chance of generalising from the first sentence to the second.

In the broadest terms, HODYNE learns the tuples which are most commonly and strongly indicative of both grammatical and ungrammatical sentences, by exposure to a training set. It should then be able to generalise and make grammaticality judgements about unseen sentences from the same grammar. It works chiefly on short-range relationships (i.e. not very many long tuples are stored), and always on neighbouring symbols. Therefore if grammaticality depended on some relationship between alternate symbols, for example, HODYNE would not pick this up very naturally. Grammaticality does indeed depend on hierarchical structural regularities, but it was believed that HODYNE might go some way towards learning these by simple composition of grammatical constituents.

2.2 Architecture

The architecture of HODYNE is very simple. Figure 1 shows a portion of a HODYNE net after training on the grammaticality problem. The number of nodes in the input layer after training depends on the lengths of tuples selected and the number of syntactic categories in the grammar. In the experiments described in this chapter, the number ranged from 35 to 217.

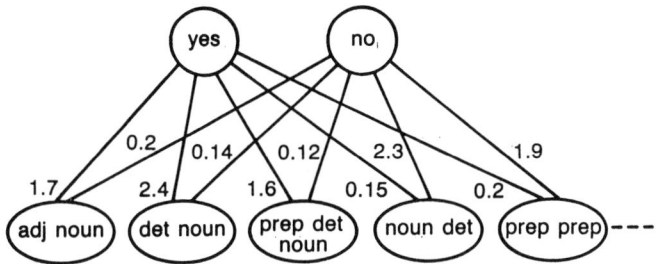

Fig. 1 The architecture of HODYNE. A portion of HODYNE trained on the grammaticality problem is shown. The weights shown are typical values. Only pairs and triples are shown for the sake of simplicity.

HODYNE is a single-layer net, with output nodes calculating a simple weighted sum of their inputs, with no thresholding or squashing function. Only the output node with the highest activation fires. There is no hidden layer. The input layer of nodes is generally large and connected by weighted links to a smaller layer of output nodes. In the case of the grammaticality problem, there are just two nodes in the output layer, yes and no, while for other problems the number of output categories, and hence output nodes, would be larger. Both layers of nodes start empty and grow dynamically during the course of learning. For the problem of grammaticality determination, the set of output nodes is obviously known in advance, and so is the set of input nodes if it is decided to have a node for every possible tuple up to the maximum tuple length chosen. There is therefore no advantage to be gained in this case from making the architecture dynamic. However, in general, any of these conditions may be broken. One may wish to add extra output categories during training, one may not know the entire training vocabulary before training starts, and one may not wish to store exhaustively every tuple encountered in training. A dynamic architecture was therefore chosen because it promised greater flexibility.

It is worth stating at this point why such an elementary architecture was chosen, when the hidden layer(s) of multi-layer nets have proved so good at effectively restructuring input data and allowing problems to be solved which are hard or impossible for traditional single-layer nets. It was decided to investigate the potential of the higher order input idea in the simplest possible architecture, so that its effects would not be confused with those of a hidden layer. In any case, it has been claimed by Pao and Beer, and Reid, Spirkovska and Ochoa [5,6] that single layer higher-order neural nets can be as powerful as MLPs. Although it is true that back-propagation allows a hidden layer representation to be learned automatically, there are advantages with a single layer net in terms of speed of learning and convergence to a global minimum (the perceptron convergence procedure of Rosenblatt [22] may be used). The authors also believe that it is a good principle to hardwire as much knowledge about the problem domain into the net architecture as possible, and the use of higher order tuples is a way of doing this which seems attractive as long as the number of atomic symbols is not very large and the combinatorics do not get out of hand.

Investigation of whether the introduction of hidden nodes helps in capturing grammatical sub-patterns, and the creation of a hierarchical net built out of HODYNE-like modules may form the basis of future work.

2.3 Algorithm

The algorithm or mode of operation of HODYNE during training will now be outlined. The training file consists of a set of positive and negative sentences of preterminals, each one followed by its correct classification yes or no. One presentation of a sentence leads to the following sequence of operations (the 'main cycle').

- The string is read from the file.

- All possible tuples are generated, between the minimum and maximum tuple lengths specified by the user.

- Each input node matching any of the generated tuples is activated (with a value of 1), and the activations of the output nodes are calculated by a simple weighted sum of the active input nodes. There is no thresholding or use of a squashing function.

- Any tuple which is not already present in the input layer is selected for incorporation into the input layer. The program allows this to be done on a probabilistic basis, as will be briefly discussed below, but in the experiments described in this paper, all new tuples were stored.

- The most active output node is found, and designated 'current__output__winner'.

- The desired response is read from the file. If this is the same as the current output winner, the latter is simply marked 'desired_response_node' as well. If it is not the same, then this node is added to the output layer if it does not already exist, and in any case it is marked as 'desired_response_node'.

- Links are created if they do not already exist between all active input nodes (including the ones just added) and the desired response node. Note that this implies that HODYNE is not fully interconnected between input and output layers.

- Weights of links are adjusted according to the learning method described below.

The training regime can be either 'brute force' where one simply runs through the entire training set time after time until performance is judged satisfactory, or 'incremental' where sentences from the complete training set are only added to the current training set when performance on the latter is satisfactory. (What is 'satisfactory' is something to be discovered experimentally, with reference to performance on the test set. It is usually found best to demand only 90% performance on the training set rather than 100%, since this gives considerably quicker training and hardly degraded performance on the test set. See below for further discussion of incremental training).

Once the net has reached a satisfactory level of performance on the entire training set, HODYNE enters test mode. In this mode the net remains fixed: no new nodes are added, no links are changed and the weights remain constant. An unseen test sentence is input from file or from the keyboard, the input nodes corresponding to tuples in the sentence are activated, activation passes to the output layer and the winning output node is calculated as before. This is compared with the desired response. The procedure is repeated for all the sentences in the test set, and appropriate statistics of performance can be generated.

At present, HODYNE chooses a single winning output node, i.e. it acts as a 1-out-of-n categoriser. However, it could easily be adapted to output a percentage score for each output node, and hence an ordered list of output judgements.

After training on a particular set of data, the current state of the net is automatically saved to file. It can then be reloaded at a later date for testing on new data, again from file or keyboard.

2.3.1 Incremental training

It was stated above that training could be either brute force or incremental. Brute force training is the standard mode of training neural nets (particularly MLPs) where one simply cycles repeatedly through the entire training set. Although this appears to work perfectly well for MLPs, it does not work at all well for HODYNE with training sets larger than toy size (the difference is no doubt linked to the different weight adjustment methods used). Even a training set of 40 strings could not always be learnt easily using brute force training. The use of incremental training was found to reduce the total number of presentations required for training to a preset criterion. In general, the larger the incremental step size (i.e. the number of strings added to the current training set each time) the less the total number of presentations required for learning a training set, but if the step size was made too big then learning would become slower again, or not happen at all. The optimum step size must be found by trial and error, since it is data dependent.

Elman [23] and Tsung and Cottrell [24] have recently published work using similar incremental training schemes.

2.3.2 Learning strategy

During the development of HODYNE several weight-adjustment strategies have been investigated, but one of them has proved much better than the others in guaranteeing that the training set can be learnt to desired criterion in reasonable time, and this is now described. Weights are only adjusted when HODYNE produces the wrong output. The links between the activated input nodes and the current output winning node ('the wrong answer') are weakened, and the links between the activated input nodes and the desired response output node are strengthened. This is shown in Fig. 2. Thus learning could be said to be through punishment followed by teaching: there is no reward for correct responses from HODYNE, since this has been found to be ineffective as a learning mechanism. The function used to alter the weights is the following:

$$w_{new} = \left(1 + \frac{\delta w_{old}}{1 + (\delta w_{old})^4}\right) w_{old}$$

where $\delta = +1$ for strengthening weights and -1 for weakening weights.

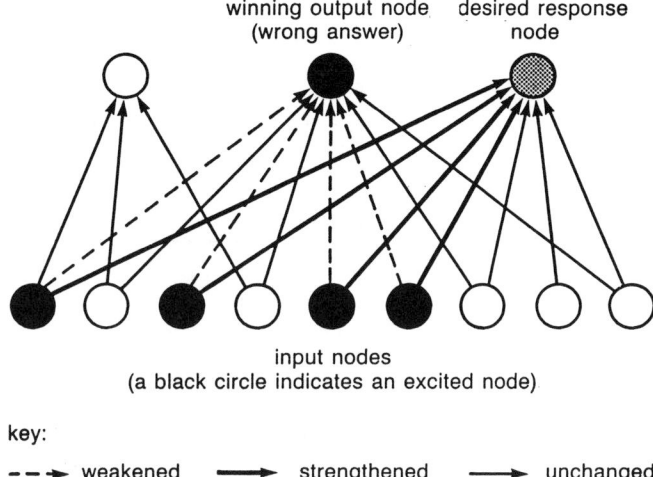

Fig. 2 Weight adjustment in HODYNE. The diagram shows how weights are adjusted when HODYNE makes a wrong answer. The strategy is 'punish & teach'.

If the expression in brackets is taken as $f(w)$, then Fig. 3 shows how it varies as a function of w. L_{max} indicates where $f(w)$ is at an extremum, and is where learning occurs at the maximum rate. (L_{max} is actually 0.76 for the simple function used: the function could be adjusted to make L_{max} equal to 1, which is the value of the weight when a link is first created, but this would make little difference to the gross effect of the function). The particular mathematical expression is not very significant; any function asymptotic to unity at zero and infinity, with an appropriate maximum or minimum in between would serve. The purpose of the function is twofold: firstly, to constrain the values of all weights not to depart too far from their initial value, and secondly, to prevent rapid unlearning of a weight value due to one or two counterexamples (the assumption is that after learning, weights will tend to take on values either to the left or to the right of the maximum or minimum in Fig. 3, where the value of $f(w)$ is not far from 1, causing the updated weight to be fairly close to the original weight).

This learning procedure performed very satisfactorily for both the experiments reported in this chapter. It is similar to the perceptron convergence procedure of Rosenblatt [22] in many ways: the chief differences being that weight updates are only made on lines leading to a single winning output unit, and the weight changes are of amounts governed by the formula above.

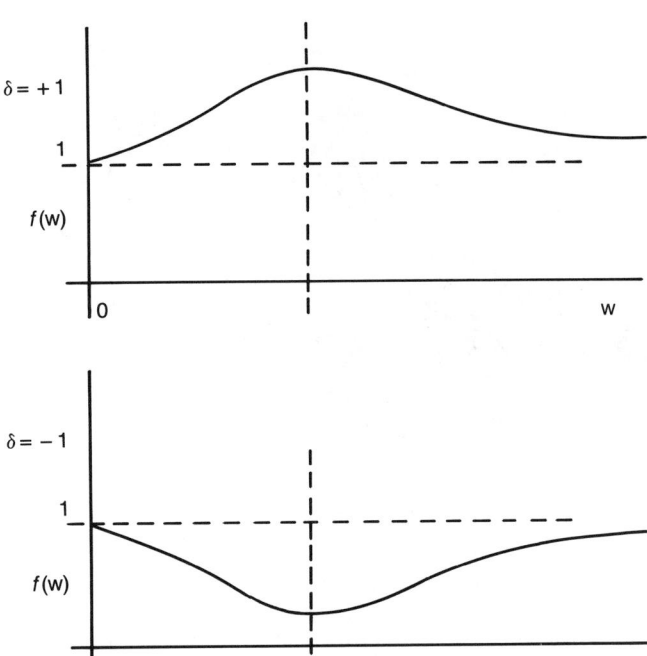

Fig. 3 The weight update formula of HOYDNE. The graph shows how the factor by which an old weight is multiplied to obtain the new weight varies as a function of the weight. It has a maximum at the value marked by L_{max} and is asymptotic to 1 as $w \rightarrow$ infinity. The top graph is for weight strengthening, the bottom graph for weight weakening.

2.3.3 Probabilistic storage of tuples

HODYNE allows the storage of tuples from input sentences into the input layer to be probabilistic, but this feature will only be very briefly described here, since in the experiments reported, all tuples up to a maximum length were stored.

The reason for probabilistic storage in general natural language processing is that the number of input nodes would grow too big for practical computation if all tuples were stored. Some means of storing only some of the tuples is required. Probabilistic storage aims to have a greater chance of storing the more generally useful tuples (often the shorter ones). The problem is that useful tuples may be thrown away. In the current experiments it was computationally feasible to store all tuples encountered during training, up to a maximum length of three.

3. APPLICATION OF HODYNE TO GRAMMATICALITY DETERMINATION

3.1 Introduction

The grammars used in this experiment were simple CFGs, and the neural net was required to make a yes/no grammaticality judgement on an input sentence, not to create a parse tree. The choice of problem, both for grammaticality as such and for the use of a grammar defined by explicit rules, is justified as follows:

- Firstly, it was wished to evaluate the performance of a neural net in an area where conventional computational linguistics has already performed well.

- Secondly, it was important to begin with a simple problem, and grammaticality determination is simpler than parsing. (The representation of the parse tree output poses problems, although the recent work of Pollack [18] is a hopeful way forward). A grammaticality test problem based on explicit rules is very well-defined and the data is easy to generate, which makes it suitable for a simple first problem.

- Thirdly, it is known that the human brain is capable of judging the grammaticality of a sentence, even when the sentence doesn't make sense. The classic example is 'Colourless green ideas sleep furiously' (Chomsky, [25]). As far as we know, the brain does not so easily create a parse tree. A useful heuristic is to give neural nets problems which humans find easy and intuitive.

- Fourthly, although it is probably true that natural English can never be captured by a set of explicit grammatical rules, rules are capable of generating a worthwhile subset of English, and enable a realistic boundary to be set up between grammatical and ungrammatical English, even if they imply a more clear-cut boundary than exists in reality. As discussed in section 5, there are plans to carry out a further grammaticality experiment using data from a natural English corpus.

- Fifthly, grammaticality determination does have some practical uses, although it is not as useful as producing a parse tree. The most obvious use is as a filter to weed out very unlikely interpretations at an early stage and prevent unnecessary processing. In the case of sentences from a written text, a medium length sentence might correspond to 10 or 20 different strings of preterminals due to lexical ambiguity, since many words have more than one possible syntactic category. These possibilities could be reduced to a much smaller number, in a very fast preprocessing step (i.e. before conventional parsing), by a neural net using grammaticality considerations alone. A traditional parser could then take over. In the case of speech input, the actual recognition of words is not 100 % accurate, and use of a neural net grammaticality checker could filter out many low probability interpretations.

3.2 Experiments with the basic grammar

3.2.1 Experimental data

Positive strings were generated from the ten-rule context-free grammar (CFG) below:

1. S → NP VP
2. NP → Det NP2
3. NP → NP2
4. NP2 → Adj NP2
5. NP2 → Noun
6. NP2 → NP2 PP
7. VP → Verb
8. VP → Verb NP
9. PP → Prep NP
10. VP → VP PP

We shall call this Grammar 1. This grammar generates basic NP-VP sentences, with prepositional phrases in noun phrase or verb phrase. Rules 4, 6 and 10 are directly recursive, and there is also indirect recursion, e.g. NP generates PP generates NP, etc. It was decided to limit recursion as follows: rules 4, 6 and 10 were not allowed to be applied twice in succession; the main NP was allowed at most one subsidiary PP; the VP was allowed at most two subsidiary PPs, one attached to the VP itself and one to a subsidiary NP. The rationale was to require the net to learn a limited degree of recursion, since this is important in natural English, but not too much since repeated recursion is rare in natural English.

With recursion limited as above, a total of 1780 unique grammatical strings of preterminals was generated, resulting from 20 different NPs and 89 different VPs. (4060 different tree structures were generated, but some of these were duplicates in terms of the strings). The longest string had 19 preterminals: det adj noun prep det adj noun verb det adj noun prep det adj noun prep det adj noun ('the black cat with the sharp claws ate the sleepy mouse with the squeaky voice with the greatest pleasure'). The shortest string had three preterminals: noun verb noun ('cats eat mice').

The 1780 positive strings were then supplemented by 1780 negative strings, produced by generating strings of length randomly selected between three and 19, and with each item randomly selected from the list of five preterminals. The strings were checked to ensure that they were indeed negative by parsing them conventionally, and it was also ensured that there were no duplicates. All strings then had a start symbol added at the beginning and an end symbol added at the end. This was regarded as legitimate assistance to the neural net in deciding on grammaticality, being equivalent to an initial capital letter and a final full stop.

The total set of 3560 strings was then shuffled randomly three times to produce three different 'master sets'. This was done both to remove bias in the order of presentation to the net, and because the positive strings were originally grouped according to similar structure due to the effect of the generating program.

3.2.2 Grammaticality experiments

After a number of preliminary runs of HODYNE with different parameters to see the sort of performance that HODYNE was giving, each of the master sets was split into a training file of 1000 strings and a test file of 2560 strings. Each of the three training sets was run with four different values of minimum and maximum tuple size, namely singletons, pairs and triples; pairs and triples; pairs only; triples only. This gave a total of 12 runs. Every run used a performance criterion of 90% during training, and an incremental stepsize of 250. This means that the net was first trained to criterion on 250 strings from the training set, then 250 more strings were added and the net trained to criterion on all 500 strings, and so on until the net reached at least 90% correct on the full training set of 1000 strings.

Table 1 shows the results from these runs, giving the tuple lengths stored, the time taken, the number of presentations for training, the number of input nodes created in the net, and the percentage correct on the test set of 2560 strings. The computer used was an Apollo DN10000 and the program is written in Pascal.

The most striking thing about these results is that in every case the test set performance is about 99% or higher. HODYNE had learnt this CFG to a high degree of accuracy from the training set and successfully generalised to a test set which was larger than the training set.

Table 1 Grammaticality determination using Grammar 1 with a training set of 1000 strings.

Data Set	Tuple lengths	Time (hrs:mins)	Presentations in training	Input nodes	Test set percentage
A	1, 2 and 3	2:21	13,750	217	99.4
A	2, 3	0:32	2,500	210	99.3
A	2	0:10	2,500	35	99.4
A	3	0:18	2,500	175	99.2
B	1,2 and 3	0:41	2,500	217	99.3
B	2,3	0:34	2,500	210	99.1
B	2	0:10	2,500	35	99.3
B	3	0:20	2,500	175	98.9
C	1, 2 and 3	0:43	2,500	217	99.2
C	2, 3	0:36	2,500	210	99.2
C	2	0:10	2,500	35	99.6
C	3	0:19	2,500	175	98.9

There does not appear to be any significant difference between the performances on the three different shuffled data sets, as would be hoped. It is also clear that the test set performance is similar for all four choices of tuple lengths, except that it is possibly a little worse for triples only. As far as time for training is concerned, and economy on input node storage, the results for pairs only are outstanding (time taken depends chiefly on number of presentations of input sentences and number of input nodes: it varies linearly with the former and to a higher power with the latter). In the case of learning this CFG, storage of pairs-only appears to give very good results, and the addition of triples does not improve performance (if anything it slightly degrades it).

It should be noted that although HODYNE was only required to learn the training set to the 90% level, it actually learnt it to over 99% (due to 'overshoot' on the final pass through the training set).

A quick inspection of the weights in the three cases where pairs only had been used showed that there was a great deal of variation. Thus the net had not converged to a particular region in weight space each time, although the performance in each case was very similar.

Having achieved good generalisation from a training set of 1000 strings, it was decided to take the three original master sets of 3560 strings and split them into training sets of 500 and test sets of 2560 strings. This was done and HODYNE was run, storing pairs only for the three data sets. The results are shown in Table 2. Test performance is still very good, but appears to have deteriorated slightly from an average of 99.4% (pairs only) with a training set of 1000 to 98.4% with a training set of 500.

Table 2 Grammaticality determination using Grammar 1 with a training set of 500 strings.

Data Set	Tuple lengths	Time (mins)	Presentations in training	Input nodes	Test set percentage
A	2	6	750	35	98.6
B	2	6	750	35	98.4
C	2	6	750	35	98.3

It was then decided to make the training set smaller and smaller, in order to discover the limits of HODYNE's ability to generalise. In order to save time, only one master set of 3560 strings was used, so the results are single runs in each case, not averages. In each case, the master set was split into two, with the stated number of strings used for training (always starting from the top of the master set) and the rest for testing. The results are shown in Table 3 (again, pairs only were stored). It was very surprising to find that with only 20 training strings, HODYNE still scored over 95% on the test set of 3540 strings, and with only five training strings it scored over 90% on the test set of 3555 strings. It was only when the number of training strings was reduced below five that test set performance was seriously degraded.

Table 3 Grammaticality determination using Grammar 1 with small training sets.

Number of strings in training set	Test set percentage
300	97.5
200	97.5
100	97.8
50	98.5
40	98.5
30	97.5
20	97.3
10	93.7
5	94.9
4	80.4
3	68.3
2	72.1
1	50.0

A final short experiment was done to see if test set performance could be pushed closer to 100% than the 99% + which had already been achieved, by demanding a higher percentage score during training. A training set of 1000 strings was used, with 2560 strings in the test set. A 100% criterion was tried first during training, but HODYNE proved unable to learn the training set in 15 hours, so that run was aborted. A 99.4% criterion was then tried during training. HODYNE learnt the training set to 99.8% but only scored 99.2% on the test set. Finally, a 99.8% criterion was tried during training. HODYNE learnt the training set to 100%, but scored only 99.3% on the test set. While not conclusive, these experiments indicated that it would be very difficult, if not impossible, to ensure that HODYNE would learn the grammar well enough to be sure of scoring 100% on the test set. (One score of 100% on the test set was achieved by the alternative strategy of having 2500 strings in the training set and a 90% training criterion. However, this was an isolated result: the average test performance with 2500 training strings showed no improvement on the results above).

3.2.3 Interim discussion

The results of the previous section indicate that HODYNE performed remarkably well at grammaticality determination using the basic 10-rule CFG, and storing pairs-only in the input layer. Three immediate lines of investigation suggested themselves, and the results from these are covered in the remainder of this report.

Firstly, it is of obvious interest to make the grammar more complex, and see how HODYNE's performance stands up. This is covered in Section 3.3. Secondly, some analysis of performance is in order, in terms of the tuples stored in the input layer, the strings wrongly classified and the weight values. This is the subject of Section 3.4. Thirdly, how would HODYNE perform if asked to distinguish grammatical strings from near-miss ungrammatical strings, rather than random ungrammatical strings, which are usually very ungrammatical? This is covered in Section 3.5, and will be seen to relate back to the analysis of Section 3.4.

3.3 Experiments with a more complex grammar: possessives and relative clauses

3.3.1 Experimental data

The grammar used in this section, henceforth referred to as Grammar 2, is essentially the same as the basic Grammar 1 of the previous section, with possessives and relative clauses added. The eventual aim is to increase the complexity of grammar incrementally until it reaches the syntactic coverage of the most comprehensive natural language computer systems. Grammar 2 is the first small step towards that goal.

Grammar 2 was written in definite clause grammar (DCG) form in Prolog, and appears below.

s	→	np, vp.
np	→	np (Rel, Prep).
np1	→	det, np2.
np1	→	np2.
np2	→	[adj], [noun].
np2	→	[noun].
vp	→	vp1, pp.
vp	→	vp1.
vp1	→	[verb].
vp1	→	[verb], np.
det	→	det3.
det	→	det1, poss.
det1	→	det3.
det1	→	det2, poss.
det2	→	det3.
det3	→	[det].
det3	→	[ ].
poss	→	[noun_gen].
poss	→	[adj], [noun_gen].
np (rel, Prep)	→	np (norel, Prep), rel.
np (Rel, prep)	→	np (Rel, noprep), pp.
np (Rel, Prep)	→	np1.
pp	→	[prep], np1.
rel	→	[rel_pro], [verb], np1.

The use of features in the DCG rules allows a greater control over recursion, but the rules are essentially simple rewrite rules. A brief description of the sentences generated from this grammar is in order. There are two extra syntactic categories compared to those in Grammar 1, namely rel_pro (relative pronoun such as 'that', 'which', 'who') and noun_gen (possessive noun form such as 'student's', 'cat's'). Thus there are seven syntactic categories in Grammar 2, adj, det, noun, verb, prep, rel_pro, noun_gen, together with the start and end categories which are placed at the beginning and end of each string to create the strings found in the files input to HODYNE.

Possessives are regarded as an expansion of the determiner, and recursion has been limited such that each possessive phrase can have at most two possessives. However, every determiner can be expanded. Thus wherever Grammar 1 had 'the black cat', Grammar 2 could have 'the student's black cat', 'the nervous student's black cat', 'cats' claws' points', or at the longest 'the nervous student's old professor's black cat'.

A general pair of rewrite rules for relative clauses are np →np, rel and rel → rel_pro, vp. However this allows looping from vp to np and back to vp via rel. This was regarded as too general for present purposes. The rules in Grammar 2 allow each np to have at most one each of pp and relative clause, and they do not allow a pp within the relative clause, which although perfectly reasonable in terms of syntactic structure (e.g. 'the book that I bought in the supermarket in the centre of town') is not really necessary for purposes of generating surface strings. Thus the most complex type of noun phrase that can be generated is something like 'the greedy cat which eats mice in the walled garden', or at the longest 'the nervous student's old professor's black cat which eats the nagging mother's silly boy's white mice in the stern magistrate's barmy husband's walled garden'.

The longest possible np is 24 words, the longest possible pp is 8 words, and the longest possible sentence is 57 words, excluding start and end, made up of np, verb, np, pp $(24 + 1 + 24 + 8)$.

It was not possible to generate sentences exhaustively directly from Grammar 2 in its DCG form, since the total number of sentences is over 10^{11}. Instead, a sentence template grammar was derived which generated exactly the same sentences. Successively generated strings bear no close syntactic relation to one another, since the template slots are filled randomly with substrings of syntactic categories, so that if one generates just a few thousand of the possible strings, they will be likely to cover the grammar fairly representatively.

The sentence template used was: np1, relprep, verb, np1, relprep, pp. This has one fixed item, the verb, and five slots. Without going into full detail, the np1 slot can be filled with one of 28 different fillers, containing different strings of det, adj, noun_gen, and noun. There is a roughly equal probability of the np1 containing zero possessives, one possessive or two possessives. The relprep slot can be filled with one of five different intermediate level fillers, containing, respectively, neither relative clause nor prepositional phrase, relative clause only, prepositional phrase only, relative clause followed by prepositional phrase, and prepositional phrase followed by relative clause. The pp slot can be filled with equal probability by nothing or by a preposition followed by np1.

2000 positive strings were generated from this template grammar, to form part of the master set.

It was necessary next to generate a set of negative strings using the same syntactic categories as Grammar 2. This was to be generated randomly, but it was not desirable simply to choose string lengths at random between 2 and 57, with equal probability, as was done in Section 3.2. Although the maximum length of string generated by Grammar 2 was 57, the average length was only about 20, and the frequency distribution of lengths has a very long thin tail at the upper end of the length range. A program was written to generate negative strings with approximately the same length distribution as the positive strings. As before, syntactic categories are picked at random from the list of seven. Each string has to be parsed to make sure that it is indeed negative.

2000 negative strings were generated in this way, and added to the 2000 positive strings to create a master set of 4000 strings. This set was of similar size to the 3560 strings which had been used in the first experiment. These strings were then randomly shuffled. Only one shuffled file was produced since the previous experiment had indicated very similar results from all three differently shuffled files. Each string was on a separate line, followed by 'yes' or 'no' on the next line, according to whether it was grammatical or ungrammatical.

3.3.2 Results for grammaticality determination using the more complex grammar

Starting from the master file of 4000 strings just described, training and test files of different sizes were constructed, simply by taking the first n strings for the training file and using the remainder for the test file. Since the previous experiments had shown that using pairs only for the tuple length gave as good results as any other choice, and was much quicker than using triples or longer tuples, the initial set of runs used pairs only, and varied the number of strings in the training file. The percentage correct criterion during training was 90%, and all pairs were again stored.

The results from this initial set of runs appears in Table 4. It can immediately be seen that the same very high accuracy in the test phase was achieved with Grammar 2 as with Grammar 1 in the previous experiment. With 100 training strings, the test set accuracy is 99.8% (8 errors out of 3900 presentations), and with only 30 training strings the test set accuracy is still 99.7% (10 errors out of 3970 presentations).

Table 4 Grammaticality determination using Grammar 2. Only pairs were stored. Time is for train + test; a sizeable fraction is for test. Number of test strings = 4000 — number of training strings.

Number of training strings	Time (hrs:min)	Presentations in training	Input nodes	Test set percentage
100	0:30	320	63	99.8
50	0:28	160	63	99.8
40	0:27	80	61	99.8
30	0:27	70	61	99.7
20	0:26	40	57	99.5
10	0:25	20	46	98.4
9	0:19	18	42	97.6
8	0:19	16	42	97.7
7	0:19	21	42	98.4
6	0:18	12	36	83.7
5	0:21	10	25	60.0
4	0:23	8	25	60.0
3	0:20	6	19	50.0
2	0:19	4	18	50.0
1	0:18	2	14	50.0

In fact the accuracy in the test phase using Grammar 2 is higher than with Grammar 1. The first four entries in Table 4 all show a test performance equal to or better than 99.7%, whereas in Table 1, using a training set of 1000 strings, the best test performance obtained was 99.6%, and the other scores using a training set of 1000 had an average test performance of about 99.2%. This is a surprising result, since Grammar 2 is more complex than Grammar 1. However, the correct interpretation of this result is unclear; the number of tuples stored in the input layer may play an important role.

It can be seen that the test set accuracy drops very fast between seven training strings (98.4%) and five training strings (60.0%). This appears to be associated with the corresponding sharp fall in the number of pairs stored in HODYNE's input layer (a drop from 42 to 25). The next section, which attempts to analyse HODYNE's performance in a limited way, sheds some light on this.

For the last three runs, with three training strings or less, and 19 pairs or less in the input layer, test set performance is only the 50% which one would obtain by random guessing.

A second, small set of runs was performed using 100 training strings, and varying the tuples stored, to see whether the fact that Grammar 2 is more complicated than Grammar 1 means that higher order tuples would give an advantage over pairs only. All runs used the same settings of the other parameters as the runs in Table 4. The results appear in Table 5. They are rather inconclusive. All three runs showed an improvement over pairs only which is possibly significant; the error rate was 4 or 5 per 3900 instead of 8 or 9 per 3900 obtained using pairs only. However, exactly the same improvement was obtained by using singles and pairs as by using pairs and triples or triples only. This clearly does not support the idea that triples as such are helping much in determining grammaticality; the improvement may equally well be due to an increase in the sheer number of nodes in the input layer. With seven syntactic categories plus start and end, the number of triples becomes very large and the net runs much more slowly. Hence it can probably be concluded that for a grammar of the complexity of Grammar 2, the use of triples (and presumably higher order tuples) is not advantageous.

Table 5 Grammaticality determination using Grammar 2.
All runs used 100 training strings.
Time is for train and test.
Number of test strings = 3900
The run for pairs only is repeated from Table 4 for purposes of comparison.

Tuple Lengths	Time (hrs:min)	Presentations in training	Input nodes	Test set percentage
1, 2	0:45	320	75	99.9
2, 3	3:24	320	456	99.9
3 only	1:53	320	391	99.9
2 only	0:30	320	63	99.8

3.4 Analysis of HODYNE'S performance at grammaticality determination

3.4.1 Introduction

HODYNE's test set performances on both Grammar 1 and Grammar 2 appear almost 'suspiciously' good. Some analysis was carried out to try and understand just why it was doing so well.

3.4.2 Investigation 1

The first investigation carried out used the results of the first experiment on Grammar 1. Three runs were singled out for examination. Here they will be referred to as runs 1, 2 and 3. All three runs used a training set of 1000 strings and a test set of 2560 strings, although Run 3 used a different shuffled training set from the other two runs. Run 1 stored singles, pairs and triples. Run 2 and Run 3 both stored pairs only. The number of errors in test phase for Runs 1, 2 and 3 respectively were 19, 18 and 10, which incidentally shows that in this case at least, the precise make-up of the training set was as significant as the lengths of stored tuples in determining the number of errors during test.

The actual strings wrongly classified on these three runs are shown in Table 6. These strings were studied carefully in an attempt to extract some patterns, and the following conclusions were reached:

- For all three runs, the average length of string wrongly classified was only about half the average length of string in the test set. This is easily understood: a shorter string must be classified on the basis of a smaller number of tuples activated in the input layer, and there is less chance for errors in the individual weights to 'average out'.

- For Runs 1 and 2, nearly all the grammatical strings rejected ended with a verb, i.e. the verb is intransitive in these strings. In the training set used for these runs, the number of positive strings ending in a verb is only two, whereas the number of negative examples ending in a verb is about 120, and as a result, verb end is connected rather strongly to no (strength 2.14, compared to a weight of 0.50 linking it to yes).

Table 6 Sample errors using Grammar 1.
The number of training strings is 1000 in each case.
The tables below show every case in which HODYNE made the wrong grammaticality judgement, out of a test set of 3560 strings on each of the three runs.
Syntactic categories are denoted by their initial letters, and start and end are omitted.

Run 1 (singles, pairs and triples)		
Is string grammatical?	String	Length of string
yes	a n p n v	5
no	n v d n v a n p v d n	11
no	v a n	3
no	p n v n	4
yes	n v	2
no	a n	2
yes	a n v	3
no	v p n v d n	6
no	v d a n	4
yes	d n v	3
yes	n p n v	4
no	n p n	3
no	a d n p d a n v a	9
yes	n p d n v	5
no	a n p n	4
yes	d n p n v	5
no	p a n	3
no	p n p n v d a n v p	10
no	n v d v d n p d a n	10

Run 2 (pairs only)		
Is string grammatical?	String	Length of string
yes	a n p n v	5
yes	a n p d n v	6
no	d p a n	4
yes	n v	2
no	a n	2
yes	a n p n v p n	7
yes	a n v	3
no	p a n v d p d n	8
yes	d n v	3
yes	n p n v	4
no	n p n	3
yes	n p n v p n	6
yes	d n p d n v	6
yes	n p d n v	5
no	d n	2
yes	d n p n v	5
no	p a n	3
no	n v d v d n p d a n	10

Table 6 (cont.)

	Run 3 (pairs only: a different training set)	
Is string grammatical?	String	Length of string
no	n p n p n v	6
no	n v d n v	5
no	a n p n	4
yes	n v p n	4
no	d d n v n v n	7
yes	n p n v a n	6
no	a n p d n v n p	8
no	p n v n	4
yes	n v a n	4
no	n p n	3

It might be supposed that splitting the syntactic category verb into intransitive and transitive verbs would improve performance, and this would be worth investigating in the future. However, on Run 3 none of the grammatical strings rejected ended with a verb. No doubt this was related to the fact that in the training set for Run 3 there were six examples of grammatical strings ending in a verb, causing verb end to be connected less strongly to no (strength 1.61, compared to a weight of 0.74 to yes). This highlights the crucial role played by the training set in determining the individual errors made during the test phase, although it apparently has much less effect on overall test set performance percentage, and casts doubt on the usefulness of strategies like splitting the category verb, which are designed to correct particular types of error.

Apart from the final verb phenomenon, no other grammatical type of pattern was observed in the errors from these three runs.

- There was no consistent pattern over these three runs as to whether the errors contained a greater number of positive strings rejected or negative strings accepted.

- For a particular grammar, the set of all possible tuples can be divided into legal tuples (those which occur in at least one grammatical string) and illegal tuples (those which occur only in ungrammatical strings). A tuple such as det verb, for example, is illegal, and the detection of this tuple alone in an input string immediately enables it to be classified as ungrammatical.

- Many of the ungrammatical strings accepted contained a fairly long grammatical subsequence, in the sense that this subsequence forms part of a grammatical string and contains no illegal tuples. For example, from Run 1 the last string accepted (wrongly) was n v d v d n p d a n (using initial letters to denote categories), of which the last seven categories form a grammatical subsequence (a complete grammatical string can most simply be formed from this subsequence of 7 categories by adding an initial n). A number of points arise from this observation. Firstly, it suggests that the current grammaticality determination task could be done using a non NN method extremely simply by checking each tuple in a test string in turn against a table of legal tuples. The task, in some senses, is not very difficult. However, this is an a *posteriori* judgement. It was not generally considered an easy task for a neural net before the investigation began. It is also useful when analysis of a neural net's performance suggests new ways of tackling a problem.

Secondly, it was observed that HODYNE does not do what might have been expected, which is to build up large weights from illegal tuples in the input layer to the output node no. Such weights are no bigger than average. However, it must be remembered that illegal tuples are only connected to no, because of HODYNE's method of creating connections, whereas legal tuples are usually connected to yes and no. This leads to a simple picture of how HODYNE can achieve quite good performance at grammaticality determination using the crudest of methods, and without any fine weight adjustment whatsoever. Suppose that all weights are fixed at a value of 1, and suppose, for example, that all possible pairs are stored in the input layer, both legal and illegal. For the current grammar, there are 35 possible pairs, of which 17 are legal and 18 are illegal. These are shown in Table 7. Suppose that all the legal tuples are connected to both yes and no, and the illegal tuples to no only. If an input string contains for example three legal tuples and four illegal tuples, then yes will receive an activation of three and no will receive an activation of seven, so the string would correctly be judged ungrammatical. If a second (grammatical) string contains five legal tuples and zero illegal tuples, then yes will receive an activation of five and no will receive an activation of five, so HODYNE would not be able to judge grammaticality. However, all that would be required for the correct answer to be given is for the links from legal tuples to yes to be slightly higher than to no. If this difference were small enough, then all grammatical strings would be accepted, but the presence of just one illegal tuple connected only to no would be sufficient to tip the balance to a rejection of the string.

Table 7 Legal and illegal pairs for Grammar 1.
The table shows the 17 legal pairs and the 18 illegal pairs which can be formed from the syntactic categories used in Grammar 1.

Legal Pairs	Illegal Pairs
adj noun	adj adj
noun verb	adj verb
noun prep	adj det
noun end	adj prep
verb adj	adj end
verb noun	noun noun
verb det	noun adj
verb prep	noun det
verb end	verb verb
det adj	det det
det noun	det verb
prep adj	det prep
prep noun	det end
prep det	prep prep
start adj	prep verb
start noun	prep end
start det	start verb
	start prep

In Investigation 2 it will be discussed whether this is the sort of thing HODYNE actually does, with reference to the actual weights in a trained net. For the moment, it is hoped that it is clear that the legal/illegal tuple distinction already sheds considerable light on how HODYNE might score so highly at the grammaticality problem, without the need for tremendously fine weight adjustments. HODYNE will already have stored most or all of the possible tuples in its input layer, and connected them up to yes or to yes and no as appropriate, after the presentation of only a small number of training strings. If the scenario which has been outlined above is roughly correct, then the mere presence or absence of links goes a long way to explaining correct grammaticality determination, without the need for accurate weight adjustment, and this is why HODYNE shows such powers of generalisation from small training sets.

3.4.3 Investigation 2

The second investigation was carried out on the results of Section 3.3 above, using the more complex Grammar 2. It was shown in Section 3.3 that the test set performance falls very sharply from 97% with 42 input nodes, to 83% with 36 input nodes, to 60% with 25 input nodes. The total number of possible pairs with Grammar 2 is 63, and it seems that with just 42 of these stored in the input layer, very good test performance is possible, but that with less than this number, test performance deteriorates sharply.

It was decided to follow up the idea about legal/illegal tuples explained above by looking in more detail at the weights of the net in Table 4 trained with 50 strings. All 63 possible pairs are present in the input layer, and of these 25 are legal and 38 are illegal. The average strength of weights from legal and illegal input nodes to the output nodes was calculated, and the results were as follows:

average strength of weight from legal pairs to yes = 1.35
average strength of weight from legal pairs to no = 1.14
average strength of weight from illegal pairs to no = 1.19

From this it is clear that the hypothesis about the average strength of weights from legal pairs to yes being greater than from legal pairs to no was borne out in practice. Apart from this, nothing very clear emerged from the examination of the weights, except for the observation that there were only six different values taken by weights, implying that very fine weight adjustment was not necessary in training.

This emphasises the earlier observation that the existence of the correct connections and the gross strength of those connections is much more important than their precise values.

3.4.4 Conclusion

The two investigations above have shed some light on how HODYNE is able to perform so well at grammaticality determination. It has been shown that the use of tuples makes this an easier problem than might have been supposed (at least as tackled in the experiments described so far) for any system, including a neural net, and that fine adjustment of weights or movement to a global minimum in weight space is not necessary. Nevertheless, the fact remains that HODYNE has learnt these grammars, which though simple, are more complex than the toy grammars commonly used, to a high degree of accuracy.

3.5 Grammaticality determination using 'near miss' negative sentences

3.5.1 Introduction

The analysis of Section 3.4 has shown that grammaticality determination is a fairly easy task for HODYNE because of the legal/illegal tuple distinction. An obvious extension to the work is to use negative strings which are derived from positive strings by just one or a few category substitutions rather than randomly generated negative strings as used hitherto. The point of this is that such 'near-miss' negative strings will contain mostly legal tuples, with just a few illegal tuples around the point of substitution, whereas randomly generated negative strings will contain a much higher number of illegal tuples, thus making the task of grammaticality determination much easier. Near-miss negative strings should give HODYNE a more demanding task. A second motivation for the use of near-miss negatives is that in some applications the task to be performed will actually involve near-miss negatives, so it is useful to study HODYNE's performance at this task.

The most difficult task would be to use negative strings in which every tuple is legal. However, assuming that all strings continue to start with start and end all strings with end, a little thought shows that the only strings satisfying this criterion are those which are initial fragments of grammatical sentences and which end with noun or verb, since the only legal pairs with end as the second item are noun end and verb end. Thus it would be limited to negative strings corresponding to incomplete sentences such as 'the black cat', 'the black cat on the mat', etc. This did not seem a very interesting exercise to perform, although HODYNE would no doubt have found it very hard, since discriminating whole grammatical strings from grammatical fragments is getting well away from the original problem specification.

It was therefore decided to use negative strings derived from positive strings by making one, two, three or four substitutions at random, and checking that the 'mutated' string was in fact negative. A program was written which makes a specified number of random mutations (substitutions) to the syntactic categories in an input string, and which does not allow 'identity mutations'. The mutated strings are parsed to ensure that they are true negatives.

A file of 2000 positive strings was generated according to Grammar 2 using the sentence template grammar described in Section 3.3.1. Four files of 2000 near-miss negative strings were derived from this file, having one, two, three and four substitutions respectively. In the case of one and two errors, some of the mutated strings were still positive, so these files were cut to 1800 strings (all negative). No check was made for duplicates, but on previous experience these are rare. Four master files were then prepared by combining the 2000 positive strings with each of the four files of negative strings in turn (or 1800 positive strings in the case of one and two errors), and randomly shuffling the order of strings. The end result was four master files whose negative strings had one, two, three and four errors respectively. From each of these master files a training set of 100 strings was split off, and the remainder of the strings were used for testing.

3.5.2 Results

Using each of the four datasets, two runs were performed. All runs stored pairs only. The first used the criterion of 90% during training, which has been used hitherto, the second used a 95% criterion to see if test set performance could be improved. All runs used a step size of 20 during training.

The results from these runs appear as Table 8. From this table some interesting conclusions can be drawn. Firstly, test set performance is still very respectable even when the negative strings have just one error (best values of 93% for four errors in negative strings to 79% for one error in negative strings), but has now fallen below the perpetual 99% + which was obtained hitherto. Secondly, there is a regular decline in performance away from the case where the negative strings have four errors to the case where they have only one error, as might be expected. Thirdly, the increase in training criterion from 90% to 95% had a noticeable effect on improving test set performance in the cases where the negative strings had only one or two errors.

It would be well worth investigating in future whether test set performance where the negative strings have only one error can be wound up any higher than 79% by increasing the training criterion still higher. It is also important to see if the use of triples or higher order tuples would improve performance. It might be expected to make more difference in this case than hitherto, since a negative string with only one error generates at most two illegal pairs, but three illegal triples, four illegal 4-tuples, etc.

It should be borne in mind when studying Table 8 that the total number of possible pairs is now 81 (9 syntactic categories including start and end; $9^2 = 81$), since start and end were allowed to appear anywhere in the negative strings after mutation (this was unrealistic from an applications point of view, but acceptable in terms of a NN learning problem). From Table VIII it can be seen that HODYNE only formed 60 of 81 possible pairs when training on the dataset containing negative strings with only one error, considerably less than with the other datasets, and this may be another reason why the test performance is lower, which should be separated out in future work.

It can also be noted from Table 8 that the number of presentations, and the time taken, to learn the training sets to criterion is now significantly higher than it was in the past using pairs only. Up to eight cycles through the current training set were required on occasion to learn to criterion (recall that incremental training is always used), which is higher than hitherto. It appears that a significant amount of weight adjustment is now required, unlike in most of the previous cases of training HODYNE on grammaticality.

3.5.3 Conclusion

The experiments of section 3.5 have tended to confirm the analysis of section 3.4 indirectly. Performance is clearly degraded by using near-miss negative strings than randomly generated negative strings. However, this is a more demanding problem, which makes more use of the features of the HODYNE algorithm, and the results are still respectable. Further investigation is required to establish the limits of HODYNE's performance at this more difficult task.

Table 8 Grammaticality determination using Grammar 2 and 'near-miss' negative strings.
Only pairs were stored.
Training stepsize = 20
Number of training strings = 100
Number of test strings = 3500 or 3900 (see text).

		Training criterion = 90%		
Number of categories wrong in negative strings	Input nodes	Presentations in training	Time (hrs:min)	Test set percentage
1	60	1900	1:00	68.2
2	72	1140	0:51	76.7
3	79	760	0:49	85.2
4	80	460	0:53	92.6

		Training criterion = 95%		
Number of categories wrong in negative strings	Input nodes	Presentations in training	Time (hrs:min)	Test set percentage
1	60	2280	1:06	79.3
2	72	2180	1:09	84.9
3	79	1860	1:09	85.7
4	80	600	0:56	92.0

4. FURTHER WORK

There are two main ways in which it is planned to extend the work on grammaticality determination. The first is to extend the formal grammar used to generate the input strings, gradually increasing the syntactic coverage, until it comes somewhat closer to natural English. The grammar rules of one of the leading natural language parsers such as the Core Language Engine (Alshawi et al, [26]) or the Alvey Natural Language Tools Grammar (Grover et al, [27]) could be used as a source. This work on more complex grammars is required, to see if HODYNE's tuple-based approach finally becomes a limitation when longer-range dependencies become more important. These grammars will have to be specifically designed with long-range grammatical features in mind, such as centre embedding. A decision will have to be made as to what type of negative strings to use.

The second extension planned is to use strings of preterminals obtained from a tagged natural language text corpus such as the Brown corpus, for both training and testing. If HODYNE performed well at this task, the need for explicit grammar rules in grammaticality determination would have been bypassed.

A tagged speech corpus such as the London-Lund Corpus of Spoken English (Svartvik and Eeg-Olofsson, [28] may be used to see how HODYNE performs at grammaticality determination on spoken English.

5. CONCLUSION

This chapter has introduced a single layer higher order neural net called HODYNE. HODYNE has shown very good results on simple context free grammaticality determination, and holds out the hope of doing the same task on natural language without the need for an explicit grammar.

ACKNOWLEDGEMENT

This chapter first appeared in 'Connection Science' and is reprinted with the kind permission of the Editor.

REFERENCES

1. Elman J L: 'Structured Representations and Connectionist Models'. Proceedings of the Eleventh Annual Conference of the Cognitive Science Society, Ann Arbor, Michigan (1989).

2. Minsky M L and Papert S: 'Perceptrons'. Cambridge, MA: MIT Press (1969).

3. Giles C L and Maxwell T: 'Learning, invariance and generalization in high-order neural networks'. Applied Optics, 26 , pp 2972—2978 (1987).

4. Giles C L, Griffin R D and Maxwell T: 'Encoding geometric invariances in higher-order neural networks'. In Neural Information Processing Systems, American Institute of Physics Conference Proceedings, D Z Anderson, ed., p 301 (1988).

5. Pao Y H and Beer R D: 'The functional link net: a unifying network architecture incorporating higher order effects'. International Neural Networks Society First Annual Meeting, Boston, Mass (1988).

6. Reid M B, Spirkovska L and Ochoa E: 'Rapid training of higher-order neural networks for invariant pattern recognition'. Proceedings of the International Joint Conference on Neural Nets, Washington (1989).

7. Machado R J and da Rocha A F: 'Handling knowledge in high order neural networks: the combinatorial neural model'. IBM Technical Report CCR076, Rio Scientific Center, IBM Brasil, Rio de Janeiro (1989).

8. Mozer M C and Smolensky P: 'Using relevance to reduce network size automatically'. Connection Science, 9, No 1, pp 3—16 (1989).

9. Bahl L R, Jelinek F and Mercer R L: 'A maximum likelihood approach to continuous speech recognition'. IEEE Transactions on Pattern Analysis and Machine Intelligence, PAMI-5, pp 179—190 (1983)

10. Fanty M: 'Context free parsing in connectionist networks'. Technical Report 174, Computer Science Department, University of Rochester (1985).

11. Selman B and Hirst G: 'A rule-based connectionist parsing system'. Proceedings of the Seventh Annual Conference of the Cognitive Science Society, Irvine, CA (1985).

12. Cottrell G W: 'Connectionist parsing'. Proceedings of the Seventh Annual Conference of the Cognitive Science Society, Irvine, Ca (1985).

13. Pollack J and Waltz D: 'Massively parallel parsing: A strongly interactive model of natural language interpretation'. Cognitive Science, 9, pp 51—74 (1985).

14. Hanson S J and Kegl J: 'PARSNIP: A connectionist network that learns natural language grammar from exposure to natural language sentences'. Proceedings of the Ninth Annual Conference of the Cognitive Science Society, Seattle, Wa (1987).

15. McClelland J L and Kawamoto A H: 'Mechanisms of sentence processing: assigning roles to constituents of sentences'. In McClelland J L and Rumelhart D E (eds), Parallel Distributed Processing: Explorations in the Microstructure of Cognition (2). Cambridge, MA, Bradford Books/MIT Press (1986).

16. St John M and McClelland J L: 'Applying contextual constraints in sentence comprehension'. Proceedings of the Tenth Annual Conference of the Cognitive Science Society, Montreal, Quebec (1988).

17. Jordan M I: 'Serial order: a parallel distributed processing approach (ICS Technical Report 8604)'. Institute for Cognitive Science, University of California, San Diego, La Jolla, California (1986).

18. Pollack J: 'Recursive auto-associative memory: devising compositional distributed representations'. Technical Report MCCS-88-124, Computing Research Laboratory, New Mexico State University, Las Cruces, NM 88003 (1988).

19. Allen R B: 'Connectionist State Machines'. Bellcore Technical Report (1988).

20. Elman J L: 'Finding Structure in Time (CRL Technical Report 8801)'. La Jolla, CA: University of California, San Diego, Center for Research in Language (1988).

21. Servan-Schreiber D, Cleeremans A and McClelland J L: 'Encoding sequential structure in simple recurrent networks'. Technical Report CMU-CS-88-183, Carnegie Mellon University (1988).

22. Rosenblatt F: 'Principles of neurodynamics'. New York: Academic Press (1962).

23. Elman J L: 'Structured Representations and Connectionist Models (CRL Technical Report 8901)'. La Jolla, CA: University of California, San Diego, Center for Research in Language (1989).

24. Tsung Fu-Sheng and Cottrell G: 'A sequential adder using recurrent networks'. Proceedings of the International Joint Conference on Neural Networks, Washington DC (1989).

25. Chomsky N: 'Syntactic Structures'. Mouton, The Hague (1957).

26. Alshawi H, Carter D M, van Eijck J, Moore R C, Moran D B, Pereira F C N, Pulman S G and Smith A G: 'Research Programme in Natural Language Processing: Final Report'. SRI International Cambridge Research Centre (1989).

27. Grover C, Briscoe T, Carroll J and Boguraev B: 'The Alvey Natural Language Tools Grammar (second release)'. Technical Report 162, University of Cambridge Computer Laboratory (1989).

28. Svartvik J and Eeg-Olofsson M: 'Tagging the London-Lund corpus of spoken English'. In Johansson S (ed), Computer corpora in English language research. Bergen: Norwegian Computing Centre for the Humanities (1982).

12

FUNCTIONAL COMPOSITIONALITY AND SOFT PREFERENCE RULES

N E Sharkey
Department of Computer Science, University of Exeter[1]

1. INTRODUCTION

The need for the development of a new representational theory has begun to be felt in recent connectionist research on natural language processing (CNLP). In a recent review of the literature [1], connectionist representations were classified into different types. Some of these were viewed as being very similar to their classical counterparts in that they contain explicit symbol tokens and/or have spatially concatenative constituent structure (e.g. localist concept notes, symbolic microfeatures, vector frames), and some are weaker (e.g. localist proposition nodes). The aim here is not to cast doubt on the value of the research using these representation schemes, but to discuss the beginnings of a new theory of representation.

A unique form of connectionist representation results from a mapping of an input space onto a space of lower dimensionality. This produces compact subsymbolic representations of the input. For example, Hinton [2] mapped propositional triples onto a lower dimensional PROP assembly using fixed random weights. Thus each triple, in a sense, recruited a set of PROP

---

[1] I would like to thank three Research Assistants in my laboratory: Richard Sutcliffe for running Simulation 1, Darren Mitchell for Simulation 2 and Paul Day for conducting the normative study. I would also like to acknowledge Don Mitchell, Ajit Narayanan and Peter Wyard for their support and suggestions.

units to represent it in a structurally implicit form. Through a learning process, it was possible to map the PROP activations back onto the higher dimensional triple space, and thus recreate the structure. Coarse coding, as Hinton called it, is discussed at length in [3].

Variations of this type of compact representation are common in the literature [4-7] and may be set up by a simple algorithm, as in conjunctive coding [8], or may be learned either by supervised [3] or unsupervised techniques [9]. Regardless of the learning technique used, the representation codes statistical regularities of the input (usually) by reducing the pattern environment to a lower dimensional feature space.

Compact subsymbolic connectionist representation is certainly different from classical syntactic structure representation. Nonetheless, this style of representation, Fodor and Pylyshyn [10] have argued, is not compositionally structured. However, as van Gelder [11] points out, Fodor and Pylyshyn are implicitly discussing only one type of compositionality: spatially concatenative composition. In this mode of composition, the spatial layout of the symbols are important (indeed crucial) for symbol manipulation and inference. Van Gelder states that for a mode of combination to be concatenative, "... it must preserve tokens of an expression's constituents (and the sequential relations among tokens) in the expression itself.".

In contrast to classical concatenative representation, compact connectionist representations may be considered to have a different mode of combination. That is, uniquely connectionist representations are not concatenative, but they may be functionally compositional nonetheless. As van Gelder [11] points out, 'We have functional compositionality when there are general, effective and reliable processes for (a) producing an expression given its constituents, and (b) decomposing the expression back into those constituents.' By **general** van Gelder means that the process can be applied, in principle, to the construction and decomposition of arbitrarily complex representations. To be **effective** the processes must be mechanistically implementable and to be reliable they must always generate the same answer for the same inputs.

It is the goal of this chapter to begin to examine the nature of functional compositionality and its use in a difficult linguistic task: structural disambiguation. Two simulations are presented here in which a standard BP net, taking whole sentences as input, is trained to perform a structural disambiguation task and generalise to novel examples. It is argued that, during learning, the net implements raw attachment preferences in the relationship between the upper and lower weights. An analysis is provided of how these preferences are implemented, and it is shown how sentence representations may be decomposed such that each individual word is assigned a raw preference value (RPV) which can then be used to indicate its structural bias. Moreover, it is shown how the activation function makes use of the raw preferences by modulating the strength of their biases in a manner that is contextually sensitive to the structural biases of the other words in a sentence.

2. THE DOMAIN

A major stumbling block in the automation of natural language processing is that natural language is pervasively ambiguous, i.e . there is a one-to-many mapping between surface strings and their representations. Consider the sentence: 'The old man chased the boy with a large stick'; the prepositional-phrase (PP), **with a large stick**, is attached directly to the verb-phrase (VP), and the sentence may be bracketed: ((The old man) (chased (the boy) (with a large stick))) i.e. the old man had the stick and he chased the boy with it. But this sentence cannot be parsed on the basis of syntactic information alone. This is because syntactically equivalent substitutions within the sentence affect the syntactic structure. For example, if 'long hair' is substituted for 'large stick', the result is that the PP, **with long hair**, would now be attached to the noun-phrase (NP) **the boy** instead of the VP. The new bracketing would be: ((The old man) (chased (the boy (with long hair)))) i.e the boy had the long hair and he was being chased by the old man. Thus, it appears that contextual variability can influence the assignment of syntactic structure.

Some linguists have attempted to develop parsing rules for getting round the problem of structural ambiguity. For example, Kimball [12] used right association in which the preferred attachment was to the directly preceding noun; and Frazier and Fodor [13] used minimal attachment in which the parse prefers an attachment in which the minimal number of nodes are created in the parse tree. Other linguists and AI researchers have attempted to solve the structural problem by attributing a more important role to the lexicon during parsing. The best attempted solutions have involved introducing syntactic preference rules [14], or semantic preference rules [15] into the lexicon. Nonetheless, it has proved difficult to develop rules that do not demand continual updating to handle new examples. And it is difficult to find a sufficient set of syntactic and/or semantic features. This chapter explores the types of lexical preference rules that can be learned from a sample set of sentences using high order statistical methods such as back propagation. To begin, a simulation is described in which a standard BP net (2-layer) learns to bracket input sentences into NP or VP attachments. This was done to find out if the learned representations could capture contextual regularities underlying the attachment task. Next, the net is analysed to find ways in which to characterise the 'soft' preference rules associated with the input vocabulary. First, the **raw** or **static** preferences are discussed in terms of Euclidean distances between the lower and upper weights in a trained net.

It is shown how these distances can be used to assign RPVs for individual words. Second, the **dynamics** of the soft preference rules are discussed by examining how they operate during the processing of entire sentences[2]. It is after all not individual words that determine a particular attachment, but their interactions with the other words in the sentences containing them. A further, 'more controlled' simulation is then described; further more controlled simulation is then presented to provide more detailed analyses.

3. SIMULATION 1

The task was to take five-word sentences as input and compute correct structural interpretations (bracketing) as output. Two input sentences and their target bracketings are shown in Example 1. There were two major components in this task: (i) mapping the input words onto the output (the autoassociative task); and (ii) bracketing the output string (the structuring task) for either noun-phrase attachment (NPA) or verb-phrase attachment (VPA).

Example 1   A simplified bracketing for NP and VP attachments

John hit dog in market → (John (hit (dog in market)))
John hit woman with stick → (John (hit woman (with stick)))

Materials. The sentence materials were made up from 29 words, shown in Table 1, distributed in the categories NOUN1, VERB, NOUN2, PREPOSITION, NOUN3. This word set was used to generate all possible 1048 strings. These strings were subjected to a human normative study with the result that the corpus was reduced to 173 meaningful sentences for training the net (55 NPA and 118 VPA sentences). A further 16 sentences (8 NPA and 8 VPA) were reserved for testing generalisation.

For input and output, a simple localist representation was chosen for each word and bracket. To preserve the structure of the input and output strings, the vector frame method [2] was employed. In this method the input vectors were conceptually divided into five partitions representing slots in a sentence frame: NOUN1, VERB, NOUN2, PREPOSITION, NOUN3. The units in each partition represent the possible slot fillers[3]. Thus the five-word input

---

[2] See [16-17] for alternative discussions on the implementation of rules in connectionist nets.

[3] There are serious restrictions with this type of representation [1]; however, in the current context, it serves the useful purpose of making the input and output representations easier to analyse.

sentences[4] were encoded in an n dimensional binary input vector (the vector frame) such that five elements were set to +1 (one in each partition) and n-5 were set to 0. The output targets consisted of a vector representation of five words from the corresponding input sentence and 5 brackets. Only two different output bracketings were employed; one for noun-phrase attachments and one for verb-phrase attachments.

Table 1 The words used to generate the training samples.

Noun1	Verb	Noun2	Prep	Noun3
John	played	woman	by	stick
	made	music	with	child
	hit	dog	in	market
	saw	money	on	demand
				telescope
				ear
				mate
				subway
				stage
				anger
				night
				park
				radio
				fraud
				lottery
				room

Architecture and learning. The back propagation learning algorithm [18] was employed in a network architecture consisting of two weight layers and three layers of units (29-20-36) as shown in Fig 1. The required number of hidden units was determined, after some experimentation, to be twenty[5].

Results. With a learning rate of 0.1 and a momentum term of 0.5, both the autoassociative and structural components of the task were learned, for all 173 sentences in the training set, in 1730 training cycles.

After the learning was completed, generalisation was tested by presenting 16 novel test sentences to the net for a forward pass with no weight adjustments. The test set consisted of 8 pairs of novel sentences. These were chosen such that each sentence in a pair differed from its partner by only one word which flipped the attachments. Two pairs of sentences differed on VERB, two on NOUN2, two on PREPOSITION, and two on NOUN3.

---

[4]Extraneous elements such as articles were removed from the sentences. This word order was held constant to enable the learning algorithm to concentrate on the main task of separating the attachments without having to develop other syntactic constraints. Such cannonical representations could easily be produced by an initial phase.

[5]There is a newly published technique for dynamically reducing the number of hidden units to a minimum [19].

After each test sentence was presented, the states of the output vector were examined for the preferred attachment. Since novel examples produce weaker output signals, the acceptance criteria for a unit to adopt the +1 state was gradually reduced until a complete bracketed structure appeared in the output. The learned representations proved to be general enough to correctly bracket the input for 11 out of the 16 test sentences. This was reasonably powerful generalisation, given the difficulty of the novel test set and the small size of the experimental sample.

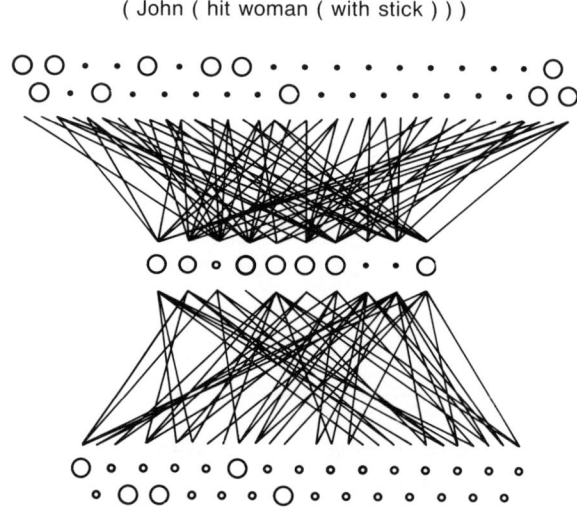

Fig. 1 The learned net with circles representing the units — their size indicates their current activity level. The lines between the circles represent weighted connections. The state of the net shows its activation after presentation of the sentence 'John hit woman with stick'.

4. ANALYSIS OF PREFERENCES

The first question to be addressed in this section is, what is the causal role of the individual words in the task of disambiguating the structures? Answering this question presents a potentially difficult problem, because the net only ever saw the words in complete sentences, and it was the complete sentences that were the patterns to be classified. So the problem amounts to finding a way to extricate the influence of individual words from the influence of the sentences that contain them.

One approach to this problem begins by examining the relationship between the upper and lower weights in the BP net. My argument is that the development of this relationship during learning implements a set of 'soft preferences' that take on the role of lexical preference rules in simulation 1. In this view, each word has, in a sense, a weighted preference that is used to 'vote' for one of the attachments. However, unlike standard preference rules, the strength of a word's vote may change according to the company it keeps, i.e. the other words in the sentence.

The importance of weight relationships may be clarified by briefly examining their development during learning. In the forward operation of the net, the input vector v is mapped onto the hidden unit vector h by the squash function $S: W_1 v \to h$ (where S is $1/1+e^{-x}$, and $x = W_1 v$). Then h is mapped onto the output vector o using the same squash function on the upper weight matrix: $S: W_2 h \to o$. Next, o is compared with the target vector t to determine its correctness. If $0 > t - o > 0$ then, in the backward operation, the error correction procedure adjusts the weights matrices W_1 and W_2 such that o is closer to t.

In order to understand how the preferences are implemented in the weights, it is instructive to note a geometric phenomenon frequently observed during the learning process. First, the upper weights, W_2, are adjusted so that the weight vectors for output units that want to be 'on' are moved closer to the current vector of hidden unit activations; and weight vectors for outputs that want to be 'off' are moved away from the current hidden unit vector. Second, the lower weights, W_1, are adjusted to push the vector of hidden unit activations even closer to the weights whose outputs should be 'on' and further away from weights whose outputs should be 'off'.

The upshot is that if an input unit should produce a '1' as output on unit A, and a '0' as output on unit B, then the projective weights for that input unit should be closer to the receptive weights of output unit A than to output unit B. This weight relationship amounts to what I shall call a 'soft preference rule'. That is, the input unit weights prefer output A and so moves closer to its weights.

Now the question is, does this analysis work for individual units (words) that are always employed as parts of larger patterns (sentences)? We can find out by examining the results from the autoassociation task in the simulation. Recall that any word that appears in the input sentence will always appear in the output. Thus, for a given word, the projective weights for its input unit should be closer to the receptive weights for its own output unit than to those of any other output units.

To support this latter point, the projective weights for the input units were plotted in the same weight space as the receptive weights for the output units. Then the squared Euclidean distance was computed from each input projective weight vector to each output receptive weight vector. An example of this analysis is given in Appendix 1 for the input word 'saw'. Input-saw is much closer to output-saw than to any other output word in the vocabulary list. This distance result was replicated across all input words with only one exception (input-made was slightly closer to output-ear (65.22) than to output-made (68.67) for which I presently have no explanation).

What the above analysis of the relationship between the upper and lower weights tells us is that the input words have a raw or static preference for producing themselves as output. This is not really surprising, but it enables us to take the next step in working out the preferences for the structuring task. First it should be noted that the structural interpretation is really carried by the positioning of the third bracket in the output. For verb-phrase attachment, the third bracket appears just before the preposition, e.g. (John (hit woman (with stick))); whereas for noun-phrase attachment, the third bracket appears just before the subject noun, e.g. (John (hit (dog in market))). We would expect these brackets to develop mutually exclusive receptive weight representations during learning. This is borne out by an examination of the weights developed in Simulation 1 as shown in Table 2. Each weight in the noun-phrase vector is approximately equal in magnitude, but in the opposite direction, to each weight in the verb-phrase vector.

To analyse the attachment preferences for each of the input words, their projective weight vectors were plotted in the same space as the receptive weight vectors of the attachment brackets (shown in Table 2). Then the squared Euclidean distance was computed between each of the projective vectors and the two receptive vectors (the results are shown in Appendix 2).

Table 2   The receptive weights for the brackets responsible for noun-phrase attachments (NPA) and verb-phrase attachments (VPA) — rounded to one decimal place. The integers across the top indicate the hidden unit numbers.

	1	2	3	4	5	6	7	8	9	10
NPA	+7.5	-3.7	-5.3	-2.2	-2.6	+5.6	-0.3	-2.9	-0.6	+2.9
VPA	-7.4	+3.7	+5.0	+2.1	+2.1	-5.8	+0.2	+2.8	+0.4	-2.9
	11	12	13	14	15	16	17	18	19	20
NPA	-1.0	+3.6	-1.6	-7.9	-1.8	-1.0	-4.3	+2.5	+1.3	+6.1
VPA	+0.7	-3.6	+1.3	+8.0	+1.4	+1.1	+4.3	-2.5	-1.3	-6.3

In this way, it is possible to tell whether a given input word preferred (was closer to) the noun-phrase or verb-phrase attachment bracketing. The distribution of preferences across word classes is given in Table 3.

Table 3 Distribution of the attachment preferences across the various word classes used in Simulation 1.

Class	NPA	VPA
VERBS	2	2
NOUN1	2	2
PREPS	2	2
NOUN3	9	7

Despite a heavy bias in the training set (118 VPA versus 55 NPA sentences), the word preferences were fairly equally divided between the two attachment classes with NPA = 15, and VPA = 13. Thus the net appears to compensate for the unbalanced training set. However it should be noted that the numbers in Table 2 do not represent absolute preferences. The projective weights for some words may be very close to the receptive weights for one of the brackets and far from the other. For example, from Appendix 2, it can be seen that the weights for the word 'saw' are much closer to the NPA bracket (15.23) than they are to the VPA bracket (20.71). In contrast, some words, such as 'money' may be almost the same distance from the NPA bracket (18.28) and the VPA bracket (18.09) with a slight bias towards VPA. Obviously, some means must be developed for indicating the strength of a word's preference. As a first step, we define *the raw preference value* (RPV) of a word as difference between the Euclidean distances, d, between the two brackets, i.e. RPV = $d_{NPA} - d_{VPA}$. Using this calculation, the RPV for 'saw' is 5.48_n and the RPV for 'money' is 0.19_v. These values clearly reflect the relative static biases of the two words. The RPV for all the words used here are given in Appendix 2.

The reason why some words exhibit weak preferences is because during learning they may be combined with other words which already have strong preferences in the target direction. Consequently, there may be only a very small change in the weights, and, as a result, weak or uncommitted words would have little or no room to acquire strong preferences. For example, the word 'money' appears more than twice as often in VPA sentences (39 times) than it does in NPA sentences (18 times) and yet it has only a very small VPA preference (RPV = 0.19_v). This is because out of its 53 appearances it occurs as the subject of the strongly NPA verb 'saw' ($RPV_{saw} = 5.48_n$) twenty-three times, and as subject of the strongly VPA verb 'money' ($RPV_{made} = 5.05_v$) thirty-two times. Thus 'made' had no room to develop strong preferences.

In the main, these raw preferences work very well. It is possible to estimate the particular attachment of a sentence simply by summing the values for the noun preferences and subtracting them from the sum of the verb preferences. If the sum is positive, the sentence is VPA, and if it is negative, the sentence is NPA. Surprisingly, this provides the correct answer for a large proportion of the training sample and exhibits as good generalisation properties as the net itself. However, like any static preferences, it fails because it is not sensitive to contextual change. Such a failure is shown in Example 2.

Example 2   Using RPVs for sentences.

$(.66_v)$ (5.48_n) (0.19_v) (0.86_v) (1.76_n)
S1: John   saw   money   on   telescope

Total $RVP_{s1} = 5.53_n$ – correct NPA

$(.66_v)$ (5.48_n) $0.19_v)$ (3.41_v) (1.76_n)
S2: John   saw   money   with   telescope

Total $RVP_{s2} = 2.98_n$ – incorrect NPA (should be VPA)

The two sentences in the example differ only on the prepositions 'on' and 'with'. The preposition 'with' should change the role of 'telescope' to be the instrument of the seeing rather than the surface on which the money sits. Although the RPV_{with} has a relative strong VPA value, it is not strong enough to overpower the RPV_{saw} which keeps the sentence as an NPA. If the sentence had been 'John saw money in night', then 'night' would overpower 'saw' and the sentence would be VPA. However, to be flexible enough, the system needs a dynamic way in which to assign preferences. This facility is already built into the operation of the net as we shall now see.

4.1   Dynamic preference values

In order to see how the attachment preference of a word modulates according to context, it is necessary to examine the function that maps the input states onto the hidden units. The function used in the simulation was the non-linear (but monotonic) sigmoidal function: $1/1 + e^{-x}$, where $x = \Sigma w_{ij}a_i$ + bias, w_{ij} is the weight from the ith input unit to the jth hidden unit, and a_i is the activation state of the ith input unit. Now, if the activation value of a hidden unit was determined by a linear combination of the binary input activation, then we could say that the preference value of an input unit in the +1 state was simply the value of the weight from it to the hidden unit. However, because the combination is non-linear we must use a less direct method to compute the preferred attachment of a word in a sentence.

Let f be the sigmoid function, x is a vector of the weighted sums of the input activations and biases for a sentence S, and x' is a vector of the weighted sums of the input activations and biases of $S-k$, i.e. the input sentence S with the kth word deleted. Then the dynamic preference value, n, of unit k to the hidden unit vector is given by:

$$v^k = f(x) - f(x')$$

We are now in a position to understand how sentence contexts affect the magnitude of a word's preference vote. To simplify matters, we shall examine a net with only one hidden unit, and with the weighted value of the kth input unit held constant at 0.5 A graph of the inputs and corresponding outputs of the hidden unit is shown in Fig. 2. To find out how the magnitude of x' affects v^k, an arbitrary point on the horizontal axis of the graph in Fig. 2 is chosen for x', the horizontal co-ordinate for x is then $x' + 0.5$. The vertical axis gives us $f(x)$ and $f(x')$. Note that the steepest increase from $f(x')$ to $f(x)$, and hence the largest value of v^k, is when $x' = 0$. The size of v^k diminishes progressively on both sides of zero.

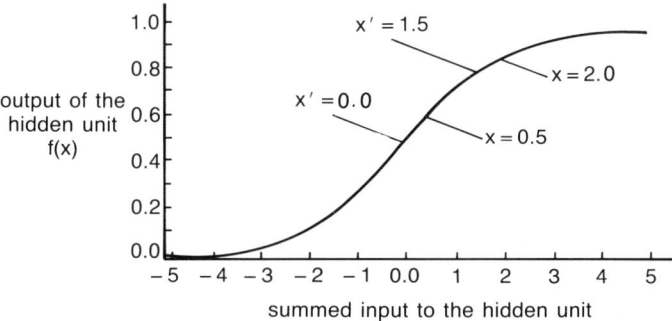

Fig. 2 A plot of the inputs and outputs to a hidden unit.

Now that we have seen how dynamic preferences operate, we shall return to examine the sentences in Example 2 in the previous section (S1: John saw money *on* telescope. S2: John saw money *with* telescope.) It was noted earlier that the raw preference values were defeated by their inflexibility for these sentences. The problem was that the word 'saw' had a very strong RPV which could not be overpowered by the change in prepositions. We now show how the dynamic preferences for the word 'saw' are modulated by the change in prepositions (see Example 2). For illustration, we shall use hidden unit 1. As can be seen in Table 2, hidden unit 1 has the largest positive weight to the NPA bracket and the largest negative weight to the VPA bracket. Thus it has a potentially large say in biasing the attachment towards NPA.

For sentence S1 (Example 2), the preference strength for 'saw' on hidden unit 1 is $v^{saw} = f(3.49) - f(1.88) = 0.10$; and for sentence S2, it is $v^{saw} = f(4.61) - f(3.00) = 0.04$. These figures show a 60% reduction in the preference strength of 'saw' from S1 to S2. Using such contextual modulation on all of the hidden units, the net computes the correct alternative output bracketing for both of the sentences even though they were not part of the training set. It is the ability to modulate the preference value of the input words that gives the net its ability on the structural disambiguation tasks.

5. SIMULATION 2

One problem with the analysis in the previous simulation was that the structural ambiguity task was made up of two components — autoassociation, and structure assignment. The autoassociative component, to some extent, masked the contributions of the individual words to the structure assignment. For example, it was not possible to get a clear picture, using cluster analysis, of the division of the sentences or words for the structuring task. Since the overall analyses were concerned mainly with structure assignment, we next ran a more tightly controlled simulation which was designed to isolate and control the variables responsible for structure assignment. Thus simulation 2 was simplified by reducing the output to two units; one representing the VPA bracketing, and the other representing the NPA bracketing.

Materials. The sentence materials were taken directly from the previous simulation. Sixty-three of the 118 VPA sentences were randomly selected and removed from the sample so that there was an even distribution of VPA and NPA strings (55 of each). All 29 of the words from the previous simulation were used here. The ordering of the sentences was randomised once before learning began.

Architecture and learning. The back propagation learning algorithm was again employed in a network architecture consisting of two weight layers and three layers of units (29-6-2). The required number of hidden units was determined, after some experimentation, to be six (this is because the autoassociation requires proportionally large numbers of hidden units).

5.1 Results and discussion

With a learning rate of 0.2 the tasks were learned, for all 110 sentences in the training set, in 740 training cycles. The resulting weight matrices and hidden unit activations for each sentences were submitted to further analyses

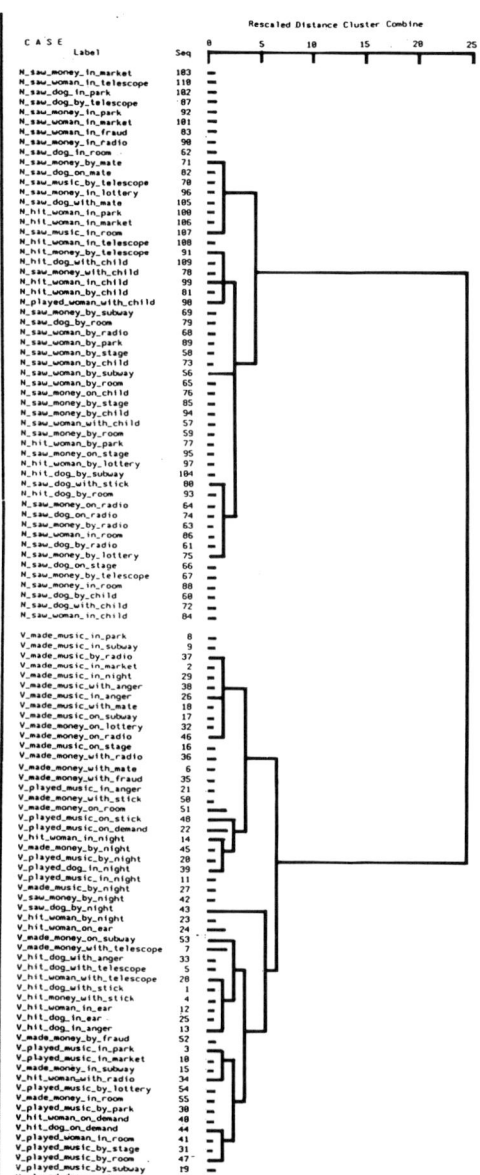

Fig. 3 Dendogram of hierarchical cluster analysis of the 110 sentences. Note the clear divisions between NPA and VPA sentences. All the sentences have had their subjects replaced by an N or a V. This letter indicates whether the sentence has an NP attachment or a VP attachment.

to examine how the representations cluster in weight space and hidden unit space as well as to extract the raw preference values.

For the analysis of the sentence representations, each sentence was presented, in turn, to the learned net and its vector of hidden unit activations was recorded. The 110 vectors of hidden unit activations were then subjected to a hierarchical cluster analysis (Ward method). A dendogram of the results is shown in Fig. 3. Two major clusters are shown in the dendogram which correspond exactly to the 55 NPA sentences in cluster 1, and the 55 VPA sentences in cluster 2. This shows that the hidden unit activation for the two attachment classes were separated by a hyperplane during learning.

The RPV for each word was collected as described in Simulation 1. The values are shown in Table 4. These RPVs divide the input words into 18 NPA biases and 11 VPA biases.

Table 4 A classification of the 29 input words according to their RPVs. The RPV for each word is shown adjacent to it.

NPA		VPA	
John	0.18n	played	3.62v
hit	1.21n	made	4.96v
saw	9.14n	music	3.59v
woman	1.96n	with	5.22v
dog	1.31n	on	2.53v
money	1.02n	demand	2.40v
by	3.18n	ear	5.02v
in	0.08n	anger	4.15v
stick	0.95n	night	10.43v
child	12.32n	radio	0.27v
market	3.35n	fraud	1.21v
telescope	1.51n		
mate	1.55n		
subway	1.52n		
stage	1.06n		
park	2.78n		
lottery	1.84n		
room	0.38n		

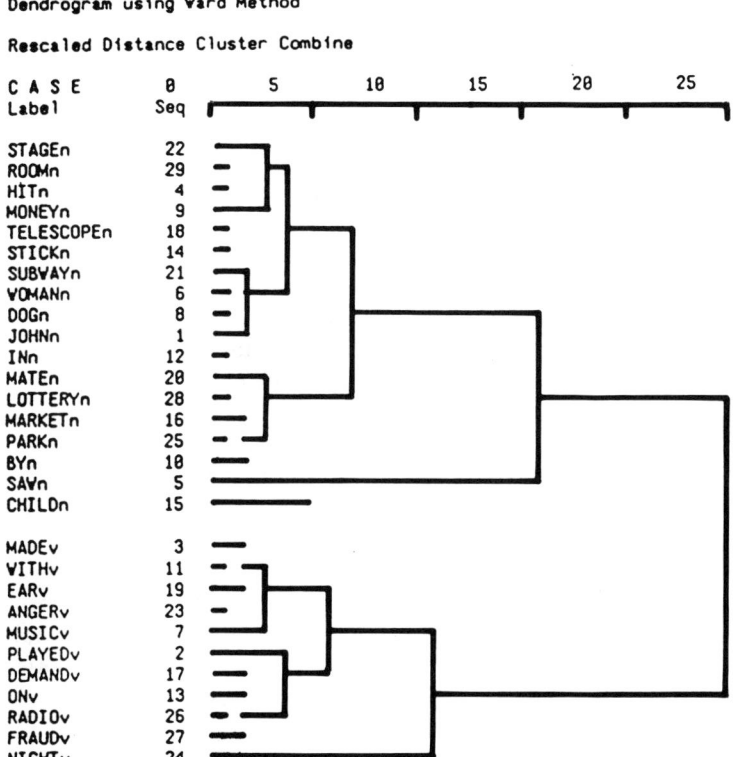

Fig. 4 Dendogram of the projective input weights for each word. The subscripts 'n' or 'v' indicate whether the raw preference bias is NPA or VPA.

The projective weight vector for each input word was collected, and these were subjected to a hierarchical cluster analysis as shown in Fig. 4. The dendogram in Fig. 4 divides neatly into two major clusters. The first cluster contains 18 weight vectors corresponding exactly to the 18 words whose RPVs were biased towards NPA. And the second cluster contains 11 vectors corresponding exactly to the 11 words whose RPVs were biased towards VPA.

6. CONCLUSIONS

The simulations presented here demonstrate how a standard BP net may be trained to perform a structural disambiguation task and how it learns to generalise to novel examples. Even though the net was trained on whole sentences it was shown that it implemented raw preferences, for each word, in the relationship between the upper and lower weights during learning. The analysis of how the raw preferences were implemented was used to assign an RPV to words that indicates the strength of their structural bias. The addition of RPVs for the the words in a sentence, turned out to produce a reasonable estimate for the correct structural assignment of a sentence. However, for many cases, like those in Example 2, the rigidity of the raw preferences prevented correct assignment.

This rigidity is overcome in the normal operation of the net, by the nature of the activation function. We showed how the activation function utilises the raw preferences in a way that is sensitive to sentence context; minor word changes in a sentence can lead to dramatic changes in the preference strength of a word. This is just the type of flexibility that is required from lexical preference rules if they are to structurally disambiguate a large variety of sentences.

Simulation 2 was designed to isolate and control factors responsible for the structural assignments in Simulation 1. First, sentences were pruned so that there were an equal number of NPA and VPA sentences. Second, the output was reduced to two units, one for each of the attachments. A hierarchical cluster analysis revealed a hyperplane that divided the hidden unit activations for the sentences into the two attachment classes. In addition, a cluster analysis of the individual projective weight vectors for the input words yielded two main clusters that correspond directly to the RPV assignments. These analyses show converging evidence for the utility of raw preference values.

Finally, the question of the compositionality of uniquely connectionist representations can be addressed in terms of the preference analysis. Imagine that a sentence is input to the disambiguation net. The active weights corresponding to each word in the input, may be thought of as a context-invariant representation of each word (though it may change slowly over time with long-term learning). These active weight representation are then composed as hidden unit activations using the sigmoid composing function described in the discussion of Simulation 1. Because of the non-linearities in this composing function, the mode of combination is context-sensitive and non-concatenative. Moreover, the simulations reported here meet van Gelder's [11] criteria for functional compositionality. That is, the simulations demonstrated general, effective and reliable processes for (a) producing an expression given its constituents, and (b) decomposing the expression back into those constituents. In addition, the compact representations on the hidden units exhibited structure sensitivity as shown in the output mapping of Simulation 1 and in the cluster analyses of Simulation 2.

This work is only a preliminary investigation of the idea of a net containing soft preference rules. So far the idea seems like a promising one for making a start on training the preference rules required for a wider range of structural and semantic tasks.

APPENDIX 1

The squared Euclidean distance between the projective weight vector for the input word 'saw' and the receptive weight vectors for all of the output words in Simulation 1.

OUTPUT WORDS	Squared Euclidean (rounded)
played	199
made	220
hit	210
saw	62 *****
woman	161
music	180
dog	157
money	166
by	169
with	171
in	166
on	140
stick	132
child	149
market	147
demand	149
telescope	128
ear	136
mate	136
subway	145
stage	131
anger	206
night	152
park	129
radio	128
fraud	122
lottery	131
room	180

APPENDIX 2

The squared Euclidean distance between the projective weight vector for each of the input words and the receptive weight vectors for the NPA and VPA brackets.

INPUT WORDS   Euclidean d

	NPA	VPA	RPV
John	17.83	17.17	0.66v
played	19.6	16.4	3.10v
made	20.35	15.3	5.05v
hit	17.09	19.31	2.23n
saw	15.23	20.71	5.48n
woman	17.61	18.65	1.05n
music	19.16	17.12	2.04v
dog	17.83	18.71	0.88n
money	18.28	18.09	0.19v
by	17.32	19.34	2.02n
with	19.72	16.31	3.41v
in	17.86	18.49	0.63n
on	18.41	17.55	0.86v
stick	17.26	19.36	2.10n
child	13.89	22.47	8.58n
market	19.18	18.19	0.99v
demand	21.79	14.83	6.96v
telescope	17.35	19.10	1.76n
ear	20.12	16.00	4.12v
mate	16.88	19.42	2.53n
subway	19.08	17.83	1.25v
stage	17.26	19.36	2.10n
anger	20.10	16.22	3.88v
night	22.00	14.76	7.24v
park	19.54	18.38	1.16v
radio	17.61	19.26	1.65n
fraud	17.66	19.16	1.49n
lottery	16.73	19.82	3.09n
room	18.38	18.89	0.51n

REFERENCES

1. Sharkey, N E: Connectionist representation techniques, AI Review (in press).

2. Hinton G E: 'Implementing semantic networks in parallel hardware'. In G E Hinton & J A Anderson (eds) Parallel Models of Associative Memory. Hillsdale, NJ:Lawrence Erlbaum (1981).

3. Hinton G E, McClelland J L & Rumelhart D E: 'Distributed representations', in Rumelhart D E & McClelland D E (eds) Parallel Distributed Processing, $\underline{1}$, pp 77—109, MIT Press Cambridge, MA (1986).

4. Touretzky D S & Hinton G E: 'A distributed connectionist production system', Cognitive Science, $\underline{12}$, (3), pp 423—466 (1988).

5. Touretzky D S & Geva G E: 'A distributed connectionist representation for concept structures', Proceedings of the Ninth Annual Conference of the Cognitive Science Society, pp 155—164 (1987).

6. Willshaw D J & von der Malsburg C: 'A marker induction mechanism for the establishment of ordered neural mapping; its application to the retinotectal connections', in Philos. Trans. Roy. Soc. Lond. B, $\underline{287}$, pp 203—243 (1979).

7. Cottrell G W, Munro P & Zipser D: 'Image compression by backpropagation: an example of extensional programming', in Sharkey N E (ed) 'Models of Cognition, A review of Cognitive Science', pp 208—240, Norwood N J (1989).

8. Kawamoto A H & McClelland J L: 'Mechanisms of sentence processing: assignment roles to constituents', in McClelland J L & Rumelhart D E (eds) Parallel Distributed Processing, $\underline{2}$, pp 272—326, MIT Press Cambridge MA. (1986)

9. Kohonen T: 'Clustering, taxonomy and topological map patterns', in Lang M (ed), Proceedings of the Sixth International Conference on Pattern Recognition, Silver Spring MD (1982).

10. Fodor J A & Pylyshyn Z W: 'Connectionism and cognitive architecture: a critical analysis', Cognition, $\underline{28}$, pp 2—71 (1988).

11. van Gelder T: 'Compositionality: a connectionist variation on a classical theme', Cognitive Science, $\underline{14}$, pp 355—384 (1990).

12. Kimball J: 'Seven principles of surface structure parsing in natural language'. Cognition $\underline{2}$ (1973).

13. Frazier L & Fodor J D: 'The sausage machine. A new two-stage parsing model'. Cognition $\underline{6}$ (1978).

14. Ford M, Bresnan J W & Kaplan R M: 'A competence based theory of syntactic closure'. In Bresnan J W, The mental representation of grammatical relations, Cambridge, MA:MIT Press (1982).

15. Wilks Y, Huang X & Fass D: 'Syntax, preference and right attachment'. Proceedings of IJCAI (1985).

16. McMillan C & Smolensky P: 'Analyzing a connectionist model as a system of soft rules'. Technical Report CU-CS-393-88, University of Colorado, Boulder (1988).

17. Hanson S J & Burr D J: 'What connectionist models learn: learning and representation in connectionist networks'. Behavioural and Brain Sciences, New York:CUP (in press).

18. Rumelhart D E, Hinton G E & Williams R J: 'Learning internal representations by error propagation'. In D E Rumelhart & J L McClelland (Eds), Parallel Distributed Processing, $\underline{1}$, Cambridge, MA:MIT Press (1986).

19. Mozer M C & Smolensky P: 'Using relevance to reduce network size automatically'. Connection Science $\underline{1}$ Pt 1 (1989).

13

APPLICATIONS OF MULTILAYER PERCEPTRONS IN TEXT-TO-SPEECH SYNTHESIS SYSTEMS

W A Ainsworth and N P Warren
Department of Communication and Neuroscience
University of Keele and BT Laboratories

1. INTRODUCTION

Previous work has demonstrated that MLPs may be used in a text-to-speech context, for example in the transcription of orthographic text to a phonemic representation. Here we report on a number of applications of MLPs; for the latter purpose, and for tasks useful in other areas of text-to-speech synthesis. In most of these we have been concerned with improving performance — by varying parameters or making structural alterations to the basic regime. As we show below, some of the techniques we have developed result in better scores.

Firstly, we describe some basic experiments using MLPs to translate orthography to a phonemic representation, varying the number of hidden units and monitoring the effect on performance. Then we describe the effects of a variety of input/output coding schemes on performance. Next we see the effect of dividing the input set into regularly and irregularly pronounced words, training separate MLPs to pronounce each set. Then we show that results can be improved by exploiting the structure of both the input and output spaces: the input space, by preprocessing words with respect to their morphology; the output space by arranging two MLPs in series, the first of which adds syllable boundary information to the input of the next. Then we report on a small MLP trained to pronounce clock times such as would occur in free text. Finally we describe an MLP which predicts the syntactic categories of isolated words, this information being useful in a broader text-to-speech context.

In all cases the MLPs we have used are of the type described by McClelland and Rumelhart [1], that is feed-forward with error back-propagation, bringing about gradient descent to a local minimum in the error space; we suggest that readers unfamiliar with this architecture refer thereto.

Various parameters can be altered to control the rate of gradient descent and the smoothness of the descent; these terms are commonly referred to as the learning rate and the momentum, respectively (see [2]). In all the experiments below, the momentum term was fixed at 0.9. In the experiments of Sections 2 and 4, the learning rate used was 0.01, but in other sections it was fixed at 0.1. This change will be explained in due course (Section 5). One other parameter, the size of the initial starting weights, was fixed within the range $[-0.5, 0.5]$.

2. TEXT TO PHONEME WITH A LARGE DICTIONARY

2.1 Introduction

Most text-to-speech systems use a set of context-sensitive rules to produce phoneme strings from grapheme strings. However, previous work using back-propagation MLPs for text to phoneme transcription was pioneered by Sejnowski and Rosenberg [3] for American English and adapted for British English by McCulloch et al [4].

2.2 Experimental details

The MLP specification was based on Netspeak, developed by McCulloch et al [4]. Seven letters were presented at the input layer of the MLP. The task is to produce a vector corresponding to the phoneme associated with the central letter of the input; the other letters can be thought of as a context. The input code was 11 bits per letter, 2 of which are set to one, the rest being zero. The first five bits of the code denote the five groups into which the letters have been split, according to likely pronunciation; the last six bits denote which element that letter is within the group. The output code had 19 bits, each corresponding to a feature which may or may not be present in the articulation of the phoneme (e.g. voiced, bilabial). Thus an output bit will be set to one if that feature is present, zero otherwise. The rationale behind these schemes is given a fuller examination in Section 3.

A dictionary of about 73 000 words was used, together with their aligned phonemic transcriptions. The alignment algorithm employed was based on that proposed by Lawrence and Kaye [5]. The dictionary was divided into 68 sections, each of which contained 10 000 characters. As the order of words in a training sequence may be important, the dictionary was sampled at random in order to produce these sections. In the cases below, MLPs were trained on 67 sections and tested on the last section. Performance was assessed using a best-guess criterion, in which the output of the MLP is deemed to be the closest valid phoneme vector to the real-valued output, by Euclidean distance.

2.3 Results

A typical learning curve for an MLP with one hidden layer of 77 units is shown in Fig. 1. It can be seen that as the system was trained on more dictionary sections the percentage of phonemes in the test set correctly transcribed gradually increased, but reached an asymptote in the 60 to 67 section region.

The results for networks varying in hidden units is shown in Fig. 2. All these MLPs have been trained over the complete set of 67 sections. It can be seen that with no hidden units 68.5% of the phonemes were correctly transcribed. With a single hidden layer the score increased from 76.1% with 10 hidden units to 87.1% with 90. With two hidden layers scores were comparable with MLPs having one hidden layer and the same total number of units.

The scores on the test section were found to be very similar to those on any training section, indicating good generalization. It is worth noting that there is no tendency to overlearn, that is to maximize score on the training set to the detriment of scores on unseen test data. This may be due to the use of such a large amount of training data.

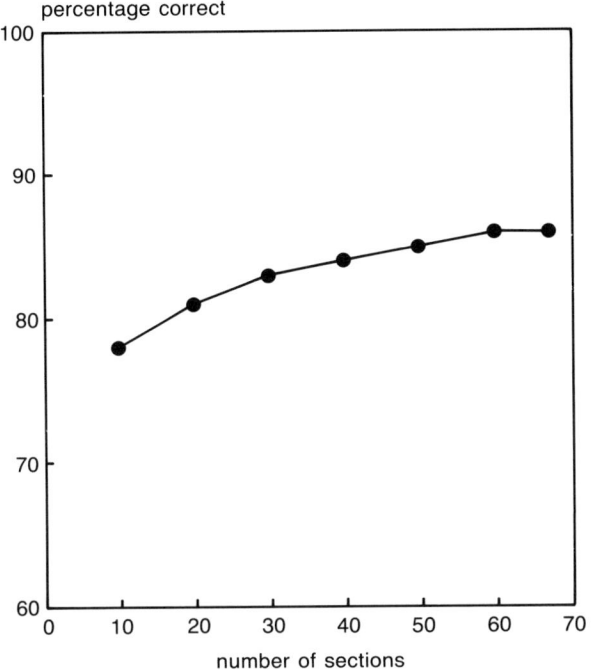

Fig. 1 A typical learning curve for the text to phoneme task.

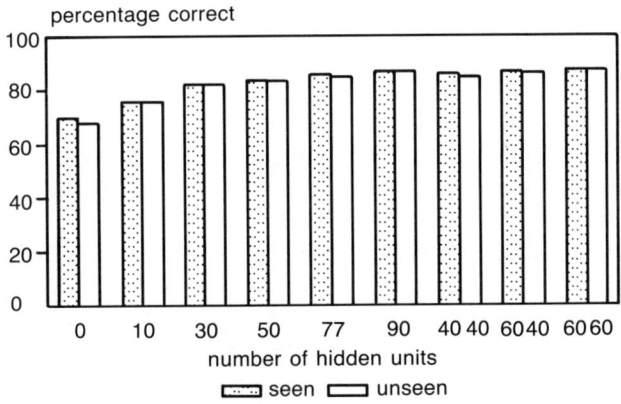

Fig. 2 Scores after training on 67 sections, for various numbers of hidden units. For each MLP the first bar shows performance on a section seen during training, the second bar performance for unseen data.

3. INPUT/OUTPUT CODING SCHEMES

The experiments described in Section 2 (above) used an 11 bits-per-letter input code and a 19-bit phoneme output code. These codes were designed to highlight features of the input and output sets thought to be relevant to the transcription task. If this is the case, then we would expect a drop in MLP performance when unsystematic codes are employed. Indeed, it has been suggested [6] that MLPs only perform the transcription task adequately because of the information they are given implicitly within the coding scheme. It is therefore of interest to systematically compare these schemes.

For a set of n characters, the minimum number of bits required to uniquely encode elements of that set is m, where m is the smallest integer such that $2^m >= n$. Conversely, the largest number of bits with which one would feasibly be prepared to code the set is n; in this case each code could contain 1 one and $(n-1)$ zeroes. Between these two extremes there are countless other ways in which to encode a set.

In these experiments a learning-rate of 0.1 was used.

3.1 Coding schemes used

3.1.1 Input — Letters

Five input coding schemes have been considered: a brief description of each is given below. At the end of each paragraph a Code-Key is given, for use with reference to Table 1, which gives the combinations of input/output schemes compared here.

- Maximally dense: the input set contains 28 characters — 26 letters, a space, and a catch-all character for miscellaneous punctuation marks. Since $2^5 = 32$, this set can be uniquely encoded using 5 bits. 5-bit codes were randomly assigned to characters of the set. (Code-Key: 5)

- Maximally sparse: this scheme uses 27 bits per letter — each letter-code contains 1 one and 26 zeroes. One vector is used for a space + punctuation character, the other 26 for the letters. This scheme is equivalent to that used by Sejnowski and Rosenberg [3]. Note that because of the computational expense involved in using such a sparse code, the context window for the input was reduced from seven to three letters under this scheme. (Code-Key: 27)

- 2-from-11, grouped by sound category: this scheme is that used in Section 2 (above). The first five bits of the code, of which 1 is set to one, indicate to which group the letter belongs; the last six bits, of which 1 is also set to one, identify individual letters within that group. Letters are grouped according to the most frequent sound category to which they will be transcribed, e.g. {A,E,I,O,U} — vowels. (Code-Key: 11)

- 2-from-11, grouped alphabetically: this scheme takes the same vectors as used in (c) above, but groups the letters alphabetically. From a phonemic point of view, this grouping is arbitrary. (Code-Key: 11*)

- Variable: this code exploits the fact that letters closer to the centre of the context window contain more information about the pronunciation of the central letter than do those letters at the edges. Here, code-length decreases with distance from the centre of the window, thus: 7-10-13-13-13-10-7. Furthermore letter-codes are chosen to maximize hamming distance between letters whose confusion cost is high. Fuller details are given in [7]. (Code-Key: V)

3.1.2 Output — Phonemes

Four phoneme coding schemes have been considered:

- Maximally dense: since the phoneme set contains 49 elements, at least 6 bits are necessary to uniquely identify these elements. Of the 64 possible 6-bit vectors, 49 were arbitrarily assigned to one phoneme each. (Code-Key: 6)

- Maximally sparse: each phoneme is represented by a 49-bit code, of which 1 bit is set to one and the other 48 are set to zero. (Code-Key: 49)

- n-from-19, by articulatory features: this scheme is that used in Section 2 (above). Each bit represents an articulatory feature which may be present or absent when the phoneme is pronounced. Examples are voiced, bilabial, nasal. (Code-Key: 19)

- n-from-19, assigned randomly: the codes from (c) above were assigned to phonemes randomly. Thus each bit can no longer be taken to represent a feature. (Code-Key: 19*)

3.1.3 Input/output combinations

Table 1 shows the nine input/output code combinations that we have compared.

Table 1 Nine input/output code combinations, identified by Code-Keys.

Experiment No:	1	2	3	4	5	6	7	8	9
I/O Code-Keys:	11/19	11*/19	5/19	5/6	V/19	27/19	5/49	11/19*	11*/19*

3.2 Results

We compare these schemes in two ways: firstly, by the shape of a typical learning curve, and secondly by t-testing the mean scores, measured over three training runs, initialized at different points in the weight space.

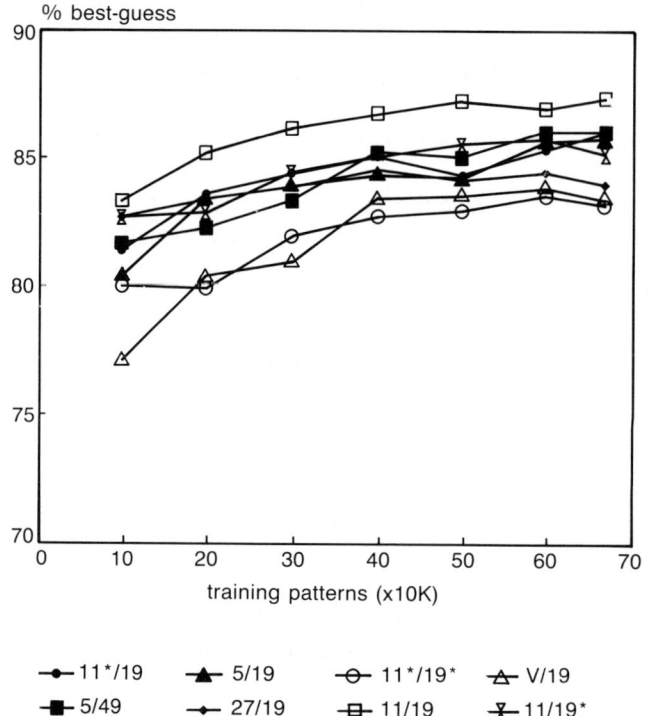

Fig. 3 Learning curves for eight different I/O schemes. The curves are identified by I/O code-keys.

3.2.1 Learning curves

Figure 3 shows the learning curves for eight of the nine different I/O schemes. We do not show the learning curve for the 5/6 combination, which performed worst of the nine schemes. Performance has been evaluated after every 10 sections of training material.

As can be seen, in most cases those MLPs which reach the higher final scores also score higher earlier in training. One might also note that the higher performance curves tend to be smoother. There does not seem to be any notable difference in the gradients of these curves.

In Table 2, we show final scores after training on all 67 sections, of all nine MLPs. Three runs have been started at different, random points in the weight-space. Note that the number of hidden units for each regime has been adjusted so that the total number of weights is approximately constant in all experiments. Thus we can be confident that the final scores are a measure of the efficiency of the I/O coding combination.

Table 2 Performance over three runs for nine I/O combinations. This also shows the MLP specifications
(Input-Hidden-Output) and total number of weights.

MLP Spec	Exp No	#WTS	I/O Keys	Score		
				Run 1	Run 2	Run 3
77-50-19	1	4869	11/19	85.7%	87.4%	86.4%
77-50-19	2	4869	11*/19	85.1%	86.0%	86.3%
35-88-19	3	4859	5/19	85.4%	85.8%	86.2%
35-116-6	4	4878	5/6	81.1%	82.4%	83.0%
73-52-19	5	4855	V/19	82.4%	83.4%	83.8%
81-48-19	6	4867	27/19	84.5%	84.0%	84.2%
35-57-49	7	4894	5/49	86.3%	86.1%	86.3%
77-50-19	8	4869	11/19*	85.4%	85.2%	84.5%
77-50-19	9	4869	11*/19*	83.2%	82.1%	83.3%

The means of these distributions have been t-tested to see whether they are significantly different. Rather than present the complete results of these tests, we give a brief summary below.

MLP performance can be divided into three groups: schemes 11/19, 11*/19, 5/19 and 5/49 perform better than the others; their performance is significantly different at the 99% confidence level. The schemes that perform worst are 5/6, V/19 and 11*/19*. Of these 5/6 is worse than the other two, at the 95% confidence level. Schemes 27/19 and 11/19* fall between these two groups.

These results can be interpreted as showing that, in general, sparse codes perform better in the text-to-phoneme task. The poorer performance of the sparse 27/19 input code could be explained by the restriction of the context window to just three letters.

Interestingly, there is no difference found between the 11/19 and 11*/19 codes, implying that the method of grouping letters according to their expected pronunciation is not significant over and above the general sparsity of the code. Performance does drop when an arbitrary rearrangement of the n-from-19 output code is used in combination with the 2-from-11 input code: this effect is more pronounced when arbitrary codes are used at both input and output. We would suggest that for this task more care is needed in choosing an output code than an input code.

Furthermore, the absolute difference in performance between the best and worst schemes is not as great as might have been expected; we suggest that where possible, sparser codes should be used, but the choice of code is not so critical. Further, no codes that we have tried lead to a drastic increase in the gradient of the learning curve.

4. REGULAR AND IRREGULAR WORDS

4.1 Introduction

Some words are pronounced regularly and some are not. It might be expected that an MLP would perform better with regularly pronounced words than with irregular ones, as the former can be pronounced according to rules. Moreover it may be able to do this with less hidden units.

A difficulty arises in deciding which words are pronounced regularly. One might think that there was a connection between regularity of pronunciation and frequency of use, that is: less common words are more regular in their pronunciation, and common words are less regular. McCulloch et al [4] chose to train separate MLPs on common and less common words. They found that, contrary to expectations, the MLP trained on common words performed the better of the two. They attributed this to a lack of unique phonemic information in the set of common words, leading to rote learning: they discovered poor generalization, in terms of perfect matches, when tested on the set of less common words. Furthermore, Ainsworth and Pell [8] found no evidence that a rule-based system's performance was linked to frequency of use, though they noted that rarer words, perhaps being longer, presented more opportunities for rules to fail.

Thus we have used the following method to divide the dictionary: first, a set of pronunciation rules was devised; then we define those words whose correct pronunciation is generated by the rules as being regular, and the rest as being irregular (see [9]).

A context-sensitive rule-based system [10] was adapted for this purpose. The system consisted of a set of rules of the form

$$(A)\ B\ (C) \rightarrow D$$

This states that a letter string 'B' preceded by the string 'A' and followed by the string 'C' is transcribed to the symbol 'D', for example:

(_) ou (se) → /aʊ/ ('grouse')
(j) ou (r) → /3/ ('journey')

This rule-based system was used to transcribe the dictionary. It performed about 8% worse than the best MLP of Section 2. It was used to split the dictionary in two: an irregular and a regular dictionary. The former contained 56 428 words and the latter contained 16 631 words.

4.2 Experimental details

These new dictionaries were divided into sections containing 10 000 characters. The regular dictionary produced 13 full-size sections and a shorter one, the irregular dictionary produced 53 full-size sections and a shorter one.

Two three-layer MLPs were set up: one to be trained with the regular dictionary and the other to be trained with the irregular one. In order to be able to make comparisons with the performance of the single MLP system of Section 2 it was decided to make the combined number of hidden units in both MLPs equal to 90. This was the largest single MLP employed and gave the best performance.

4.3 Results

In the first experiment each MLP had 45 hidden units. As training progressed MLP performance increased: the MLP trained on the regular dictionary scored 95.9% and the MLP trained on the irregular dictionary scored 83.6%. MLPs appear to perform better with regularly pronounced words. It seemed likely that the MLP trained on the irregular dictionary would require more capacity than the MLP trained on the regular one, so it was decided to change the distribution of the hidden units: two new MLPs were formed, one with 20 hidden units and one with 70 hidden units. The 20 hidden unit MLP was trained on the regular dictionary, giving a final score of 91.8%, and the 70 hidden unit MLP was trained on the irregular dictionary, scoring 85.6%. The learning curves of the four MLPs are shown in Fig. 4.

The two pairs of MLPs were then joined together to produce two 3-layer MLPs, each having 77 input units, 90 hidden units and 19 output units. Connecting the input units to the hidden units is straightforward, but connecting the hidden units to the output results in two biases for each output unit. These values were added together to produce an MLP of standard architecture. This was the technique used by McCulloch et al [4] to combine the common/less common MLPs mentioned above (Section 4.1).

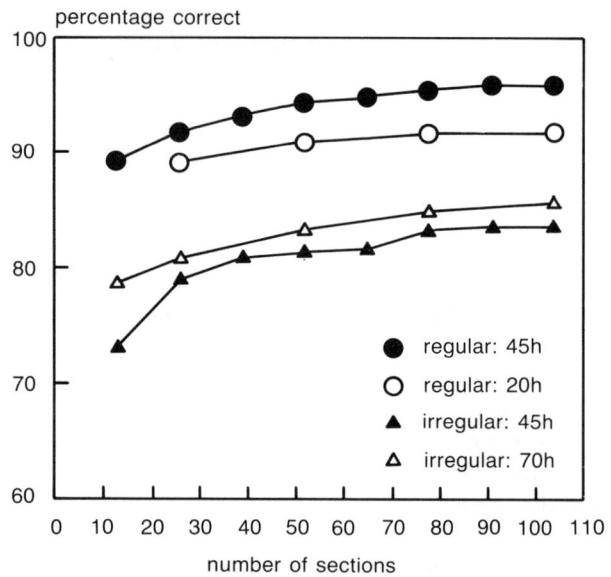

Fig. 4 Learning curves for MLPs trained on regular and irregular words, with different numbers of hidden units.

The combined 45 + 45 MLP had an initial score of 82.5%. It was trained further, with sections of the original dictionary. After a complete pass of all 67 sections the score increased to 87.5%. This is only slightly higher than the score with a similar sized MLP trained only on the original dictionary (87.0%). The combined 20 + 70 MLP, similarly retrained, produced a final score of 88.1%, though its best performance was 88.5%, after training on 60 sections. The learning curves of both these MLPs are shown in Fig. 5.

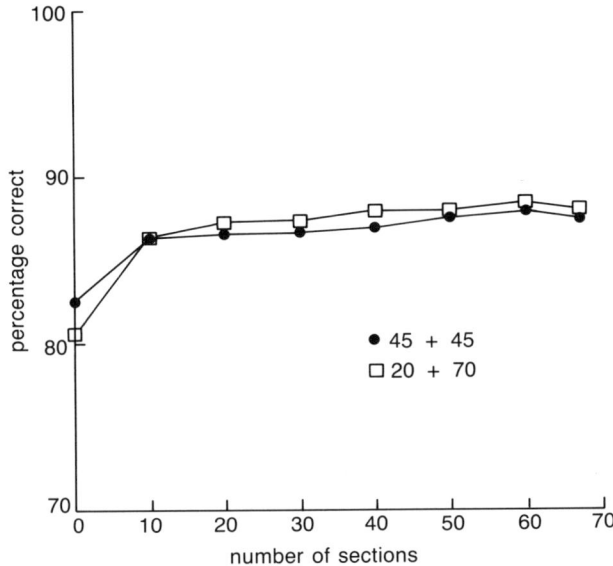

Fig. 5 Learning curves for combined regular/irregular MLPs, for two different distributions of the 90 hidden units.

4.4 Discussion

Using a rule-based system to construct regular and irregular dictionaries resulted in better performance for an MLP trained on the regular dictionary. However, combining MLPs, one trained on each, and further training of the combined MLP resulted in a small improvement compared with training a similar sized MLP on the complete dictionary.

5. MLPs IN SERIES: SYLLABLE BOUNDARY INFORMATION

The methodology underlying the experiments of the previous section can be seen as that of subdividing the input space into regular and irregular words in order to place two (in general, any number) MLPs in parallel, each of which operates on part of the whole input set. This approach provokes the question as to whether MLPs can profitably be arranged in series; the output of one MLP being used as input to the next. To realise such an architecture we might choose a sub-task X, and proceed thus:

$$\text{Text} \rightarrow X; \quad X \rightarrow \text{Phoneme}.$$

Here we use our knowledge of the mapping involved, in particular that words can be broken down into syllables, to proceed thus:

$$\text{Text} \rightarrow X; \text{Text} + X \rightarrow \text{Phoneme}.$$

When we take the task X to be marking syllable boundaries within words, we can envisage the architecture in Fig 6:

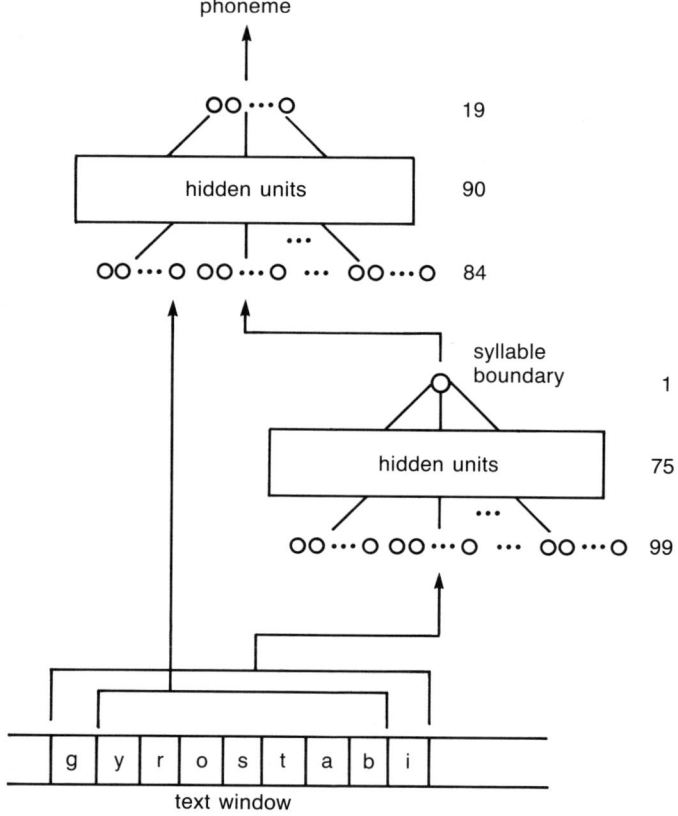

Fig. 6 Architecture for the MLPs in series, incorporating a Text → Syllable Boundary MLP.

Figure 6 shows a 9-letter text window as input to an MLP whose task is to output a 1 if the central letter lies at the start of a syllable, and 0 otherwise. This information is then used to augment a 7-letter text window at the input of a further MLP, whose task is to produce the phoneme corresponding to the central letter of the window. The lower MLP will be referred to as a Text → Syllable MLP, the higher one as a Text + Syllable → Phoneme MLP.

One can see that syllable boundary information can be useful by considering these examples: marking the word 'hothouse' as 'hot-house' indicates that the letter combination 'th' is not to be pronounced /θ/, but that the 't' and the 'h' are to be articulated separately as /t/ and /h/. Less obviously, marking the word 'cowshed' as 'cow-shed' indicates that it is a shed for cows rather than the past tense of the verb 'to cowsh'. Hence the 'ed' combination will be pronounced /ed/ rather than /t/.

5.1 MLP performance

Using the top-scoring 77-90-19 Text → Phoneme MLP (of Section 1) it was found that performance could be reliably maximized at just above 88% by using a learning-rate of 0.1. Results at this level were found to be consistent, varying only slightly with different random starting weights. Three runs are shown in Table 3.

Table 3 Three runs for a Text to Phoneme MLP, Learning-rate = 0.1.

Task	MLP Spec.	#WTS	Run 1	Run 2	Run 3
Text → Phon	77-90-19	8749	88.3%	88.2%	88.1%

Prior to training an MLP to perform the Text → Syllable Boundary task, it was decided to train an MLP to perform the Text + Syllable Boundary → Phoneme task when given perfect syllable boundary information. Thus we can establish whether such information, which we have seen to be of theoretical use (above), is of use in practice. For this purpose, an MLP with 84 input units is needed, rather than 77: to each 11-bit letter code was added a twelfth bit, set to 1 if the letter lay at the start of a syllable, and 0 otherwise. The number of hidden units was reduced from 90 to 84, giving approximately the same number of weights as the standard 77-90-19 MLP. Results for three runs are given in Table 4.

Table 4 Three runs for a Text + Perfect Syllable → Phoneme MLP.

Task	MLP Spec.	#WTS	Run 1	Run 2	Run 3
Text + Perfect Syll. → Phon.	84-84-19	8755	90.0%	89.8%	89.9%

We can see that the presence of syllable boundary information results in a marked improvement over the top Text → Phoneme MLP; we can conclude that syllable boundary information is useful in the text to phoneme transcription task.

To realise the architecture seen in Fig. 6 we now require an MLP to predict where syllable boundaries should be placed in text; such an MLP needs only one output unit — an activation of greater than 0.5 can be interpreted as placement of a syllable boundary. Preliminary experiments indicated that a context window of 9 letters is most suitable for this task. In Table 5 we show the performance of three separate runs, measured in terms of total bits correct, true-positives and true-negatives. The test set (unseen) contained 9311 patterns of which 1707 were syllable boundaries and 7604 were not.

Table 5 Three runs for a Text → Syllable Boundary MLP.

Task	MLP Spec	#WTS		Run 1	Run 2	Run 3
Text → Syll. Boundary	99-75-1	7576	Total Bits:	97.1%	97.2%	96.9%
			True +ves:	91.9%	93.2%	94.4%
			True −ves:	98.3%	98.1%	97.5%

Though the scores are high it was thought that errors may be occurring at precisely those places which are crucial to correct text to phoneme transcription, as in the examples above. Therefore it remained to be seen whether such derived, imperfect syllable boundary information would be of any use to the MLP trained on perfect information. Thus the output of these Text → Syllable Boundary MLPs was fed into each of the Text + Perfect Syllable → Phoneme MLPs (Table 4), for an unseen test set, realising the architecture of Fig. 6. Since three runs had been performed for both types of MLP, we have 9 possible combinations. In Table 6 the three runs of the lower MLP (Text → Syllable Boundary) are given horizontally, and the three examples of the higher MLP (Text + Syllable Boundary → Phoneme) are given vertically:

Table 6 Nine combinations of MLPs in Series architecture, for three runs of each component MLP.

		Text → Syllable Boundary (99-75-1)		
		Run 1	Run 2	Run 3
Text + Syllable Boundary → Phoneme (84-84-19)	RUN 1	88.8%	88.7%	88.6%
	RUN 2	88.4%	88.4%	88.7%
	RUN 3	88.6%	88.7%	88.5%

We can see that much of the gain reaped by providing perfect syllable boundary information at the input is lost when imperfect MLP output is used. Against an average score of 88.2% for the Text → Phoneme MLP (Table 3),

and an average of 89.9% for the Text + Perfect Syllable Boundary →
Phoneme MLP (Table 4), the nine scores in Table 6 have an average of
88.6%, with a peak of 88.8%.

When we consider that the latter figure is an increase of 0.5% over the
top Text → Phoneme MLP score, it can be seen to be worthwhile; though
small, this increase is significant at the 99.9% confidence level.

It seems likely, as mentioned earlier, that the Text → Syllable Boundary
MLP will make errors in precisely those circumstances in which correct
syllable boundary information is most useful. Thus an MLP trained on perfect
syllable boundary information is unlikely to produce the correct phoneme
when erroneous syllable boundary information is used as input. It might be
thought possible that an MLP trained on imperfect data, such as those
produced by the Text → Syllable Boundary MLP, rather than perfect data,
may learn to use this information when it is correct, but ignore erroneous
syllable boundary input.

Thus we can train an 84-84-19 MLP with syllable boundary information
as output by the existing Text → Syllable Boundary MLPs. We have three
such MLPs (Table 5) which vary significantly in their true-positive/true-
negative performance. Table 7 shows the results of training Text + Syllable
Boundary → Phoneme MLPs using the syllable boundary data generated
by each of these MLPs.

Table 7 Results for three training runs of Text + Syllable Boundary → Phoneme MLPs, using output of three Text → Syllable Boundary MLPs.

Task	MLP Spec	#WTS	Trained Using Output of Text → Syllable Boundary MLP		
			Run 1	Run 2	Run 3
Text + Syllable Boundary → Phoneme	84-84-19	8755	88.5%	88.5%	88.8%

Table 7 shows a top score (88.8%) and an average score (88.6%) identical
to that when (as in Table 6) an MLP trained on perfect syllable boundary
information is tested using imperfect syllable boundary data as generated
by the Text → Syllable Boundary MLP.

It is worth noting that the top score in Table 7 results from training with
data generated by that Text → Syllable Boundary MLP which scored highest
in terms of true-positive predictions; this MLP scored the worst of the three
in terms of total bits correct and true-negatives. This is in contrast to results
obtained from training with perfect syllable boundary information, followed
by testing with imperfect information: in that case the top score was obtained
with output of the Text → Syllable Boundary MLP scoring best in terms
of true-negatives.

5.2 Conclusions

We have seen that it is possible to improve on top-end MLP performance by arranging MLPs in series, the first of which performs a sub-task known to be relevant to the whole task of text-to-phoneme transcription. Were that sub-task performed perfectly the gain in performance would have been about two percentage points; in fact the MLP does not perform this sub-task perfectly, and the gain in performance is about half a percentage point. Though this gain is small it is statistically significant.

We have found no advantage in training the upper MLP of the two in series on perfect data or on imperfect (MLP output) data, given that it is to be tested using MLP output.

6. MORPHOLOGICAL PRE-PROCESSING

6.1 Introduction

Morphological information, that is the derivation of words from their constituent morphs, or units of meaning, has been used in rule-based text-to-speech systems, e.g. MITalk [11]. This approach to speech synthesis exploits the link between the pronunciation of whole words and the pronunciation of the individual morphs.

It was therefore decided to investigate the possibility that morphological analysis could be of use within the alternative, connectionist approach to speech synthesis, using MLPs.

Though the level of morphological analysis undertaken by Allen et al was well beyond the scope of this project, it remains pertinent to investigate to what extent MLP performance can be influenced by relatively straightforward pre-processing.

The investigation took the following course: firstly, suitable dictionaries were drawn up, comprising roots, prefixes and suffixes. A decomposition algorithm was then used to analyse words in terms of these morphs. This done, output of the decomposition was coded into a form suitable for input to an MLP. Then various MLPs were trained on this input, and the results compared with those for undecomposed words.

6.2 The dictionaries

Three dictionaries were needed. Firstly, a list of 128 prefixes and 263 suffixes was taken from Haldeman [12]. A simple computer program was written to strip one prefix and one suffix from each word in the dictionary, and the remainder of the word was filed. Where these 'roots' were found to occur more then once, they were retained; in this way about 8000 'roots' were listed. This list was hand-edited: implausible morphs were deleted and near-misses retained in corrected form. This process left about 5000 entries in the root dictionary.

6.3 Decomposition

Whole words were decomposed as follows: firstly, the word is checked against the root dictionary to see if it is (a) listed therein, or (b) composed entirely of roots listed therein. If not, affixes are removed, and after each removal the remainder of the word is checked against the roots. If this check succeeds the decomposition is recorded, and if not the process of affix removal and checking continues iteratively.

Certain spelling changes are known to occur at morph boundaries, e.g.

'bid' + 'ing' → 'bidding'

The decomposition algorithm took some of these into account, including insertion of double letters (as above), deletion of 'e' before certain suffixes, and transposition of 'y' to 'i' in certain roots. Spelling changes at prefix boundaries were assumed not to take place.

The process described can, in general, lead to many possible decompositions for a single word. Though there is no simple rule to tell which one is morphologically correct, some selection criteria must be employed. The criterion used here was 'least total number of letters in the affixes'. This criterion leads to selection of long root-strings (though not necessarily long roots) and short affix-strings (though not necessarily short affixes).

The output of the decomposition program, in the case of the word 'uncowshedising', looks like this:

P66cow/shedS116S118

The string 'P66' means prefix number 66, that is 'un-'. 'S116' denotes suffix number 116, that is '-ise' (note insertion of an 'e' here). Multiple roots are separated by the slash '/' character. All remaining lower case letters make up roots.

6.4 Experimental details

Letter codes were 12 bits long, of which 11 bits were the usual group/member code discussed above (Section 3), and a twelfth bit was set to zero, in order to simplify distinction from affix codes.

Each affix was also given its own 12-bit code. Details of the coding scheme used will not be given here, but each code reflected the consonant/vowel constitution of the affix. The last bit of each code was set to one, for reasons mentioned in the preceding paragraph.

MLPs were presented with the standard 7-unit window, of which the central letter was to be transcribed to a phoneme. The scheme used here allows more information to be presented within this window than with the standard MLP, since letter-combinations can be represented as a single 12-bit affix code.

MLPs were not required to pronounce affixes, which were instead scored by a look-up table. Letters inserted by the decomposition algorithm had a null phoneme as their target, letters deleted are not required to be pronounced, and transposed letters had the same target as that letter from which they were transposed.

Under this regime MLPs needed 84 ($=7*12$) input units and 19 output units. In these experiments we used either 50 or 90 hidden units.

Comparisons were made between MLPs trained/tested on decomposed words, words that could not be decomposed, and the whole set of words under the usual MLP regime of earlier sections.

6.5 Training and test data

Because of the time cost associated with the decomposition process, the training and test sets used here are smaller than those of other experiments.

6.5.1 Training set

10 000 words comprising 78 616 characters were submitted to the decomposition program, minus hyphenated and apostrophized words. Of these words, 68% could be decomposed and 32% could not. When converted to inputs and targets for an MLP, the decomposed words produced 36 985 patterns and the rest produced 25 016 patterns. Note that a decomposed word will produce less patterns then when undecomposed, since affix-strings are condensed into a single character and not required to be pronounced.

6.5.2 Test set

MLP performance was tested on an unseen section of the dictionary. Containing 7896 characters originally, it produced 3464 decomposed patterns and 2837 undecomposed patterns.

6.6 Results

In Fig. 7 we show the learning curves for MLPs trained exhaustively, over many presentations of the entire training sets. All three MLPs have dimensions 84-50-19. The curve marked 'all' is the performance of a standard MLP trained on the same, limited set of words without submission to the decomposition process.

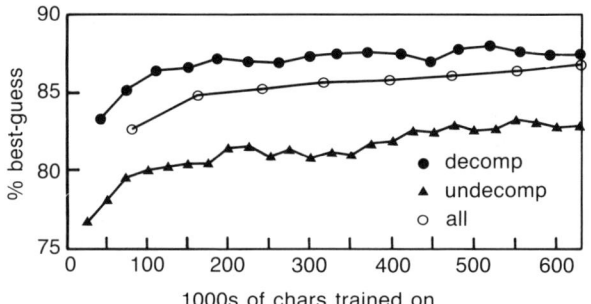

Fig. 7 Learning curves for MLPs trained on decomposed words (decomp), words which resisted decomposition (undecomp) and both sets (all) under the standard regime.

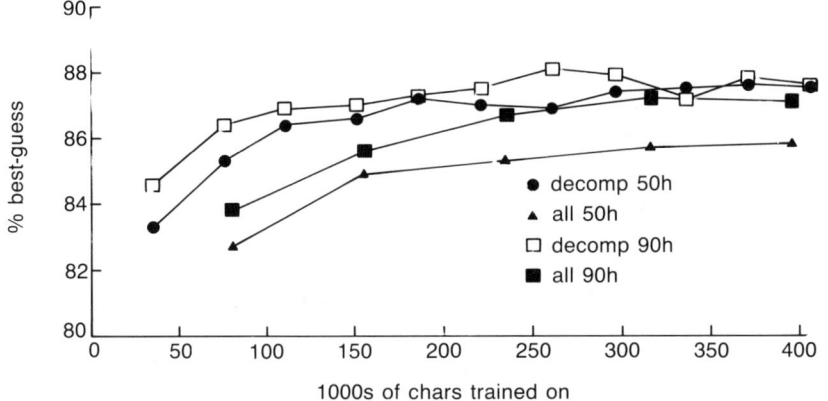

Fig. 8 Learning curves for MLPs trained on decomposed words (decomp) and under the standard regime (all), for 50 and 90 hidden units.

In Fig. 8 we show a comparison between lines marked 'decomp' and 'all' in Fig. 7, and lines for similarly trained MLPs with 90 hidden units.

Finally we show performance for the prefix and suffix look-up tables, on the unseen section.

Table 8 Performance of the prefix and suffix look-up tables.

Pref:	386/434	88.9%
Suff:	1103/1257	87.7%
Total:	1489/1691	88.1%

6.7 Discussion

Two points might be raised, to illustrate the difficulty in comparing these results with those of other sections. Firstly, the training sets used here are smaller than used in other experiments; training on smaller sets could impair generalization capabilities of MLPs. Furthermore, in comparison of the 'decomp' and 'all' results (Fig. 6), it should be noted that the relative size of these sets is 37:79, possibly flattering the generalizing capabilities of the standard MLP.

It can be seen from Fig. 7 that decomposition as a pre-processing technique improves MLP performance in the earlier stages of training. However, this gain becomes minimal as (a) learning reaches saturation, and (b) from Fig. 8, when higher-performance MLPs (with more hidden units) are used.

Such techniques will be useful in situations where training time is expensive and thus only a limited amount of training epochs is possible.

Also notable is that words which resist decomposition appear to be less easily pronounced, as can be seen by comparing the 'all' and 'undecomp' lines in Fig. 7.

Further work in this area might be aimed in the following direction. An MLP could be trained to perform the decomposition, and this processed output could then be used as input to a further MLP, whose target would be a phonemic representation. This is a similar scheme to that described in Section 5 where MLPs are arranged in series, though more complex.

7. PRONUNCIATION OF CLOCK TIMES

In the process of reading text aloud a good deal of implicit knowledge is required. Not only must one pronounce words, but it is necessary to interpret abbreviations, either by expanding them or by translating them into pronounceable words according to convention. A particularly common abbreviation is a sequence of digits. The correct pronunciation of digits, however, is extremely context dependent. The digit '2' is an abbreviation for the word 'two' when written in isolation, but it is shorthand for 'twenty' when written in the string '27'. With the sequence '2nd' the whole group of characters represents the word 'second'.

When applying MLPs to the problem of mapping input strings composed of digits to output strings composed of words, problems such as three-digit number pronunciation, e.g.

'320' → 'three hundred and twenty'

were found to be solvable by MLPs with no hidden units: i.e. the mapping in question is linear. The same was found to be true of cardinal number pronunciation. (For fuller details see [13].)

One set of mappings from digit strings to words was found to be more difficult, that being the pronunciation of 12-hour clock times, e.g.

'12.34' → 'twenty six minutes to one'
'8.15' → 'quarter past eight'

We shall therefore expound the experiments performed to get 3-layer MLPs to perform this mapping.

7.1 MLP design

24 input units were used, arranged thus:

> 1 unit for tens of hours,
> 9 units for hours,
> 5 units for tens of minutes,
> 9 units for minutes.

The output representation was more complex, requiring 39 units in all, set out as follows:

> 1 unit for the word 'quarter',
> 1 unit for the word 'half',
> 1 unit for the word 'twenty',
> 19 units for the words 'one' to 'nineteen' (minutes),
> 1 unit for the word 'minute',
> 1 unit for the plural sound /s/ after 'minute',
> 1 unit for the word 'past',
> 1 unit for the word 'to',
> 12 units for the words 'one' to 'twelve' (hours),
> 1 unit for the word 'o'clock'.

7.3 Results

As has been mentioned, the mapping appeared to be impossible for a 2-layer MLP, so a number of 3-layer MLPs were tried, with varying amounts of hidden units. Figure 9 shows the performance of these MLPs. All of them were both trained and tested on the complete set of 720 possible pairs of input and target vectors.

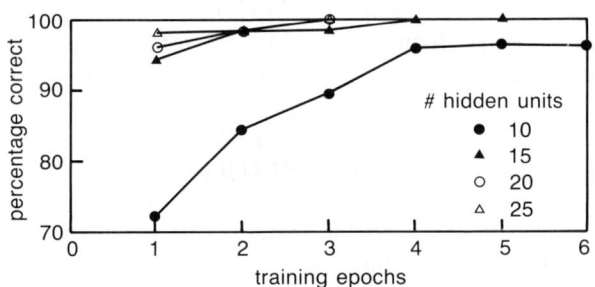

Fig. 9 Learning curves for the clock-times problem, with various numbers of hidden units.

When fully trained, the 24-15-39 MLP was purged of unnecessary connections, in that smaller weights were removed. It was found that removing all weights such that $-1 < w < 1$ left performance unimpaired, with a total of 725 weights remaining.

One can see that the mapping is non-linear by examining the subset of possible mappings consisting of the four input vectors 2.00, 2.40, 3.00, 3.40. When we look at the desired output of the unit representing 'three' hours in these cases, we get the following table:

Table 9 Desired activation of the 'three' (hours) output unit, for the times 2.00, 2.40, 3.00, 3.40.

2h	3h	40m	'three'
1	0	0	0
1	0	1	1
0	1	0	1
0	1	1	0

The desired activation of the 'three' hours output unit can be seen to be an exclusive-or of the 3h and 40m inputs, and an exclusive-nor of the 2h and 40m inputs. This sub-mapping is thus not linearly separable, so neither is the complete mapping.

7.4 Conclusion

We have seen that MLPs can be useful in the wider text-to-speech context by expanding abbreviations, in particular clock-times, to their correct wordstrings, where the mapping involved is non-linear. Since such abbreviations are by no means rare in free text, this represents an important step in building a connectionist, in particular an MLP-based, text-to-speech system.

8. CLASSIFICATION BY SYNTACTIC CATEGORY OF ISOLATED WORDS

To produce synthetic speech which sounds natural, it is essential to segment longer sentences into breath groups and to assign appropriate intonation contours to these segments [10]. To this end knowledge of the syntactic role played by each word in a sentence will be necessary in a complete text-to-speech system. Though the addition of part-of-speech information to an existing pronouncing dictionary requires little additional space, connectionist text-to-speech systems require alternative means for syntactic analysis. Here we report on a connectionist classifier, trained to predict parts of speech from orthography. We have found that the scores obtained for unseen words, with networks of less than 5000 weights, are high enough to provide a storage-efficient alternative to a grammatical dictionary. These scores compare favourably with those of a simple set of rules.

8.1 Scoring methods

The seven commonest parts of speech in the dictionary are adjectives, nouns, verbs, adverbs, pronouns, conjunctions and prepositions. An output unit can be assigned to each one of these categories, making a total of seven output units for the MLP. Many English words may be used as different parts of speech according as their context varies; the MLP target for each word will thus consist of x ones and $7-x$ zeroes, where x is the number of categories in which that word may be used.

When using seven such categories there are a possible 128 combinations for the output (though most of these will not be representative of any words). For scoring the output of an MLP we can calculate which of these 128 possible vectors is closest to the MLP output (by Euclidian distance); we then have three different scores:

(i) the percentage of output bits correct,
(ii) the percentage of true-positives,
(iii) the percentage of true-negatives.

Since most of the target bits will be zero in a large test set, methods (i) and (iii) give misleadingly high scores. In the context of a text-to-speech system the most useful measure of a classifier's performance is thought to be the percentage of true-positives, given that the classifier does not invariably output ones. As MLPs are trained to minimize mean squared error such behaviour has not been observed. In monitoring the effect of varying MLP parameters, e.g. number of hidden units, the scoring methods (i) and (iii) have been useful however, as shown in Section 8.4 below.

8.2 Breakdown of the word corpus

The training and evaluation of the various MLPs was carried out using a corpus of 5,6,7,8,9 and 10-letter words, roughly 5500 of each word-length. The distribution of syntactic categories within this corpus is shown in Table 10.

Table 10 Distribution of syntactic category throughout the word corpus.

Adj	*Verb*	*Noun*	*Adv*	*Prep*	*Conj*	*Pron*
21%	18%	58%	3%	0.1%	0.1%	0.1%

Further analysis shows that most words in the corpus can be grouped into one of eight combinations of the above categories, for example: words ending with 'ing' are commonly classified as 'adjective, verb or noun'. Such analysis was exploited in writing a set of rules for syntactic classification, but for the purposes of MLP-based classification the architecture described in Section 8.1 was found to be more effective than that alternative in which one output unit is used to represent each common combination of categories.

8.3 MLP performance

8.3.1 Experimental details

The input coding used 11 bits per character, hence a five-letter word needed 55 input units to represent it. It was found convenient to split the corpus into two sections, the first consisting of all the 5,6 and 7-letter words and the second consisting of all the 8,9, and 10-letter words. Preliminary experiments indicated that splitting the corpus further, e.g. into six sections by word-length, did not improve performance, whereas the higher performance for longer words (see below for details) was obscured when all the words were combined to give one large set. The number of input units needed for training/testing on the first section was 77, and for the second section was 110.

Within the above regime two variables were manipulated: firstly, the number of hidden units was varied in order to optimize performance; secondly we looked at whether left- or right-justification, within the input window, of shorter words is better for training.

All MLPs were trained using a learning-rate of 0.1 and a momentum term of 0.9.

8.3.2 Results

Figure 10 shows the learning curves for MLPs trained on (a) shorter and (b) longer words. The size of the training sets, in both cases, is 15 000 words (5000 of each word-length); the test sets are composed of 1500 unseen words (500 of each word-length). Testing takes place after each training epoch for a total of ten epochs. Performance is shown here in terms of percentage true-positive outputs. Each graph shows learning curves for MLPs with various numbers of hidden units. Shorter words have been left-justified.

One can see that performance is about five percentage points higher for the longer words, the peaks being at 78.5% for 5,6 and 7-letter words compared to 84.0% for 8,9 and 10-letter words. Though test performance can vary with the syntactic distribution of the test set, such results were found to be typical for left-justified input.

We can gain insight into MLP behaviour for this task by examining the performance of one of the above MLPs in greater detail: Fig. 11 shows the curve of the 110-50-7 MLP (8,9 and 10-letter words); this one line is now broken down into performance for each of the four commonest syntactic categories.

We can see that the MLP scores higher the commoner the category. One might also note that the peaks for each category occur at different stages of the training process. This could be of interest were one concerned to optimize performance on one particular category.

The graphs in Fig. 12 each show two curves, one in which shorter words have been left-justified and one in which they have been right-justified. The x-axes shows the number of hidden units in the MLPs, which has been varied; performance, on the y-axis, is measured by finding the peak value over 10 training epochs. These graphs are for MLPs trained and tested on 8,9 and 10-letter words, and show true-positive, true-negative, and total bits correct scores.

282 TEXT-TO-SPEECH SYNTHESIS SYSTEMS

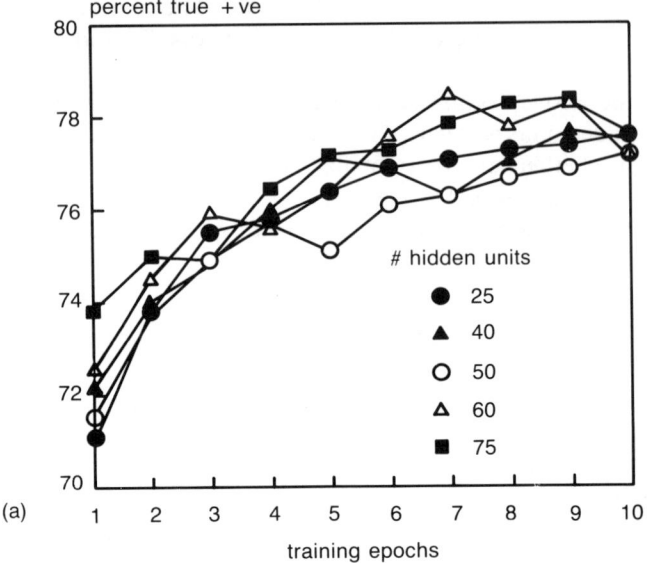

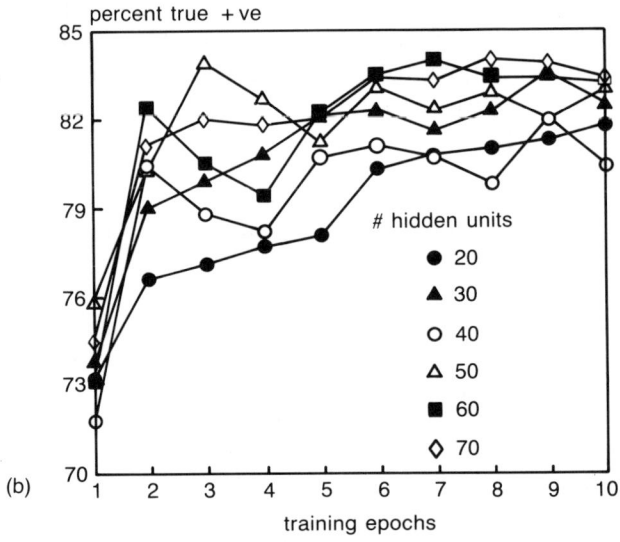

Fig. 10 Learning curves for MLPs predicting syntactic category of (a) 5, 6 and 7-letter words, (b) 8, 9 and 10-letter words. Both graphs show various numbers of hidden units; all words have been left-justified.

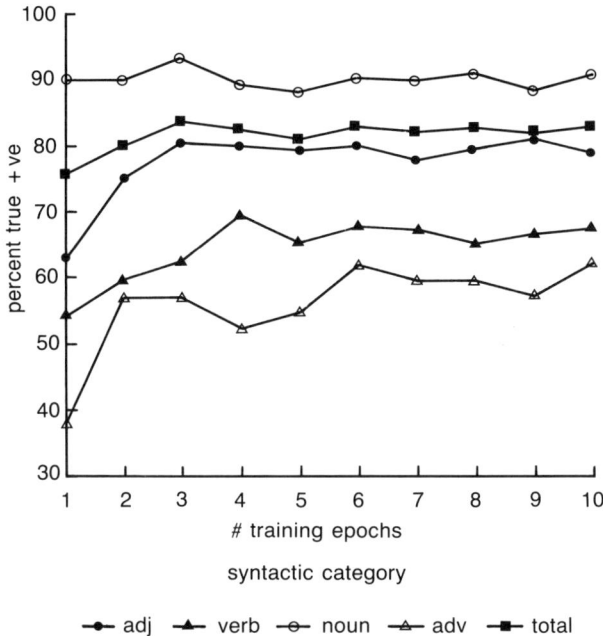

Fig. 11 Performance of the 110-50.7 MLP broken down by syntactic category.

One can see (a) that right-justifying the input words enables an MLP to classify more words accurately, leading to a top score for longer words of 87.9%. This figure is not improved upon by increasing the number of hidden units, however; it seems that the extra weights are instead used to decrease the number of false-positive outputs (b), leading to a rise in total bits correct (c), thus decreasing mean squared error. It can also be seen that increasing the number of hidden units beyond 50, in the case of right-justified words, does not lead to any better classification.

8.4 Conclusion

The higher performance of MLPs trained on right-justified words might imply that most syntactic information is contained in word-endings (see also [14]). Subsequent examination of weight distribution in trained MLPs would tend to confirm this: many of the MLPs trained have been successfully purged of up to half their weights with no drop in true-positives and no rise in false-negatives. In these cases the majority of those weights remaining were found to be connected to the word-ending input units.

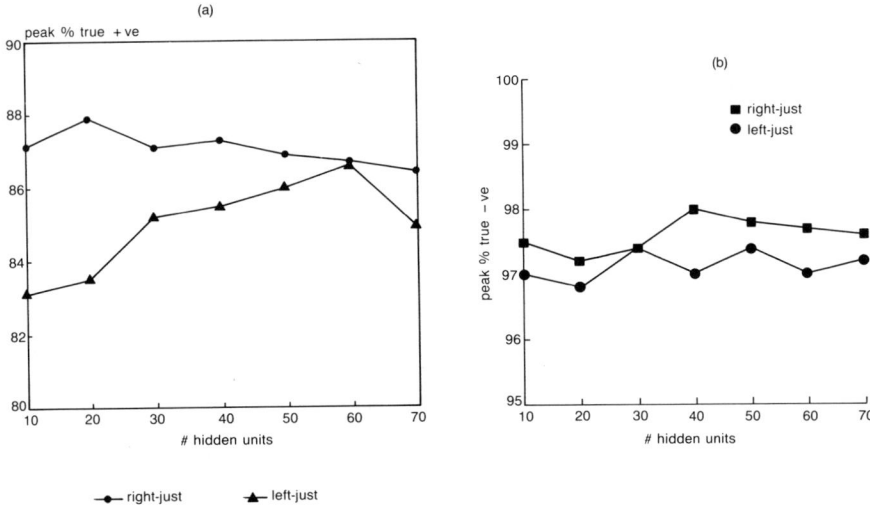
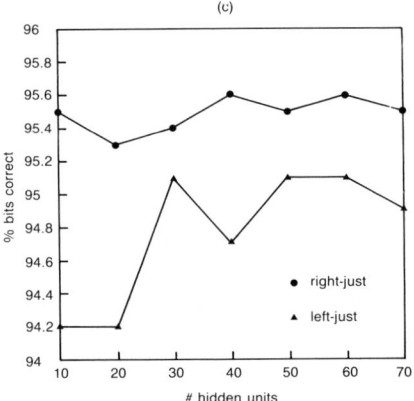

Fig 12 Peak percentage scores, over 10 training epochs, for 8, 9 and 10-letter words, right-justified.
(a) True positives   (b) True negatives   (c) Total bits correct.

With the above findings in mind, a simple set of word-ending rules was drawn up and applied to the MLP test sets, e.g.

'IF a word ends in 'LY' THEN it is an ADVERB'.

The default category, should no rule be applicable, was that of noun. The rules were thought to cover the most frequent 'word-ending to syntactic category' inferences. On shorter words the rules scored 72.6%, about 6% below the top MLP. On longer words the rules scored 84.8%, about 3% below the top MLP. The drop in performance differential between rules and MLP for longer words is consistent with the thesis that most of the syntactic information resides at the end of a word; shorter words will contain less such information, thus disabling the rule-base, whereas the MLP classifier will be able to pick up other residual clues, whatever they may be.

MLP scores of about 88% are thought to be encouraging for syntactic classification in the context of the storage efficiency and swift execution-time of a connectionist, non dictionary-based text to speech system. Moreover we would suggest that these scores are not the highest obtainable by MLPs and that further development of these experiments should lead to even better classification.

9. SUMMARY AND CONCLUSIONS

In this chapter we have shown how MLPs can be used in many of the modules of text-to-speech systems. Most importantly perhaps, it has been found that orthographic to phonemic transcription can be performed with a phoneme score of nearly 90% for a dictionary of over 70 000 words. Such a dictionary requires about 1.5 Mbytes of memory to store the orthographic and phonemic versions of each word, yet the largest MLP employed to perform this translation task (77 input units, 90 hidden units and 19 output units) requires less than 35 Kbytes to store its weights. This suggests that the use of MLPs for orthographic to phonemic transcription could reduce the storage requirements of this part of a text-to-speech system by a factor of more than 40 compared with one based on dictionary look-up.

The experiments on input/output coding confirmed that sparse coding leads to higher performance than dense coding, but the difference is relatively small provided that the number of hidden units is chosen so that the number of weights remains the same. These experiments also revealed that the pseudo-phonemic input coding used by McCulloch et al [4] in NETspeak did not perform significantly better than an arbitrary coding scheme with the same number of input units.

The possibility of training several MLPs separately to perform a sub-task, then connecting them together in parallel or in series to perform the complete task has been shown to be feasible. However, the gain in performance obtained by this technique was found to be minimal, at least for orthographic to phonemic transcription. Training one MLP on regularly pronounced words and another on irregularly pronounced words resulted in improved performance for the regular MLP, as might be expected, but combining the two in parallel led to a performance which was similar to that obtained by a similar sized MLP trained on the complete dictionary. However, training an MLP to insert syllable boundaries in text, then using text which had thus been segmented into syllables as input to a second MLP did result in a small but statistically significant increase in performance.

As segmenting words into syllables appeared to increase performance another form of segmentation, morphological analysis into roots and affixes, was investigated. This has previously been shown to be superior to other systems for rule-based synthesis [11]. An algorithm was developed for decomposing words into their constituent morphemes. This was successful in decomposing nearly 70% of the words in the dictionary. An MLP trained to transcribe these decomposed words performed better than one trained on the complete dictionary; however, this improvement was reduced with more training and with increasing the number of hidden units. Further work in this area is required.

There are other tasks which have to be performed in a text-to-speech system as well as orthographic to phonemic conversion. One of these is expanding abbreviations such as dates and times into pronounceable words. It has been found that an MLP can be trained to expand digital clock times such as '12.15' into 'quarter past twelve'. Two layers of variable weights are required with at least 15 hidden units in order to obtain 100% accuracy.

Finally it has been shown that MLPs may be used to predict the syntactic category of isolated words. Normally this would be done by means of a dictionary, but if an MLP is used to perform the orthographic to phonemic conversion the dictionary can be dispensed with and the storage requirement reduced by a factor of 40; in these circumstances other means of determining syntactic category must be employed. In the module of a text-to-speech system which deals with prosody some form of parsing is required in order to segment text into breath groups and to assign appropriate intonation contours. It has been found that an MLP may be trained to predict the syntactic category of a word with a success rate of nearly 90%. Moreover it was found that higher scores were obtained with the words right-justified, suggesting that the most significant information for this task resides in word-endings. A simple rule system based on word-endings was devised to predict syntactic categories, but the best MLP performed 6% better than this algorithm.

Thus we have shown that MLPs may be employed to perform many of the tasks required in order to generate speech from text. There are other tasks, such as the determination of intonation contours and the conversion from the phonemic representation to the acoustic signal, which it may be possible to perform using MLPs or other neural networks. Further work is required to determine the advantages or otherwise of this approach.

ACKNOWLEDGEMENTS

We are indebted to BT Laboratories who provided both the financial support and the dictionary for this research.

REFERENCES

1. McClelland J L & Rumelhart D E: 'Parallel Distributed Processing', MIT Press (1986).

2. McCulloch N, Ainsworth W A & Linggard R: 'Multi-layer perceptrons applied to speech technology' in Speech and Language Processing (C Wheddon & R Linggard, eds), Chapman & Hall, London (1990).

3. Sejnowski T J & Rosenberg C R: 'Parallel networks that learn to pronounce English text', Complex Systems, 1, pp 145—168 (1987).

4. McCulloch N, Bedworth M & Bridle J: 'NETspeak — a re-implementation of NETtalk', Computer Speech and Language, 2, pp 289—301 (1987).

5. Lawrence S G & Kaye G: 'Alignment of phonemes with their corresponding orthography', Computer Speech and Language, 1, pp 153—165 (1986).

6. Tattersall G D: 'Neural networks and speech processing', in Advanced in Speech, Hearing and Language Processing (W A Ainsworth, ed), JAI Press, pp 107—146 (1990).

7. Tombs J: 'A more representative coding for NETspeak', RIPR Tech Rep RIPRREP/1000/69/89, RSRE, Malvern (1989).

8. Ainsworth W A & Pell B: 'Regularity of pronunciation and word frequency in English', Proc SPEECH 88, 7th FASE Symposium, Edinburgh, pp 975—980 (1988).

9. Ainsworth W A & Pell B: 'Connectionist architectures for text-to-speech systems', Proc Eurospeech 89, Paris, 1, pp 125—128 (1989).

10. Ainsworth W A: 'A system for converting English text into speech', IEEE Trans AU-21, pp 288-290 (1973).

11. Allen J, Hunnicutt M S & Klatt D: 'From text to speech: the MITalk system', Cambridge University Press (1987).

12. Haldeman S S: 'Affixes in their origin and application, exhibiting the etymologic structure of English words', Philadelphia, Butler (1865).

13. Ainsworth W A & Warren N P: 'Pronunciation of digit sequences in text-to-speech systems', Connection Science 2(3), pp 245—253 (1990).

14. Elenius L & Carlson R: 'Assigning parts-of-speech to words from their orthography using a connectionist model', Eurospeech 89, Paris, 1 , pp 534—537 (1989).

Part 4: Implementation

HARDWARE IMPLEMENTATION OF NEURAL NETWORKS: AN INTRODUCTION

D J Myers
BT Laboratories

1. INTRODUCTION

Neural networks imply a requirement for massive fine-grained parallelism, with very high levels of interconnection and simple processing at each node. It is from this parallelism that they derive their power. From biology comes the analogy of the human or animal brain, which can be viewed as an implementation in a technology with a very low switching speed (of the order of milliseconds) but which allows massive interconnection. Such systems appear to perform recognition tasks in fractions of a second, corresponding to only a small number of parallel operations.

The applications oriented experiments described in Parts 1,2 and 3 of this book have been performed using workstations or other general purpose computers, running simulation programs written in C or another high level language. The simulations use floating point computation, with high precision and wide dynamic range (an exception to this is the work of Woodland described in Chapter 7).

The intrinsically parallel structure of neural networks maps poorly on to conventional Von Neumann computer architectures. Therefore these architectures are not suitable for implementing real-time systems except for the case of smaller pre-trained networks with less demanding real-time constraints such as the alphabet recogniser of Chapter 7. The mismatch between the parallelism required for neural networks and the performance of sequential computer architectures is exacerbated as networks increase in size. As a consequence there is much research activity in the implementation area, investigating technologies which allow the parallelism of neural networks to be mapped into hardware.

A brief description of the main areas of investigation is given in this introduction, followed by a summary of the work currently being undertaken at BT Laboratories, introducing the chapters in this section.

2. DESIGN ISSUES

When considering hardware implementations, a number of questions need to be answered. These include the problems of input-output (I/O), how to interface such sub-systems to conventional digital systems such that their parallelism can be fully exploited, how to implement training, and the adequacy of the computational accuracy, dynamic range and resolution attainable.

In Chapter 14 Vincent looks at the effects of restricted dynamic range and precision on the performance of the backpropagation training algorithm, and suggests some techniques, suitable for hardware implementation, which can be used to improve that performance. The results of this work are exploited in the chip architecture described in Chapter 15.

3. IMPLEMENTATION APPROACHES

A number of technologies have been proposed for the implementation of neural net systems, including analogue very large scale integration (VLSI) digital VLSI, opto-electronics and optical technologies. Each of these has some advantages and disadvantages.

3.1 Analogue VLSI

Analogue VLSI has received much attention as a potential implementation technology for neural networks, because of the relative compactness and speed of analogue circuits compared to digital. For instance analogue multiplication can be implemented using a Gilbert four quadrant multiplier [1] which requires only a handful of transistors, two orders of magnitude fewer than an 8 bit parallel digital multiplier, and which performs multiplication two to three orders of magnitude faster.

Such compact circuits mean that neural networks of reasonable size can be implemented in a single chip. Analogue technology provides great scope for innovation, and a number of novel implementation techniques have been proposed, including the use of pulses to signal neuron activation [2] which is claimed to have some biological plausibility. Some interesting work on modelling biological systems such as the cochlea has also been undertaken [3].

Potential problems with analogue implementations include limited dynamic range, resolution and precision, the difficulty of implementing analogue memory for weight storage and the difficulty of incorporating training. A further potential problem is that of efficiently interfacing systems with large numbers of analogue inputs to conventional host systems, to enable the full speed of the net to be exploited. In addition, because most of the systems developed to date have been relatively small scale, there is some uncertainty as to how well the technology will scale for larger networks.

Work at BT Laboratories, in conjunction with the Universities of Edinburgh and Dundee, is investigating the use of programmable amorphous silicon as a method of achieving reliable long-term analogue weight storage [4].

3.2 Digital VLSI

Conventional digital VLSI is a mature, and therefore reliable technology. Neural networks implemented using this technology are based on simple processor array architectures with either a processor-per-synapse [5] or a processor-per-neuron organisation. The attractions of using this technology to implement neural systems are that precision can be arbitrarily specified, it is possible to implement any training/learning algorithm, and the effects of scaling up an implementation are predictable.

Digital implementations are larger and slower than analogue implementations, nevertheless they represent the most reliable and lowest risk path from high level simulation to hardware implementation of a real-time neural network. In Chapter 15 Myers, Vincent and Orrey present the design of a chip based on a processor-per-neuron architecture, which allows on-chip training using the backpropagation algorithm. It is primarily intended for the production of a real-time facial feature location demonstrator based on the work described in Chapters 1 and 2, but should find wider application as a general purpose building block for neural systems.

3.3 Optical and opto-electronic technologies

Optical and opto-electronic architectures are potentially very fast, and do not have the communication bottleneck problem associated with essentially two-dimensional electronic implementations. Completely optical systems can be bulky, and require very precise alignment. In Chapter 16 Barnes, Healey et al describe a high speed opto-electronic implementation of a neural network with the potential to be compactly integrated as a robust system component. The high speed of this architecture can be exploited to allow the network to be trained using a form of simulated annealing [6]. This approach to training could point the way to a class of algorithms suitable for analogue networks where speed of operation can be exploited. The chapter also discusses potential advanced opto-electronic architectures, which further exploit the potential of optical intercommunication.

REFERENCES

1. Eberhardt S, Duong T and Thakoor A: 'Design of Parallel Hardware Neural Network Systems from Custom Analog Building Block Chips' IEEE/INNS Int Joint Conf on Neural Networks, Washington, (1989).

2. Murray A F and Smith A W: 'Asynchronous VLSI Neural Networks using Pulse-stream Arithmetic' IEEE Journ Solid State Circuits, $\underline{23}$, No 3 (June 1988).

3. Mead C: 'Analog VLSI and Neural Systems', Addison-Wesley (1989).

4. Reeder A A, Thomas I P, Smith C, Wittgreffe J, Godfrey D, Haito J, Owen A, Snell A, Murray A, Rose M and LeComber P: 'Application of Analogue Amorphous Silicon Memory Devices to Resistive Synapses for Neural Networks' Proc 2nd Int Conf on Microelectronics for Neural Networks, Munich (16-18 October 1991).

5. Ramacher U: 'Systolic Architectures for Fast Emulation of Artificial Neural Networks', IEEE Int Conf on Neural Networks, San Diego (July 1988).

6. Wood D: 'Training High-speed Opto-electronic Neural Network Hardware', Optics Communications 82, $\underline{3}$, 4, pp 236—240 (1991).

14

FINITE WORDLENGTH, INTEGER ARITHMETIC MULTILAYER PERCEPTRON MODELLING FOR HARDWARE REALIZATION

J M Vincent
BT Laboratories

1. INTRODUCTION

The implementation in hardware of neural networks such as the MLP raises questions concerning the representation of the parameters of the network. If an analogue implementation is being contemplated, it is necessary to know whether the inherent dynamic range and accuracy achievable with the components being used (e.g. resistor or capacitor values) will be adequate to achieve the desired performance of the net.

In the case of a digital implementation, this translates to choosing number representations (e.g. floating point or fixed point) and optimising storage wordlengths, communication and computational bandwidths so that the desired performance is achievable whilst minimising the hardware cost.

This chapter describes a digital hardware model of an MLP with backpropagation learning. The model uses fixed point arithmetic and is based on the architecture of the VLSI integrated circuit known as HANNIBAL (hardware architecture for neural networks implementing backpropagation learning) described in Chapter 15. This is a digital building block chip for constructing MLPs with on-chip backpropagation learning [1]. The model was used to investigate the effects of modifying storage wordlengths and other parameters of the chip, and the results of experiments with this model were used to develop the specification of the chip. In addition, experiments with the hardware model have resulted in the development of some novel techniques to improve the performance of finite wordlength implementations. These are also described.

Although the model is targeted at a specific architecture, the results obtained from it give a more general idea of the accuracy of representation required in trainable hardware implementations.

2. THEORY OF FIXED-POINT NEURAL COMPUTATION

2.1 Neuron activation

2.1.1 Hardware organisation and activation equations

An MLP contains layers of nodes where the bottom layer is an array of input nodes, the top layer is an array of output nodes and the other layers contain hidden nodes. Each hidden node or output node is a non-linear neuron, fully connected to nodes in adjacent layers via weighted synapses.

The response of the j-th neuron to an I-dimensional input vector, $(x_1,...x_I)$, is to output an activation level, a_j. If the neuron is in the first hidden layer then the input vector is the pattern vector, p, being classified. For other layers the input vector is formed by the activations from the previous layer. The activation, a_j, is formed by passing a linearly weighted sum of inputs, s_j, through a sigmoidal non-linearity $f(\ )$:

$$s_j = w_{j0} + \sum_{i=1}^{I} w_{ji} x_i \qquad \ldots (1)$$

$$a_j = f(s_j) = \frac{1}{1+e^{-s_j}}. \qquad \ldots (2)$$

2.1.2 Fixed-point formats

All computations in the neuron circuits are carried out in fixed-point arithmetic. Hence all inputs, outputs, weights and intermediate values are fixed-point numbers. Specific formats for inputs, outputs and weights are described below.

Inputs and outputs of neurons are fractional and share a common format. Inputs are of two types: either activations from other neurons or pattern vector elements. Note that this may require pre-scaling of pattern vectors. Inputs and outputs are represented by fractional 2's complement bytes. Therefore, values are in the following ranges:

$$-1 \leq p_i \leq 1-2^{-7} \qquad \ldots (3)$$

$$0 \leq a_j \leq 1-2^{-7}. \qquad \ldots (4)$$

The user can choose between one of two word sizes for weights, 8 or 16 bits. If weights are stored on-chip the maximum number of synapses, for a given silicon area, is inversely proportional to word size. Therefore the 8 bit/weight option allows twice as many synapses at the expense of increasing quantization error.

Weights are represented by 2's complement words. The dynamic range is controlled by varying the number of integer bits, I_w, which may be preset to 1, 2 or 3. With B bit/weight the dynamic range is:

$$-2^{I_w-1} \leq w_{ji} \leq 2^{I_w-1}(1-2^{1-B}). \qquad \ldots (5)$$

Because large numbers of on-chip weights require significant amounts of RAM, it is important to have as few bits per weight as is practical. Only low precision is required for neuron activation, as has been shown in previous experiments [2]. However, on-chip learning requires higher precision; this is discussed in detail in section 2.2. Therefore, the number of bits per weight is determined by the requirements of on-chip learning.

The robustness of activation levels to quantization error is inherent in the non-linearity of neurons. Suppose the weighted sum, s_j, has error Δs_j due to quantization error. Thus the activation, a_j, has error Δa_j which may be approximated as:

$$\Delta a_j \approx \frac{da_j}{ds_j} \Delta s_j \qquad \ldots (6)$$

where from equation (2)

$$0 \leq \frac{da_j}{ds_j} \leq \frac{1}{4}. \qquad \ldots (7)$$

Thus the non-linearity attenuates quantization errors. The slope of the non-linearity is usually somewhat smaller than ¼ because weights and weighted sums tend to be large after training and the slope decreases as $|s_j|$ increases.

2.1.3 Circuit characteristics

Figure 1 is a block diagram of the digital sub-circuit which computes the activation level. Characteristics of this sub-circuit are discussed below.

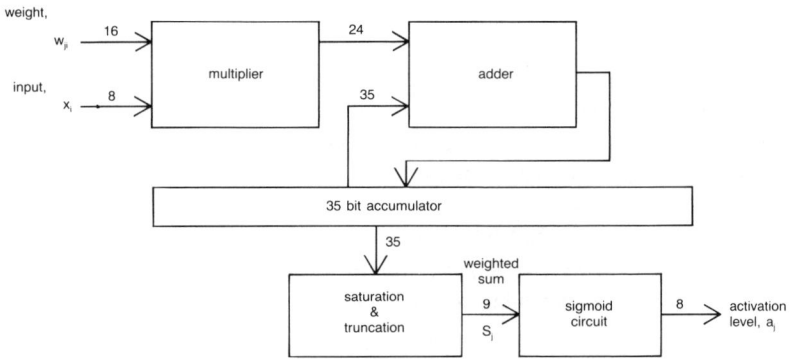

Fig. 1 Block diagram of activation circuit model.

The multiplier forms each product, $w_{ji}x_i$, in turn. The w_{ji} operand can be up to 16 bits wide whereas the activation or pattern operand can be up to 8 bits. In the sub-circuit model it is assumed that the products are accumulated in a 35 bit accumulator allowing up to 2048 synapses per neuron without ever saturating the weighted sum, s_j. Many of the most significant bits in an accumulator of this length would hardly ever be used. However, they are a relatively low architectural overhead. Furthermore, by allowing for any possible accumulation, it is not necessary to resort to statistical arguments for deriving a suitable accumulator bit length, thus avoiding a risk in the design.

Following accumulation, the weighted sum of inputs, s_j, is limited and truncated to 9 bits and sent to the sigmoid sub-circuit. The saturation level for the limiter is $s_{sat} = \pm 8$, requiring 4 integer bits. This is a sensible value in view of the required precision of the output. The saturation level is large enough to ensure that only those values of s_j are saturated, that would anyway have resulted in an extreme activation level. Since the output has 7 bits of precision (see equation (4)), the saturation level for negative inputs to the sigmoid should satisfy the following:

$$\frac{1}{1+e^{S_{\text{sat}}}} < 2^{-7} = \frac{1}{128}. \qquad \ldots (8)$$

$$\therefore s_{\text{sat}} < 4.84.$$

After saturation and truncation a weighted sum, s_j, is represented as a 9-bit signed number with 5 fraction bits. Greatest precision is required in the central part of the sigmoid curve where the slope is at its maximum, $\frac{1}{4}$. Therefore to achieve a precision of 7 fraction bits for a_j requires a precision of just 5 fraction bits for s_j and so the above 9-bit representation of s_j is sufficiently accurate.

The sigmoid curve is approximated by a piecewise-linear function based on a highly efficient design with low complexity [3]. The gradient, $y_j = \frac{da_j}{ds_j}$, of each line segment is a negative power of 2:

$$y = 2^{-Y} \qquad \ldots (9)$$

where Y is an integer from 2 to 6. This value is required during on-chip training. Note that this allows multiplication by y to be easily implemented with a bit shifting operation.

2.2 On-chip backpropagation

2.2.1 Backpropagation equations

In section 2.1, the weight values were assumed to be known for a given pattern recognition problem. However, prior to useful recognition, the weight values need to be learnt. The weights can be learnt off-line using any desired learning scheme, and pre-loaded into chip RAM. Alternatively the weights can be learnt on-chip using backpropagation [4]. This section describes how backpropagation is designed into neuron circuits despite limited precision.

With on-chip learning, weights are up-dated after each pattern vector is presented. For each weight, w_{ji}, a weight increment, $\Delta w_{ji}(n)$, is calculated after the n-th presentation

$$w_{ji}(n) = w_{ji}(n-1) + \Delta w_{ji}(n). \qquad \ldots (10)$$

If $w_{ji}(n)$ goes outside the allowed dynamic range, then $w_{ji}(n)$ is set to the minimum or maximum allowed value.

In some variants of backpropagation weight increments are accumulated over an epoch and then added to weights. For a hardware implementation this would require twice the amount of on-chip memory. Experiments have indicated that any advantages of this method of up-dating do not warrant a doubling of memory or halving of the number of synapses. For the same reasons a momentum term has not been considered.

In backpropagation a weight increment is a product of a learning rate, η, an error term, δ_j, and the corresponding input, x_i

$$\Delta w_{ji} = \eta \delta_j x_{ji}. \qquad \ldots (11)$$

If the j-th neuron is an output neuron then

$$\delta_j = y_j(t_j - a_j) \qquad \ldots (12)$$

where

$$y_j = \frac{da_j}{ds_j} \qquad \ldots (13)$$

and t_j is the desired output from the j-th neuron. Otherwise, if the j-th neuron is in the l-th layer then

$$\delta_j = y_j \sum_{k=K}^{K+N} w_{kj} \delta_k \qquad \ldots (14)$$

where neurons in the $(l+1)$-th layer are indexed from K to $K+N$.

Prior to learning, weights are randomly initialised. The dynamic range of initial weights must be somewhat smaller than the total dynamic range. This allows weights to grow without encountering saturation early on. In simulation experiments the dynamic range of initial weights is restricted to one-eighth of the total range. Therefore, assuming a B bit weight wordlength from equation (5), the weights are initialised in the range:

$$-2^{I_w - 4} \leq w_{ji} \leq 2^{I_w - 4}(1 - 2^{4-B}). \qquad \ldots (15)$$

2.2.2 Calculation of error terms and weights

In digital 'processor per neuron' architectures there is generally one computation circuit per neuron, such as that shown in Fig. 1, with data being fed sequentially from processor to processor. This leads to restrictions on the wordlength used for error terms. Firstly, there is the need to transfer sums of weighted errors, $\sum_k w_{kj} \delta_k$, across the data bus. Secondly, error terms are restricted by the capacity of the multiplier.

In forming the error term, δ_j, products of the form $w_{kj}\delta_k$ must be accumulated as expressed below

$$e_j(n) = \sum_{k=K}^{K+n} w_{kj}\delta_k \qquad \ldots (16)$$

$$\delta_j = y_j e_j(N). \qquad \ldots (17)$$

The product $w_{kj}\delta_k$ must be supplied by the k-th neuron which, in general, is not in the same processor as the j-th neuron. Therefore, partial sums of products, $e_j(n)$, need to be transferred across the data bus. e_j is restricted to the same number of bits as the data bus, 16 bits in the case of HANNIBAL, using saturation and truncation.

Multiplication by the sigmoid derivative, y_j, is equivalent to right shifting by 2 to 6 bits. The extra number of bits needed for lossless representation is equal to the difference between the maximum and minimum bit shifts as illustrated in Fig. 2. Therefore, a suitable representation of δ_j is from 16 to 20 bits.

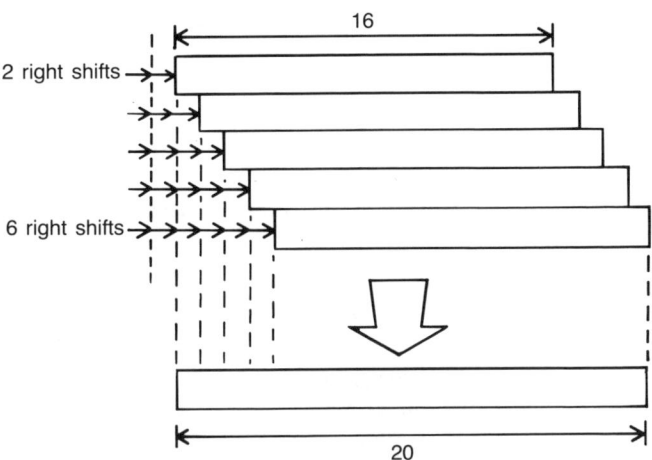

Fig. 2 Diagram showing that the required number of extra register bits equals the difference between the maximum and minimum number of bit shifts.

The multiplier accepts an 8 bit operand and a 16 bit operand as shown in Fig. 1. In forming the product $w_{ji}\delta_j$, the weight is chosen to be truncated to 8 bits of precision and so it is convenient to always restrict δ_j to 16 bits.

The error term given by equation (17) has a dynamic range controlled by the number of integer bits, I_δ:

$$-2^{I_\delta-1} \leq \delta \leq 2^{I_\delta-1}(1-2^{-15}). \qquad \ldots (18)$$

Values for I_δ are needed which are suitable for many types and sizes of net. This is discussed below for nets with a single hidden layer.

Consider, firstly, a net with one output node. It can be shown that, with the piecewise linear activation function used, error terms of output neurons always satisfy the following inequality:

$$|\delta| \leq \frac{3}{16} < 2^{-2}. \qquad \ldots (19)$$

Consequently, it may be shown that error terms in the hidden layer satisfy the following if there is one output neuron:

$$|\delta| \leq \frac{3}{64} 2^{I_w-1} < 2^{I_w-5}. \qquad \ldots (20)$$

Therefore, with one hidden layer and one output neuron, a sufficiently large value for I_δ is:

$$I_\delta = \max(-1, I_w - 4). \qquad \ldots (21)$$

At the other extreme architectures such as HANNIBAL allow over 1024 synapses per neuron. To prevent saturation with 1024 synapses per neuron, 10 more integer bits are required, that is

$$I_\delta = I_w + 6. \qquad \ldots (22)$$

However, this gives a precision of 2^{I_w-10} which is insufficient as demonstrated below. Consider an error term of the form $\delta_j = y_j w_{kj} \delta_k$. At initialisation y_j, w_{kj}, δ_k are typically around $\frac{1}{8}, \frac{1}{32} 2^{I_w}, \frac{1}{8}$ respectively. Therefore the precision needs to be better than 2^{I_w-11} to preserve typical values.

A compromise is taken between $(I_w - 4)$ and $(I_w + 6)$, that is $I_\delta = I_w + 1$. This choice is plausible from a statistical perspective. If we assume that, with a large number of output nodes, error terms in the output layer have zero means and are statistically independent, then the standard deviation of n weighted error terms,

$$\sum_{k=K}^{n} w_{kj} \delta_k, \qquad \ldots (23)$$

is $\sqrt{n}$ times that of one error term, $w_{kj}\delta_k$. With $n = 1024$, $\sqrt{n} = 2^5$. Therefore, if $I_\delta = I_w - 4$ is adequate with one output neuron, then this argument suggests the following is a good choice:

$$I_\delta = (I_w - 4) + 5 = I_w + 1. \qquad \ldots (24)$$

A suitable dynamic range for $e_j(n)$ can be derived by similar arguments. Since $\delta_j = y_j e_j(N)$, $e_j(n)$ requires two more integer bits than δ_j. Thus

$$I_e = I_w + 3$$

$$-2^{I_e - 1} \leq e_j(n) \leq 2^{I_e - 1}(1 - 2^{1-B}). \qquad \ldots (25)$$

In order to calculate a weight increment, Δw_{ji}, an error term, δ_j, is multiplied by the learning-rate, η, and an input, x_{ji}. Both η and x_{ji} are represented by 8 bit numbers and are consistent with the capacity of the multiplier. x_{ji} is signed whereas η is unsigned. η has a dynamic range which includes small and comparatively large values

$$2^{-6} \leq \eta \leq 4(1 - 2^{-8}). \qquad \ldots (26)$$

2.2.3 Dithering and auto-scaling

In this section two novel methods are discussed for improving performance during on-chip training: dithering of weight increments to allow reduced weight wordlengths, and auto-scaling of weights to extend their dynamic range without increasing memory.

The wordlengths of weights must be sufficiently large to avoid the net becoming untrainable, a problem which occurs when the maximum calculated weight increment determined by the training algorithm is less than a single quantisation step. In general a weight increment will tend to decrease as training converges. An idealised curve of weight increment versus time is shown for illustrative purposes in Fig. 3(a), together with the quantised value, $\Delta \hat{w}$, using magnitude truncation. It can be seen that when the value of Δw falls below a quantisation step the value of $\Delta \hat{w}$ becomes zero, and no further modification of the weight is possible. If this is true for all weights then no further training can take place.

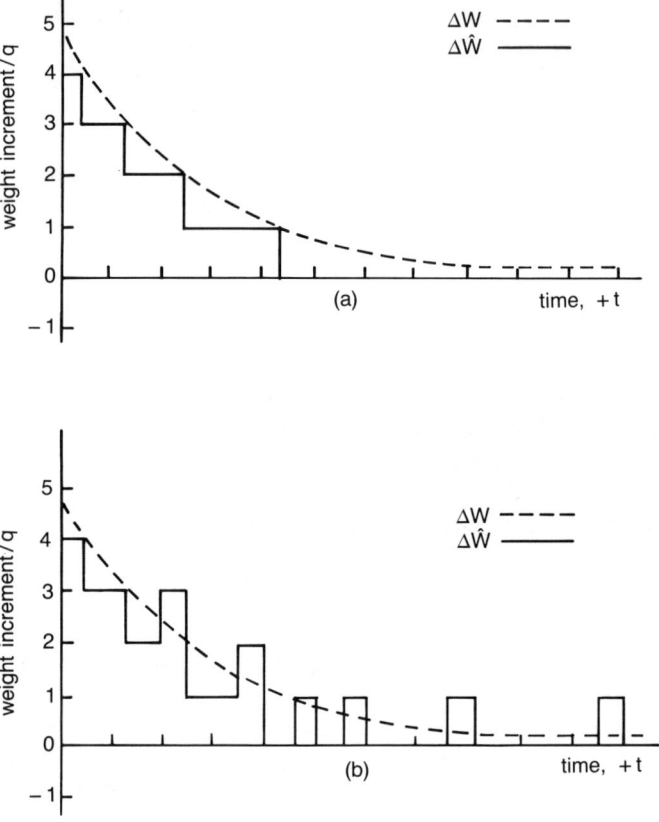

Fig. 3 (a) Idealised weight increment value ΔW and quantised value ΔŴ.
(b) Idealised weight increment value ΔW, and quantised value ΔŴ after adding noise prior to quantisation.

An approach which limits the weight resolution is to add noise when updating weight values prior to truncating and storing the weight. This introduces a probabilistic element into the weight updating. This is illustrated in Fig. 3(b), which when compared with Fig. 3(a) shows single quantisation level transitions being made probabilistically. Considering for the present only positive values of weight increments, if the noise source has a uniform probability distribution in the range 0 to q (where q is a single quantisation step) then the probability of transition is proportional to the quantisation error $|\Delta w - \Delta \hat{w}|$. If Δw is greater in magnitude than one quantisation step then the $\Delta \hat{w}$ component of Δw is added deterministically into the weight, whilst the $|\Delta w - \Delta \hat{w}|$ component is added probabilistically. When Δw is smaller than the first quantisation step weight updating becomes entirely probabilistic, preventing permanent attenuation to zero. A pseudo-random binary sequence (PRBS) generator can be used as the noise source. PRBS generators approximate the desired distribution function and can be produced using only a few shift-register elements and exclusive-NOR gates. These produce sequences of length $2^N - 1$ where N represents the number of shift register elements. For the simulations discussed here a PRBS generator with eight elements, shown in Fig. 4, was selected which computes a separate pseudo-random number for each weight during an up-date cycle. This is done by clocking the PRBS generator at the same rate as weight up-dating.

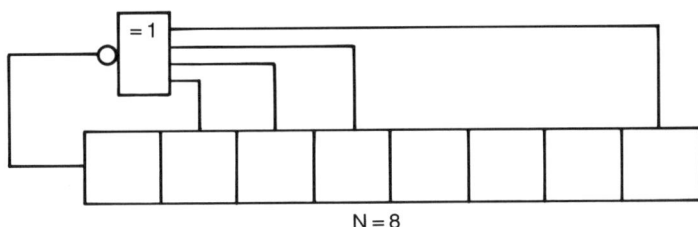

Fig. 4   PRBS generator of length 255.

Figure 5 shows the results of simulations of the technique, displaying training time versus weight wordlength for a character recognition problem (described later in section 3.2). Without dither, learning fails below 11 bits per weight, whereas dither allows learning with as few as 5 bits per weight.

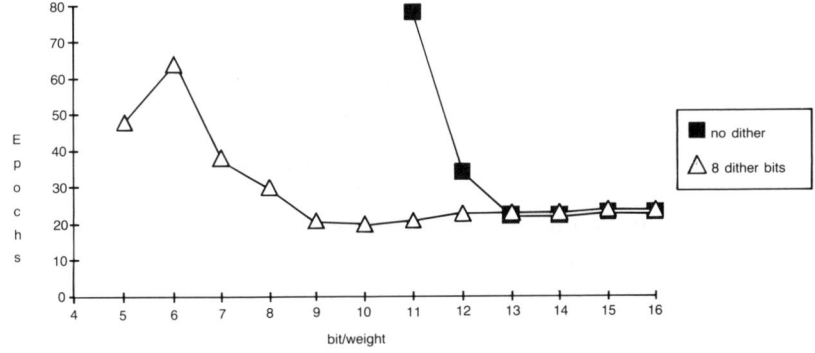

Fig. 5   Training time, in epochs, versus weight wordlength for a character recognition problem.

A limited dynamic range of weights has been shown to improve generalization [3]. However, in some applications the chosen dynamic range could be too small, in which case backpropagation suffers excessive saturation. The auto-scaling option prevents this without having to increase the number of bits per weight. A scale factor, 2^{n_j}, is introduced into the non-linear activation function,

$$a_j = \frac{1}{1 + e^{-2^{n_j} s_j}} \qquad \ldots (27)$$

where n_j is an integer ranging from 0 to n_{max} and is initialized to 0.

During weight up-dating a flag is set if any of the weights of the j-th neuron are saturated and if $n_j < n_{max}$. If the flag is set then during the next updating cycle the j-th neuron's weights are halved and n_j is incremented:

$$w_{ji} := w_{ji}/2, \qquad 0 \le i \le I_j$$
$$n_j := n_j + 1. \qquad \ldots (28)$$

The halving of weights is compensated by incrementing n_j, and each auto-scaling operation doubles the dynamic range but halves the precision. The loss of precision only slightly affects performance because neurons are robust to weight quantization. Furthermore, prolonged weight saturation is prevented. The effective dynamic range of the weights is increased to:

$$-2^{n_{max} + I_w - 1} \le w_{ji} \le 2^{n_{max} + I_w - 1}(1 - 2^{1-B}). \qquad \ldots (29)$$

In experiments auto-scaling was found to give a closer agreement with unrestricted floating-point.

3. SIMULATIONS

3.1 Statistical treatment of performance data

The aim of the simulations was to compare the fixed point hardware description model with the floating-point model of computation. The simulations cover a variety of problems and MLP sizes. The models can be compared by measuring the misclassification rates for training and test sets. Misclassification rate is defined as the percentage of a pattern set which is misclassified.

Performance is partially dependent on the initial set of weight values. This is true for floating-point as well as finite wordlength models. Therefore it is necesary to repeat simulations using randomly generated initial weight values and statistically treat the performance data.

Let the training simulations be repeated S times for each computational model. All training parameters are the same except for the random initial weight values. The sample mean, $\bar{E}$, and standard deviation, σ, of the error rates are calculated for training and test sets. Standard error, ϵ, is the experimental error of $\bar{E}$.

$$\epsilon = \frac{\sigma}{\sqrt{S}} \qquad \ldots (30)$$

If ϵ is sufficiently small, the mean error rate can be quoted with the desired number of significant figures, otherwise standard error must also be quoted.

Let $\bar{E}_F$ be a sample mean for floating-point and $\bar{E}_H$ be the corresponding sample mean for a hardware descripton model. $\bar{E}_F$ and $\bar{E}_H$ can be objectively compared although the standard deviations, σ_F and σ_H, should also be taken into account.

Sample means and deviations can be used to calculate confidence levels which quantify hardware performance. A formula for confidence should embody a user's criteria for good and bad performance. Different applications may require different criteria. An example is given below.

Suppose a maximum error-rate, E_{max}, is specified. If $\sigma_H \ll \bar{E}_H$ then assume an approximately normal distribution. This assumption can be checked with tests using the χ^2 distribution. The confidence level, C, is the probability that the error-rate for test data is smaller than the maximum specified.

$$C = Pr(E_H \leq E_{max}) = \Phi(u)$$

$$u = \frac{E_{max} - \bar{E}_H}{\sigma_H} \qquad \ldots (31)$$

$\Phi(u)$ is the cumulative distribution function of a standardised normal variable, u. If $\sigma_F \ll \bar{E}_F$ and the aim is to emulate floating-point computation to a tolerance, k, then:

$$E_{max} = (1+k)\bar{E}_F \qquad \ldots (32)$$

where $k = 50\%$, say.

$$u = \frac{(1+k)\bar{E}_F - \bar{E}_H}{\sigma_H} \qquad \ldots (33)$$

The following sub-sections include tables of statistically treated results for four different problems. Confidence levels are quoted in the tables where S is large enough and $\sigma_H \ll \bar{E}_H$. Simulations were performed on an Apollo DN10000 computer with a vector processor. The vector processor could be used for the floating-point model but not the hardware description models. Much processing was required because of the large number of simulations and the detailed hardware modelling, particularly for large nets. The choice of sample size, S, was problem dependent because of differing computational complexity.

3.2 Character recognition problems

In this problem bit-mapped characters are to be classified irrespective of font. There are four characters ('A','B','C','D') each drawn from four fonts. Bit-maps are corrupted by complementing individual bits with probability P_B. There are C corrupted examples of each exemplar bit-map in a training set or a test set. Therefore, data sets each consist of 16C pattern vectors. Each pattern vector corresponding to the 64 pixels in each bitmap. Zero valued input bits are mapped to -1 and ones are mapped to $(1-2^{-7}) = 0.992$. For the results presented below the learning-rate was 0.1, the net contained 5 hidden nodes, and each training simulation lasted 100 epochs. Simulations were carried out 100 times per computational model.

Table 1 compares hardware models with floating-point for 2.5% bit noise and three corrupted pattern vectors per exemplar (C=3). Table 2 shows performance figures for $P_B = 10\%$, and six corrupted pattern vectors per exemplar (C=6), which is a more testing problem. In Table 1 error-rates for the fixed point hardware model are 0% or very small unless $I_w = 3$. Confidence levels were not calculated because the condition $\sigma_H \ll \bar{E}_H$ did not hold. Table 2 shows good performance by the hardware models although there is degradation if $I_w = 3$. Performance with 8 bit/weight and dither is as good as with 16 bit/weight.

Table 1 Character Recognition Problem, 2.5% Bit Noise

Model	Iw	Training Set		Test Set	
		Mean error rate /%	Standard deviation	Mean error rate /%	Standard deviation
Floating-point	1	0	0	0	0
	2	0	0	0	0
	3	0	0	0.27 ± 0.08	0.82
16 bit/weight	1	0	0	0	0
	2	0	0	0.063 ± 0.04	0.36
	3	0	0	2.20 ± 0.25	2.54
8 bit/weight plus dither	1	0	0	0	0
	2	0	0	0.08 ± 0.05	0.51
	3	0.04	0.03	1.52 ± 0.19	1.87

Table 2 Character recognition problem, 10% bit noise.

Model	I_w	Training Set		Test Set		Confidence level /%
		Mean error rate /%	Standard deviation	Mean error rate /%	Standard deviation	
Floating-point	1	0	0	7.66 ± 0.11	1.09	—
	2	0	0	7.65 ± 0.14	1.41	—
	3	0.17 ± 0.04	0.38	7.86 ± 0.18	1.8	—
16 bit/weight	1	1.04 ± 0.06	0.59	5.98 ± 0.09	0.9	> 99.9
	2	0.08 ± 0.03	0.28	6.28 ± 0.13	1.34	> 99.9
	3	0.35 ± 0.06	0.63	9.42 ± 0.24	2.44	83
8 bit/weight plus dither	1	1.00 ± 0.06	0.59	5.83 ± 0.12	1.24	> 99.9
	2	0.05 ± 0.02	0.23	5.89 ± 0.17	1.74	99.6
	3	0.25 ± 0.04	0.45	8.74 ± 0.24	2.4	90

3.3 Yes/no speech problem

In this problem "yes"/"no" utterances are to be classified independent of speaker. Each utterance is represented by utterance segmentation followed by low order linear prediction. Three features are extracted from each of 5 segments to give a 15-dimensional feature vector. Each element of the vector is represented as a variable 8 bit value. The training set consists of 381 "yes" utterances and 417 "no" utterances. The test set consists of 301 "yes" utterances and 319 "no" utterances.

Table 3 shows results using 5 hidden nodes and a learning-rate of 0.1. Simulations were carried out 100 times per computational model. Good performance was obtained with two and three integer bits ($I_w = 2,3$). The digital models were worse at classifying training data but better at generalization than floating-point. Error-rates for hardware models were higher with one integer bit ($I_w = 1$) as indicated by lower confidence levels. Note that the error-rates are more spread out for hardware models than floating-point, as indicated by the columns of standard deviations. Again there is little difference between 8 bit and 16 bit hardware models.

Table 3 "Yes"/"No" Speech Problem

Model	Iw	Training Set		Test Set		Confidence level /%
		Mean error rate /%	Standard deviation	Mean error rate /%	Standard deviation	
Floating-point	1	6.04	0.05	5.65	0.02	—
	2	6.04	0.03	5.65	0.02	—
	3	6.05	0.08	5.63	0.07	—
16 bit/weight	1	8.14 ± 0.04	0.43	8.41 ± 0.05	0.51	55
	2	7.29 ± 0.02	0.20	4.85 ± 0.06	0.56	> 99.9
	3	7.19 ± 0.04	0.43	5.35 ± 0.04	0.35	> 99.9
8 bit/weight plus dither	1	7.98 ± 0.04	0.36	8.66 ± 0.05	0.59	36
	2	7.07 ± 0.02	0.22	5.07 ± 0.04	0.43	99.6
	3	6.52 ± 0.02	0.24	4.99 ± 0.04	0.39	> 99.9

3.4 Bar coder

This is the first example of a large but somewhat artificial problem containing 1024 inputs and 1024 outputs. The aim here is to show that the hardware models work well even with large numbers of active synapses and accumulated error terms.

Each input vector, p, is a randomly generated array of 1024 binary bits. The desired output vector, t, forms a bar graph with an array of ones at one end and an array of zeros at the other. The length of the array of ones equals the frequency of ones, n, in the input array

$$n = \sum_{i=1}^{1024} p_i$$

$$t_i = \begin{cases} 0, & l < i \leq 1024 \\ 1, & i \leq l \end{cases}$$

Input 0s and 1s are mapped to -1 and $(1-2^{-7})$ respectively.

There is just one hidden layer. Given infinite precision, a solution exists with just one hidden neuron irrespective of the dimension of the input vector. If all weights in the first layer are the same then the linear weighted sum is a linear function of n, and each output node acts as a simple comparator. However, because the piece-wise linear sigmoid circuit used has only 128 possible outputs, so at least two hidden neurons are required to give a lossless representation of n.

Results are shown in Table 4 using two hidden neurons, a learning-rate of 0.1 and 1000 patterns in both training and test sets. Fifteen simulations were carried out for each computational model each lasting one hundred epochs. The number of integer bits was set to one ($I_w = 1$).

There are two types of performance measures to choose from. The first type is the percentage of mis-classified pattern vectors and the second is the percentage of incorrect output bits. In the former case, correct classification corresponds to perfect counting. With a very large number of output nodes, even a very small bit-wise error-rate is likely to result in a high mis-classification rate. Therefore, bit-wise error-rates are more meaningful for this problem and they are quoted in Table 4. The tables show that the hardware models give virtually equal performance as each other, as well as being marginally better than floating-point. Confidence levels are correspondingly high.

Table 4 Bar Coder Problem

Model	Training Set		Test Set		Confidence level /%
	Mean error rate /%	Standard deviation	Mean error rate /%	Standard deviation	
Floating-point	1.17 ± 0.01	0.024	1.24 ± 0.01	0.025	—
16 bit/weight	1.21	0.018	1.22 ± 0.01	0.027	> 99.9
8 bit/weight plus dither	1.21	0.018	1.22 ± 0.01	0.028	> 99.9

3.5 Entropy coder

This is the second large net problem with 1024 inputs and 1024 outputs. The aim of this problem is to entropy code binary sequences, a harder problem than the bar coder. An input array is an array of binary bits and the aim is to reproduce the input vector at the output nodes.

There is one hidden layer containing M nodes and each hidden neuron outputs an 8-bit word. The array of words forms a compact code. Elements of the input vector are statistically independent and the probability of a one is p. Outputs of hidden neurons are always positive and so the sign bits can be ignored. Therefore, 1024 bits are compressed into $7M$ bits. The bit-rate is allowed to be just above the entropy, $H(p)$.

$$\frac{7M}{1024} > H(p) = -p \log_2 p - (1-p) \log_2(1-p)$$

$$M > 1024 H(p)/7$$

With a probability level of 0.2, entropy is 0.722. Therefore M should satisfy the inequality $M > 105.6$. Consequently M was chosen to be 120. Simulations were carried out using the following settings:

Learning-rate, $\eta = 0.1$,
500 pattern vectors per data set,
50 epochs per simulation,
$S = 4$ simulations per computational model.

Simulations for this problem are computationally intensive, hence only four simulations were carried out per model.

Bit-wise error-rates are listed in Table 5. They are around 0.02% for floating-point and 0.1% for hardware description models. There is no difference in performance between 8-bit and 16-bit models. Therefore 8 bit/weight would require 1.875 Mbits of weight storage whereas 16 bit/weight would require 3.75 Mbits of weight storage. This illustrates the usefulness of the dithering option for very large nets.

Table 5 Entropy Coder

Model	Iw	Training Set Mean error rate /%	Test Set Mean error rate /%
Floating-point	1	0	0.013 ± 0.002
	2	0	0.019 ± 0.001
	3	0	0.021 ± 0.003
16 bit/weight	1	0.078 ± 0.001	0.096 ± 0.001
	2	0.078 ± 0.002	0.087 ± 0.009
	3	0.098	0.098
8 bit/weight plus dither	1	0.078 ± 0.001	0.095 ± 0.002
	2	0.079 ± 0.002	0.090 ± 0.005
	3	0.085 ± 0.003	0.080 ± 0.003

4. CONCLUSIONS

This chapter has discussed the computational issues involved in the design of digital neural networks, with particular reference to the HANNIBAL chip. An analysis of finite wordlength fixed-point MLPs has been presented for neuron activation and on-chip learning. In particular, suitable dynamic ranges and precisions have been specified for inputs, weights, error terms and weighted sums. A novel dithering technique allows the halving of weights from 16 to 8 bits or less thereby potentially doubling the available number of synapses. Another novel technique, auto-scaling, prevents saturation of weights during training.

The hardware description model was tested with four different problems using up to 1024 inputs and 1024 outputs. A statistical technique was developed for measuring the influence of weight initialisation on performance.

This allowed a proper comparison of hardware description models with unrestricted floating-point computation. Simulations showed little difference in performance between them.

The model has enabled the HANNIBAL neural net chips to be specified, and novel features such as dither and autoscaling to be included. The successful simulations mean we can have confidence in our design for solving real world problems.

REFERENCES

1. Myers D J, Brebner G E: 'The implementation of hardware neural net systems', Proc IEE 1st Int Conf on Artificial Neural Networks, Conf pub No 313, pp 57—61, (16—18 October 1989).

2. Woodland P C: 'Weight limiting, weight quantization and generalization in multi-layer perceptrons', Proc IEE 1st Int Conf on Artificial Neural Networks, Conf pub No 313, pp 297—300, (16—18 October 1989).

3. Myers D J, Hutchinson R A: 'Efficient Implementation of Piecewise Linear Activation Function for Digital Neural Networks', Electronics Letters, 25, No 24, pp 1662—1663, (23rd November 1989).

4. Rumelhart D E, McClelland J L: 'Parallel Distributed Processing Volume 1: Foundations', The MIT Press Cambridge, Ma (1987).

15

A VLSI ARCHITECTURE FOR IMPLEMENTING NEURAL NETWORKS WITH ON-CHIP BACKPROPAGATION LEARNING

D J Myers, J M Vincent, D A Orrey
BT Laboratories

1. INTRODUCTION

In this chapter the development of a CMOS integrated circuit known as HANNIBAL (hardware architecture for neural networks implementing backpropagation algorithm learning) [1] is described. The chip can be used as a building block for efficiently implementing large neural networks. Although any network topology is allowed, it is intended for implementing MLPs. As its name implies, it allows training to be performed via the backpropagation algorithm. This chip does not provide explicit inter-neuron connections, but has its communication bandwidth tailored to match that of digital host systems with which networks are likely to communicate in envisaged applications.

HANNIBAL features on-chip weights storage and allows large networks to be constructed by cascading chips, with little support circuitry required.

2. COMPUTATIONAL AND COMMUNICATION REQUIREMENTS

A range of interconnection or communication topologies have been proposed for neural networks. Two of the more common are (i) fully connected nets, as shown in Fig. 1(a), where each neuron communicates with every other neuron, and (ii) layered nets, where communication is only provided between layers, as shown in Fig. 1(b). An example of a fully connected net is the Hopfield associative memory [2], and the MLP is an example of a layered net.

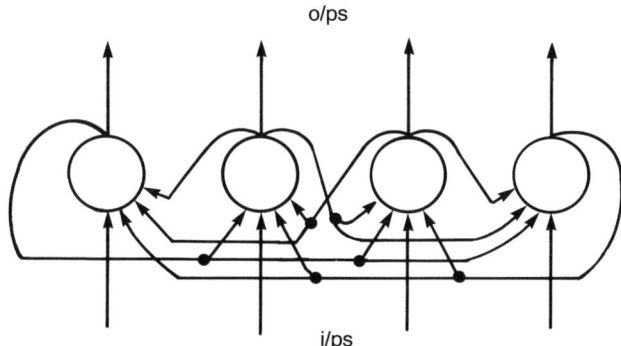

Fig. 1a   Fully connected net.

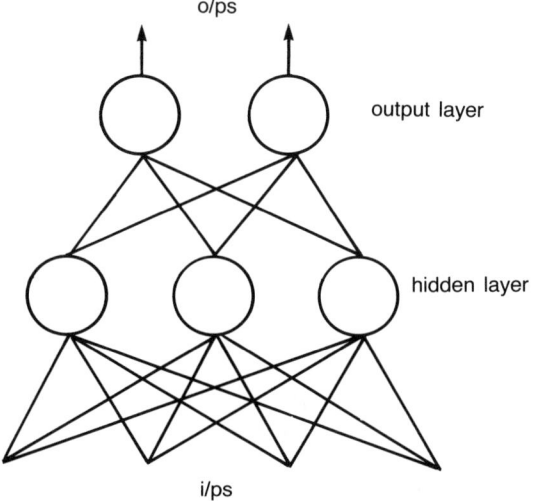

Fig. 1b   Layered net.

The communication requirements of layered nets are much less demanding than those of fully connected nets. However if hardware is to be flexible, it needs to provide the capability for full intercommunication. If this is done by providing physical interconnections or 'wires' then a system of N neurons will require N^2 connections.

The computational requirements of a neural network fall into two categories as follows.

- Evaluation of the output of the net (forward pass).
- Evaluation of an updated set of weight values for the net, as defined by the training algorithm.

A range of training algorithms exist. The training is often a more computationally intense activity than the evaluation of the output of the net, and requires a richer set of operations. The computational requirements (i.e. the nature of the computations) for the evaluation of the net output are relatively restricted and unchanging from net to net.

2.1 Evaluation of the net output

For the forward pass the computation required at each node varies with the neuron model being used. However, the model being considered here is the simple, widely used model shown in Fig. 2. Referring to Fig. 2, for neuron j this requires the following computations:

1. Weighting of inputs y_i by weights w_{ij}.

2. Summation of weighted inputs plus a threshold t_j of neuron j to form o_j:

$$o_j = \sum_i w_{ij} \cdot y_i + t_j \qquad \ldots (1)$$

3. Evaluation of the activation function output $y_j = f(o_j)$.

The model also requires the ability to store N weights values.

The activation function is a non-linear function that may take a number of forms. The function most frequently made use of is the sigmoidal function:

$$y_j = (1/(1 + e^{(-o_j)})) \qquad \ldots (2)$$

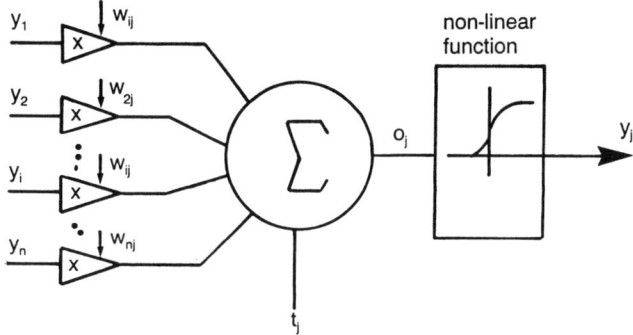

Fig 2. Simple neuron model.

Therefore a simple digital processor dedicated to the evaluation of the neuron function would consist of N words of weights memory, a fast parallel multiplier to form the products $w_{ij}.y_i$, and an accumulator to form the sum of products o_j, followed by a circuit to evaluate y_j, the output of the activation function. The inputs y_i to the processor are provided sequentially. Such a 'node processor' (NP), which is shown schematically in Fig. 3, is at the core of the HANNIBAL architecture.

2.2 The backpropagation training algorithm

As previously stated, a number of training algorithms exist. Each has its specific computational requirements, which will impact on the network hardware requirements for a trainable net. The backpropagation algorithm [3] for training MLPs requires that an error signal be propagated back through the layers from the output layer. This affects the communications requirements of the net. By comparison, the Boltzmann machine algorithm [4] requires only 'local' information and therefore may be more suitable (in this regard) for hardware implementation. The backpropagation algorithm has been selected for incorporation into the HANNIBAL chip because it is arguably the most popular neural net training algorithm in current use. In particular it is being used in the work on facial feature location described in Chapter 1. A real-time hardware demonstrator for facial feature location is one of the intended applications of the HANNIBAL chip.

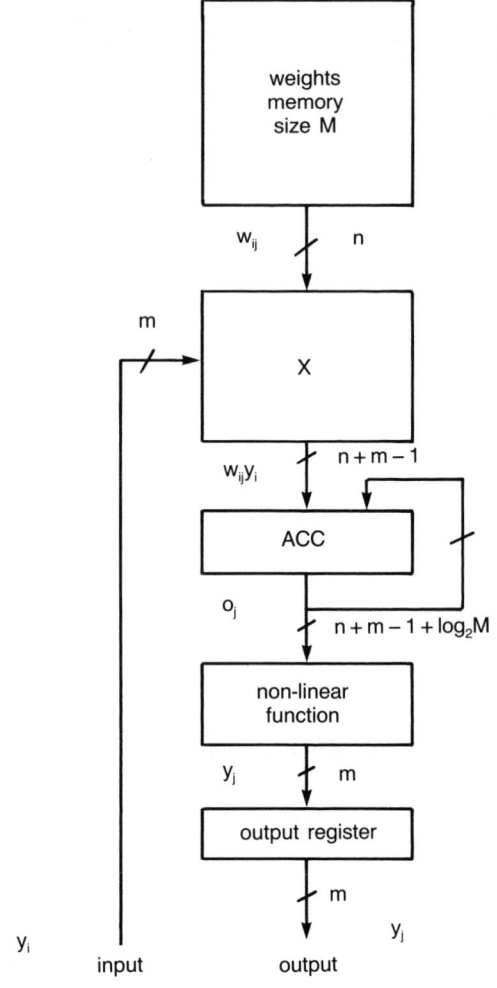

Fig. 3 Basic node processor structure.

The simplest form of the backpropagation algorithm is as follows:
For the jth node in the output layer:

$$\delta_j = (e_j - y_j) \cdot y_j \cdot (1 - y_j) \qquad \ldots (3)$$

where y_j is the output of node j, and e_j is the expected output of node j. The weight connecting the ith node in the layer below to the jth node in the output layer is then modified as follows:

$$w_{ij}(n+1) = w_{ij}(n) + \eta.\delta_j.y_i \qquad \ldots (4)$$

where v is a constant known as the learning rate. For layers below the output layer (known as hidden layers), the form of (4) remains the same, but the calculation of δ is more complex. For the jth node in the first hidden layer (i.e. one below the output layer):

$$\delta_j = y_j(1-y_j). \sum_k \delta_k.w_{jk} \qquad \ldots (5)$$

where the summation is over all the nodes in the output (or in general, all the nodes in the layer above).

From these equations it is clear why the algorithm is known as backpropagation, and also why it might be considered difficult to implement in hardware; the δ values for hidden nodes are obtained by propagating back and summing δ values from layers above, weighted by the strengths of the node connections. The calculation of equation (3) requires information local to each output node, but calculation of equation (5) requires distributed information. What is worse, the summation in equation (5) is the exact opposite of the summation required in the calculation of the output of the net (equation (1)) in that it requires the weights values associated with the output of a particular node, whereas the forward pass summation at each node requires the weights associated with the inputs to the node. If the simple digital node processor described in section 2.1 is being used, each of the weights values required to evaluate equation (5) will reside on a different processor.

In a popular variant of the backpropagation algorithm, a momentum term is included in the weight updating equation, giving it the following form:

$$w_{ij}(n+1) = w_{ij}(n) + \eta.\delta_j.y_i + m.\Delta w_{ij}(n) \qquad \ldots (6)$$

where $\Delta w_{ij}(n) = w_{ij}(n) - w_{ij}(n-1)$, and m is a constant known as the momentum coefficient. The inclusion of the momentum term has important implications for the hardware; it becomes necessary to store either $\Delta w_{ij}(n)$ or $w_{ij}(n-1)$, significantly increasing memory requirements. Because of the large hardware overhead, and because simulations on a range of test problems based on feature location and recognition in binary and greyscale images showed that the use of a momentum term showed little, if any, performance improvement, this feature was not included in the HANNIBAL design.

3. HANNIBAL ARCHITECTURE

A number of possibilities exist for multi-processor architectures which implement VLSI neural networks. Almost all are based on the realistic assumption that each processor has only a single multiplier, and therefore can only operate on incoming data items sequentially — i.e. that it has the basic capabilities of the node processor described in section 2.1.

Assuming that each processor in an architecture is sequential, then it is redundant to provide communication resources that present the processor with more than one data item at a time. The goal of the communication strategy employed is to keep all processors operating at as close to 100% efficiency as possible. The computational requirements outlined in section 2, plus the communication strategy employed will define the additional functional requirements of the processor, and thus the circuitry required.

Two types of architecture have been considered; (i) Processor per connection (or "synapse") architectures, and (ii) Processor per neuron architectures. Architectures in the first category were rejected because they are too hardware intensive, and for other reasons discussed elsewhere [5]. The HANNIBAL chip is based on a processor per neuron architecture.

3.1 Processor communication in forward pass mode

For networks with many node processors (as described in section 2.1 and shown in Fig. 3), a bus based (global bus or bus per layer) communication scheme could be adopted, in which a single node processor (NP) captures the bus and broadcasts its output to all the other NPs, but this is unattractive due to the need to drive many NP inputs from a single NP output. The problem increases with the size of the network.

In order to overcome this scaling problem, pipelined communication is employed for HANNIBAL with data being fed to and read from each NP via the use of linear arrays of shift-registers as shown in Fig. 4. The throughput rate of the shift-registers is matched to the computation time of the NP. In this scheme two shift-registers are provided; an input and an output register. The computation scheme and timing are also shown for the simple single layer example in Fig. 4. Note that the input values are used immediately they arrive at a node processor. The use of separate input and output registers together with the provision of a temporary storage register (not shown in Fig. 3) in each node processor to hold calculation results, permits pipelining, i.e. new input data can be input to a layer before it has completely evaluated its outputs related to the previous input vector.

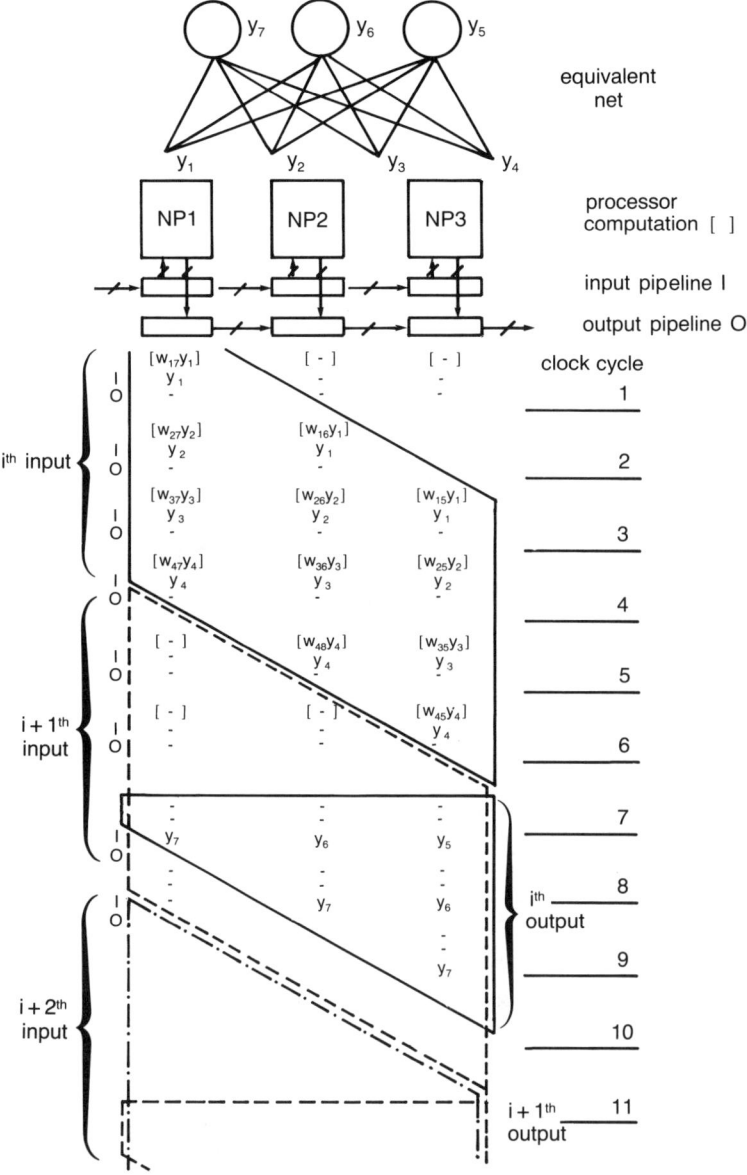

Fig. 4 Linear array of NPs implementing single layer net.

The structure of Fig. 4 is easily extended to cope with multiple layers. The requirement is for the results calculated by a collection of NPs

320 A VLSI ARCHITECTURE

implementing one layer of a multi-layer net to be passed as input to the next layer. This is achieved by connecting the output register of the lower layer to the input register of the upper layer at the layer boundary such that the output of the lower layer forms the input to the next. This is illustrated in Fig. 5, which shows two layers, one of three NPs and one of two, connected together.

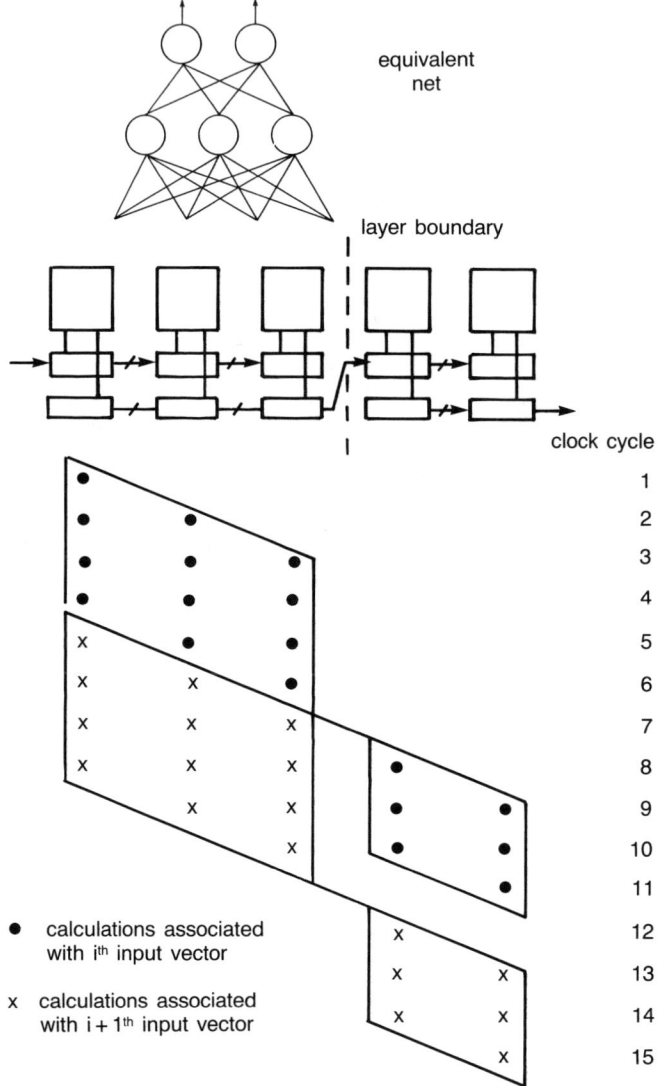

Fig. 5   Implementing multi-layer nets on the linear array.

The structure of Fig. 5 can be maximally pipelined (input vectors fed in continually) if the number of inputs is greater than the number of units in the first layer, and the number of NPs in each succeeding layer monotonically decreases.

3.2 Incorporating backpropagation training

The linear shift-register architecture described above has been developed based on the computational requirements of the forward pass through the net. To allow training using backpropagation the architecture needs to be extended. This requires that the communication shift-registers be made bi-directional in order that data can be communicated from the upper layers of the net back through to the lower layers.

From Equation (3) it can be seen that in order to evaluate δ_j for the jth node of the output layer, the expected output of that node, e_j, must be provided to the NP. This is achieved by clocking the values into the shift register array in the reverse direction from the output end. In addition the NP must be extended to allow the calculation of Equation (3).

In order to evaluate δ_j for the jth node of a hidden layer a weighted summation is required as shown in Equation (5). If this summation is performed local to the node j of the layer concerned a number of undesirable effects could result. Firstly, if only the values δ_k from the layer above are propagated back, each node will be required to store not only the weight values associated with all its inputs, but also the weight values associated with its fan-outs. This doubles the weight storage requirement, and duplicates the storage of each weight. A further serious problem is associated with ensuring that the pairs of stored weight values, which are stored on different NPs, keep in step during training.

These problems are overcome by evaluating the product $\delta_k.w_{jk}$ at each node of the layer above, and propagating the results back. However this scheme still has the drawback that for many cycles the average efficiency of the array in terms of simultaneous processor utilization drops to that of a single NP because only one NP at a time in the lower layer can evaluate the summation of Equation (5).

The solution to the problem adopted in the HANNIBAL architecture is to form the product $\delta_k.w_{jk}$ in the kth NP in the layer above, and perform the summation over all k in a distributed manner as the values are propagated back across that layer. This involves providing an adder at each NP in the backpropagation path in the upper layer. The NP will contain an adder (its accumulator) in any case, so the backpropagation path in the upper layer is routed through this. On reaching the layer boundary, the summations will

322 A VLSI ARCHITECTURE

have been completed. These are propagated unchanged through the lower layer. Thus two modes of backward flow are required. These are illustrated in Fig. 6 for a net of 3 hidden nodes and 3 output nodes. The calculation scheme for the backpropagation phase is also shown. Note that the two register pipelines are commoned together when feeding data back in this way. A further backpropagation mode exists in which only the direction of flow of the input registers is reversed. This is used to feed expected output values e_j into the net during training (see Equation (3)).

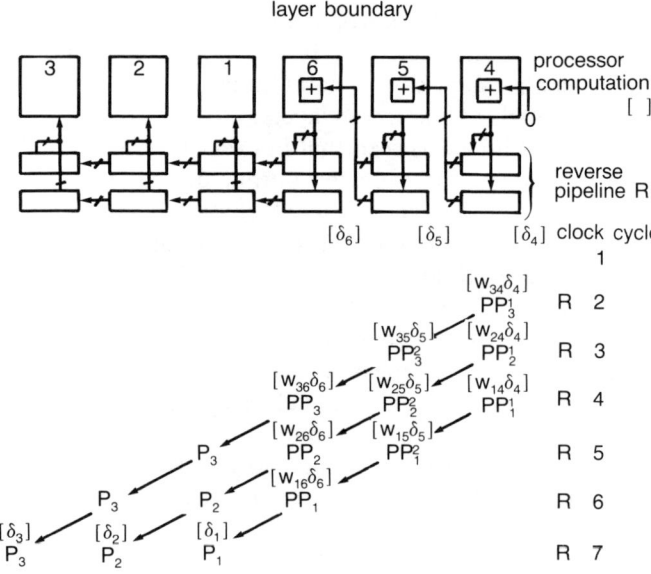

$P_j = \sum_k \delta_k w_{jk}$ summed over all nodes in layer

PP_j^l = partial sum (up to l^{th} term) of P_j.

Fig. 6 Backpropagation of erros in linear array.

The efficiency of the architecture is lower during training than during the forward pass, however the use of distributed computation stops it from falling too low. Exact figures for efficiency in terms of percentage processor utilisation depend on the dimensions of the net that is mapped on to the architecture.

4. WORDLENGTH SELECTION AND ARCHITECTURAL ENHANCEMENTS

Having settled on the basic architecture for HANNIBAL, it is necessary to determine suitable data and weight storage wordlengths and wordlengths of internal and intermediate data values, in order to ensure that the design achieves the required performance at the lowest cost in terms of hardware required. To this end a finite wordlength model of the architecture has been constructed in a high level language (C), in which the effects of varying the wordlengths, accumulator size, and other parameters internal to the node processor can be simulated, as well as simulating variable width communications paths between NPs. Its performance on a range of test problems was compared with full floating point simulations in order to determine suitable design parameters for the HANNIBAL chip.

As a result of these simulation experiments, this finite wordlength model was enhanced in ways that map elegantly into hardware, in order to achieve performance comparable to the floating point simulation. A full description of these simulations is given in another chapter (Chapter 14, by J M Vincent).

The wordlengths selected and some of the more significant of the enhancements are discussed below.

4.1 Input and output wordlengths

Because the architecture, though general purpose, is intended primarily for applications involving feature location in greyscale images, the width of the input data is set at 8 bits. Therefore the input and output registers are both 8 bits wide. During training an accumulating sum-of-products (see equation (5)) is propagated back. This needs greater than 8 bit precision. During this phase it is possible to common up the input and output registers, to form a 16 bit backpropagation path. Simulations show that this provides adequate accuracy.

4.2 Dither

Given that HANNIBAL has on-chip weights storage, the resolution of the weights has a significant impact on chip area. It has been shown [6] that for pre-trained nets quite coarse weight quantization, and therefore quite small wordlengths, can be used. Unfortunately, much larger weight wordlengths are required, to allow for small incremental changes in weights values during training. If the wordlength is too short, the network freezes well before it reaches the optimum solution.

HANNIBAL allows the choice of two weights wordlengths; 16 bits and 8 bits. In order to allow satisfactory training with 8 bit weights, an optional technique known as dither can be used during training. This consists of adding pseudo-random noise, generated by a simple 8 bit pseudo-random binary sequence generator, during the evaluation of the updated weight value (Equation (4)). This is performed in the accumulator of the NP at high precision, prior to truncation back to 8 bits. The noise is added in the bit positions below the truncation point, and its effect is to allow probabilistic updating of the weight when increments become small. Note that this use of noise is very different to the concept of adding noise to the training data to improve generalisation.

4.3 Auto-scaling

When using a fixed point binary data representation, with finite wordlengths, the allowable dynamic range (maximum positive and negative values that data items can take) has to be set. For example, input data to the HANNIBAL chip is constrained to lie in the range -1 to $(1-2^{-7})$. Simulations show that restricting the weights values to a maximum magnitude of 4 (w_{ij} in the range -4 to $+4-2^{-5}$) results in no serious degradation of performance when compared with the full floating-point model.

HANNIBAL has options to restrict weights values to half and one quarter of the above weights ranges, allowing an increase in precision of one and two bits respectively (i.e. halving or quartering the minimum quantization step size).

In order to ensure that precision is maximised at each NP during training, HANNIBAL has a further option known as auto-scaling. In this option each NP is initialised to interpret its stored weights values as being in the range -1 to $+1-2^{-7}$. If, during weight updating, any weight value stored on that NP saturates (reaches the limit of the dynamic range) then during the next update cycle weights (and thresholds) are halved after updating and prior to being stored back in memory. When the weights are subsequently used to evaluate the forward pass output of the NP, the output of the accumulator must be doubled in order to give a consistent result. This process can be repeated one further time, if saturation is again detected. The process of auto-scaling can be envisaged as re-expressing Equation (1) in the following way:

$$o_j = 2^{n_j} \cdot (\sum_i (2^{-n_j} \cdot w_{ij}) \cdot y_i + (2^{-n_j} \cdot t_j)) \qquad \ldots (7)$$

where $n_j = 0, 1$ or 2. Note that each NP operates auto-scaling independently, so the weight range in operation at each NP is independent. The use of auto-scaling gives network performance very similar to the full floating-point model.

4.4 Activation function

The digital implementation of the activation function of Equation (2) can be done in a number of ways. Perhaps the obvious method of evaluating it is by table lookup, in which the finite wordlength value o_j is used as an address to look up an appropriate value of y_j, stored in a read-only memory (ROM). Assuming 16 bit addresses and 8 bit data this would require 0.5 Mbit ROM, which would potentially consume a significant amount of chip area.

In order to significantly reduce this overhead a seven segment piecewise linear approximation to the sigmoid function has been developed which maps compactly into an integrated circuit realisation [7], which also gives the derivative of the activation function $y_j(1-y_j)$ (see Equations (3) and (5)). Each of the segments has a gradient which is a power of 2. The form of the approximation is shown in Fig. 7, with the true sigmoid plotted for comparison.

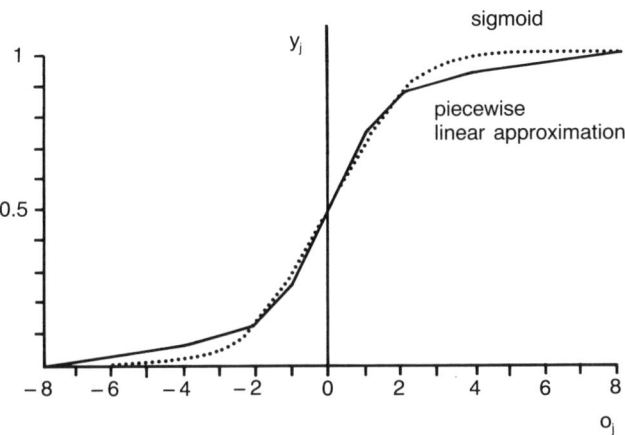

Fig. 7 Piecewise-linear approximation to sigmoid.

The seven segment piecewise linear approximation has been built into the finite wordlength model used to verify the hardware, and has shown comparable performance to the ideal sigmoid.

5. CHIP DETAILS AND OPERATION

The HANNIBAL chip consists of 8 node processors, which are being integrated into a single 9 mm by 11.5 mm CMOS integrated circuit. The chip is designed in a sub-micron (0.7μm) technology, and contains 0.75 million transistors, and is designed to operate at 20 MHz, or up to 160 M connections per second. The chip is cascadeable to build up larger networks — a 50 chip PCB giving performance of up to 8 G connections per second. The chip can also be multiplexed, under some circumstances, to allow each NP to operate as up to 4 neurons.

5.1 Memory

Each NP is provided with 9216 bits of memory for weights storage, which can be configured as either 512 17 bit words, or 1024 9 bit words. Each word consists of a weights value plus a flag bit. The flag bit is used to indicate whether or not the connection exists, allowing the implementation of layers and/or nets which are not fully connected. The memory in each chip can be flexibly allocated to allow the chip to be operated as n NPs each with ($4096/n$) 16 bit weights values (or ($8192/n$) 8 bit weights values, where $n = 1,2,4,8$. This allows the implementation of nets containing neurons with up to 8192 inputs.

5.2 Multiplexing

In some applications, the memory available to each NP, and the speed of operation of the chip may be significantly greater than is required. In such circumstances the memory in each NP can be partitioned into up to four sectors of any size within the constraints of the maximum memory size. The NP can then be multiplexed to operate as up to four 'virtual' neurons. This requires that the entire NP array is set up as a single physical layer. The output of the array is fed back to the input, and the entire array is multiplexed to form, in sequence, the layers of the 'virtual' MLP to be implemented. Multiplexing cannot be used in conjunction with training; it is restricted to forward pass calculation only.

5.3 The complete node processor

Figure 8 shows the main functional blocks for the complete node processor. In addition to the weights memory, the following blocks are identified:

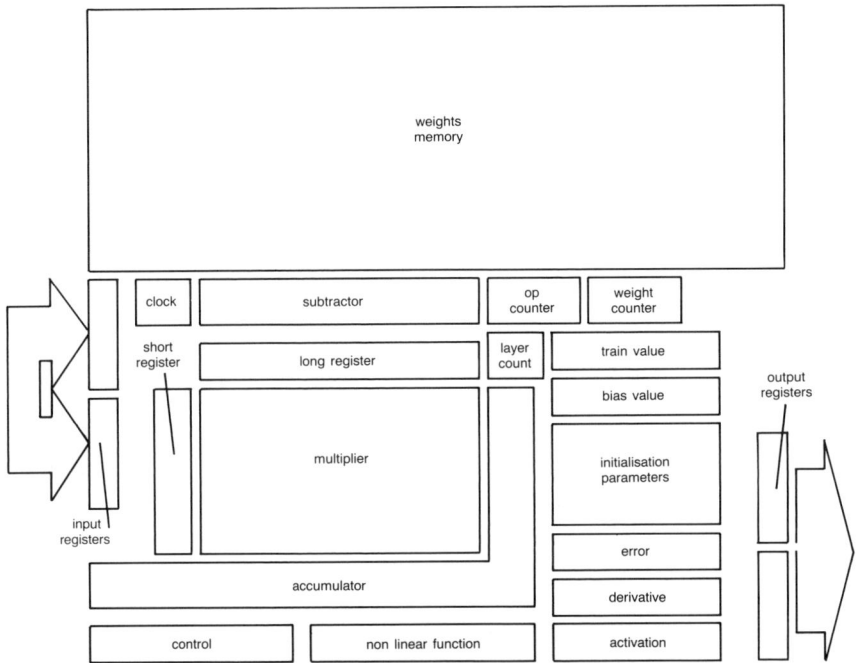

Fig. 8 Major functional blocks.

- 16 × 8 bit fast parallel multiplier with associated long and short input registers.

- 32 bit accumulator capable of being pre-loaded with a 16 bit threshold or bias value t_j (see Equation (1)).

- 8 bit subtractor for evaluating $(e_j - y_j)$ (see Equation (3)).

- Bypassable non-linear activation function generator which also generates gradient of activation function.

- 16 bit op(eration) counter for timing and control.

- 16 bit weight counter for generating addresses for weights memory.

- 8 bit train value register for storing learning rate or training gain factor η (see Equation (4)).

- 4 × 16 bit bias value registers for storing bias or threshold values for up to 4 'virtual' neurons.

- 16 bit error register for storing δ_j (see Equations (3) and (5)).

- 8 bit activation value register for storing y_j during training.

- 8 bit derivative register for storing $y_j.(1-y_j)$ during training.

- Initialisation parameter registers, used to store a number of parameters used in the setting up, timing and control of the NP, including information such as position of the NP in the network to be executed, and the size of weights memory used.

- 16 bit input and output registers and bi-directional data ports capable of being operated as 2 8 bit ports.

The NP also requires a control circuit to sequence its operation, and a local 2 phase clock generator.

5.4 Chip operation

When one or more HANNIBAL chips are used to implement a neural network, the individual processors must first be initialised. This is achieved by using global control signals to load configuration information into each NP, followed by initial values for the weights memories. If the net is not being trained, these values will have been pre-calculated.

After initialisation the net can be set up to execute in forward pass mode (pre-trained), or can be trained by cycling through forward pass/backpropagation/weight update modes, again controlled by external global signals. There is also a facility for unloading weights values from the NPs, which allows weights values to be stored after training.

Control of all these operations is very straightforward, with only four global control signals required. These signals are also used to set up a range of modes which are used for chip testing.

6. CONCLUSIONS

The digital architecture presented in this chapter, and the HANNIBAL chip based upon it, are intended to provide the building block for implementing neural networks for real-time applications. The sequential pipelined communication strategy used results in high performance and ease of communication with digital host systems.

The innovative features in the architecture, including the use of dither and a compact activation function circuit, result in efficient use of silicon real-estate without compromising performance.

REFERENCES

1. Orrey D A, Myers D J, Vincent J M: 'A High Performance Digital Processor for Implementing Large Artificial Neural Networks', Proceedings of Custom Integrated Circuit Conference CICC'91, San Diego, Ca (12—15th May 1991).

2. Hopfield J J: 'Neural Networks and Physical Systems with Emergent Collective Computational Abilities' Proc. Nat. Acad. Sci. USA (1982).

3. Rumelhardt D E, Hinton G E, Williams R J: 'Learning Internal Representations by Error Propagation' in Rumelhardt D E, McClelland J L, (eds), 'Parallel Distributed Processing' 1 MIT Press, Cambridge, Ma pp 318—362 (1986).

4. Graf H P, de Vegvar P: 'A CMOS Implementation of a Neural Network Model', Proc. Stanford Conf. on Advanced Research in VLSI Design, MIT Press Cambridge, Ma (1987).

5. Myers D J, Vincent J M, Oldfield J K, Orrey D A: 'Digital Approaches to Neural Network Implementation', IEE Colloquium on VLSI Signal Processing Architectures, Digest No. 1990/95 (31st May 1990).

6. Woodland P C: 'Isolated Word Speech Recognition Based on Connectionist Techniques' Br Telecom Technol. J. 8 No. 2 (April 1990).

7. Myers D J and Hutchinson R A: 'Efficient Implementation of Piecewise Linear Activation Function for Digital VLSI Neural Networks' Electronics Letters 25 No. 4 (1989).

16

AN OPTO-ELECTRONIC NEURAL NETWORK PROCESSOR

N Barnes, P Healey, P McKee, A W O'Neill,
M A Z Rejman-Greene, E G Scott, R P Webb, and D C Wood
BT Laboratories

1. INTRODUCTION

We have seen in previous chapters that typical neural network models comprise large numbers of relatively simple processing elements (PEs), usually arranged in layers, with massive interconnectivity between the layers. The processing elements usually perform simple nonlinear transformations on their summed inputs and feed the results to many processors in the next layer by means of the weighted interconnections. Hardware realisations must emulate both the parallelism and massive interconnectivity of these models. Digital electronics is now capable of extremely large complexity and functionality in a very small space; however, massive interconnectivity is very difficult to implement with this technology. Optics, on the other hand, offers massive interconnectivity, both spatial and temporal, but is very limited in terms of logical complexity. Hardware realisations of artificial neural networks will require both complexity and connectivity and thus the most practicable solution may be a sensible mixture of both technologies. Hybrid opto-electronic hardware, with optics performing the interconnectivity and the electronics carrying out the processing, offers significant potential speed advantages for large neural networks. These advantages can be used either to enable a pre-programmed network to recall at very high speed, or could be used to reduce significantly the training time. This chapter describes the first high speed opto-electronic neural network demonstrator constructed at the BT Laboratories [1] and explores the optics/electronics tradeoffs for future hardware realisations.

Since the optimum solution is likely to be a hybrid between optics and electronics, it is important to establish an efficient interface technology. A solution to this problem is emerging for the related task of serving the ever increasing communications requirements both within and between VLSI chips. Communications places a substantial overhead on the chip area and power consumption, that grows rapidly with the scale of integration. This communications bottleneck can be overcome by using parallel optical interconnects to exploit the third dimension [2]. Such applications require high-speed transducers which are physically small, dissipate little power and present low electrical loading to the electronic circuits. These requirements are met by arrays of multiple-quantum-well (MQW) surface modulators optically 'wired' to a common remote source [3]. By taking this approach, rather than using an array of optical emitters such as LEDs or lasers, power dissipation problems in the transmitter array are avoided. (Further architectural advantages of this approach will be discussed later.)

Opto-electronic solutions, however, only make sense if we have an efficient and practicable optical 'wiring' technology. To this end, we are developing a range of computer originated passive optical elements to perform such functions as beam splitting (fan-out), weighting, and light collection (fan-in) [4].

It is likely to be some time before opto-electronic technologies will be capable of implementing very large neural network processors, but their early deployment could be for modest sized problems (of the order of 100 neurons) requiring very fast processing. Such networks could find application in future managed telecommunications transmission and switching network control systems.

The following sections describe the fundamental operations required in typical neural network models, a novel opto-electronic architecture and the associated implementation technology developed at BTL.

2. NETWORK MODEL

A basic operation, fundamental to the operation of most neural network models, is the matrix-vector product. That is, each PE or 'neuron' calculates the total stimulation arriving at its inputs via weighted interconnections from other PEs or system inputs (which are labelled $x(j)$) and forms an activation signal, $y(i)$, which it then passes on to other PEs or system outputs via further weighted interconnections (see Fig. 1.)

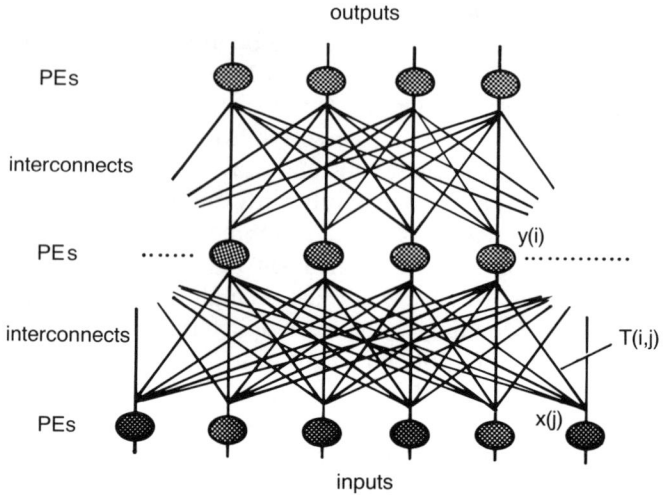

Fig. 1 Layered model of artificial neural networks.

That is

$$y(i) = S\{\sum_{j=1}^{N} T(i,j).x(j)\} \quad \ldots (1)$$

where, $y(i)$ represents the output of the i-th PE in an upper layer in response to the nonlinearly transformed $S\{.\}$ sum of the weighted outputs from the N PEs, $x(j)$ $\{j \in 1,...N\}$, in the layer below. $T(i,j)$ represents the inter layer interconnection strength between processing elements j and i. When viewed across all PEs in a particular layer, the resulting computation can be represented by a matrix-vector product operation

$$y = S\{T.x\} \quad \ldots (2)$$

where bold upper and lower case letters correspond to two-dimensional matrices and one-dimensional column vectors respectively. $x = [x(1), x(2)...x(N)]^T$ and $y = [y(1), y(2)...y(M)]^T$ for typographical reasons, column vectors will be represented in transpose notation within the text.

Figure 2a shows the 'classical' optical architecture for the realisation of equation (2), where the input and output vectors are arranged spatially in a one dimensional (1-D) format. This architecture is relatively simple to implement when the fan-out/in interconnection functions between the input/output vectors and the weight matrix *T* are replaced by one-to-one interconnections between 'electrical' replications of the 1-D input and output vectors, as shown in Fig. 2b. The architecture shown in Fig. 2b allows the three functional planes to be stacked in a compact sandwich effectively eliminating the interconnection problem; alternatively, the planes may be interconnected by simple imaging optics.

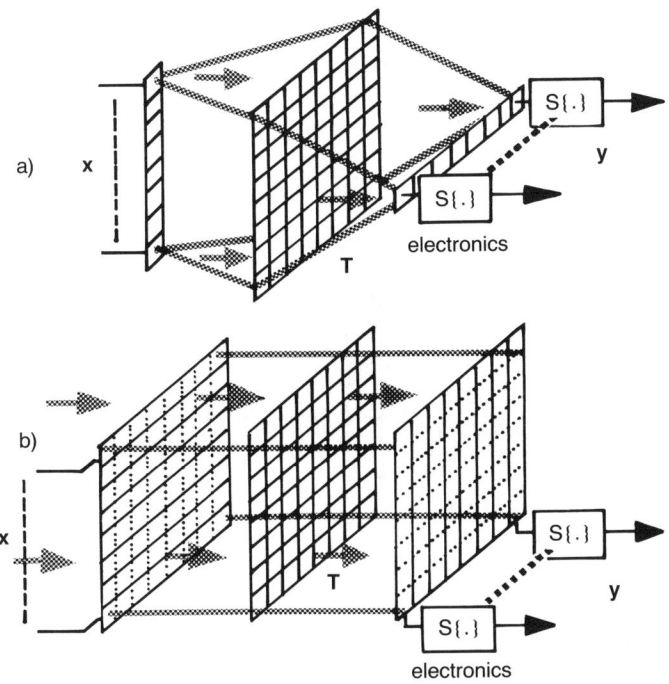

Fig. 2 (a) Classical matrix-vector architecture,
(b) Modified architecture employing replication of the I/P and O/P vectors.

3. AN OPTO-ELECTRONIC NEURAL NETWORK DEMONSTRATOR

To date, most opto-electronic neural network expriments have been based on the architecture shown in Fig. 2b [5,6]. The input vector is usually arranged to drive an array of light emitting diodes (LEDs) or liquid crystal modulators. The resulting intensity modulated optical beams carry a series of replicas of the input vector signal to the interconnection weight matrix *T* — which is commonly a fixed transparency mask. The resulting weighted beams are then collected on an array of photodiodes connected to current summing preamplifiers. The nonlinear transfer function is nearly always performed in the post-detection electronics.

The network that has been developed differs from previous implementations in having several novel features which open up the possibilities for performance improvements and integration. The use of optical modulators, instead of light emitters, gives much more flexibility in the design of an optical matrix-vector processor since the ordering of the first two planes in Fig. 2b is then unimportant. Thus, the weight matrix can be brought outside the opto-electronic layers allowing the opto-electronic devices to be stacked closer together as a general purpose opto-electronic subassembly. The application program stored in the external weight matrix can be determined, and possibly reconfigured, at later time.

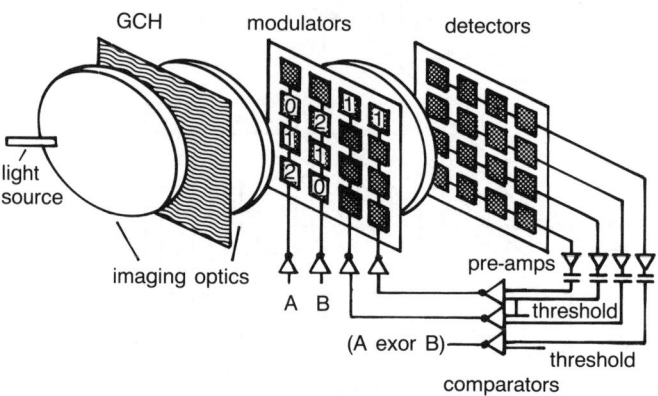

Fig. 3 Opto-electronic hardware demonstrator, preprogrammed to implement the Exclusive-OR function.

MQW optical modulators fabricated in indium phosphide (InP) semiconductor material have the advantage of a transparent substrate at their operating wavelength (1.5 μm), allowing the modulator array to be used in transmission without etching, thus simplifying the optical configuration. Two dimensional arrays of InGaAs/InP based MQW surface modulators driven by standard high-speed CMOS are employed in the experimental artificial neural processing system. Transition times were fast enough for 100 MBit/s operation and the potential exists to increase the operating speed to many

GBit/s. Apart from being much faster than LED or liquid crystal modulator arrays, MQW diodes may also offer advantages in terms of hybrid integration in the route towards an optical 'neurochip'. Figure 3 shows the modified architecture employed in the experiments.

The interconnection weight matrix is stored externally in a computer generated hologram (CGH) which transforms the optical power supply beam into a two dimensional (2-D) array of appropriately intensity coded optical beams. This 2-D array of weighted beams addresses the modulator array on the input plane. The 1-D input vector replication function is performed by connecting each element of the input vector to a linear array of optical modulator diodes. After passing through the modulator diodes, the beams are imaged onto a linear array of connected photodiodes, arranged orthogonal to the modulator arrays. The fan-in function on the output side of the network is performed by summing the photocurrents from the array of connected photodetectors with transimpedance amplifiers. These amplifiers have AC coupled outputs, to eliminate the DC voltages that are associated with the unmodulated beams from the input devices. The amplifiers have a transimpedance of 7 kΩ and produce a voltage swing of approximately 8 mV peak-to-peak, for the modulation of a unity weight spot.

A more compact 'neurochip' version of Fig. 3 is shown in Fig. 4. In this case, the optical modulators and detectors are fabricated on opposite sides of the same substrate by double-sided epitaxy (DSE) [9] and hybrid-integrated with the electronic components.

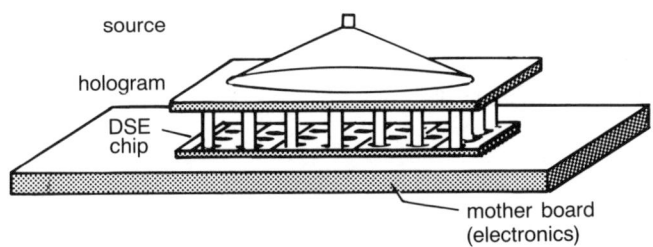

Fig. 4 'Neurochip' architecture.

The external application program (weight matrix) is simple to replace mechanically and/or optically, for example; a range of application programmes could be stored on different regions of a translating slide or disc. And, since the application programs can be stored as Fourier holograms, which have inherent shift invariance, their alignment with respect to the optical system is non critical. Alternatively an array of switchable laser sources arranged to illuminate different regions of the hologram would allow rapid (nanosecond) reconfiguration of the processing function. The latter capability, combined with the speed advantage of optoelectronic systems, could be employed in the realisation of larger networks through the extensive use of time multiplexing.

To explore the new architecture (Fig. 3), we built an optical network to recognise exclusive-or (EXOR) combinations in two input data streams. Simple, two-layer MLP networks to recognise EXOR combinations are well known [7]. Figure 5a shows the example on which we have based the network. Each of the nodes receives the weighted sum of inputs from the previous level. A signal is passed to the next level, or not, depending on whether this weighted sum is above, or below, some threshold. As the weights are coded here as different optical intensities in the beams they must take positive values. We therefore represent the weights in the form of a positive definite matrix, minus a uniform bias, determined by the input signals. The negative bias is used to set the threshold value in the output comparators [8]. Figure 5b shows how this unipolar form is implemented here. The threshold at the second layer is set by the sum of the signals from the two input nodes.

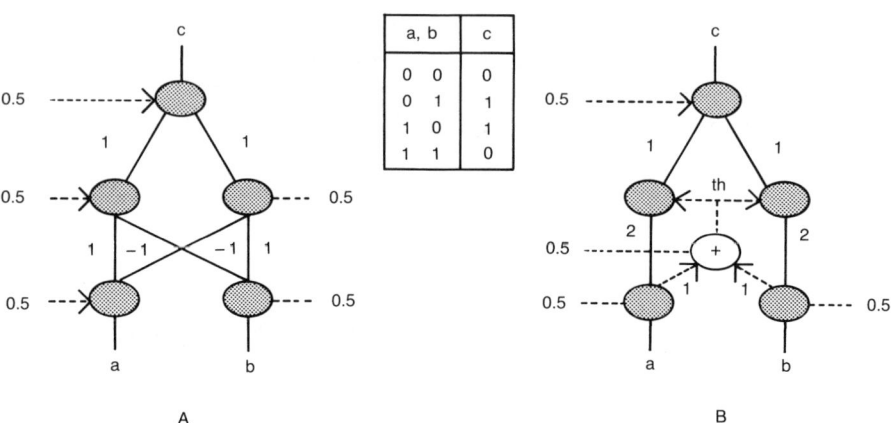

Fig. 5 A: MLP for EXOR and, B: Unipolar equivalent.

To form the interconnection weight matrix for the EXOR problem, the hologram is required to produce input beams with weights of zero, one and two units. A two layer logical network is mapped onto a single layer physical realisation by feeding the results from the first logical layer back onto unused input modulators which are then employed in the second logical layer of the network. Figure 3 shows the design and indicates the relative strengths of the optical weights. In our implementation the common drives to the modulators are connected in a slightly different way, to take better account of the symmetries in the output from the hologram. Only eight of the 16 available MQW modulator/detector pairs in the experimental hardware are actually used.

The optical network recognises EXOR patterns in the two input data streams and is currently capable of being clocked at rates in excess of 50 MBit/s. There is no detectable dependence on the bit sequence, when a 'return to zero' (RZ) data format is used. If the RZ format were not used, the AC coupling would prevent consecutive levels being detected and it would cause the average level of the bit patterns to affect the required DC threshold bias. Figure 6 shows the two, 16 bit, input data patterns and the resulting EXOR output from the network.

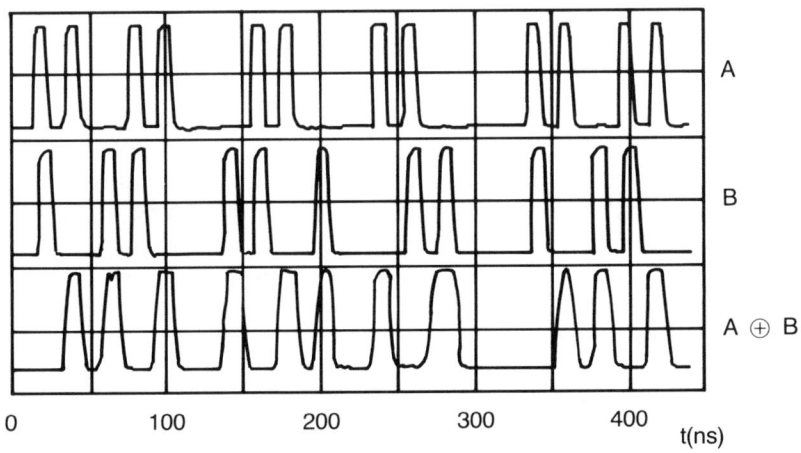

Fig. 6 EXOR input and output waveforms.

4. MQW SURFACE MODULATORS

The MQW structure is shown in Fig. 7, it comprises 200 57 Å InGaAs wells separated by 57 Å InP barriers grown on an InP substrate by gas-source MBE. On it were formed 4×4 planar arrays of 60 μm diameter modulators on 125 μm centres, each connected by a metallisation pattern to a separate bond pad at the edge of the array. (Growth and fabrication details may be found in [10]).

An array was mounted in an 18-pin chip carrier, drilled to allow optical transmission, which was surface-mounted onto a printed circuit board carrying standard high-speed CMOS drive circuitry. High-speed CMOS was chosen because it offered the best combination of speed, operating voltage and power consumption of the standard logic families.

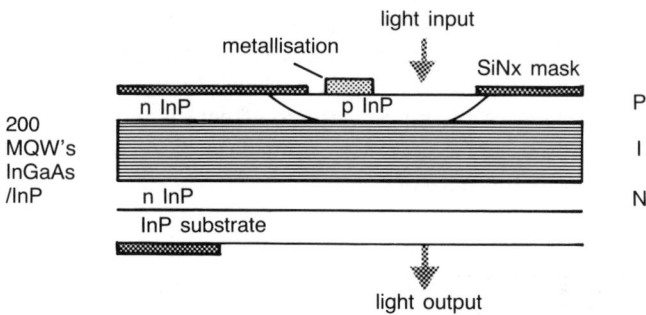

Fig. 7 MQW surface modulator (not to scale).

The insertion loss of the modulators, measured against voltage at various input wavelengths, is shown in Fig. 8. From these curves, it can be seen that the largest obtainable modulation depth with a 6 V drive (the maximum available from the high-speed CMOS) was 1.7 dB at 1.519 μm with a 15 V bias added to the drive voltage. However, the largest output signal was found at the slightly longer wavelength of 1.524 μm where, although the modulation depth dropped to 1.5 dB, the insertion loss reduced from 5.4 dB to 2.6 dB. The half-peak-signal wavelength range was 13 nm (Fig. 9), allowing the use of standard Fabry-Perot lasers.

The modulation depth may be increased to 3 dB with 30 V drive [10]; alternatively, modulators may be grown on both sides of the substrate by double-sided epitaxy, doubling the available modulation depth [9]. (Operating in reflection, via substrate entry and reflecting electrodes, would also improve the modulation characteristics.) Even without these modifications, the 1.7 dB modulation depth achieved corresponds to less than 5 dB power penalty compared with complete extinction. A detector-limited measurement has shown the modulator 10-90% transition times to be less than 2 ns and, since the total capacitance of each modulator plus remote bond pad is only 1.5-2 pF, operation at many Gbit/s should be possible with a suitable drive circuit. The negligible electrical load presented by these devices makes drive buffers unnecessary, therefore close integration will allow modulation at the internal operating speed of the fastest logic chips. The rise and fall times achieved with commercial high-speed CMOS were 3.4 ns, significantly faster than normally obtained because of the low capacitive load presented by the modulators and fast enough for operation at 100 Mbit/s.

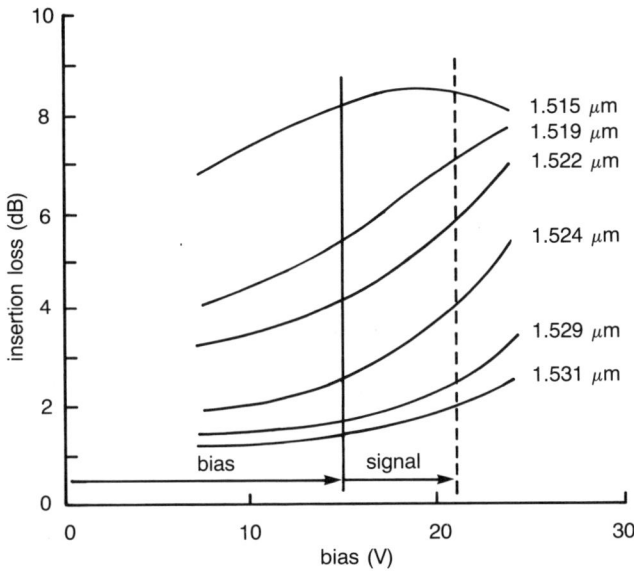

Fig. 8 MQW modulator insertion loss.

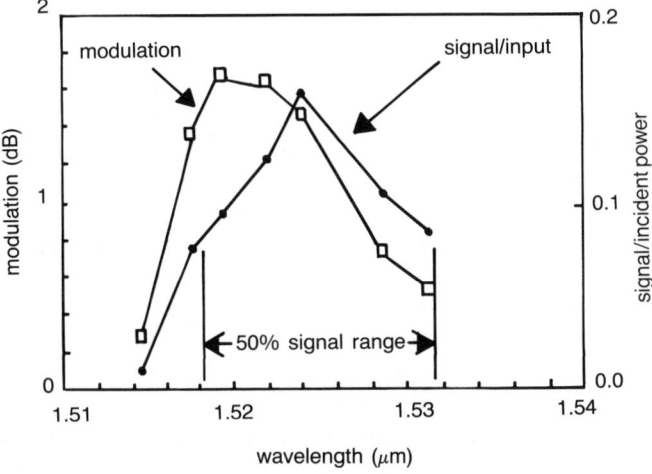

Fig. 9 MQW modulator wavelength range (measured with 6 V drive on 15 V bias).

5. COMPUTER GENERATED HOLOGRAM

The hologram is designed to work in the Fourier transform plane between a pair of collimating/focusing lenses. It is made as a binary phase hologram with a pattern of 0 and π phase shifts etched into a quartz glass substrate. The pattern is composed of a number of repeats (here 20×20) of a single cell design. This single cell is broken up into 256×256 pixels, the phase shifts of these pixels are determined by a simulated annealing technique, to minimise the error in the chosen spot pattern [4]. The cell dimensions determine the angular separation of the spots. Roughly 75% of the incident light energy goes into the designed spot pattern, resulting in individual spots with intensities of about 0, 20 and 40 μW, with the intended ratio of 0:1:2 accurate to around 2%. This accuracy is limited at the moment by Fabry-Perot effects in the quartz glass, the design accuracy is better than 0.1%. We have recently produced quad-phase holograms which have the advantage of removing the need for inversion symmetry in the target response, whilst retaining the efficiency of the earlier binary-phase devices.

6. ALTERNATIVE ARCHITECTURES

Individually, (and in small arrays) the optical modulator diodes and detector photodiodes offer very high speed (order GHz) and low power performance. When connected in large arrays, however, the build up of capacitance will reduce this performance advantage. Hence, a major limitation of the architecture described so far is that the number of opto-electronic interface devices (modulators and detectors) grows as the number of synapses, ie as N^2.

Clearly, the performance degradation associated with large arrays of connected high speed opto-electronic devices would be minimised if purely optical, rather than opto-electronic, techniques could perform both the fan-out and the fan-in functions. Fan-out, or equivalently replication, is relatively simple to implement optically. The computer originated Fourier optics described earlier perform exactly this function on the input optical power supply beam. In that case, not only is the input beam replicated in two dimensions, the individual replications are also intensity weighted. Here, all that is needed are uniform replications of the input image. Thus, in principle, the modulator array may be reduced from N^2 to N, the dimensions of the input vector (image). The row/column architecture, however, does not lend itself to simple fan-in optics design — a new approach is required. The following discussion will develop practical solutions to both the fan-out and fan-in optics design by concentrating on simplifying the fan-in optics design.

It will be shown that the fan-in optics may be simplified by: (i) collecting the weights associated with the input to each PE into a compact group for subsequent spatial integration; (ii) employing the shift invariant properties of Fourier holograms to provide position independent fan-in; or, (iii) using the well known multi-imaging properties of 'fly's eye'/spherical lens combinations [11]. To gain these advantages we must arrange the PEs in each layer on a two dimensional plane. Equation (1) in a two dimensional co-ordinate system becomes:

$$y(i,j) = S\{\sum_{k=1}^{N_1} \sum_{l=1}^{N_2} T(i,j,k,l) \cdot x(k,l)\} \quad \ldots (3)$$

where the output and input PEs are indexed by i,j and k,l respectively. In the following discussions we will assume that the numbers of PEs in each direction is the same; ie, a square array where $N_1 = N_2 = \sqrt{N}$. In matrix notation equation (3) may be cast into two equivalent formulations, each reflecting a different systems architecture:

$$y(i,j) = S\{\text{Weight}[T_{i,j} \otimes X]\} \quad \ldots (4a)$$

or,

$$Y = S\{\sum_{k,l} x(k,l) \cdot T_{k,l}\} \quad \ldots (4b)$$

where bold upper case characters indicate two dimensional matrices. $\otimes$ means take the Hadamard product (mutually multiply the elements of the adjacent matrices), and the Weight[.] of a matrix is sum of all matrix elements. Matrices T_{ij} and T_{kl} contain the synaptic weights associated with each output and input PE respectively (i.e. the elements of T_{ij} and T_{kl} are contained in $T(i,j,k,l)$, given ij and kl respectively). The representations in equations (4a) and (4b) are particularly useful for optical implementations since we can now view the input field X and output field Y as two dimensional images comprising $\sqrt{N} \times \sqrt{N}$ and $\sqrt{M} \times \sqrt{M}$ PEs respectively. Thus, equation (4a) indicates that the input image X is copied to each output PE where it is masked by the interconnection weight matrix $T_{i,j}$ associated with that PE. An equivalent representation, equation (4b), is to form the output image Y by collecting the contributory images cast by the interconnection matrices $T_{k,l}$ associated with each input PE. Thus, there are two equivalent system architectures based on image formation implicit in equation 4, and these will now be considered in some detail.

Before we explore these new architectures, it should be noted that a trivial modification in the way the modulators and photodiodes are connected (e.g. by arranging the photodetectors into square, rather than linear arrays) and regrouping the modulators would transform the 1-D architecture shown in Fig. 2b into this 2-D format. However, there would be no significant advantages resulting from this modification since the physical size of the network and the number of opto-electronic interfaces would remain unchanged. A significant advantage would result if the photodetector dimensions, hence capacitance, could be reduced by demagnifying (or by spatially integrating) the image of the PE input signal $T \otimes X$, onto a small area photodetector. This improvement could be worthwhile since it would retain most of the advantages offered by the existing set-up. The following subsections describe significantly improved realisations.

6.1 Designs based on input image replication

The first solution is based on equation (4a). Figure 10 shows the optical arrangement which is similar to that proposed by Monahan et al in 1977 [11]. The input image X may be formed by either a 2-D array of optical modulators, as described earlier, or by a 2-D array of surface emitting lasers.

The input image is replicated by the computer generated Fourier phase hologram such that the weight matrix T_{ij} associated with each PE in the higher level receives one copy. The resulting Hadamard product ($T_{ij} \otimes X$) is then either spatially integrated by a microlens or tapered lightpipe (Fig. 10a), or demagnified (Fig. 10b), onto the associated photodetector which after electronic processing yields $y(i,j)$. The main drawback of the modified system is that the interconnection weight matrix T must now be returned to its usual position between the optical modulator and detector devices. Practically, T would now take the form of transmission mask or spatial light modulator (SLM), so it would also loose the inherent alignment simplicity and efficiency of the shift-invariant hologram employed previously. However, a liquid crystal spatial light modulator (SLM) could be employed in this position allowing dynamic reconfiguration of the weight matrix, hence flexibility and trainability. This architecture is compatible with the high speed hardware-based training algorithm developed at BTL [12]. An alternative architecture, which is compatible with holographic weight matrices is implicit in equation (4b).

ALTERNATIVE ARCHITECTURES   343

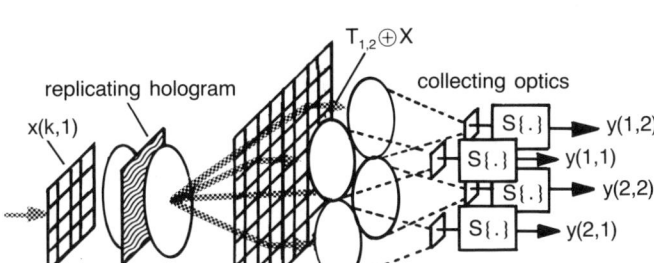

(a)

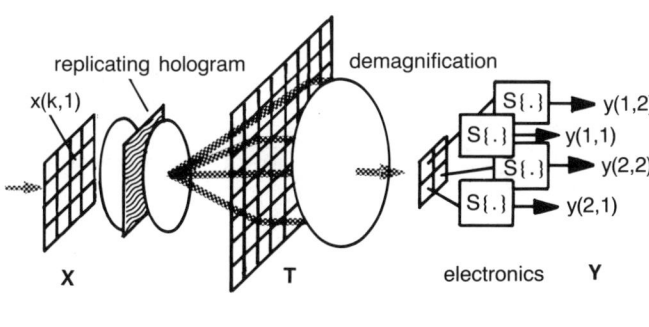

(b)

Fig. 10 Designs based on input image replication employing, (a) an array of spatial integrators, and (b) a demagnifying lens arrangement, to perform the fan-in.

6.2   Designs based on output image formation

Equation (4b) may be used to describe an equivalent representation of an opto-electronic 'neural network' which also minimises the size and capacitance of the interface transducers by performing the replication and fan-in functions in the optical domain. Figure 11a shows a schematic representation of this architecture.

Each element $x(k,l)$ of the input image is arranged to modulate an optical beam, emanating from either a surface laser or diode modulator, which in turn addresses a submatrix $T_{k,l}$ of T via its associated collimating microlens. In fact, $T_{k,l}$ could be stored as a computer generated Fourier phase hologram. Thus, T would be designed as a multi-facet phase hologram such that a common Fourier transform lens placed on its output side will cast all contributory images onto a common detector array. (In the longer term, the preprogrammed holographic weight matrices shown in Fig. 11a could be replaced by real-time holographic materials such as the photorefractives.) Alternatively, the $T_{k,l}$ submatrices could be stored in image-plane form (Fig. 11b), in which case a common objective lens would be required to collect all such submatrix images and bring them into focus on the photodetector array [13]. In principle, this objective lens architecture could also be made programmable. Of the two approaches to output image formation, the Fourier plane approach has the greatest optical power efficiency, is moderately shift-invariant and therefore simpler to set up, but is much more difficult to make programmable.

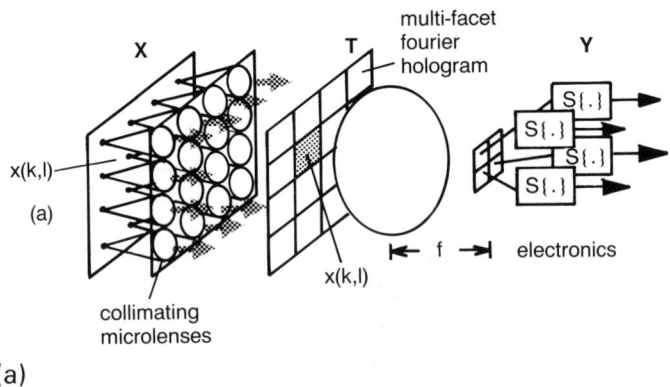

(a)

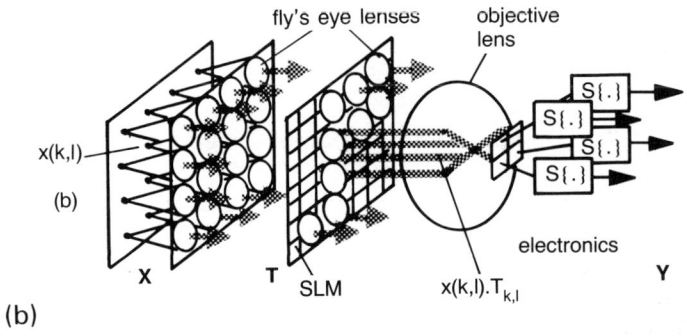

(b)

Fig. 11 Designs based on output image formation. (a) employing multi-facet Fourier hologram, and (b) employing fly's eye/objective lens combination.

Multi-layer neural network models can be mapped onto a single-layer 2-D hardware realisation by employing the spatial multiplexing techniques described earlier; i.e, by using spare input devices (see Fig. 3). The 2-D architecture shown in Fig. 11a is particularly efficient in this respect since it avoids the undesirable isolation of input devices that can occur with other layouts (e.g. in the EXOR network shown in Fig. 4, half of the input modulators are unusable). In Fig. 11a, **any** input devices not used in the first layer can be arranged to efficiently illuminate second layer outputs via their associated holographic weight matrices, etc for additional layers.

The alternative architectures described above should be capable of supporting networks of at least 64 inputs and 16 outputs organised as 8×8 and 4×4 arrays respectively, operating at speeds of many 10s of MBit/s. In both designs, great care must be taken to ensure that the fanned in beams add on an intensity basis by employing either mutually incoherent sources or spatial/angular multiplexing techniques to avoid coherent mixing in the photodetector plane. Of the two design philosophies, the systems based on input image replication, shown in Fig. 10, are preferred for near term demonstrators since they are the most compatible with the high speed hardware-based training algorithm [12].

6.3 Future developments

Attempts to access the huge spatial and temporal bandwidth of optical interconnects have only just begun. The network designs described here allow the trade-offs and relative advantages of employing optical interconnect technologies in modest sized ($\approx$ 100 'neurons') artificial neural networks to be established. The ultimate size of opto-electronic neural networks will be very much larger than this, although they are likely to remain limited by the interface-transducers and weight-matrix technologies and their associated packaging issues.

In the longer term, more compact systems could be built using volume holography. The architectures shown in Figs. 10 and 11 are implementing the fourth rank tensor equation (3) in a practicable but not the most efficient way. As the diagrams show, the weight matrix $T(i,j,k,l)$ is implemented as a two dimensional array of sub matrices. By using angular, rather than spatial multiplexing, it is possible to superimpose all of these sub matrices into a single volume-holographic recording material, equal in size to a single sub matrix (rather like stacking a pack of cards) — leading to a dramatic reduction in the physical size of the network. Volume holograms holding up to 500 stored images (equivalent to sub matrices) have been demonstrated [14]. Since in principle, the input/output images could be at least 100×100 elements square (surface emitting laser arrays of this size have already been demonstrated in the laboratory [15]), the opto-electronic neural network could grow to around 10^4 inputs feeding 500 neurons. This is clearly a long term perspective, our immediate plans are much more modest.

7. CONCLUSIONS

Opto-electronic 'neural network' hardware implementations have been described which minimise the number of opto-electronic interfaces by exploiting the functions which optics finds relatively simple to implement. This approach should optimise the mixture of electronics and optics since it exploits the advantages of both to the full: electronics providing the logical complexity and optics providing the interconnectivity and also possibly the memory. In the near future, the approach will be one of optical 'breadboarding' with a modest degree of hybrid integration of the optical and electronic subsystems. Compact packaging architectures, compatible with the neural network architectures described in this chapter, are beginning to emerge [16], but it is likely to be some time before all of the necessary fabrication facilities are established and evaluated. The ultimate objective being a robust and portable neuro-processor card, or chip if possible.

REFERENCES

1. Barnes N, Healey P, McKee P, O'Neill A W, Rejman-Greene M A Z, Scott E G, Webb R P and Wood D: 'High Speed Opto-electronic Neural Network', International Topical Meeting on Optical Computing, Kobe, (1990), 10K2 (post-deadline) & Elect Lett 26 pp 1110—1112 (1990).

2. Goodman J W: 'Optical Interconnections for VLSI systems', Proc IEEE 72, No 7 pp 850—866 (1984) & 'Optics as an Interconnect Technology', in Optical Processing and Computing Academic Press; Ed A Henri, pp 1—32 (September 1989).

3. Webb R P and Rejman-Greene M A Z: 'A Parallel Interconnect Demonstration Using A 4×4 Array Of MQW Modulators', International Topical Meeting on Optical Computing, Kobe, (1990), 10E3 & '16-Channel Parallel Optical Interconnect Demonstration with an InGaAs/InP MQW Modulator Array', Elect Lett 26 pp 1126—1127 (1990).

4. Dames M P, McKee P, Wood D and Dowling R J: 'Design and Fabrication of Efficient Optical Elements to Generate Intensity Weighted Spot Arrays', IEE Colloquium on 'Optical Connection & Switching Networks for Communication and Computing', Digest No: 1990/076 pp 14/1—14/3 (1990).

5. Ohta J, Takahashi M, Nitta Y, Tai S, Mitsunaga K, and Kyuma K: 'GaAs/AlGaAs Optical Synaptic Interconnection Device for Neural Networks', Optics Letters, 14, No 16 pp 844—846 (1989).

6. Von Lehmen A, Paek E G, Carrion L C, Patel J S, and Marrakchi A: 'Optoelectronic Chip Implementation of a Quadratic Associative Memory', Optics Letters, 15, No 5 pp 279—281 (1990).

7. Rumelhart D E, Hinton G E and Williams R J: 'Learning Internal Representations By Error Propagation', in Rumelhart D E, and McLelland J L (Eds): 'Parallel Distributed Processing' MIT Press Cambridge, Ma (1986).

8. Jang J-S, Jung S-W, Lee S-Y, and Shin S-Y: 'Optical Implementation of the Hopfield Model for Two-Dimensional Associative Memory', Optics Letters, 13, pp 248—250 (1988).

9. Rejman-Greene M A Z and Scott E G: 'Packaged 2×2 Array of InGaAs/InP Multiple Quantum Well Modulators Grown By Double-Sided Epitaxy', Electronics Letters 26, pp 946—948 (1990).

10. Rejman-Greene M A Z, Scott E G and McGoldrick E: 'Planar 3×3 Array of GaInAs/InP MQW Surface Modulators Grown By Gas Source MBE', Electronics Letters 24, pp 1583—1584 (1988).

11. Monahan M A et al: 'Incoherent Optical Correlators', (Section 2D) Proc IEEE 65, pp 121—129 (1977).

12. Wood D C: 'Training High Speed Opto-electronic Neural Network Hardware', Optics Communications 82, No 3,4, pp 236—240 (1991).

13. Jackson A S: 'A New Approach to the Utilization of Opto-Electronic Technology', COMPCON, San Francisco, CA, pp 251—254 (Feb 1974).

14. Staebler D L, et al: 'Multiple storage and erasure of fixed holograms in Fe-doped LiNbO3', Applied Physics Letters, 26, No 4 pp 182 (1975) & A Marrakchi, et al: 'Dynamic holographic interconnects with analogue weights in photorefractive crystals', Optical Engineering, 29, No 3 pp 215—224 (1990).

15. Jewell J L, et al: 'Surface-Emitting Microlasers for Optical Microcommunications', in SPIE's OE/BOSTON'90 Conference. Paper 1389-33. 4-9 November 1990 & R P Stabile, et al: 'Two-dimensional edge and surface emitting semiconductor laser arrays for optically activated switching', ibid, Paper 1378-14. (Also see related papers 1389-31, 1389-34 and PLO6.)

16. Jahns J & Huang A: 'Planar integration of free-space optical components'. Applied Optics, 28, No 9, pp 1602—1605 (1989).

Part 5: Architectures

ARCHITECTURES: AN INTRODUCTION

C Nightingale
BT Laboratories

1. BRIEF REVIEW

Proposed new neural net architectures and theoretical approaches reflect the multidisciplinary nature of the research community. The very diverse tools used for carrying out theoretical investigations in neural nets go far beyond those discussed in this book, and cover a very wide range of subjects. A brief review of examples of some of the research in the different areas may be of benefit to the reader interested in pursuing the theme. Predicate logic has played a significant part, especially in establishing the limitations of simpler neural nets in the famous book of Minsky and Papert [1]. Extensions of the capabilities of more complex neural nets have involved work in functional analysis of the mappings generated by multilayered non-linear networks. An example of work of this type in function approximation may be seen in Poggio [2]. The nonlinear dynamics of many physical systems has given birth to a number of optimisation techniques — simulated annealing for example [3] — and provides a basis for the study of dynamical response nets with feedback. Many nets are based on principles known from probability and statistics, and the performance of neural net classifiers in particular is related to that of optimal statistical classifiers [4]. Much of the original interest in neural nets was generated by new knowledge of the animal brain acquired by neuroscientists, and the reverse engineering approach to neural net design is based firmly in biology. A recent account of the modelling of real neurons can be found in [5]. Similarly cognitive aspects of the attempt to build learning machines relate strongly to experimental psychology and psychophysics and a number of discussions of these topics are to be found in [5] and [6]. The very breadth of knowledge required to take in the whole field of neural computing is now probably more than one person can hope to cover. Although the main focus of this book has been in the application of well known neural paradigms to some practical problems in telecommunications and related fields, this latter part of the book presents some new architectures, some biologically inspired neural models, and a study of dynamical aspects of neural nets. No attempt has been made to cover the very diverse fields comprehensively — such an endeavour is beyond the scope of this applications-oriented book.

2 NODE GROWING NETS

Although systems in which all the weights in a net are varied simultaneously have been shown to be successful they are usually computationally intensive, and to some extent reverse the role of processing and memory as found in biological systems, where memory seems to play a more dominant role than processing. In addition, nets in which fixed numbers of nodes are chosen in advance have distinct drawbacks both from an input representation point of view and from the point of view that choosing the appropriate number of internal nodes becomes a matter of trial and error. Nets in which the number of nodes may grow during the training of the net therefore have some attractions. Indeed there are applications for neural nets in which it is not easy to present data as a fixed number of inputs. Although in image applications it is intuitively reasonable to deal with a retina which consists of an array of inputs, binary or otherwise, in other applications, for example natural language processing, this is not so evident. If words or microfeatures are used there is every advantage in using a net whose input layer grows during the training phase. Nets have also been studied in which the fundamental problem of classification is addressed by the growth of internal nodes of the net, even though the net may have a fixed number of inputs. Much of this work is based on biologically-based nets in which feedback is an inherent part of the net — see [7] for example. The dynamic topology net described by Nightingale in Chapter 17 allows nets to grow both on the input layer, the internal layer and on the output layer, but avoids the complexities of feedback which requires the treatment of nonlinear differential equations involving time in their formulation, and which may not necessarily add any extra capability to a net.

3. STOCHASTIC NETS

N-tuple nets introduced by Aleksander [8] have played an important role in the development of image processing neural nets. Such nets have often concentrated on binary inputs, but it is possible, for example using Minchinton cells, to use grey level analogue input to such nets. In Chapter 18 Bishop has used a stochastic search technique to map features into the search space. The problem addressed was an eye location problem, though not using the standard data described in the image processing section.

4. BIOLOGICALLY INSPIRED NEURAL NETS

Rather than developing as accurate a model as possible for a single neuron it is possible to use a realistic, though stylised, model of a biological neuron and to examine the behaviour of such neurons when they are connected together into systems. In Chapter 19 Linggard makes a step in this direction, examining the firing sequences in such networks, and considering the possibilities for using the sequences to store information. Again the question of the accuracy of the model, and the advantages gained by its closer approach to a biological neuron are critical, and further work to establish the long-term value of the node sequence networks described in this chapter will be welcome.

5. FEEDBACK IN DYNAMIC RESPONSE NETWORKS

One of the reasons for the popularity of the feedforward net, as exemplified by the MLP, is the ease with which the network response can be calculated. It is sufficient to calculate the outputs from each node using the node equations, for each layer of the network until the network outputs are known. Networks with feedback require that some process be carried out whereby a steady state network response to an input is obtained. The problems of teaching such nets are then compounded by the fact that between each cycle of weight modification it may be necessary to converge a finite difference iteration to obtain the network response in order to calculate a new error value. Such nets may also be unstable, in that the output grows indefinitely, or it may be that oscillations between two or more possible output values occur. Such instabilities could, in principle, occur in the middle of a training regime, so that an incremental change of weight values may render a previously stable net unstable. Even in spite of these difficulties it is desirable to be able to train a net having arbitrary connections between its processing elements, since some degree of memory and order sensitivity can be induced by this means. In Chapter 20 Olafsson examines methods for obtaining stable nets and training them using difference equations derived from the differential equations which characterise the dynamic behaviour of the net.

REFERENCES

1. Minsky M L and Papert S A: 'Perceptrons' MIT Press, Cambridge, Ma (1969).

2. Poggio T and Girosi F: 'Networks for approximation and learning' Proc IEEE 78 , No 9, pp 1481—1497 (Sept 1990).

3. Hinton G E and Sejnowski T J: 'Learning and relearning in Boltzmann Machines' in 'Parallel Distributed Processing', Rumelhart D E and McClelland J L, eds, MIT Press, Cambridge, Mass (1986).

4. Wan E A: 'Neural Net Classification: A Bayesian interpretation', IEEE Trans on Neural Nets, 1 , No 4, pp 303—305 (Dec 1990).

5. Anderson J A and Rosenfield E: 'Neurocomputing: foundations of research', MIT Press, Cambridge, Ma (1988).

6. Rumelhart D E and McClelland J L: 'Parallel Distributed Processing' MIT Press, Cambridge, Ma (1986).

7. Grossberg S: 'Competitive learning: from interactive activation to adaptive resonance', Cognitive Science 11 , pp 22—23 (1987).

8. Aleksander I, Thomas W V and Bowden P A: 'Wisard: a radical step forward in image recognition', Sensor Review, pp 120—124 (July 1984).

17

A DYNAMIC TOPOLOGY NET

C Nightingale
BT Laboratories

1. INTRODUCTION

One interesting aspect of neural nets is their flexibility in applications. They can be applied to problems in which the low-level functions of the brain — early vision for example — are modelled, and in other cases to problems where it seems that higher order functions are emulated — natural language processing being an important example. A difficulty in these latter cases is the method of inputting language to a machine. The most popular neural paradigms usually require that a fixed number of numerical inputs are specified, and every input pattern must be represented in this way. A simple sentence which can be drawn from the whole vocabulary of the English language is difficult to apply to a net of this type. One approach is to use microfeatures in which a reasonably large vocabulary is seen as consisting of words which are represented by microfeatures drawn from a smaller fixed-size vocabulary, as in McClelland [1]. These microfeatures usually turn out to be words, but each can be seen as exciting an input node with some varying degree of intensity. Other ways of treating words might include the use of restricted vocabularies, or even simple binary coding of words in which no measure of closeness between word-meanings is possible — see [2].

One method of experimenting with nets in which words are to be to be the basic input features, but where it is not wished to specify a limited vocabulary in advance, is to follow the principle of a net which can add new nodes to its input as it encounters new words. The drawback of this method is that it becomes difficult to apply the backpropagation algorithm to the net whilst the input, hidden and output layers are varying in size. The difficulties are not insuperable, and several algorithms have been described in which new nodes can be added during training as in, for example [3]. The nets described here use a modification of the perceptron learning rule. A simple single-layer form of such a net is described here, but shown to be limited to solving easy problems. An extension of the net is then described in which hidden cluster-nodes as well as input nodes are created in response to difficult problems. A method of forcing some sensitivity to order on the net is also described and some preliminary results given. Then two test problems in natural language are tackled; grammaticality, and limited domain translation.

2. SIMPLE FORM OF DYNAMIC TOPOLOGY NET

When the net starts it consists of only a single output node which fires in response to any input. As it receives new and unfamiliar inputs, the net instantiates new nodes as necessary. Therefore after the simple form of dynamic topology net (DTN) has been running for some time it will consist of a layer of input nodes, connected by a set of connections to a single layer of output nodes, as shown in Fig. 1a. The connections from input to output do not exist between every input/output pair, but each connection possesses a weight. Inputs consist of any text entities that are desired. If words are used as the lowest level features, then a complete input could be a phrase or sentence, for example. Each node in the input corresponds to some feature of an input that has been applied to the net previously, and when a new input is applied which includes some of these features these nodes will become excited. Any unknown features contained in the input play no part in the determination of the net's output, but are retained in memory during the subsequent cycles of connection-weight modification, and are ultimately connected to some appropriate output. Each output node is a typical neural processor, as shown in Fig. 2 in which the excitation is given by equation (1).

$$y = \sum_{i=1}^{n} w_i x_i \qquad \ldots (1)$$

Although no nonlinear activation function appears here, the competitive algorithm ensures that a notional thresholding operation occurs which is automatically set to cut off all but the strongest firing output cell.

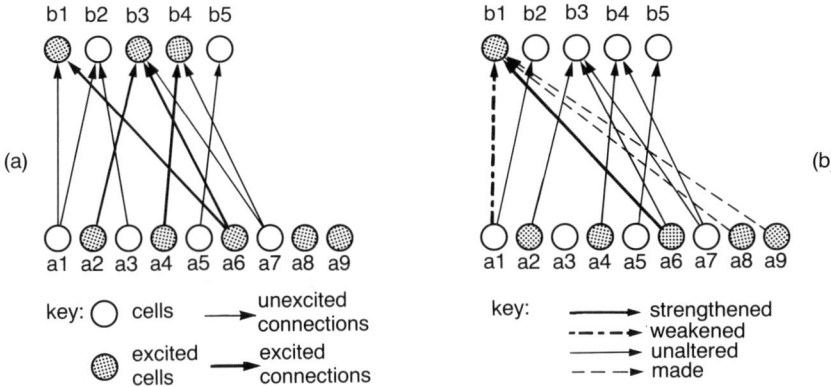

Fig. 1 a) Interrogate stage — On presentation of the input (a2 a4 a6 a8 a9) the cell which responds to each of the elements fires as shown. In the case of a8 and a9 no cell exists which responds to these cells, so two new cells are created. The output cells b1 b3 and b4 become excited by the rule of equation 1 and that which responds most strongly (b1 say) fires, and the other excited output cells are inhibited. When the cell fires, some action particular to the cell is performed.

b) Reward stage — In the case that b1 is a correct response, the user may reward the net to reinforce the correct response to the given input.
Rewarding the net causes connections to be altered as shown, with a6-b1 strengthened, since both a6 and b1 fired, a1-b1 weakened, since a1 did not fire, with other existing connections unaltered. Two new connections a8-b1 and a9-b1 are made.

The algorithm works, in its single-layer mode, by following the flow-diagram shown in Fig. 3 which is described in the next section.

2.1 Algorithm

Referring to Fig. 3 the algorithm works as follows:

2.1.1 Learning cycle

Ready1: At position 6 in the interaction cycle the system is in its start state and the user has the choice of proceeding via 1, 2 or 3.

356 DYNAMIC TOPOLOGY NET

Interrogate: At position 1 of the interaction cycle assume the net configuration is as shown in Fig. 1a.

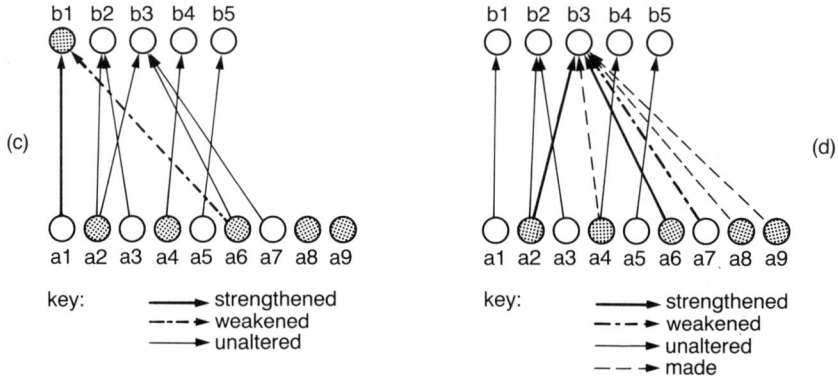

Fig. 1 c) Punish — In the case that b1 is an incorrect response, the user may punish the net to inhibit this response to the given input. In this case conversely to reward it is a1-b1 which is strengthened, a6-b1 is weakened and no new connections are made.

d) Teach — If the net has been punished it may then be taught the correct response to the previous input. If b3 were the expected answer then connections with excited input nodes a2 and a6 are strengthened. In addition new connections from b2 to excited input cells which are not connected (a4 a8 and a9) are made, and connections to unexcited cells a7 are weakened. In the event that the expected answer is none of the existing outputs then a new cell, b6, for example would be created, and these operations performed with b6 in place of b3.

A new input is given to the net which excites some of the cells in the input layer, say a2, a4 and a6, which fire, and instantiates two new cells a8 and a9. The cells {a2, a4, a6, a8, a9} are known in the net as the current short term memory (CSTM). Several cells in the output layer (b1, b3 and b4) are excited by the firing of the CSTM cells via appropriate existing interconnections e.g. {a2-b3, a4-b4, a6-b1 and a6-b3}. The output layer behaves exactly like a cluster in competitive learning [4] in that one cell then dominates the others and inhibits all outputs except its own. In principle this should be done by fully connecting the output layer with inhibitory connections, and using some dynamic feedback system to stabilise the net when only a single cell remains firing. In practice this is cumbersome, and does not contribute to either the ease of implementation or the understanding of the net's behaviour. Therefore a simple global function which identifies the cell which fires most strongly is applied, for the purpose of simplification. Suppose it is b1 that dominates in our example. This cell then fires and produces a certain action in the net. This action will normally mean printing an output, but can include other things. Unlike competitive learning there is no weight modification at this stage.

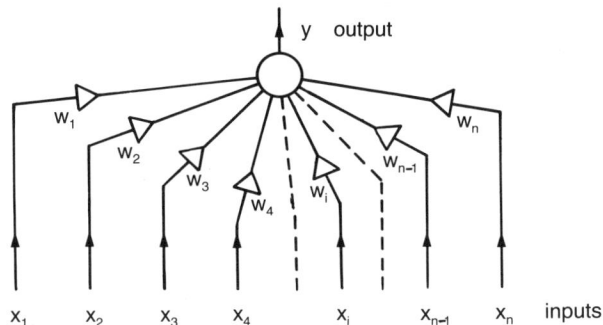

Fig. 2 A cell in the output layer in the simple form of DTN. In the extended DTN this cell would be in one of the clusters in the intermediate layer. There is no nonlinear activation function, since the output is inhibited by interactions amongst all the output cells, rather than by a threshold or logic-function.

The program now returns to Position 6. The supervisory aspect of the net is brought into play at this stage. The supervisor determines the correctness of the response. In the event that the response is correct the net can either be left unmodified, or it can be rewarded. If the response is incorrect then the net should be punished, where punishment is a weight modification process which makes the incorrect response less likely for the given input. In the event that the response is considered neither correct nor incorrect then the net can be left unmodified and further inputs can be tried.

Reward: At Position 2 assume the net is as shown in the example in Fig. 1b and has output the correct response. The user rewards the net, and the connections are modified in the following way:

Connections to the excited output node which are not carrying a signal are weakened, e.g. a1-b1.
Connections to the newly instantiated nodes are made, e.g. a8-b1, a9-b1.
Connections to excited output nodes which are carrying a signal are strengthened, e.g. a6-b1.
Other connections are unaltered.
The algorithm then returns to 6.

Punish: At position 3 in the interaction cycle, the net as shown in Fig. 1c, has produced an incorrect response, so the user punishes the net, and the connections are modified in the following way:

> Connections to excited output node which are not carrying a signal are srengthened, e.g. a1-b1.
> Connections to excited output node which are carrying a signal are weakened, e.g. a6-b1
> Other connections are left unaltered.
> The cycle then proceeds to Position 5.

Ready2: At this stage the user has the choice of proceeding to position 4 or returning to Position 6.

Teach: At Position 4 the user gives the expected output for the net to learn: for example assume that b3 is the expected output as shown in Fig. 1d.

> Teach proceeds as for reward-making connections between all CSTM cells and expected output cell which do not already exist, e.g. a4-b3, a8-b3 and a9-b3.
> Connections are strengthened between CSTM cells and expected output cell, e.g. a2-b3, a6-b3
> Other connections to given cell are weakened, e.g. a7-b3.
> Go to position 6.

2.1.2 Weight modification

The method of altering the weights is a modification of the method used in competitive learning [4] except that instead of strengthening connections in such a way as to reinforce the existing tendencies of the net as is done in competitive learning, the procedure is controlled so that only desired responses are strengthened and undesired responses are weakened.

In competitive learning it is usual to normalise the weights, but in the DTN a different strategy is adopted, as shown in equation (2).

$$w_{new} = \left(1 + \frac{\mu \delta w_{old}}{1 + (\mu \delta w_{old})^4} \right) w_{old} \qquad \ldots (2)$$

where $\delta = +1$ causes strengthening, and $\delta = -1$ causes weakening, μ governs the position of the maximum.

Figure 4 shows graphs of the weight modification functions, for strengthening and weakening. The effect of this weight modification function

SIMPLE FORM OF DYNAMIC TOPOLOGY NET

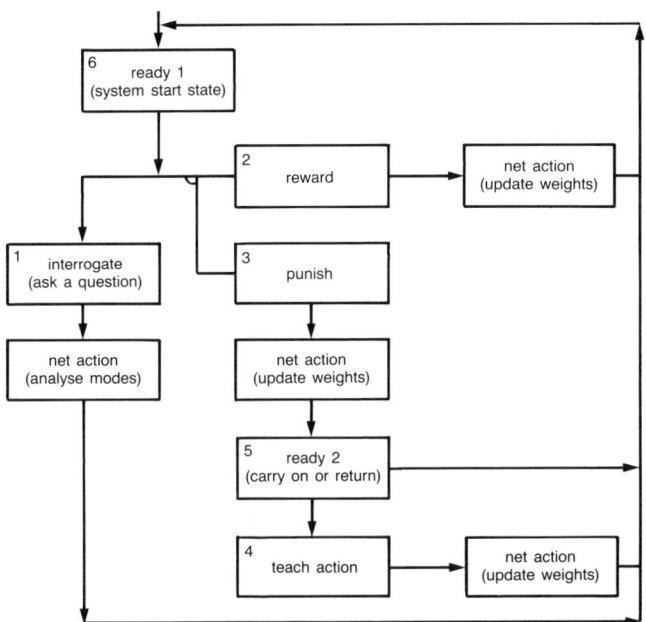

Fig. 3 Flow chart for DTN learning cycle. At the net action blocks, some modification to the net topology or connection weights takes place. At the other blocks the user inputs data to the net, and causes flow control to move to another block.

is that when first instantiated weights are easy to alter, but when a lot of weakening or strengthening has taken place the strengths tend to saturate, and do not easily increase or decrease. This prevents weights from becoming too dominant, but ensures that if a weight has been constantly strengthened it is not easily weakened. Unlearning is therefore difficult, though possible.

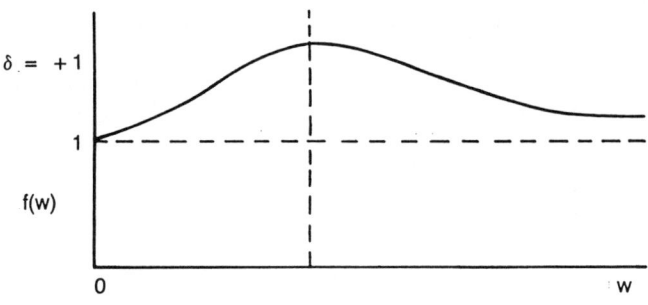

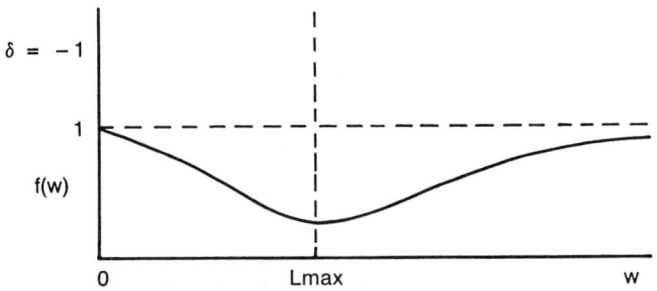

Fig. 4 The figure shows plots of the function f(.) of equation 2. Weights are altered by an amount proportional to the value of f(w) where w is the current weight value. This means that connection weights are easy to alter for values of about L_{max} and it is this value at which new connections are set. For much larger or smaller values of connection weights the function gives values of near unity, so that the weights are difficult to change.

3. INTERNAL NODE CREATION

It is easy to show that the net in the above form cannot learn even rudimentary difficult problems such as XOR. The extended form of DTN has an additional capability of creating internal nodes to cope with what appear to a single layer net as contradicatory inputs. If such nodes were created frequently, and for cases where a single-layer net could cope if enough training were given, then the net would be swamped with a large number of unnecessary internal nodes, and what would have been created would be nothing more than a very large memory. If on the other hand such cell creation is usually only performed when necessary, to cope with complex data, then a net with such a capability could be expected to learn difficult problems without using excessively large amounts of memory. A mechanism whereby such extra nodes can be introduced sparingly, but appropriately is given below.

3.1 Broadcast parameters

All communication in the net so far described is local, if the convention adopted for the competitive output layer is accepted. Other parameters are now introduced which need to be transmitted to all the cells in an intermediate cluster at the same time, or to all the cells in the whole intermediate layer. These can be seen as analogous to some of the chemical agents which affect behaviour in biological nets such as adrenalin, although no pretence is made that these parameters or any other features of the net, operate in a biologically plausible way.

Two parameters are introduced which are only analogous to these chemical indicators in the brain in that they can be broadcast to all cells or a large group of cells simultaneously:

C_e : A parameter affecting all internal cells which measures the current tendency of the net to create new cells. (Cell creation excitation).

C_t : A parameter which is applied to a new entity (an output **cluster**) and which governs the level of excitement that is required to increase the size of the particular cluster to which it applies. (Cell creation threshold).

In the DTN C_e is related to the number of punishments the network has received compared to the number of interrogations. If the network has given a number of correct answers and received few punishments the network will be in a state of low C_e and will be unlikely to instantiate any new cells. In the event of it having received a lot of punishments the network gets into an excited state with a high value of C_e and will frequently instantiate new cells in appropriate clusters.

C_t is related to the number of cells in a given output cluster. If the cluster is large, it will be resistant to the creation of new cells. This means that the net will not instantiate cells very easily in a large cluster, so that there is a natural tendency towards economical cell use. According to the bounds on these parameters a net can be quick or slow to learn new complex concepts, but the slower nets will ultimately be capable of more learning for less memory.

3.2 Clusters

Figure 5a shows a part of a DTN in which two cells are excited by an input (a1 a2 a3) residing in short term memory. The correct response should be for cell CR1 to fire, triggering output cell CR, but assume that this is not the case, and that IR1 fires instead triggering incorrect response IR. The user punishes the net and connections are varied according to the algorithm described above. The net is then told that the output CR was correct, and further tests take place. The highest output in the cluster of CR at the time of output-determination (in our case, since there is only one, it is that of CR1) is compared with that of the winning excitation which is that of IR1. The following logical step then is made:

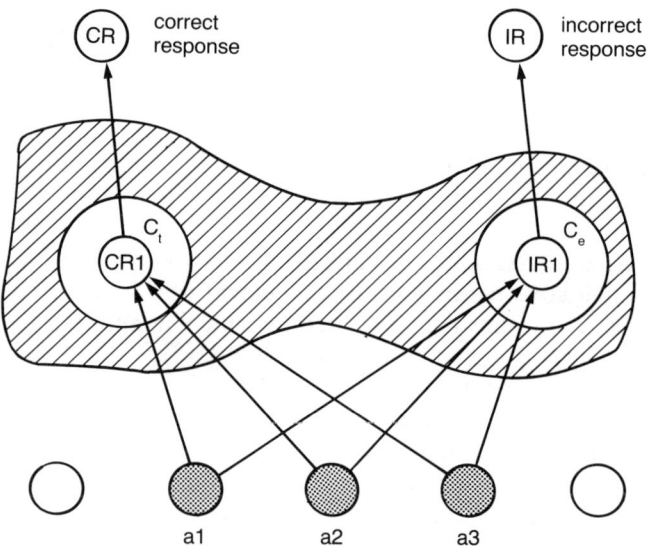

Fig. 5a The conditions under which a new intermediate node will be created in a cluster are shown in the Fig. T (not shown) is a parameter which depends upon the two broadcast parameters C_e (the current tendency for new cells to be created by the net) and C_t (the threshold below which, for a particular cluster, no new cluster cells will be created). T tends to be large for high C_e and low C_t. CR1 is the firing strength of the cluster cell connected to the expected cell CR, and IR1 is the firing strength of a cell connected to the incorrect output cell IR. C_e will be high after a high frequency of punishments, C_t will be high for a cluster with many cells.

If Excitation (CR1) < T.(Excitation (IR1)), where $T = T(C_e, C_t)$, then a new cell, CR2, is instantiated in internal cluster CR and appropriate connections made, as shown in Fig. 5b.

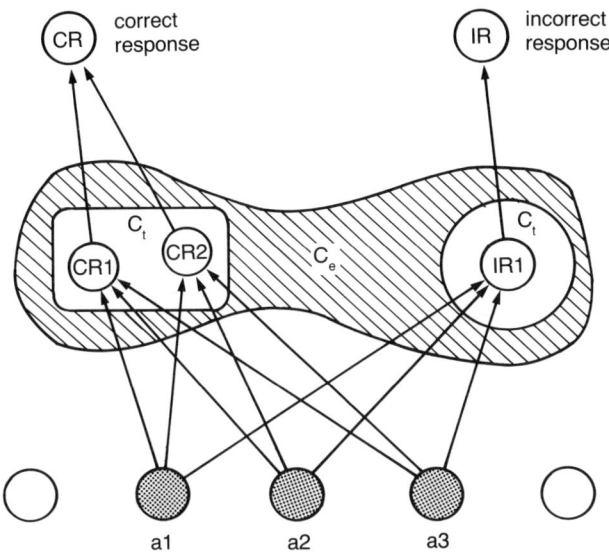

Fig. 5b In the case that CR < T.IR a new cell CR2 is introduced to the expected response cluster, and this cell will be likely to fire if the same input is encountered. The output cells CR and IR are simply OR functions which fire given any active input.

3.3 Familiarity

Figure 6 shows another mode of the net. Input cells excited by frequently encountered (familiar) inputs which are connected to a large number of internal clusters can be made to fire more weakly. This feature is included on the principle that the more outputs to which a feature is connected, the less discriminatory it is likely to be. It is little more than an *ad hoc* rule which has improved the performance of the net in practice. It leads, in linguistic applications, to the ignoring of input words like 'the' 'is' and 'and', which at this simple level do not carry much information. In some problems this mode is very useful, and turns the net into an automatic keyword weighting system. This diminution of the contributions of familiar inputs can be taken to a further extreme in the interests of reducing the number of excited output nodes, and hence processing time. An inverse attentional threshold, below which weakly firing input cells are inhibited from firing at all, rises gradually, during uneventful interrogations (no punishment or reward). This greatly reduces the number of internal excited cells and reduces the search time for the competitive determination of the winning cell. The attentional threshold can be reset on reward. The net then functions more or less exactly as a keyword driven algorithm. The exact details of these modes are not important for the general principle of this type of DTN.

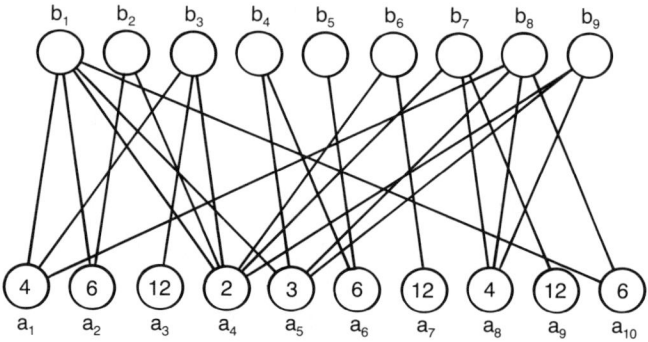

Fig. 6 Familiarity — In this figure the method by which the firing strengths of highly connected (familiar) input cells are reduced is shown. The firing strength of a4 is automatically reduced in proportion to the number of output cells to which it is attached. This gives cells which may carry less information less weight in the competitive phase. The firing strengths of the cells in the input layer are shown in the nodes.

4 ORDER SENSITIVITY

Nets like the MLP have a built in sense of order in the presentation patterns — for example the input pattern 10000 to a five-input-node MLP would not give the same output as the pattern as 00100, although for some purposes, when the input data is intrinsically a stream, as in speech, a further sense of ordering is required, so that each separate pattern has some relation to what has gone before. In the case of the DTN, even primitive pattern ordering is lacking. In binary images for example, ordering (in two dimensions) carries almost the whole information. In language an input set of, for example, 'Mary likes John' would have exactly the same pattern of excitation as 'John likes Mary'. Surprisingly enough, even in some limited domain translation exercises this order insensitivity has not been seen as particularly problematic. Sentences like 'The heater in my hotel room doesn't work' may sound strange if jumbled up — like 'The hotel in my work doesn't heater room' but a DTN seems to easily sort out the intended meaning. Even so, it is easy to think of examples which would fail, and it is evident that any English language oriented neural net needs to have some method of recognising order. Grammaticality, in particular, which can be used in aiding speech recognition is heavily dependent on word order.

From the basic DTN paradigm two methods of introducing word order have been developed. The first, described in detail in [5], uses the principle of n-tuples where in addition to single words, pairs, triplets or higher order groups are used to define cells. This method, related to other higher order nets like Sigma-Pi nets [6] moves slightly away from the idea of highly interconnected sets of very simple processors operating in parallel. The other method uses the principle of position-marking to retain memory of order. In its simplest and perhaps least useful form it merely position-marks each word in an input with a number to correspond to its position in a phrase or sentence. This absolute position-marking does not produce either an intuitively reasonable, nor a utilitarian net. A more powerful preprocess can be applied to input phrases such that words are position-marked with their approximate position in the sentence, and the position-marked words retained in addition to the original position-unmarked words. A sentence like, for example 'the black cat stalked the cunning diseased rat' is preprocessed to yield the following set of tokens, in no particular order (stalked2 cunning the2 diseased3 cat1 stalked the the1 black1 black rat black1 cat diseased cunning3 cat 2 cunning2 rat3). This example allows words to be perceived as somewhere near the beginning of the phrase with position-mark 1; somewhere around the middle with position-mark 2; and somewhere round the end with position-mark3. This multiplies the possible size of the input layer by three, which is still very much less than would be the potential size of a net which retained pairs, triplets or higher n-tuples. The degree to which the order is to be resolved depends on how many of the position-marking integers are allowed. In extremum, as many position-marks as words in a sentence can be used, but as well as greatly increasing the potential size of the net some generalisation can be lost. If, for example, the 'diseased rat' sentence above were position-marked with eight integers, then the cat1 would evidently become cat3. If subsequently a sentence like 'the alert black cat stalked the cunning diseased rat' then the cat3 token would become cat4, and there would be no sense that both sentences had the word cat more or less at the beginning of the sentence, so an obvious relationship between these almost identical inputs would be lost. Of course the crudeness of the 3-position-mark resolution would probably confuse the meanings of sentences like 'This month Kasparov and Karpov met for the fourth time in a world championship and after a long struggle Kasparov beat Karpov' and 'This month Karpov and Kasparov met for the fourth time in a world championship and after a long struggle Karpov beat Kasparov'. This is because both Karpov and Kasparov would get position-marked as 3 in the terminating clause thereby destroying an important feature of the sentence. But no doubt humans find the two sentences somewhat more difficult to distinguish than shorter ones, and the gains for short sentences are great.

5 SOME RESULTS

5.1 Grammaticality

A simple CFG equivalent to the transition network of Fig. 7 was used to generate 20 sentences and a further twenty sentences which were not grammatical according to the CFG were constructed, in all cases using word categories rather than words. Each node in the transition net was visited only once, and sentences varied in length between 2 and 7 symbols. Similarly, random selections of between 2 and 7 symbols were generated to produce the ungrammatical sentences. The net used an absolute ordering, which was a reasonable policy for this problem, in that order is highly significant for English grammar.

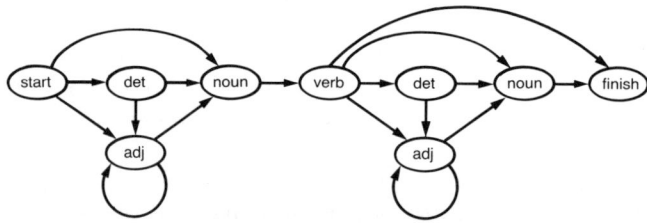

Fig. 7 The figure shows a transition network equivalent to the context free grammar used in the grammaticality tests.

Initially the sets were input in alternating fashion, with a positive sentence followed by a negative sentence through all 40 sentences in repetitive cycles, but this method failed to train the net. Success rates of about half — which is no better than random — were obtained, after which the net did not improve. A method of training whereby the net was trained fully on progressively larger subsets of the 40 sentences was then used and with this approach after 575 training steps the net learned the complete set of 40 sentences. Although this is a superficially positive result, it is evident that such a net would have great difficulty in learning constituent strings like (det adj noun) if they could crop up an any absolute position in a sentence, and for that reason this application of the DTN was not pursued.

5.2 Limited domain translation

Many rule-based automatic translation systems are being developed [7], but many of them have difficulty coping with ungrammatical inputs, an area where the generalisation properties of a neural net give it some advantage.

At the present state of development it is not reasonable to test the DTN as a general translation system, but for a limited domain, such as phrasebook translation for hotel reservation, or rail travel enquiries, a neural net solution may be feasible.

An advantage of such a neural net approach to translation would be that a net could be trained by anyone who spoke both source and target language, with an appropriate method of data collection, and would not require skilled programming by language experts. In cases where it is economic to spend a lot of resources on a powerful translation program, for example in a Japanese-English context, it would be feasible to implement an elaborate classical language translation algorithm. In cases where languages spoken by smaller groups of less economic strength are involved, it may well be advantageous to use a neural net aided translator. Any such net would, of necessity, produce the intended output phrase in the source language as well as the target language so that serious mistakes could be filtered out.

A project for testing the DTN for a limited domain translation was undertaken by Morton [8]. The domain of travel bookings was selected amongst others as being a useful application, yet with a sufficiently restricted range to give a possibility of a successful outcome. The domain selected was rail booking and enquiries. In the preliminary experiments reported here no actual translation was attempted, but the ability of the DTN to map a range of varied inputs onto single correct responses is sufficient to prove the point. It proved possible, with some difficulty, to train the net to the task required, although the domain was more limited than would be useful with a practical system. Queries were selected from a small database concerned with train travel:

Destination	*Time*	*Via*	*Fare*
Edinburgh	Twelve	York	Fifty pounds
Glasgow	One	Preston	Forty-five pounds
Liverpool	Two	Crewe	Twenty-five pounds
Leeds	Three	Peterborough	Twenty-four pounds
Nottingham	Four	Kettering	Twenty pounds
Birmingham	Five	Milton-Keynes	Fifteen pounds
Swansea	Six	Cardiff	Twenty-six pounds
Bristol	Seven	Reading	Eighteen pounds
Exeter	Eight	Plymouth	Thirty-five pounds
Southampton	Nine	Basingstoke	Thirty pounds
Brighton	Ten	Gatwick	Ten pounds

A sample interaction with the program is given:

Can you tell me what time the train to Edinburgh leaves?
TWELVE

Do you happen to know where the train to Nottingham stops?
KETTERING

Would you tell me where the Exeter train stops?
PLYMOUTH

I don't suppose you happen to know what the fare to Southampton is?
THIRTY POUNDS

I wonder whether you could tell me what time the Edinburgh train leaves?
TWELVE

Would you tell me what time the Glasgow train is supposed to leave?
ONE

Do you happen to know where the Liverpool train stops?
CREWE

I don't suppose you know what the Nottingham fare is supposed to be do you?
TWENTY POUNDS

Do you happen to know what the Nottingham fare should be?
TWENTY POUNDS

Can you tell us what time the Swansea train is supposed to depart?
SIX

I wonder whether you could give me the departure time of the train to Bristol?
SEVEN

As can be seen the net scored 100% on this particular set of questions. In this limited domain it was able to produce error-free performance on free entry of questions. With so small a database it is feasible to have a reliable net if training is done carefully. The net only acted as a simple demonstrator for this task and may not easily scale to more complex phrase-book translation domains. Some work on the phrase-book translation using a higher-order version of the net is described in [5], in which much more quantified testing of a DTN using n-tuples is given.

6 CONCLUSIONS

A net which can be used for some tasks in natural language processing, having indefinitely extendable vocabulary, has been described. The net functions by adding nodes to both input layer, and to an intermediate layer of clusters. The net is designed so that there will not be an uncontrolled proliferation of nodes in the hidden layer, and yet such nodes will be introduced in cases where the net cannot learn a new input/output pair with its current topology. A simple method for introducing some ordering information has been described.

The results of applying the net to two simple problems in natural language processing have been given.

REFERENCES

1. McClelland D E and Kawamoto A H: 'Mechanisms of Sentence Processing: Assigning Roles to Constituents of Sentences'. Parallel Distributed Processing 2 McClelland J L and Rumelhart D E (Eds) Cambridge, Ma MIT Press (1986).

2. Allen R B: 'Several Studies on NL and Back-propagation', Proceedings of the International Conf on Neural Networks 2 , pp 335—341, June 21-24 San Diego CA (1987).

3. Lee S and Rhee M K: 'A Gaussian Potential Function Network With Hierarchically Self-Organising Learning' Neural Networks 2 , No 4 (1991).

4. Rumelhart D E and Zipser D: 'Feature Discovery by Competitive Learning'. Parallel Distributed Processing. 1 , McClelland J L and Rumelhart D E (Eds) MIT Press Cambridge, Ma (1986).

5. Wyard P and Nightingale C: 'A Single Layer Higher Order Neural Net and its application to context free Grammar Recognition', Connection Science 2 , No 4 (1990).

6. Rumelhart D E, Hinton G E and McClelland J L: 'A framework for parallel distributed processing'. Parallel Distributed Processing. 2 , McClelland J L and Rumelhart D E (Eds) Cambridge, Ma MIT Press (1986).

7. Slocum J: 'A Survey of Machine Translation: its History, Current Status, and Future Prospects' Machine Translation Systems. J Slocum, (Ed) Cambridge, England: Cambridge University Press (1989).

8. Morton K, Coulston M and Gerrihy G: 'Translation English to French Limited Domain Translation using Dynamic Topology Net'. Internal BT Report (1989).

18

THE STOCHASTIC SEARCH NETWORK

J M Bishop and P Torr
Department of Cybernetics, University of Reading

1. STOCHASTIC SEARCH

1.1 Introduction

A fundamental difficulty when using neural networks applied to pattern recognition, is the problem of stimulus equivalence — the invariance of symbolic information independent of transformation within a search space. For example, symbolically, the letter A remains an A irrespective of its position, size or orientation within an image field. Adult humans can generally recognise patterns accurately, despite such transformations and distortions. Classically it has been hypothesised that this ability is due to a normalisation process that occurs before the classification process begins.

One criticism of the network paradigm has been that there is no clear mechanism by which such normalisation can occur, since at first sight such unstructured systems do not provide any mechanism for attention — the focussing of analysis onto a subset of a larger pattern. This chapter describes two network solutions to this normalisation process — Hinton mapping and stochastic networks, which give an introduction to the analysis of stochastic networks and illustrate their use in locating features in grey-scale images.

The problem of stimulus equivalence is a specific example of a best fit constraint satisfaction search, where the target pattern has been mapped into the search space, using translational, rotational or scale transformations. The goal of a system that can solve such problems is to ascertain the inverse mapping from search space to pattern. For example, in the situation where a letter has been rotated in a visual field, the inverse mapping would be the angle of rotation $\{\theta\}$, if it had been translated then the inverse mapping would be its cartesian co-ordinates $\{X, Y\}$, etc. One solution to this problem is a technique described by Hinton [1], summarised below.

1.2 Hinton mapping

A Hinton mapping network consists of two sets of feature detectors, canonical and retinocentric (see Fig. 1). Mutually excitatory connections link the canonical detectors with higher order detectors such as letter detectors, in the manner of the interactive activation and competition (iac) model [2].

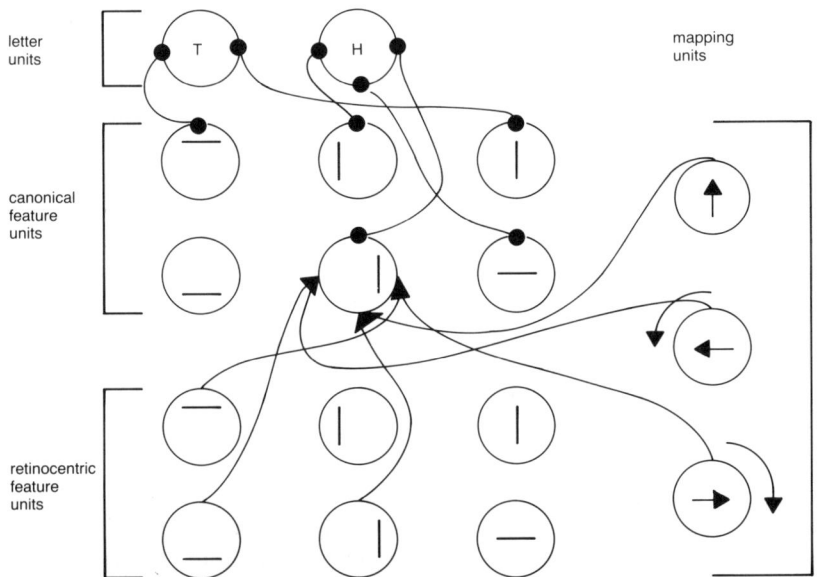

Fig. 1 Hinton mapping network.

Hinton describes a method for mapping retinocentric feature patterns into canonical feature patterns. Although the general application to three dimensional visual problems involves normalising six degrees of freedom, a simplified version which corrects for a one dimensional rotational transformation is described here.

Central to Hinton mapping are fixed, **static**, mapping cells which implement potential mappings into the search space. There is one such cell **for each possible mapping into the search space**. Interactive activation and competition between cells ensures that the mapping which yields the best fit of the model into the search space will receive the most activation. After a few iterations, unless the model is symmetric, this mapping will become dominant.

Considering the situation in which a letter has been rotated clockwise by ninety degrees, a mapping system is required that will transmit activation from the activated retinocentric feature detectors to the relevant canonical detector, offset by a counter clockwise rotation of ninety degrees.

In Fig. 1, three different mapping cells are shown, producing zero, plus ninety and minus ninety degree rotational shifts. Activity on mapping cell $[x]$ produces one of two multiplicative inputs to a canonical cell, the other being from the corresponding retinocentric cell offset by $[x]$ degrees. Thus for a canonical cell to receive input activation, a retinocentric cell must be active together with a mapping cell corresponding to the rotation of the retinocentric feature relative to the canonical feature. If only one of these cells is active, either a mapping cell or a retinocentric cell, then no activation will pass to the canonical cell. Thus the mapping cell effectively selects mappings from input space to normalised space.

If the correct rotational mapping is known in advance then it is possible to activate the corresponding mapping cell enabling the network to map from retinal to normalised co-ordinate space. Object recognition thus becomes:

- select a mapping, perhaps on the basis of prior knowledge,
- activate corresponding mapping cell,
- analyse degree of match between retinocentric stimuli and higher order features.

This process is repeated until the best match is found. The above technique is simply a sequential implementation of the standard normalisation and compare procedure and does not offer any improvement in performance over traditional methods.

The advantage of the above technique is that by using Hinton mapping cells it is possible to perform the search for the correct mapping in parallel. This is accomplished by using a further set of multiplicative connections to choose the correct mapping for a pattern given the retinal input and correct normalised pattern of activation.

Simultaneous activation of a central feature and a retinal feature is evidence that the mapping is correct. Thus, by allowing central and retinal cells that correspond under a specific mapping to project back to a multiplicative connection on the mapping cell, the activation of the mapping cell can be reinforced. Spurious conjunctions will occur, but correct mapping cells will in general receive more activation than the incorrect ones (unless there is ambiguity due to symmetry). By allowing mapping cells to compete, so that the ones receiving the most activation win, the network will eventually converge onto the correct mapping.

Initially when the retinal input is presented, all the mapping cells are partially active. Each retinal feature then stimulates partial activation to the canonical features corresponding to it over all mappings. The correct mapping allows the correct canonical cell to be partially active. Interactive activation between the canonical cells and the higher order cells will then reinforce the correct mapping relative to the background noise. This process alone can be sufficient for correct identification. However, the multiplicative connections on the canonical cells between the retinocentric cells and the mapping cells force further suppression of the noise. This process swiftly converges onto the correct interpretation of the pattern, as well as the correct canonical representation and correct mapping, purely from the retinal input.

However, examining the requirements of Hinton's scheme, we see that if the pattern is defined by a set of $[M]$ features, and the search space consists of a set of $[Z]$ features, then $[Z]$ *static* mapping cells are required in the network. The number of mapping cells, $[Z]$, will increase polynomially with the number of degrees of freedom of the search. Thus in many situations, where the search space is very large, Hinton mapping is not a practical solution.

Stochastic searching [3], a technique for solving constraint satisfaction problems, evolved from a study of Hinton mapping, but only requires $[M]$ mapping cells.

1.3 The stochastic search

Stochastic searching is a search technique which uses a random diffusion process to find the best fit of a given data model within a specified search space. The data model and the search space are defined in terms of atomic data units (ADUs) between which comparisons can be made. For example, when searching for the best fit of a string of numbers within a larger string, the ADUs may be the digits that comprise the strings.

Unlike Hinton mapping, where each mapping cell defines a fixed mapping, stochastic searching uses a network of variable (**dynamic**) mapping cells to test possible mappings of the model in the search space. Each cell defines one potential mapping of the model in the search space. There is one such cell for each ADU of the model. A random diffusion process ensures that mappings which appear successful are spread to other cells.

Stochastic searching is inherently parallel in nature; empirical evidence [4] suggests that the algorithm is probabilistically bounded by $O(\text{Log}(T_r))$, where T_r, the time ratio, is the ratio of the size of the model to the size of the search space. This chapter includes recent work by the authors providing an introduction to the formal mathematical analysis of network behaviour.

1.4 Method

Stochastic searching is an iterative two phase process, involving the testing of cell mappings and the diffusion of successful mappings across to other cells. The general procedure of the search is:

INITIALISE (mappings);

REPEAT

    TEST (mappings);

    DIFFUSE (mappings);

UNTIL TERMINATION;

Mappings describes the $[M]$ mapping cells which define potential mappings of the object into the search space. Each mapping cell becomes **active** or **inactive** according to the currently perceived accuracy of **its** mapping of the model in the search space.

Cell mappings are first **initialised** to specific values. These values will usually be random unless extra information is available to cluster the mappings around a specific area.

During the **test** phase each cell's activity changes to reflect the currently perceived accuracy of its present mapping. The accuracy of a mapping is usually defined by a local comparison between a randomly selected group of ADUs from the model and **the corresponding ADUs from the search space defined by that mapping**.

Diffusion spreads mappings from active cells to inactive cells by a stochastic selection process. Diffusion can either be synchronous, whereby all mapping updates occur simultaneously, or asynchronous, where the cells update individually. In the networks described in this chapter all updates are synchronous.

A stochastic network **terminates** when its mapping cells are at equilibrium, that is, the distribution of mappings into the search space becomes constant. In some cases, for example when the ADUs in the search space are badly distorted by noise, or when the model is not within the search space, equilibrium may never be reached.

1.4.1 Initialisation

The initialisation of the mapping cells is determined by any a-priori knowledge of the problem that can be usefully applied.

If stochastic searching is to be used in an environment where there is no a-priori knowledge of the search space, then the **new map** process consists of assigning all mappings randomly (or at regular intervals through the search area). Advance knowledge of the search space enables mappings to be suitably biased. Two common examples of a-priori knowledge are:

- The time ratio of the search is greater than one ($[M] > [Z]$).

  This occurs if the number of potential mappings into the search space is less than the number of ADUs in the model. For example, classifying a model into one of $[k]$ sets ($[Z] = k$), where $[k]$ is less than the size of the model $[M]$.

  In this situation, it is certain that during initialisation at least one of the mapping cells will exhibit the correct (best fit) mapping of the model into the search space.

- The previous position of the model is known.

  This is sometimes of use in scenarios where the model is unlikely to move in large discontinuous jumps. For example, successive images of a ball or an aircraft in flight.

  In this situation the initial mappings can be biased towards the last known position of the model.

1.4.2 The test phase

The test phase of the search evaluates the mappings currently defined by the mapping cells. The test for each mapping cell usually comprises the selection of $[j]$ ADUs from the model, ($1 \leq j \leq M$), which are compared with a set of $[j]$ ADUs from the search space, pointed to by the cell. The result of the test is either a unanimous or a majority decision of the $[j]$ ADU comparisons. (NB. The test phase of the hybrid stochastic search, described in section 3, uses an n-tuple RAM neuron to make this comparison).

To avoid becoming trapped in a local minimum, at each iteration every mapping cell searches for a random section of the model. Thus when testing mapping [m] using segment [i] of the model, [j] ADUs of the model at position [i] are compared with [j] ADUs from the search space at mapping [$m+i$], where [i] is a random offset between [0 and M-1].

If the comparison is successful the mapping cell goes **active**, otherwise it remains **inactive**.

1.4.3 The diffusion phase

The diffusion phase enables an active cells' mapping to cross to an inactive cell via a stochastic selection procedure. Each **inactive** cells' mapping is redefined as follows:

- another cell is randomly selected from the network of mapping cells,

- if the selected cell is active then its mapping diffuses to the inactive cell,

- if the selected cell is also inactive then a completely new mapping into the search space is chosen using the new map function (see initialisation).

1.4.4 Termination

The simplest termination condition that can be used is to sum the number of mappings that point to the same position within the search space. The algorithm terminates when this sum [Q] exceeds a given threshold. A problem with this technique is that it requires a specific threshold to be defined before use. If the model is very distorted, or there is more than one similar instance of the model in the search space, then the sum may never exceed this threshold and hence the algorithm will never terminate.

A more sophisticated termination condition is to use a stability criterion. That is, when [Q] remains constant within specified bounds, over a number of iterations, the network is said to have reach equilibrium whereby each of the [Q] cells will define the best fit mapping into the search space. However, this condition alone is not sufficient to guarantee correct operation, since until the best fit mapping emerges and begins to diffuse across to other cells, [Q] will remain consistently low.

A general technique that has been used successfully is a combination of threshold and stability criteria, i.e. an initial activation threshold is set and the system operates until this threshold is reached. Then the system is monitored until the distribution of mappings becomes stable.

1.5 An example

To illustrate the operation of a stochastic search a small search will be described.

The problem is to derive the position of a small symbolic pattern [123] within a search space consisting of a string of eight digits [76512329]. The model pattern can be decomposed into three symbols, ADUs (1,2,3), hence ($M = 3$). The search space consists of the eight possible mappings of [123] in [76512329] (given wrap-around at the boundaries), hence ($Z = 8$), and thus the time ratio for the search is ($M/Z = 3/8$).

The example illustrates the network converging in three iterations (on average it would take around 2.54). Given random initialisation, at iteration one, each cell has a (1/8) probability of selecting the correct, best-fit mapping. Figure 2 shows the situation at iteration 1, one cell is testing mapping [0] with an offset of 1. Hence, the ADU pointed to in the search space is {6} which is compared with an ADU from the model pointed to by this offset, {2}. As the comparison is negative ({6} ≠ {2}), the cell remains **inactive**. The second cell is testing mapping [4] using an offset of 0 and thus compares {2} with {0}, hence it remains inactive, the third tests mapping [7] with an offset of 2, so comparing {6} with {3} and also stays inactive.

After this test phase, stochastic diffusion attempts to propagate successful mappings across the network. Each inactive cell selects another cell at random and if active the active cells mapping is transferred to the inactive cell. At this point none of the cells are active, thus each cell simply selects a new mapping at random into the search space.

At iteration two, one cell has selected the correct mapping, and hence becomes active. Now, during the diffusion phase the two inactive cells each have a (1/3) probability of selecting the one active cell. The probability that both will select it is (1/3 * 1/3 = 1/9), the probability that one will select it is (2 * 1/3 * 2/3 = 4/9) and the probability that neither will select it is (2/3 * 2/3 = 4/9).

At iteration three, all three cells in the network have settled on the correct mapping {3}.

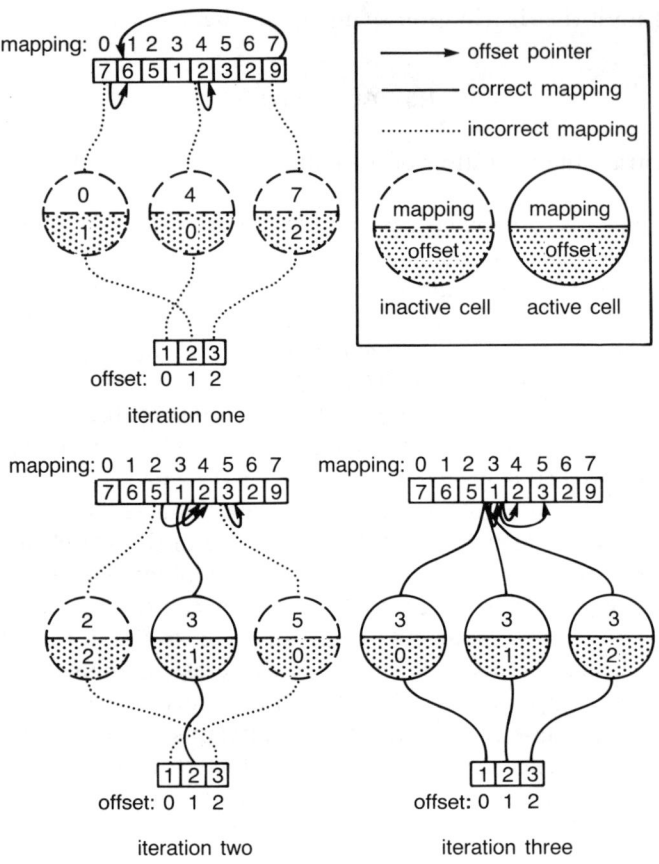

Fig. 2 An example search.

2. ELEMENTARY ANALYSIS OF STOCHASTIC DIFFUSION

Background

The complete analysis of stochastic diffusion is outside the scope of this chapter, however a theorem concerning stochastic diffusion will be proved to illustrate the general method of analysis. It is first useful to demonstrate that stochastic diffusion will converge when there is no noise.

Let the model comprise of M ADUs.
Let **alphabet size** be the number of possible states an ADU can occupy.

Let the number of iterations be N.
A cell is **active** when its mapping points to the 'correct' location of the model in the search space.

2.1 Theorem one

Under conditions of no noise and infinite alphabet size, given one cell active at iteration one, the network is certain to converge completely, that is all mapping cells will reach the 'active' state.

Let $\theta(K, N)$ be the probability that k cells are inactive at iteration n. If at iteration n, k cells are inactive

$$\theta(k,n+1) = \left(\frac{k}{M}\right)^k \qquad \ldots (1)$$

(Since to remain inactive, each inactive cell must select a fellow inactive cell)
Let this quantity be called α ($\alpha < 1$ since $k < M$)

$$\theta(k,n+2) = \left(\frac{k}{M}\right)^{2k} = \alpha^2 \qquad \ldots (2)$$

$$\theta(k,n+q) = \left(\frac{k}{M}\right)^{qk} = \alpha^q \qquad \ldots (3)$$

$\therefore$ Since $\alpha < 1$, $\theta(k,n+q) \to 0$ as $q \to \infty$ $\forall k$

$\therefore$ Network will converge.

The analysis of stochastic diffusion uses stochastic matrices and Markov chains. The nomenclature used is that defined by [5].

2.2 Theorem two

Under conditions of no noise and infinite alphabet size, given one mapping cell active at iteration one, the algorithm behaviour can be described by a homogeneous Markov chain defined by the stochastic matrix $[D]$.

Let $\rho(X, N)$ be the probability of X mapping cells active at iteration N.
If at iteration n, x mapping cells are active, and k cells are inactive ($k = M - x$), then

$$\rho(x,n+1) = \left(\frac{M-x}{0}\right)\left(\frac{M-x}{M}\right)^{M-x}\left(\frac{x}{M}\right)^0 \qquad \ldots (4)$$

$$\rho(x,n+1) = \binom{k}{0} \left(\frac{k}{M}\right)^k \qquad \ldots (5)$$

Where $\rho(x,n+1)$ is the probability that x are active at iteration $(n+1)$

$$\rho(x+1,n+1) = \binom{M-x}{1} \left(\frac{M-x}{M}\right)^{M-x-1} \left(\frac{x}{M}\right)^1 \qquad \ldots (6)$$

$$\rho(x+1,n+1) = \binom{k}{1} \left(\frac{k}{M}\right)^{k-1} \left(\frac{M-k}{M}\right)^1 \qquad \ldots (7)$$

$$\rho(x+q,n+1) = \binom{M-x}{q} \left(\frac{M-x}{M}\right)^{M-x-q} \left(\frac{x}{M}\right)^q \qquad \ldots (8)$$

$$\rho(x+q,n+1) = \binom{k}{0} \left(\frac{k}{M}\right)^{k-q} \left(\frac{M-k}{M}\right)^q \qquad \ldots (9)$$

The above expression defines the transition probabilities, d_{ij}, of a Markov chain $[D]$, giving the probability of moving from state $[i]$ to state $[j]$ due to stochastic diffusion (see Table 1). The matrix of transition probabilities $[P]$ at the nth iteration is thus defined [6] by:

$$[P_n] = [D]^n \qquad \ldots (10)$$

where P_{ij} is the probability of moving from state $[i]$ to state $[j]$.

All the states with [0] to $[M-1]$ cells on are **transient** states in the above Markov chain. These transient states represent x units being active ($k = M-x$). The probability of remaining in each transient state is:

$$\alpha = \left(\frac{k}{M}\right)^k \qquad \ldots (11)$$

$\therefore$ there is a $(1-\alpha)$ chance that each transient state will never be entered again.

Let $\gamma(k,\beta)$ be the probability of staying in a transient state $[k]$ for β iterations.

$$\gamma(k,\beta) = \alpha^\beta(1-\alpha) \qquad \ldots (12)$$

$\therefore$ for any given transient state $[k]$, the time periods in state $[k]$ follow a **geometric** distribution with finite mean:

$$\mu = \left(\frac{1}{1-\alpha}\right) \qquad \ldots (13)$$

Given no noise, the state with $[M]$ mapping cells active is **recurrent** and the system will remain in this state with a probability of one.

2.3 Summary

The above analysis deals only with basic stochastic diffusion, however it can be simply extended to fully describe a stochastic search by similarly considering the effects of reselection, noise and alphabet size.

3. THE HYBRID STOCHASTIC SEARCH NETWORK

3.1 Locating features in grey-scale images

An example of a problem involving pattern invariance in which stochastic searching has been successfully used is that of locating eye positions within grey scale images of human faces. An adult human has little difficulty in locating eye positions from a facial image, even though these positions could be anywhere within the image field. This is a difficult task in machine vision since facial features do not generally comprise hard edges and lines [7]. The hybrid stochastic network, a combination of a stochastic search network and an n-tuple network, has been shown to accurately locate all eye features on which it has been trained, and also achieve over 60% success in the general problem of locating eye features on which it has not been explicitly trained.

One of the aims of the feature location work described in this and other chapters is to produce real-time hardware demonstrators [7]. The hybrid stochastic network comprises of two systems, both of which can be easily implemented in dedicated hardware.

3.1.1 A System to classify the desired feature

The n-tuple method of pattern classification, first proposed by Bledsoe and Browning [8] and implemented in hardware as the WISARD system [9], has significant advantages over traditional methods of simple pattern classification [10]. A thorough introduction to the n-tuple technique of pattern classification is given in [10], a brief resume of which is given below.

The data to be classified are stored as an array of boolean values. This array is then sampled, according to some predefined schema (usually either randomly or sequentially), with [n] such samples forming one n-tuple. The data can be either exclusively sampled, such that each value is used only once, or oversampled by a factor of (m), where each value is used (m) times.

To learn a pattern, the (n) boolean values from each sample are used to form an n-bit address into an array (or RAM), where there is one such RAM per n-tuple sample, and a boolean TRUE value is stored at this location. To classify an image, the data are sampled as before. However, instead of storing a TRUE value at each defined location, a count of the TRUE values stored at these addresses is maintained. This count is the system response to an unknown pattern. After training with a set of patterns, such a network is able to classify patterns **not in the training set**. If these new patterns are 'similar' to those in the training set, then the system has **generalised** successfully. Such systems can differentiate between facial images at video speed. Hence it was decided to utilise n-tuple RAMs to perform the test phase of the stochastic search.

3.1.2 A system to search for the desired feature

The simplest form of feature location would be to scan the classifier sequentially over the search space, however a video image of 256*256 pixels is a large space to traverse, requiring 2^{16} sequential comparisons (iterations). However, by using stochastic search, as described in section 1, a typical analysis only requires around 30 iterations (see Fig. 4a), and when simulated sequentially on an Acorn Archimedes, takes only around one and a half minutes to locate the feature.

3.2 N-tuple feature classification

There are two particular problems associated with using simple n-tuple cells to classify grey level eye images — dealing with the grey level data, (simple binary coding cannot be used because of its non-linearity), and over-saturation (the network requires a lot of training in order to successfully generalise).

3.2.1 Grey Level Data

3.2.1.1 Thermometer coding

An established technique to convert grey level information into binary information suitable for addressing the RAM neurons is thermometer coding (1 in N coding). This technique consists of expanding an N bit grey level into a pattern of $2N$ binary pixels. Thermometer coding has the desirable property that a small change in pixel intensity causes a small change on the pattern to be classified, however it also has the undesirable property of expanding the search space exponentially with the resolution of the grey level used. This dramatically increases the amount of learning that must be carried out in order to correctly classify an object over a range of lighting conditions.

3.2.1.2 Minchinton cells

Minchinton cells describe a family of analogue preprocessing units that can be successfully used with n-tuple nets [11]. In the simplest case they consist of a digital comparator which is used to sample two randomly chosen points of the input pattern, the cell firing if $(P_i > P_j)$. It can be shown that:

- if the input pattern is sufficiently oversampled, none of the grey level information is lost,

- the output of the cell is immune to global DC changes in the input pattern.

Hence Minchinton cells were used to convert the grey level data into binary data.

3.2.2 Saturation

The stochastic search technique ideally requires a very sharp response from the feature classification system as the time to converge in an stochastic search increases rapidly as the response of the classifier to non-features rises. This would nominally require the tuple size to be large or the amount of learning small. However, both of these actions reduce the ability of the n-tuple network to generalise.

3.2.2.1 Adaptive n-tuple networks

To improve on the standard n-tuple behaviour a system for controlling the saturation in each RAM was used. This system differs from the standard single layer n-tuple learning in that, instead of storing a BOOLEAN value at the address defined by the micro feature of the image covered by the RAM, a count is maintained of how frequently that micro-pattern has been observed during training. At the end of the learning period only the addresses containing the highest (l) counts will cause the given RAM to fire. Thus by control of (l) there is a mechanism for effectively controlling saturation in each RAM.

3.3 Network architecture

Figure 3a shows a schematic block diagram of the hybrid stochastic network. The input video image is first digitised to a resolution of 256*256 pixels at an accuracy of 8 bits. A selection of points from this grey level data is processed by an array of Minchinton cells (Fig. 3b), the selection being controlled by the stochastic mapping cells. Each n-tuple RAM thus receives binary data from a given mapping into the search space. The response of the RAM to this data comprises the test phase of the stochastic search. The diffusion phase then reallocates stochastic cell mappings dependent on their success.

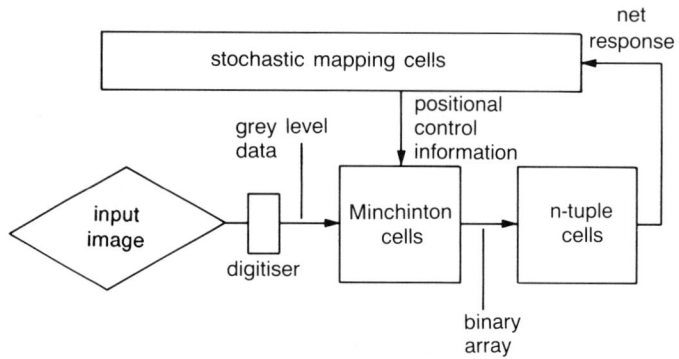

Fig. 3a Block diagram of hybrid stochastic network.

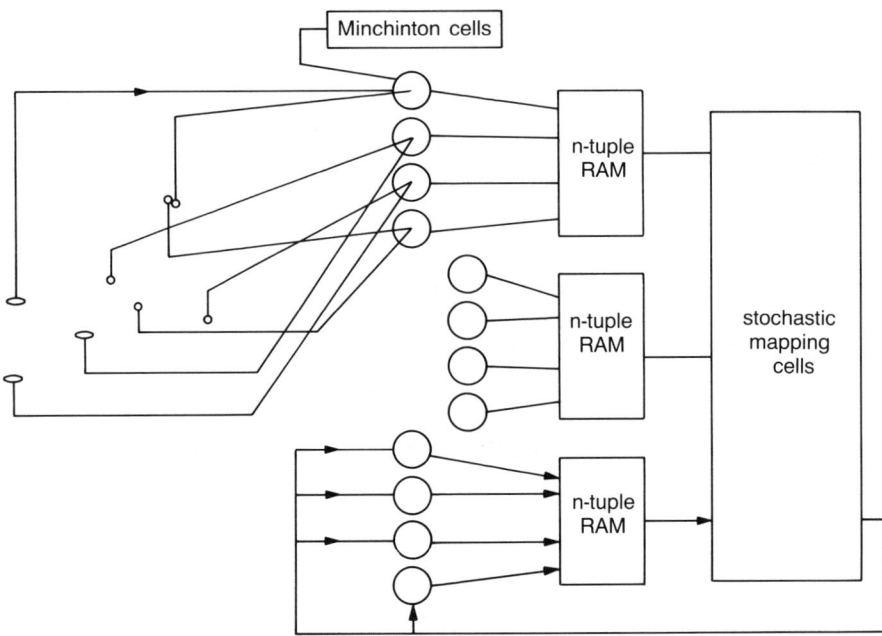

Fig. 3b The hybrid stochastic network.

3.4 Experiments

Due to hardware limitations it was unfortunately not possible to use the test data provided by BT Laboratories, as it was not in a form readable by the Archimedes computer on which the system was developed. However, by filming a set of subjects in similar conditions [7], a close approximation to that data was obtained.

The test data used comprised 64 video images of forward facing human faces, digitised to a resolution of 256*256 pixels at an accuracy of eight bits. The images were vaguely normalised to the centre of the screen. The subjects chosen were both men and women of various ethnic origins. There were no restrictions on their clothing, beards or make-up.

3.4.1 Location of 'trained' facial features

This test was a simple preliminary evaluation of the network's ability to locate a facial feature on which it had been trained. This involved training the network on one set of eyes then testing the system on a different image of the same face.

The system correctly located both eyes on each occasion it was tested.

3.4.2 Location of 'untrained' facial features

The second experiment tested how well the hybrid network located eyes on which it had not been previously trained. This involved training the net on 32 subjects (64 eyes) with their pupils approximately central, and testing the system using a different set of 32 subjects.

This experiment was repeated three times. Each training session lasted approximately three hours and each test session five hours. The tuple sizes used were (i) four, with a saturation level of two (i.e. only two addresses in each RAM would cause the cell to fire); and (ii) eight, using saturation levels of eight and ten. The results are summarised in Fig. 4 (t is the tuple size and l is the degree of saturation). It can be observed from Fig. 4a that, with a tuple size of eight ($t=8$) the network usually converged in about 30 iterations. This figure also illustrates how convergence is reached more rapidly with a high tuple size and low saturation ($t=8$, $l=8$). This is due to the stochastic search operating more efficiently with a sharp filter response. However Fig. 4b shows a converse effect, as the largest number of correct convergences occur when the filter is relatively blurred ($t=8$, $l=10$). This is due to the n-tuple cells generalising more efficiently over the untrained eye images with the higher RAM saturation.

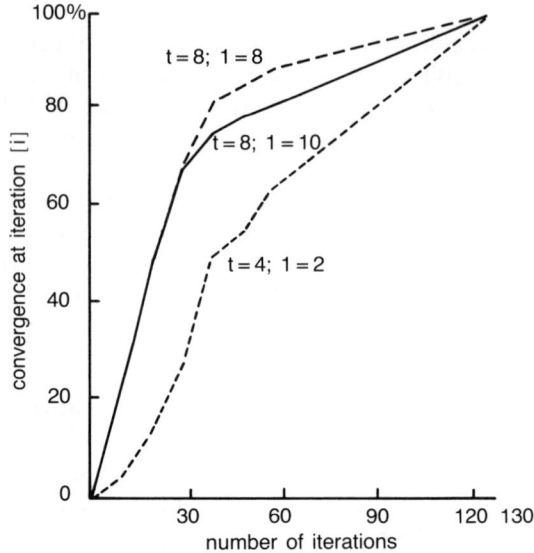

Fig. 4a Convergence of hybrid stochastic network.

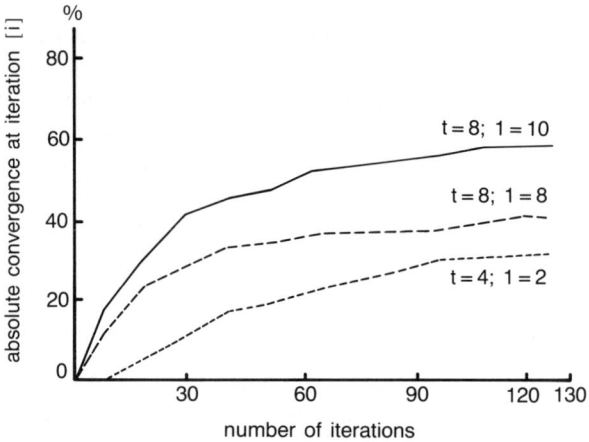

Fig. 4b Absolute performance of hybrid stochastic network.

3.5 Summary

The investigation of the hybrid stochastic network has demonstrated the feasibility of using such an architecture for feature location, however more research needs to be carried out to improve the performance of the system, and to investigate its behaviour in more general situations. The network developed was able to locate eye features in over 60% of cases tested. The current system used no explicit knowledge of where the facial features were likely to be in the image.

The performance of the hybrid stochastic network described was limited not by the stochastic search, but by the n-tuple classification sub-system. Overall system performance could be substantially improved if the classifier had a sharper rejection of non features but better generalisation of untrained correct features.

REFERENCES

1. Hinton G E: 'A parallel computation that assigns canonical object based frames of reference', Proc 7th IJCAI (1981).

2. McClelland J L: 'Retrieving general and specific knowledge from stored knowledge of specifics', Proc 3rd Conf Cognitive Society, Berkeley, CA (1981).

3. Bishop J M: 'Stochastic searching networks', Proc 1st IEE Conf on Artificial Neural Networks, pp 329—331, London (1989).

4. Bishop J M: 'Anarchic techniques for pattern classification', PhD Thesis, Reading University, pp 5—14 (1989).

5. Cox D R & Miller H D: 'The theory of stochastic processes', Chapter 3, Chapman & Hall, London (1965).

6. Cox D R & Miller H D: 'The theory of stochastic processes', Chapman & Hall, London pp 79, (1965).

7. Welsh W J, Woodland P C & Myers D J: 'A set of test problems for assessing neural net algorithms', BTL, Martlesham Heath, UK (1989).

8. Bledsoe W W & Browning I: 'Pattern recognition and reading by machine', Proceedings of the Eastern Joint Computer Conference, pp 225—232 (1959).

9. Aleksander I, Thomas W V & Bowden P A: 'WISARD: a radical step forward in image recognition', Sensor Review, (July 1984).

10. Aleksander I & Stonham T J: 'Guide to pattern recognition using random access memories', Computers & Digital Techniques, 2, No 1, pp 29—40 (1979).

11. Bishop J M, Minchinton P R & Mitchell R J: 'The Minchinton cell — Analogue input to the n-tuple net', Proc INNC '90, Paris (1990).

19

NODE SEQUENCE NETWORKS

R Linggard
School of Information Systems, University of East Anglia

1. INTRODUCTION

A major inspiration for the study of neural networks is the existence of very powerful, natural computers in the form of animal nervous systems. Foremost amongst these is the human brain — a neural network whose processing capacity is far in excess of any man-made machine. Because of the potential applications of neural networks in tasks hitherto performed exclusively by humans, there is a huge commercial interest in bringing such machines to a state of useful operation as soon as possible. This has encouraged some research workers to concentrate on the shorter term problems of applying neural network machines, rather than on investigating basic principles which, at present, are far from being fully understood. Consequently, the emerging field of neural networks is characterised by many premature applications: by machines which, though practical and useful, are distinctly un-brain-like in their architecture and somewhat limited in performance.

At the present time, artificial neural networks rarely perform as well as even the simplest of animal brains, and the question of how large numbers of autonomous cells can be interconnected to form a functional information processing system, is still wide open. Indeed, were it not for the existence of animal nervous systems such an idea might even be thought impossible. There is still some virtue, therefore, in attempting to model biological neurons and their interconnection, in the hope that the emergent properties will throw some light on the fundamental principles of complete nervous systems.

This chapter describes a study of simulated neural behaviour in which the model of the neuron is reduced to its simplest operational form. Using computer simulations, it is shown that when arrays of these simplified neurons are connected together by inhibitory synapses, they fire in stable sequences. It is possible to show, mathematically, that such sequences are equivalent to minimum energy states of the network, and that the system as a whole can function as an associative memory. In biological terms, these stable states form the basis of patterned behaviour, and it is shown that even for small numbers of neurons, the number of possible behaviour patterns is very large.

2. BACKGROUND

The study of animal nervous systems is a vast subject, drawing on the resources of many different, and disparate, scientific disciplines. At the system level, experimental psychologists attempt to understand behavioural responses of complete and sectioned nervous systems to controlled stimuli. At the system component end of the scale, neuro-physiologists and anatomists study the action and structure of neurons, networks of neurons and their synapses [1]. At the molecular level, the detailed operation of excitable cells and transmitter substances are being investigated by micro-biologists, physiologists, and pharmacologists [2,3]. More recently, physicists, computer scientists and engineers have turned to animal nervous systems for inspiration in their studies of parallel processing [4]. This has consisted mainly in simulating networks of neurons with greater or lesser degrees of fidelity. This present chapter follows in this tradition.

As a result of half a century of intense study, a great deal is known about how neurons function at the cell level, and how nervous systems operate both functionally and disfunctionally in living animals. The great gap in our knowledge is at the sub-system level, where a significant number of highly inter-connected neurons are functioning as a unit (ganglion) in a complete nervous system. What is known, is that such units exist, and in some cases the exact function of a particular ganglion is known. What is not known, is how such functionality is achieved in terms of the known properties of individual neurons and their synapses.

The work described here is part of an attempt to find unifying principles which will account for the operation of a ganglion in terms of the action of individual neurons, and may, perhaps, lead to an explanation of how connections of ganglia can constitute a complete nervous system. In searching for such principles, two rather strong assumptions have been made, which are worth mentioning if only because they have considerably reduced the search space.

The first assumption is that only the gross behaviour of a neuron is important in determining its functionality when massively inter-connected within a ganglion. It seems unlikely that every aspect of the complex biochemistry of a nerve cell is a functional characteristic of its interaction with thousands of other cells. Of course, without the biochemical reactions the cell would not function as a cell, but taking its internal behaviour for granted, its external behaviour is what determines its functionality as a member of a ganglion.

In this chapter, the biochemistry of the cell is regarded simply as the means whereby the cell achieves its functional characteristics. To this end, the internal state of the neuron is modelled by a single variable. In this one variable is subsumed all the variations in chemical concentrations and membrane potentials within the cell. This internal variable generally decays with time, so that when it falls below a certain threshold value, it causes the neuron to fire. This firing, which is instantaneous, is communicated to other neurons by an external binary pulse which simultaneously resets the internal variable to a fixed value. Again, synapses are modelled only in functional terms, and inhibitory or excitatory connections into a neuron cause the internal variable to rise and fall.

With these simplifications, the neuron functions as a relaxation oscillator which fires (and resets) when the (unspecified) internal state variable crosses a threshold. Neither absolute nor relative refractory periods are modelled, so that neuron-reset is simultaneous with the firing event. This simplification is justified by earlier studies in which refractory period was modelled, and which showed no significant difference in behaviour.

The second assumption is that any theory of neuron and ganglion functionality must pass the test of 'evolvability'. That is, there must be an evolutionary path, at each stage of which neurons and ganglia must be functional — there can be no jumps in functionality. The brains of humans and those of higher mammals are, undoubtedly, extremely complicated. If, as is assumed, they evolved from the much simpler nervous systems characteristic of lower animals, then an understanding of the higher might be approached via an investigation of the lower. Thus, in this chapter, simple connections of neurons are modelled without any attempt to include sensory input, and a single ganglion is assumed to constitute a functional system. This corresponds to an extremely simple form of life in which nerve cells are also muscle cells, and the effect of nervous action is simply to cause movement.

Other work in this field has attempted to model the oscillating neural networks found in the nervous systems of invertebrates [5]. These have been called 'central pattern generators' and are instrumental in governing rhythmic motor behaviour; for example, insect wing beats [6] and the gastric mill in the lobster stomach [7]. This chapter considers a much simpler system corresponding to life-forms in which the mediation of behaviour by sensory input is minimal.

3. THE NEURAL MODEL

3.1 The processing node

The neuron is modelled as a 'processing node', hereafter referred to as a 'node' to distinguish it from a real biological nerve cell, which will be called a neuron. A node is characterised by two variables; an internal-state variable, V, which is a real number, and an external variable, B, which is Boolean. For convenience B is either zero or one. Figure 1 shows the arrangement.

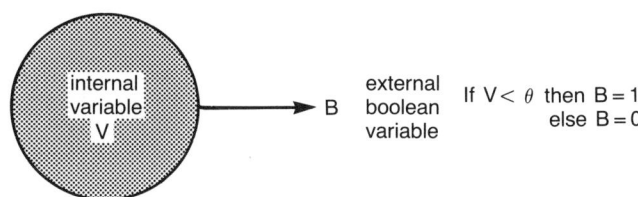

Fig. 1 The neuron as a processing node.

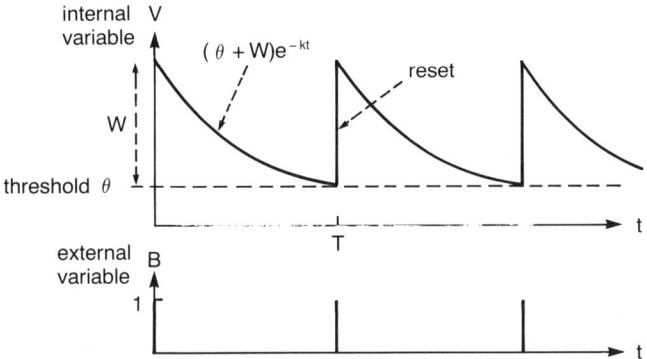

Fig. 2 The processing node as a relaxation oscillator.

The internal-state variable, V, decays exponentially with time until it reaches a threshold value θ, at which point the output variable, B, is set to one. This event is called a 'node firing' and immediately after it the node resets itself, that is, B switches back to zero and V is brought back above threshold by addition of a constant, W. An isolated node of this kind acts as a relaxation oscillator; V decays to threshold causing B to switch to one and V to be augmented by the amount W, bringing its value above threshold so that, as B resets to zero, the decay process begins again. This sequence of events is illustrated in Fig. 2. The time taken for the node to fire and for the internal variable to reset is assumed to be zero. The output pulse at B

is thus a true impulse. This is obviously impractical even for the fastest electronic machine; however, the omission of switching delays simplifies the mathematics without introducing any essential difference in system behaviour.

The exponential decay of the internal variable V can be described by the equation

$$V = (\theta + W) e^{\frac{-t}{q}} \qquad \ldots (1)$$

where t is the time variable and q is the decay time-constant.

The period of relaxation, T, is thus

$$T = q \ln\left(\frac{\theta + W}{\theta}\right) \qquad \ldots (2)$$

In this model of neural behaviour, the decay time-constant, q, and the threshold value θ, are assumed to be the same for all nodes. The reset constant, W, is assumed to vary from node to node in a random manner, so that in an array of such nodes the periods of relaxation will be randomly distributed. Hence, without any interconnections (synapses), the node firings are unsynchronised, and the nodes will fire in a randomly changing sequence.

3.2 Node interconnections — synapses

Synaptic inputs to a node caused by the firing of other nodes, are modelled as disturbances to the value of the node's internal-state variable, V, as follows.

An inhibitory synapse from node j, to node i, adds a value, W_{ij} to the value of V_i, every time node j fires. This prolongs the decay time of V_i, to threshold, thereby lengthening its period of relaxation, and reducing its rate of firing.

An excitatory synapse from node j to node i, subtracts a value W_{ij} from V_i, every time node j fires, thereby shortening the decay time of node i and increasing the rate of firing.

Inhibitory and excitatory synapses can be modelled in the same equation by making the sign of W_{ij} either positive (inhibitory) or negative (excitatory). The reset constant, W, also fits into this representational scheme if it is viewed as an inhibitory 'self-weight' which adds W to V_i whenever node i, itself, fires. Thus, W can be written as W_{ii}, and a given network of nodes together with the synaptic connections can be characterised by a weight matrix, $[W_{ij}]$. This arrangement is illustrated in Fig. 3.

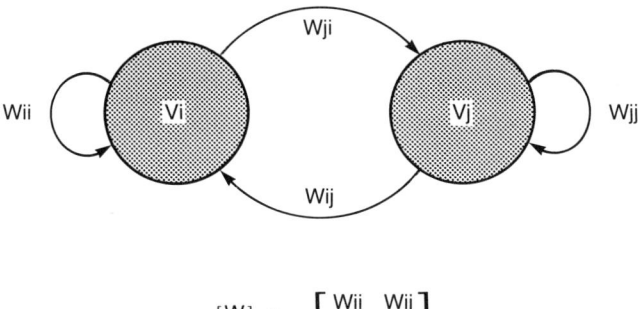

$$[W] = \begin{bmatrix} W_{ii} & W_{ij} \\ W_{ji} & W_{jj} \end{bmatrix}$$

Fig. 3 Weight matrix and synaptic arrangements.

Fig. 4 shows one cycle of reset and decay for a node i, with the reset event as time zero. The equation of decay, without synapses, is given by

$$V_i = (\theta + W_{ii}) e^{\frac{-t}{q}} \quad \ldots (3)$$

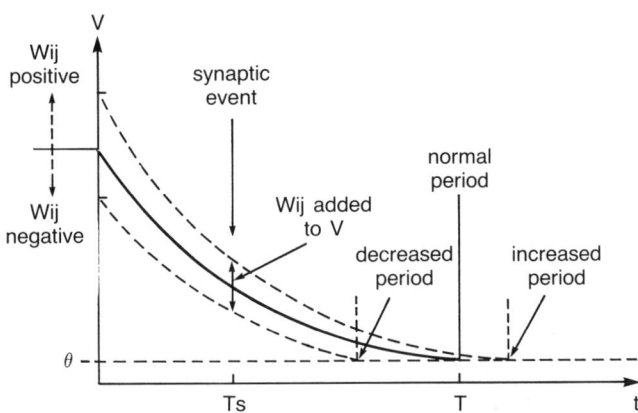

Fig. 4 Effect of synaptic event on the relaxation period.

If, at time $t = t_j$, the Node j fires, there is a synaptic event. The above equation is then only valid up to the time $t = t_j$, thereafter the equation is modified by the addition of the synaptic weight value W_{ij} giving

$$V_i = (\theta + W_{ii}) e^{\frac{-t}{q}} \quad 0 < t < tj \quad \ldots (4)$$

and

$$V_i = ((\theta + W_{ii}) e^{\frac{-tj}{q}} + W_{ij}) e^{\frac{-(t-tj)}{q}} \quad tj < t < T \quad \ldots (5a)$$

where T is the total relaxation period. This can be rewritten as

$$V_i = (\theta + W_{ii} + W_{ij}\, e^{\frac{tj}{q}})\, e^{\frac{-t}{q}} \qquad tj < t < T \qquad \ldots (5b)$$

Comparing this with equation (3), we see that the effect of the synapse is to introduce a component $W_{ij}\, e^{\frac{tj}{q}}$ into the decay equation. This means that the firing time of a node relative to the other nodes in a network depends, not just on the weight values, but also on the firing times of the other nodes. For a network with fixed weight values, the nodes may, or may not, settle down into a firing sequence which is stable. However, if a stable sequence is established, then the actual firing times of the nodes are uniquely determined by the weight values, the decay time-constant and the threshold value of the network.

For a network of nodes connected by inhibitory weights, this relationship is analysed mathematically in the appendix.

3.3 Inhibitory versus excitatory synapses

In its effect on the firing time of a node i, the synaptic weight value, W_{ij}, is modified by the factor, $e^{\frac{tj}{q}}$, which depends on tj, the firing time of node j relative to node i. An effective, modified self-weight, Wm, can be found by considering W_{ij} to be projected back in time (see Fig. 4) to the reset event of node i, and adding to W_{ii}.

$$Wm = W_{ii} + W_{ij}\, e^{\frac{tj}{q}} \qquad \ldots (6)$$

Since, from equation (2), $T = q\, \ln(\theta + Wm)$, the effect of Wm on the relaxation period T, depends on the sign of W_{ij}, that is, whether the synapse is inhibitory or excitatory. If W_{ij} is positive, then the relaxation period is increased, firing rate is decreased and the synapse is inhibitory. If W_{ij} is negative, then the relaxation period is decreased, firing rate is increased and the synapse is excitatory.

The actual magnitude of the change in relaxation period of a node i, due to a synaptic input from node j, is dependent not only on the value of the synaptic weight W_{ij}, but also on the exponential decay factor $e^{\frac{tj}{q}}$ and hence on the firing time tj of node j. This means that the longer the interval between the firing of node i and node j, the greater the effect the synapse W_{ij}, has on the relaxation period of node i.

It has been found, in computer simulations, that there is a tendency for a network to fire in a stable cycle and to maximise the cycle repeat period. This means that, if the weights are positive (inhibitory), then the tj will tend to increase — thereby increasing the inhibitory effect inherent in the $e^{\frac{tj}{q}}$

term. Alternatively, if the weights are negative (excitatory), then the t_j will tend to decrease — thereby decreasing the excitatory effect of the $e^{\frac{t_{ij}}{q}}$ term. The result of this, is that, with inhibitory synapses the firing times between nodes will tend to be as long as possible. With excitatory synapses the firing times will be as short as possible and the nodes will tend to fire in rapid succession.

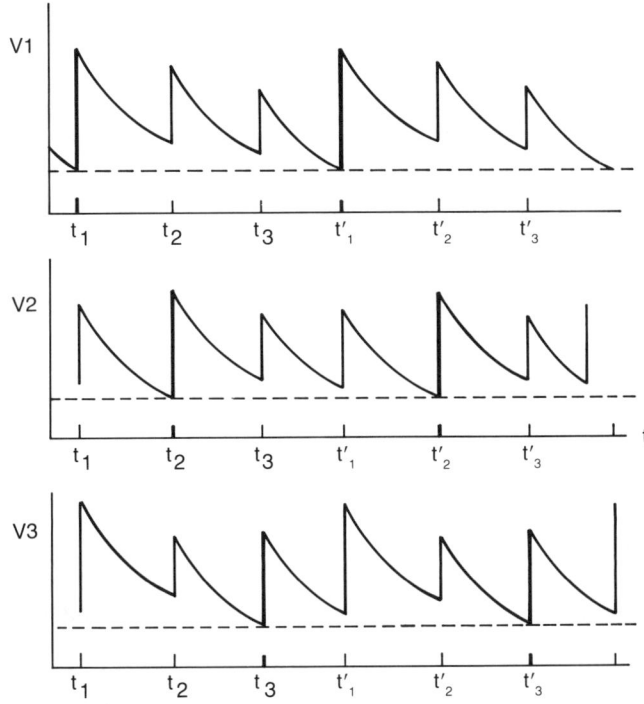

Fig. 5 State variables for a three node network.

The internal state variables for each node of a three node network are shown in Fig. 5. In this illustration all the weights are inhibitory. It is worth noting that the tendency of a network to maximise the cycle period does not depend on the decay of the internal state variable being exponential. It is clear from Fig. 5 that any monotonic, concave, decaying function will produce the same kind of behaviour. (A linear decay makes the synaptic effects independent of firing times.) However, the assumption of an exponential function is not all that unrealistic in the context of biochemical reactions, and it certainly makes the mathematical analysis in the appendix much more tractable.

4. NETWORK BEHAVIOUR

4.1 Sequential firing in network simulations

When several nodes are connected together by synaptic weights, the relaxation period of a given node i, is governed by three factors;

- its own self-weight, W_{ii}
- the synaptic weights from other nodes, W_{ij}
- the relative firing times of the other nodes.

In computer simulations it has been found that, with networks of interconnected nodes in which the weight matrix is fixed, there is a tendency for the firing sequence to change until the nodes are able to fire in a stable sequence. That is, until the nodes fire at the same frequency and in a fixed phase relationship.

It was found that networks with excitatory synapses quickly establish a firing sequence in which the nodes fire in rapid succession (sometimes simultaneously) after which there is a pause before the firing pattern is repeated. This is called a 'relay' sequence since most of the nodes simply relay the firing of one node.

On the other hand, it was found that networks with inhibitory synapses change sequence relatively slowly before settling down into a stable firing pattern in which node firings are spaced out fairly uniformly throughout the cycle of repetition.

Networks with both inhibitory and excitatory synapses showed a mixture of these two types of behaviour. Typically, some groups of nodes fire together in relay sequence, and several of such groups fire in a stable sequence.

In view of the more interesting behaviour of networks with inhibitory synapses, and the difficulty of analysing networks with excitatory synapses, the remainder of this paper is devoted exclusively to inhibitory networks. It is convenient in this respect to define four kinds of stable sequence for an inhibitory network consisting of n nodes.

- Simple sequence — each node fires once per cycle of the sequence.
- Sub-sequence — some nodes do not fire — that is, the sequence length is less than n.
- Super-sequence — some nodes fire more than once per cycle — that is, the sequence length is greater than n.
- Complex sequence — a combination of sub- and super-sequence.

This phase-locking, or self-synchronising, tendency is very strong and an inhibitory network with quite wide variations in its weight values can usually find a sequence in which it can continue to fire indefinitely. Such a sequence is called a stable sequence, and, for a given network, there will usually be many stable sequences in which it can fire.

An unstable sequence is one in which the network will not fire indefinitely. If a network is started in an unstable sequence, then the between-node firing times will change, causing the firing sequence to change until a stable sequence is established. Once a stable sequence has been established, the between-node firing times do not change. In some networks, usually ones with wide variations in weight values, there are no stable simple sequences.

Node sequence networks of this kind are dynamic networks in that the internal-state variables of the nodes change continuously. However, if firing sequences are considered as states, stable sequences may be defined as states in which dynamic equilibrium has been established. Thus, a network with many stable states can be regarded as a multi-state system. It will be shown later that such states correspond to energy-dissipation minima of the system.

4.2 Stable sequences in inhibitory networks

It is shown in appendix 1 that when an n-node inhibitory network fires in a simple, stable sequence then the times, t_i, at which the nodes fire with respect to some arbitrary reference, can be related to the weight matrix by the eigen relationship given in equation (21) (see appendix).

$$M\mathbf{a}_i = \lambda \mathbf{a}_i \quad \ldots\ldots (21)$$

Where $\quad a_i = e^{\frac{t_i}{q}} \ (i = 1..n)$

and M is a matrix which depends only on the synaptic weights, W_{ij}, and the threshold constant θ. The period, T, of one cycle of repetition of the sequence is given by

$$\lambda = e^{\frac{T}{q}}$$

The matrix equation (21), of order n (the number of nodes), is derived assuming a particular firing sequence — in this case 1,2,...n. Essentially, it represents a set of n simultaneous equations, and as such it has n solutions. That is, there are n values of λ, and n sets of values a_i, (and hence timings, t_i) which satisfy the relationship described by the equation. Obviously, if the nodes are firing in time sequence the actual firing times t_i must be in order of value, that is, $t1 < t2 < t3 < ... < tn$. Of the n possible values of λ (and hence periods, T), the largest is called the principal eigenvalue and the corresponding set of a_i values is called the principal eigenvector.

In simulations of networks of this kind, it has been found that the timings which the network invariably takes up for a particular sequence, is the set which corresponds to the principal eigenvalue and the principal eigenvector. That is, the period of the firing sequence has the longest possible duration.

4.3 Minimum energy dissipation

If the firing of a single node is considered to consume a finite amount of energy E, then the total energy dissipated by an n node network in one cycle of a simple sequence is nE. The power, or rate of energy dissipation, of the network in such a state is thus nE/T. Since a network always takes up the maximum value of A, and hence of T (the cycle period), the rate of energy dissipation, (nE/T), of the network is minimised for that particular sequence. A stable sequence is, therefore, an energy dissipation minimum of the system.

The number of different sequences which are possible for an n node network is equal to the number of different ways the nodes can be numbered, that is, $(n-1)!$. In general, not all these sequences will be stable. However, for a network with many stable sequences (states), the stable sequences represent energy dissipation minima of the system into which it will settle after a disturbance.

As an example, consider the four node network shown in Fig. 6, in which the nodes have been labelled 'A', 'P', 'T' and '-'. There are thus $(n-1)! =$ 6 possible sequences, which are, -APT, -TAP, -PAT, -ATP, -TPA and -PTA. (The sequences 'APT-', 'PT-A', 'T-AP' and '-APT', are considered to be rotations of the same sequence. The '-' symbol is included to delimit words and in discussions on sequences will always appear as the first symbol).

For any particular stable sequence, for example, '-APT', there are four different sets of firing times which could give a stable sequence. In a simulation of the network, with threshold set at one and the weight values as shown in Fig. 6, the cycle time and firing times adopted by the network were those corresponding to the principal eigenvalue and principal eigenvector.

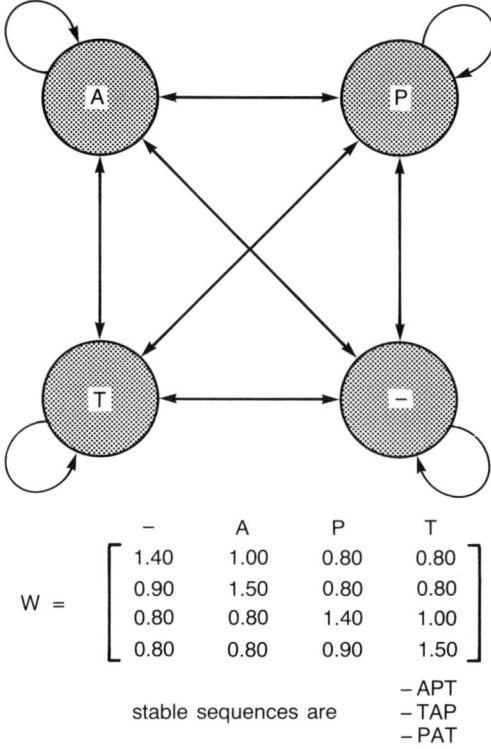

Fig. 6 The -APT network.

5. ASSOCIATIVE MEMORY

5.1 Content addressable memory

Associative memory is sometime referred to as 'content addressable memory' because each item of data acts as its own memory address. In write mode, each item of data activates a memory location. In read mode, an input item (address) invokes the information that the memory location has, or has not, been activated. An important property of associative memory is its ability to deal with noisy or incomplete input. In the case of noisy input, a corrupt version of a stored item of data is input to the memory which responds by outputting the correct version. For incomplete input, the memory responds with the complete data item. In order to do this without ambiguity, it is necessary that all the possible address locations are not used, and that the ratio of used to unused locations is very low.

5.2 Associative recall

The characteristics of node sequence networks suggests that they could function as associative memory if simple sequences are regarded as potential memory locations. For an n node network, there are $(n-1)!$ different possible repeating sequences in which the network can fire. Of these, only a small fraction need be stable to give a large storage capacity. For example, if $n = 10$ there are $9! = 362\,880$ different possible sequences. If only 10% of these are stable this still permits over 36 000 stored items. Thus, the input (corresponding to any sequence from the original set of 362 880 possible sequences), causes the network to respond with the 'nearest' stable sequence.

In order to be able to store information, the stable states of a node sequence network must be selectable by manipulation of the weight values. Each item of data to be remembered is associated with a sequence which is then made stable by selecting appropriate weight values for the network. It seems reasonable to assume that it will be relatively easy to choose weight values to make a set of similar sequences stable, and indeed, experiments confirm this. What is not obvious is how to choose weight values to produce an arbitrary set of stable sequences; that is, to find an adequate learning rule. However, there appears to be no theoretical reason why weight values should not exist which will make any possible set of sequences stable.

So far, attempts to find an infallible learning rule have failed. In experiments with networks having only a small number of nodes, heuristic methods were used to find appropriate weight values. Experiments with numbers of nodes greater than seven were hampered by the difficulty in checking out the stability of all possible sequences.

5.3 The '-APT' network

A particularly convenient way of investigating the capacity of node sequence networks to act as associative memory is to label the nodes with letters of the alphabet so that sequences can be used to spell out words. The 'legal' words are sufficiently random to be a good test of a system's ability to have an arbitrary set of stable states.

As an example, consider the four node network already introduced in section 4 and shown in Fig. 6, in which the nodes have been labelled 'A', 'P', 'T' and '-'. Of the six possible sequences, only three are selected as 'legal' words, these are '-APT', '-PAT' and '-TAP'. By adjusting the weight values of the work, it is possible to make these legal words the stable sequences of the network. It is easily confirmed that, if the network is started in an unstable sequence, its firing times will change until it falls into a stable sequence.

5.4 The '-STAR' network

In an experiment with a fully interconnected, five node network, the nodes were labelled '-', 'S', 'T', 'A', 'R'. With five nodes, the total number of possible sequences is (5-1)! = 24. (The sequence '-STAR' is considered to be the same as 'R-STA', 'AR-ST', 'TAR-S' and 'STAR-'). With all cross-weight values set to the same value, all 24 sequences can be made stable.

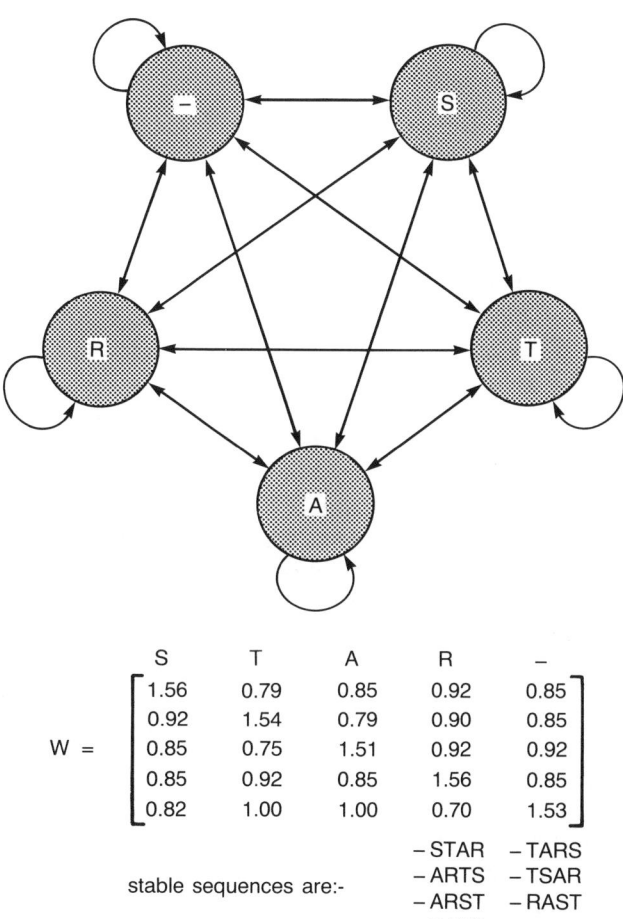

$$W = \begin{bmatrix} S & T & A & R & - \\ 1.56 & 0.79 & 0.85 & 0.92 & 0.85 \\ 0.92 & 1.54 & 0.79 & 0.90 & 0.85 \\ 0.85 & 0.75 & 1.51 & 0.92 & 0.92 \\ 0.85 & 0.92 & 0.85 & 1.56 & 0.85 \\ 0.82 & 1.00 & 1.00 & 0.70 & 1.53 \end{bmatrix}$$

stable sequences are:-
 -STAR   -TARS
 -ARTS   -TSAR
 -ARST   -RAST
 -RATS

Fig. 7 The -STAR network.

By adjusting the weight values appropriately, it is possible to make only seven sequences stable. These can be chosen to be 'legal' words, such as '-STAR', '-TARS', '-ARTS', '-TSAR', '-ARST', '-RAST' and '-RATS'. This network and its weight values are shown in Fig. 7.

Again, if the network is started in an unstable sequence the firing times change until a stable sequence is established. For example, if the network is started in '-TASR', then the node firing times adjust themselves until the nodes 'R' and 'S' change places in the sequence, and the stable sequence '- TARS' is established.

6. DISCUSSION

6.1 Justification

The model of the neuron proposed here is extremely simple. Nevertheless, such neurons, when connected together in a network, show a strong tendency to organised behaviour. This 'emergent property' takes the form of sequential firing, such that the nodes of the network fire in sequence, with fixed phase relationships and a fixed total period. A given network may be able to fire in many different stable sequences, and when started in an unstable sequence, the network will change sequence until it 'finds' a stable sequence, in which it will continue to fire indefinitely. It has been shown that a stable sequence is, effectively, an energy dissipation minimum of the system.

Networks of this kind have been called 'node sequence networks'. The particular set of sequences which are stable for a given network, is governed by its weight matrix, and this set can be changed by changing the weight values. The number of possible sequences that a network may take up is $(n-1)!$, where n is the number of nodes. This expression increases so rapidly that networks with only a small number of nodes may have, potentially, very large numbers of stable sequences. This makes them ideal for use as associative memory.

6.2 Physiological plausibility

Node sequence networks are physiologically plausible for very simple animals whose nervous systems consist of only one type of excitable cell. This applies to primitive animals in which excitable cells are not specialised into sensory neurons, motor neurons and muscle cells, as they are in higher animals. These primitive cells contract on firing and thereby cause movements of the animal's body. Networks of cells of this kind would have an evolutionary advantage if they could fire in co-ordinated sequences rather than at random. For example, the peristaltic movements of tube-like sea creatures are produced by a wave of contraction passing along the animal. This type of sequential firing is easily explained by node sequence networks.

Again, it seems plausible that cells of this kind could have evolved from more primitive forms. Originally, such cells would not need to have highly developed axons, dendrites and synapses in order to function; it is only necessary that, on firing, the cells release an inhibitory transmitter. The transmission of this chemical by diffusion, and the different distances of the cells from each other, would give the effect of different synaptic weights. The weight values of these effective 'synapses' would then correlate with cell spacing and anatomical shape.

Given a small nervous system in which each cell can contract on firing, it is not unreasonable to assume that certain stable sequences of firing/contraction would produce beneficial behaviour. It could then be expected that random genetic mutation and natural selection would produce animals in which such behaviour patterns would be an inherited characteristic. The node sequence idea may also have some relevance in explaining the action of smooth muscle in higher animals. For example, the gut muscle in most animals is essentially a tube which operates by autonomous peristaltic contractions. The heart muscle too, is an autonomous muscle characterised by rhythmic waves of contraction.

6.3 Behaviour and behaviour patterns

The functioning of node sequence networks is very simple and very robust; it seems, therefore, quite plausible as a model for primitive nervous systems. However, the simplicity of its operation does not preclude a wide variety of possible behaviour patterns, as the following analysis will show.

Let a particular stable, simple sequence be defined as a 'behaviour'. (In a primitive animal this would correlate with a particular movement, for example, a peristaltic contraction). An n node network has $(n-1)!$ different simple sequences which may or may not be stable, that is, it has $(n-1)!$ potential behaviours. Let any particular set of selected sequences be called a 'behaviour pattern'. It is interesting to calculate the total number of different behaviour patterns which are possible for an n node network. The number of potential behaviours (sequences), $b = (n-1)!$. If a set s, of these b potential behaviours are chosen as a behaviour pattern, then for a particular value of s, the number of different ways of choosing s behaviours from the b possibilities is given by

$$\frac{b!}{(b-s)!\, s!}$$

If all values of s are considered, from 0 to b, then the above expression must be summed for $s=0$ to $s=b$. The total number p, of different behaviour patterns, is thus given by

$$p = 2^b = 2^{(n-1)!}$$

The power of the $2^{(n-1)!}$ function can be appreciated by considering its value for $n = 3$ to 6.

n	$(n-1)!$	$2^{(n-1)!}$
3	2	4
4	6	64
5	24	1.7×10^7
6	120	1.3×10^{36}

The number of different behaviour patterns becomes very large for values of n above 7.

For example, in the -APT experiment, only 3 of the 6 possible sequences are made stable. The behaviour pattern chosen was the 'legal' words, but could have been any 3 of the possible 6. There are 20 different ways of choosing the 3 states from the 6 possibilities. That is, there are 20 different behaviour patterns each consisting of 3 behaviours. However, to calculate the total number of different behaviour patterns, it is necessary to consider behaviour patterns consisting of 1, 2, 3, 4, 5 and 6 behaviours.

If a behaviour pattern consists of only one behaviour, then there are only 6 possibilities; for 2 behaviours there are 15 possibilities; for 3 behaviours there are 20; for 4 there are again 15; for 5 there are again 6; and for 6 there is only 1. If we include the pattern which consists of zero behaviours, there are a total of 64 different behaviour patterns.

6.4 Future work

In the model of the neuron model proposed here, the decay factor and threshold are assumed to be constant and the same for all neurons. Global variation of either of these factors should produce effects on the behaviour of the whole network. This is akin to the influence of drugs or hormones, and it would be interesting to investigate these effects on a node sequence network.

Networks which include excitatory synapses have been largely excluded from this study. In networks of inhibitory synapses, only one neuron may fire at any one time. By including some excitatory synapses it is possible for the firing of one particular neuron to be relayed to other neurons so that its effect is magnified. It has been noted that local excitatory synapses cause groups of neurons to fire more or less together as part of a longer stable sequence. This makes possible a certain degree of redundancy since the loss of one neuron in a group does not destroy the overall firing pattern. These effects are, as yet, unexplored.

The assumption that a node sequence network may have any arbitrary set of simple sequences made stable, needs to be proved, or disproved. Such a proof, if positive, ought to lead to a learning rule. Since experiments have shown that it is relatively easy to make sets of similar sequences stable, the question of arbitrary sequences needs to be related to the idea of 'sequence similarity'. In particular, it would help to have an adequate definition of similarity in this sense. With large numbers of nodes the memory capacity of a node sequence network is, at least theoretically, enormously large. However, since simple sequences are n nodes in length, for large n, the duration of the sequence period becomes a limiting factor. It is therefore more realistic to utilise the shorter, sub-sequences as the units of memory. The mathematics of sub-sequences is complex and is at present under investigation. It would be particularly interesting to find out how sub-sequences interact with each other.

Given that primitive animals could evolve useful behaviour patterns, as described above, the question then arises — how can the animal change from one particular behaviour to another, at the appropriate time? For example, how can it change from feeding behaviour to moving behaviour? Obviously, some kind of sensory input is required, which acts on its neural network so as to stimulate the appropriate firing sequence. This suggests another role for excitatory synapses and the topic is under investigation at present.

ACKNOWLEDGEMENTS

The author is grateful to many colleagues for guidance, comments and inspiration over many years. However, particular thanks are due to Gavin Smyth who wrote a suite of software to evaluate the existence of stable sequences and investigated the problem of learning algorithms.

REFERENCES

1. MacGregor R J: 'Neural and Brain Modeling', Academic Press (1987).

2. Kuffler F W, Nicolls J G & Martin A R: 'From Neuron to Brain', Sinauer Associates Inc. (1984).

3. Shepherd G M: 'Neurobiology', Oxford University Press Inc. (1988).

4. Rumelhart D E & MacClelland J L: 'Parallel Distributed Processing', MIT Press Cambridge, Ma (1986).

5. Roberts A & Roberts B L: 'Neural Origins of Rhythmic Movements', Cambridge University Press (1983).

6. Ryckebusch S, Bower J M & Mead C: 'Modeling Small Oscillating Biological Networks in Analog VLSI', in Advances in Neural Information Processing Systems 1, Morgan Kaufmann Inc, pp 384—393 (1989).

7. Selverston A I & Moulins M: 'The Crustacean Stomatogastric System', Springer-Verlag, New York (1987).

APPENDIX 1

If, at time $t = ti$, node i fires, and at time $t = tj$, node j fires into node i with weight Wij, equations (4), (5) and (6) can be modified as follows;

$$V_i = (\theta + W_{ii}) e^{-\frac{(t-ti)}{q}} \quad ti < t < tj \quad \ldots (7)$$

and $$V_i = ((\theta + W_{ii}) e^{-\frac{(tj-ti)}{q}} + W_{ij}) e^{-\frac{(t-tj)}{q}} \quad tj < t < T \quad \ldots (8a)$$

where T is the total relaxation period. This can be rewritten as

$$V_i = (\theta + W_{ii} + W_{ij} e^{\frac{(tj-ti)}{q}}) e^{-\frac{(t-ti)}{q}} \quad tj < t < T \quad \ldots (8b)$$

The effective self-weight of node i is

$$Wmi = W_{ii} + W_{ij} e^{\frac{(tj-ti)}{q}} \quad \ldots (9)$$

and the relaxation period, T, is given by

$$\theta + W_{ii} + W_{ij} e^{\frac{(tj-ti)}{q}} = \theta e^{\frac{T}{q}} \quad \ldots (10)$$

Considering only simple sequences, it is possible to derive the necessary conditions for stable sequences. If, in the general case, the nodes i, j, etc fire at times ti, tj, etc and the network is fully connected, then the total effective weight for each node i is thus,

$$Wmi = \Sigma_j W_{ij} e^{\frac{(tj-ti)}{q}} \quad \ldots (11)$$

This is related to the relaxation period, T, by

$$\theta + \Sigma_j W_{ij}\, e^{\frac{(tj-ti)}{q}} = \theta\, e^{\frac{T}{q}} \qquad \ldots (12)$$

If the nodes fire in a simple, stable sequence then the relaxation period of each node must be the same. Hence for each node i, there is an equation of the above form. However, before such a system of equations can be solved to give the firing times $ti, \ldots tj$, it is necessary to take account of the fact that these firing times may occur in consecutive cycles.

As an example, consider the three node network whose firing arrangements are shown in Fig. 5. For each node i, the equation relating weights to firing times is given by equation (12). The form of this equation shows that the threshold, θ, acts as a scaling factor for the weights, and the expression can be simplified by defining normalised weights as

$$w_{ij} = \frac{W_{ij}}{\theta}$$

The normalised equation is therefore

$$1 + \Sigma_j w_{ij}\, e^{\frac{(tj-ti)}{q}} = e^{\frac{T}{q}} \qquad \ldots (13)$$

The corresponding equations for each of the three nodes are

$$1 + w_{11}\, e^{\frac{(t1-t1)}{q}} + w_{12}\, e^{\frac{(t2-t1)}{q}} + w_{13}\, e^{\frac{(t3-t1)}{q}} = e^{\frac{T}{q}} \qquad \ldots (13a)$$

$$1 + w_{21}\, e^{\frac{(t'1-t2)}{q}} + w_{22}\, e^{\frac{(t2-t2)}{q}} + w_{23}\, e^{\frac{(t3-t2)}{q}} = e^{\frac{T}{q}} \qquad \ldots (13b)$$

$$1 + w_{31}\, e^{\frac{(t'1-t3)}{q}} + w_{32}\, e^{\frac{(t'2-t3)}{q}} + w_{33}\, e^{\frac{(t3-t3)}{q}} = e^{\frac{T}{q}} \qquad \ldots (13c)$$

Here the times $t1, t2, t3$ are in one cycle and $t'1, t'2$ are in the next cycle. Note that $T = t'i - ti$. Separating t and t' variables gives

$$(1 + w_{11})\, e^{\frac{t1}{q}} + w_{12}\, e^{\frac{t2}{q}} + w_{13}\, e^{\frac{t3}{q}} = e^{\frac{t'1}{q}} \qquad \ldots (14a)$$

$$(1 + w_{22})\, e^{\frac{t2}{q}} + w_{23}\, e^{\frac{t3}{q}} + w_{13}\, e^{\frac{t'1}{q}} = e^{\frac{t'2}{q}} \qquad \ldots (14b)$$

$$(1 + w_{33})\, e^{\frac{t3}{q}} + w_{31}\, e^{\frac{t'1}{q}} + w_{32}\, e^{\frac{t'2}{q}} = e^{\frac{t'3}{q}} \qquad \ldots (14c)$$

It is convenient at this stage to define new variables as follows

$$e^{\frac{t1}{q}} = a_1 \quad e^{\frac{t2}{q}} = a_2 \quad e^{\frac{t3}{q}} = a_3 \quad \ldots\ldots (15a)$$

$$e^{\frac{t'1}{q}} = a'_1 \quad e^{\frac{t'2}{q}} = a'_2 \quad e^{\frac{t'3}{q}} = a'_3 \quad \ldots\ldots (15b)$$

and $e^{\frac{T}{q}} = \lambda$ ..... (15c)

The equations can now be written

$$(1+w_{11})\,a_1 + w_{12}\,a_2 + w_{13}\,a_3 = a'_1 \quad \ldots\ldots (16a)$$

$$(1+w_{22})\,a_2 + w_{23}\,a_3 + w_{21}\,a'_1 = a'_2 \quad \ldots\ldots (16b)$$

$$(1+w_{33})\,a_3 = -w_{31}\,a'_1 - w_{32}\,a'_2 + a'_3 \quad \ldots\ldots (16c)$$

This can be expressed in matrix form as

$$W_u a = W_l a' \quad \ldots\ldots (17)$$

or as

$$M_a = a' \quad \ldots\ldots (18)$$

Where W_u is an upper triangular matrix and W_l is a lower triangular matrix related to the normalised Weight matrix W by

$$W_u - W_l = W \quad \ldots\ldots (19)$$

and $M = W_l^{-1} W_u$ ..... (20)

Since the sequence is stable with period T, then

$$t'_i = t_i + T \text{ and } a'_i = a_i \lambda$$

or as

$$M_a = \lambda_a \quad \ldots\ldots (21)$$

This is an eigen equation. For an n node network, there are n solutions. The values of λ are the eigenvalues and the largest of these is the principal eigenvalue, and its corresponding vector a is the principal eigenvector.

In simulations of node sequence networks, it has been observed that when a stable sequence is established, its period T corresponds to the principal eigenvalue and the firing times correspond to the principal eigenvector.

If a_i is the principal eigenvector, then the node firing times t_i, are given by

$$t_i = q \, ln(a_i)$$

If the sequence is stable then the ti must be in value order, that is $t1 < t2 < t3$ etc. This is a necessary but not sufficient condition for stability. It is also necessary that the values of the internal state variables Vi do not fall below threshold between firing times. That is, the values of Vi at times tj must be greater than threshold. The matrix of Vi at firing is given by

$$[V_i(t_j)]$$

The diagonal elements of this matrix will be equal to threshold, θ. For stability, the off-diagonal elements must be greater than θ.

20

SOME DYNAMICAL PROPERTIES OF NEURAL NETWORKS

S Olafsson
BT Laboratories

1. INTRODUCTION

In this chapter we review some essential dynamical properties of neural networks. We work towards a definition of neural networks formulated as dynamical systems and give reasons for our study of particular differential equations. The time evolution of various models is discussed and some conditions for convergence towards equilibrium states analysed. The feedforward dynamics of the models considered is identical to the ones considered by various authors in the recent past. However, the models considered here have different stability criteria and the dynamics of the backpropagation are modified. The stability of these states is discussed by using the concept of terminal attractors as introduced by M Zak. We show that some of the dynamical models lead in their static limit to the recursive feed forward structure of MLPs. Preliminary results on a speech recognition problem are given.

The present state of research into neural networks is rather unsatisfactory because our understanding of the temporal behaviour of most neural models is very limited. Most software implementations of neural network models ignore time as a real variable completely only considering the changes that take place in the network's quantities in discrete steps and according to prescriptions different to the temporal law by which the network would be governed when formulated as a dynamical system.

Because many of the tasks one wants neural networks to deal with can be described as processes that occur in time, a real aim would be to have a neural network that could learn or access stored memory in real time, i.e. as the processes are happening. A neural network that is capable of achieving this sort of aim lies far in the future, but the first steps have been taken a long time ago and lie, we believe, in the realms of the mathematical theory of dynamical systems.

In recent years several authors have tried to apply the principles of dynamical systems on the mathematical formulation of neural networks [1,2,3]. The mathematical concept of a dynamical system is by now well defined but its initial formulation goes back to the works of Poincare, Lyapunov and in more recent years Rene Thom, Smale, Hirsh and others. For a general introduction see [4]. One of the essentials of the modern approach to dynamical systems is its qualitative nature, i.e. considerable information about a system's dynamical behaviour can be achieved without actually solving the differential equations that govern it. This fact is very important if one keeps in mind that most of the equations are nonlinear and therefore their exact solutions are not known.

The number of papers dealing with neural networks as dynamical systems has increased rapidly over the last few years. So far most works deal only with neural networks of discrete valued neurons with symmetric weight couplings. Neural networks consisting of neurons with only two states have received particular attention, as these can easily be studied on the basis of the statistical theory of the Ising model and other models with properties similar to spin glasses [5,6]. There have been few theoretical explorations of the properties of analog networks and only little systematic comparison of these to their discrete counterparts has been undertaken. A recent notable exception is a work by Shiino and Fukai [7]. These authors have studied analog networks of the Hopfield type by using mean field models of spin glasses. As real neurons have a continuous input-output transfer function, the biological significance of the discrete models is not obvious [8]. How the transfer function affects the performance of the network is not clear as yet and therefore one does not know whether the difference between digital and analog neural networks is computationally significant. Nevertheless several authors have pointed out the benefits of analog computation in various applications [9].

Neural networks of spin glass type are not trained but rather their weight connections are fixed as linear combinations of the patterns to be stored by the network. The theoretical foundation of these networks is by now well understood. On the other hand, the network that has been most successful in software implementation for various recognition purposes is the MLP trained by the method of backpropagation developed by Rumelhart et al [10]. It therefore appears to be desirable to develop further the theory of these networks and in particular try to introduce time as a real variable. This approach leads us to treating neural networks as dynamical systems. A variety of neural models have been considered, but because of the aforementioned success of MLPs we will mainly restrict our study to those that present a 'natural' generalisation of MLPs. This point will be explained later.

Strictly speaking the method of backpropagation is only applicable to layered, feed-forward networks. An extension of this rule to networks with feedback was attempted by Rumelhart et al, with the result that unlimited amount of memory is required for each unit. Recently some authors have managed to derive a learning rule for recurrent networks with feedback which is local, i.e. the data needed for updating of the weight coefficients can be obtained from the units connected by the weights [11,12].

Recently some interesting results have been published by M Zak [13] where the concept of terminal attractors has been introduced into a dynamical theory of neural networks. Some aspects of these works will be discussed in this chapter and in particular the aspect that has to do with convergence towards states of infinite stability in a finite time. It appears that a proper implementation of these models could considerably improve training and avoid the problems of local minima.

In section 2 we discuss some basic properties of dynamical systems with emphasis on those aspects important for neural networks. Here we state briefly the theorem of Lyapunov which gives sufficient conditions for the system to converge towards states of equilibria. In section 3 we review some basic principles of neural networks and establish carefully a notation and a formalism essential for their treatment as dynamical systems. In section 4 we discuss some stability properties of dynamical networks and consider possible use of perturbation techniques. Section 5 discusses some properties of recurrent neural networks and in particular their nonlocality, and how it can be circumvented by the introduction of the associated dynamical system of Pineda. We further point out that Pineda's network is equivalent to some approximation of the initial network. Section 6 discusses briefly the various kind of attractors that can occur in a dynamical system. Terminal attractors as introduced by M Zak are the subject of section 7 but their incorporation into the dynamics of neural networks is discussed in section 8. In section 9 we show that MLPs can be viewed as a static limit of the dynamical systems considered in section 3. In section 10 we give a short review of some recent literature on the dynamical theory of neural networks. In section 11 we describe some of the experiments done so far and give the results.

2. DYNAMICAL SYSTEMS — A SHORT REVIEW

A dynamical system is generally formulated as a system whose time dependent quantities are described by vectors in some multidimensional space. These quantities can be anything needed to describe the quantitative behaviour of the system in question, ranging from the position of a particle in some physical space, to the electrical potential of a nerve or the concentration of some particular chemical compound within chemical reaction systems.

The dynamical system is at any given time t characterized by some multidimensional state vector $x(t) = (x_1(t), x_2(t), \ldots, x_n(t))$. The state vector which is a function of time is subject to differential equations which in the general case are of the form

$$\frac{dx_i}{dt} = f_i(x_1(t), \ldots, x_n(t); F(t); t). \qquad \ldots (1)$$

The last argument is to be included if the system has explicit dependence on time. F stands for any other external or internal variables that influence the dynamics of the system.

A state vector $x_c = (x_1, \ldots x_n)$ that satisfies the condition $\dot{x}_i = 0$ for each of its components is called a singular or a critical point of the dynamical system, described by equation (1). Singular points are also called stationary or equilibrium points as they present constant solutions to equation (1). Generally we will be interested in neural systems that gradually develop towards equilibrium points and therefore the study of the system's behaviour in the neighbourhood of x_c is of particular importance.

A mapping $\phi: R \to R^n$ from the time axis into the state space which satisfies

$$\frac{d\phi}{dt} = f(\phi(t)), \qquad \ldots (2)$$

is called a solution of equation (1). Usually the solutions to nonlinear dynamical equations are only known locally, i.e. in some surrounding $U(x_o)$ of a point x_o. An equilibrium point x_c is called stable if for every t_o and any $\epsilon > 0$ there exists a $\delta(\epsilon, t_o)$ so that $|x(t_o) - x_c| < \delta$ implies that $|x(t) - x_c| < \epsilon$ for all $t > t_o$. In other words a solution $x(t)$ that starts in some appropriate neighbourhood $U(x_c)$ of x_c stays in that neighbourhood for ever. The point x_c is called asymptotically stable if from $x_c \neq x(t) \epsilon U(x_c)$ it follows that $x(t) \to x_c$ as $t \to \infty$.

As mentioned we are particularly interested in the behaviour of the dynamical system described by equation (1) in the neighbourhood of critical points, rather than searching for global solutions, which in most cases is a very difficult and so far an unsolved problem. The local behaviour of equation (1) can be studied by linearising it in the critical points. To pursue this analysis we expand equation (1) in a Taylor series around x_o. Set $x = x_o + y$, then $\dot{y}_i = \sum_j \frac{\partial f_i}{\partial x_j}|y_j + O(y^2)$. With $\Omega_{ij} \equiv \frac{\partial f_i}{\partial x_j}|$ this takes the form of the linear matrix equation (we ignore higher order terms)

$$\dot{y}_i = \sum_{j=1}^{n} \Omega_{ij} y_j. \qquad \ldots (3)$$

To solve this equation one typically tries as solution

$$y_i(t) = y_{i,o} \exp(\lambda t), \qquad \ldots (4)$$

which after inserting into equation (3) leads to

$$\sum_{j=1}^{n} (\Omega_{ij} - \lambda \delta_{ij}) y_j = 0, \qquad \ldots (5)$$

where $\delta_{ij} = 1$ if $i = j$ and 0 otherwise. The problem is therefore reduced to finding the eigenvalues of the characteristic equation

$$|\Omega - \lambda I| = 0. \qquad \ldots (6)$$

I is the unity matrix. After the matrix Ω has been diagonalised as $\Omega_{ij} = \delta_{ij} \lambda_i$ the solution of equation (3) is given by

$$y_i(t) = \sum_{k=1}^{n} a_{ik} \exp(\lambda_k t), \qquad \ldots (7)$$

where the constants a_{ik} are fixed by the initial conditions. The characteristics of the motion are therefore determined by the values of the real parts of λ_i. The solutions define stable states if $Re\ \lambda_i < 0$ for all i and unstable states if $Re\ \lambda_i > 0$ for at least one index i. The case $Re\ \lambda_i = 0$ will correspond to oscillations of constant amplitude.

In this work we are mainly interested in neural networks as dynamical systems that converge towards some stable and time independent states. They are therefore dissipative systems that converge onto a lower dimensional state space volumes as time increases. The stability of a dynamical system can also be investigated without actually solving the differential equations (3) or the eigenvalue equation (5). A widely applied stability criteria is given by the following theorem of Lyapunov:

If x_c is an isolated critical point of the dynamical equation $\dot{x}_i = f_i(x_1, x_2, ..)$ then x_c is stable if in a neighbourhood $U(x_c)$ of x_c there exists a scalar positive definite function $V(x)$ so that $\frac{dV}{dt} \leq 0$. V is called a Lyapunov function of the system and we have $\frac{dV}{dt} = \nabla V \cdot \dot{x}$, by applying the chain rule.

In general there is no systematic way for constructing Lyapunov functions but a great number of interesting dynamical systems have a Lyapunov function associated with them. An example is given by the so called gradient systems whose dynamics are governed by equations of the form

$$\dot{x}_i = f_i(x_1, x_2, ...) = -\frac{\partial W}{\partial x_i}, \qquad \ldots (8)$$

from which we find

$$\frac{dW}{dt} = \sum_{i=1}^{n} \frac{\partial W}{\partial x_i} \dot{x}_i = -\sum_{i=1}^{n} \left(\frac{\partial W}{\partial x_i}\right)^2 \leq 0. \qquad \ldots (9)$$

The system therefore gradually evolves towards a stable state or an attractor and W plays the role of a Lyapunov function. The problem with most attractors, i.e. normal attractors, is that it takes the system a very long time to reach equilibrium and they are often not stable. Slight perturbation in the system's parameters, such as the weight connections, can drive the system out of these equilibrium states.

3. DYNAMICAL NEURAL MODELS — BASIC PRINCIPLES

So far most neural dynamical models considered are either restricted to a time dependence for the neural activation at fixed weight values (activation dynamics) or the neural activation is fixed in time and the weights allowed to evolve according to some nonlinear neural dynamics (weight dynamics). These equations are of the form

$$\dot{x}_i = F_i(x_i, w_{i1}, w_{i2}, ...), \qquad \ldots (10)$$

for neural dynamics with constant weights or

$$\dot{w}_{ij} = G_{ij}(w_{ij}, x_1, x_2, ...), \qquad \ldots (11)$$

for weight dynamics with constant activation levels.

For neural networks that are to be trained for certain recognition tasks both of these network models are likely to be far too restricted. We therefore study a more general model which describes the time evolution of the weights coupled with running neural activation dynamics. This option is far more complicated than models of pure activation or weight dynamics because in this case one has to study a set of highly nonlinear coupled differential equations.

The nonlinear elements which make up the neural network are the processing units associated with each neuron or node in the network. The neurons process signals received from other neurons in the network or from some external stimuli. If $x_j(t)$ is a time dependent variable which describes the activation level of the jth neuron in the network then the sum $\xi_i(t) = \sum_{j=1}^{n} \omega_{ij}(t) x_j(t)$ describes the input signal received by the ith neuron from other neurons in the network. The sum $\xi_i(t)$ may contain external stimuli as will be discussed. ω_{ij} is the weight connection between the ith and the jth neuron. As mentioned before the weights ω_{ij} are time dependent quantities just as the activation levels $x_i(t)$. The nature of this time dependence is model dependent and will be discussed later.

The processing done by the neurons is described by a nonlinear function f. For example the processing in the ith neuron maps the received input into the value

$$\xi_i(t) \rightarrow f_i(\xi_i(t)), \qquad \ldots (12)$$

which describes the activation level of the neuron after the processing has been done. The index i on the activation function indicates that the neural processing may vary from one neuron to another. If the neurons receive no inputs we assume that their activation levels decrease according to the simple exponential decay

$$x_i(t) = x_{i,o} \exp(-A_i t), \qquad \ldots (13)$$

where A_i fixes the decay rate and $x_{i,o}$ the initial activation level.

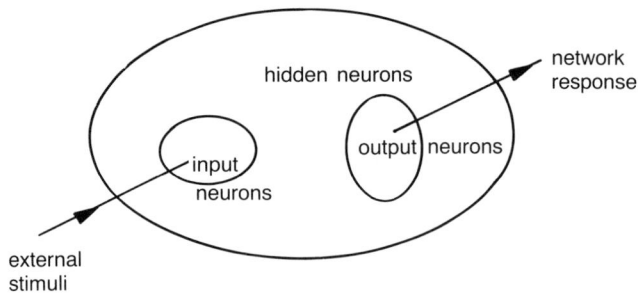

Fig. 1 Schematic picture of the network.

Even though we do not prefer to think of the network's neurons as having any particular geometrical arrangement, we do make distinction between three essentially different types of neurons. These are the input neurons I that receive signals or stimuli external to the network, the hidden neurons H that do the actual neural processing and the output neurons O whose activations measure the network's response to the external inputs. The inputs I_i only affect the input neurons directly and therefore $I_i = 0$ if $i \notin I$.

On the basis of these assumptions we assume that the time evolution of the activity of the ith neuron is governed by the differential equation

$$\dot{x}_i = -A_i x_i + B_i f_i(\sum_{j=1}^{n} \omega_{ij} x_j + I_i) = F_i(x, \omega), \quad \ldots (14)$$

where A_i and B_i are some positive constants and I_j presents the inputs to the network. The exact dependence of the neural processing on the variables ω_{ij} and x_j depends on the particular model considered, but in equation (14) it is assumed that the processing is nonlinear in both variables. This is by no means the case in all models as will be discussed below. The reasons for our particular interest in the model equation (14) is that its static limit, for a particular choice of weight connections, can be associated with feed forward networks of MLP type which have been subject to very extensive studies. The details of this static limit will be discussed in section 9.

Another model that has been studied extensively in the literature [14] is described by the dynamical equation

$$\dot{z}_i = -A_i z_i + \sum_j \omega_{ij} g(z_j) + I_i . \quad \ldots (15)$$

This model is simpler than equation (14) and has consequently been a favoured model amongst several theoretical researchers. The most obvious and significant difference between the two models is that the first is directly nonlinear in the weight connections and the latter only linear. However in the activation case, there is a relation between the two models which we will briefly discuss. By making the transformation (we assume for the sake of simple notation, that the x_j's have been redefined to include the external stimuli)

$$z_i = \sum_j \omega_{ij} x_j, \quad \ldots (16)$$

and assuming the existence of the inverse weight matrix ω_{ij}^{-1} equation (15) can be written as

$$\frac{d}{dt}(\sum_j \omega_{ij}^{-1} z_j) = -A_i \sum_j \omega_{ij}^{-1} z_j + B_i f(z_i). \quad \ldots (17)$$

Here we have had to assume that all the A_i's have the same value. Only if ω_{ij} is time independent can we multiply equation (17) by ω_{ij} to end up with

$$\dot{z}_i = -A_i z_i + B_i \sum_j \omega_{ij} f(z_j), \qquad \ldots (18)$$

which is an equation of the same structure as equation (15).

The reverse transformation from equation (15) to equation (14) is simple and will not be worked out in detail here. It is important to realise that equations (15) and (16) are only equivalent in activation dynamics where the weight connections are kept at constant values. In pure weight dynamics or even in combination of activation and weight dynamics the equations (15) and (16) present different systems.

In the most general case the external inputs I_i, $i\epsilon I$, would be time dependent functions of some known or unknown form. In this case it seems natural to introduce two timescales for the system, one which dictates the time dependence of the external stimuli and another timescale that describes the network's response (inertia with respect) to this stimuli. To be able to introduce some sort of training or recognition procedure it appears to be necessary to assume that the temporal changes in the external inputs are slow compared with the time it takes the network to respond to the inputs, i.e. settle in equilibrium. Given that this is the case, we assume that before the external inputs change considerably the network has enough time to settle in equilibrium states that are given by the equation

$$x_i^o = \left(\frac{B_i}{A_i}\right) f_i(\xi_i^o), \qquad \ldots (19)$$

with

$$\xi_i^o = \sum_{j=1}^{n} \omega_{ij} x_j^o.$$

As the external inputs are supposed to change on a far slower timescale than the network's activation we can consider the inputs to be at constant value in the timeperiod (interval) it takes the neurons to settle in equilibrium states. Consequently we can consider I_i in equation (14) to be a constant in the time period it takes the network to settle in states that satisfy equation (19). Only after making this basic assumption on the existence of stationary states are we in a position to define a learning algorithm which, by properly adjusting the weights ω_{ij}, forces the network to develop towards fixed desired outputs. The problem can be formulated as follows: we assume that at some time zero the network is in an initial state characterised by the activation vector x_o and the weight matrix ω_{ij}. Next the input nodes receive the input values I_i, $i\epsilon I$. The training procedure consists of continuously adjusting the weight connections so that the network evolves towards some stable state x_c whose values at the output nodes have the desired target values t. What we actually do is to move the equilibrium states towards some position close to the targets. The values of x_c along the hidden units are not required to develop towards any particular targets. For this purpose one defines an error function E which usually contains a quadratic function of the difference between the target and the actual output values of the output nodes. The simplest possible error function is therefore of the form

$$E(x_o) = \frac{1}{2} \sum_{j \epsilon O} (t_j - x_j^o)^2, \qquad \ldots (20)$$

where x_j^o is a solution to equation (19).

Even though this simple expression is the most commonly chosen error measure there are a whole variety of other possible choices for an error function which can be more efficient for training purposes of some particular neural models. One of these is of the general form

$$E = E(x_o) + \frac{1}{2} \sum_{ij} m_{ij} \omega_{ij}^2 + \sum_{ij} h_{ij} \omega_{ij}. \qquad \ldots (21)$$

Both the terms $\frac{1}{2} \sum_{ij} m_{ij} \omega_{ij}^2$ and $\sum_{ij} h_{ij} \omega_{ij}$ can be exploited to support locality of calculations [15]. The coefficients m_{ij} relate to the momentum term frequently used in simulation experiments on MLPs. Only in this general formulation is there a momentum matrix, i.e. a different value for the momentum rate for each weight connection.

Equations (14) or (15) cannot give a complete description of the neural dynamics as they do not include the temporal changes for the weights. Therefore our next step is to make some assumptions on the dynamics of the weights in the weight space. A learning process consists of minimizing the error and this can be achieved by the method of steepest descent. Here the weights evolve in weight space along paths that are directed antiparallel to the partial derivatives $\partial E / \partial \omega_{ij}$. Therefore the time evolution is given by the equations [12]

$$\frac{d\omega_{ij}}{dt} = -\eta \frac{\partial E}{\partial \omega_{ij}}. \qquad \ldots (22)$$

Here, $\eta > 0$ is the step or the learning rate and its magnitude determines the speed with which ω_{ij} changes in the opposite direction of $\partial E / \partial \omega_{ij}$. This equation generalises the method of steepest descent as it is applied in the backpropagation method of MLPs.

After the network has been initialised (i.e. after the initial values of the neural activations and the weights have been fixed), the dynamical behaviour of the neural network in response to the external stimuli $I_i(t)$, $i \epsilon I$, and under the constraint to develop towards the desired outputs t_i, $i \epsilon O$, is in principle completely described by the equations (14) or (15) and (22). These two equations constitute a set of coupled nonlinear equations which cannot, so far, be solved analytically. Note that equation (22) is a gradient system which, because of the Lyapunov theorem as discussed in section 2, gradually evolves towards an equilibrium. From the relation

$$\frac{dE}{dt} = \sum_{ij} \frac{\partial E}{\partial \omega_{ij}} \frac{d\omega_{ij}}{dt} = -\eta \sum_{ij} (\frac{\partial E}{\partial \omega_{ij}})^2 \leq 0, \qquad \ldots (23)$$

we see that the error function plays the role of the Lyapunov function. The stability of the weight dynamics is therefore guaranteed even though nothing has as yet been said about the stability of the reached equilibrium. The stability of the activation dynamics is a far more difficult issue and as far as we are aware no general criteria that guarantees its stability has been derived. Cohen and Grossberg [1] have constructed Lyapunov functions for some dynamical models and Hopfield [16] has proved that a symmetry condition on the weights guarantees stability for some models (see section 10).

4. STABILITY PROPERTIES OF NEURAL NETWORKS

In the previous section we showed that the weight dynamics are guaranteed to evolve towards equilibrium. In this section we discuss briefly how one can assess the stability properties of the activation dynamics.

When studying neural networks as dynamical systems several important questions related to stability have to be analysed. Only a few of them can be addressed here and those that we consider to be of a particular importance are the following.

- How does the stability of the network depend on the various network parameters?

- Are there any bifurcations present?

- Does the network possess attractors and what is their nature?

By performing the stability analysis of section 2 for the neural system

$$\dot{x}_i = -A_i x_i + B_i f_i (\sum_{j=1}^{n} \omega_{ij} x_j + I_i) = F_i(x, \omega), \qquad \ldots (24)$$

we end up with a matrix Ω of the form

$$\Omega_{ij} = (-A_i \delta_{ij} + B_i \sum_k \Lambda_{ik} \omega_{kj}) \, , \, \Lambda_{ik} = f'(x_{i,o}) \delta_{ik}. \qquad \ldots (25)$$

The eigenvalues therefore depend on the weights ω_{ij} which are functions of time and consequently the stability of a given point is a function of time.

It is beyond our present ambition to solve these equations analytically but it is in order to point out how one could proceed by applying perturbation techniques as they are frequently used in various fields in applied mathematics.

First we make the observation that the the matrix Ω is split into two parts, a diagonal component, $D_{ij} = -A_i \delta_{ij}$ and another which has only off diagonal elements $T_{ij} = B_i f'(x_{i,o}) \omega_{ij}$. This follows from the fact that the diagonal elements of the weight matrix have been put equal to zero to avoid neural self interaction. There are various ways of making the values of the matrix T small compared with the diagonal elements of D. First we can put $B_i < A_i$, secondly we can introduce a gain parameter (inverse temperature) in the argument of the activation function, i.e. replace the argument $\sum_j \omega_{ij} x_j$ by $(\frac{1}{\tau}) \sum_j \omega_{ij} x_j$. Then $f' = \frac{1}{\tau} f(1-f)$ when f is of the symoid type and therefore the derivative can be made smaller by increasing τ. Thirdly we can put some restrictions on the possible values of the weights that can evolve during the training process. Given that this can be done the zeroth order approximation for the time evolution of the locally linearized system is given by

$$x_i(t) = x_{i,o} \exp(-A_i t). \qquad \ldots (26)$$

If the matrix elements of T are far smaller than those of D we consider T as a minor disturbance and try to estimate its effects on the evolution of the neural system.

5. RECURRENT NETWORKS

The method of backpropagating error is, strictly speaking, only applicable to feed forward networks. Recently several authors [11,12,17] have discussed how the backpropagation method can be generalised in the presence of feedback.

In this section we discuss some properties of neural networks whose dynamics were discussed in the previous section. We assume that the neural activation dynamics are governed by equation (14) and that the weights develop according to an equation of the form equation (22). The two equations fix, in principle, the time evolution of the network totally. As a neural activation function we can consider any nonlinear function of the sigmoid type, for example

$$f(x) = \frac{1}{1+\exp(-x)} \text{ or } f(x) = \tanh(x). \qquad \ldots (27)$$

We start by evaluating the partial derivatives of the error function, which we will take to be of the form given by equation (20). Then

$$\frac{\partial E}{\partial \omega_{ij}} = - \sum_{j \in O} (t_j - x_j^o) \cdot \frac{\partial x_j^o}{\partial \omega_{ij}}. \qquad \ldots (28)$$

To further evaluate this expression we have to calculate $\partial x^o_j / \partial \omega_{kl}$. To do this we make use of the expression in equation (19). After some calculation we find (we have put $A = A_i$, $B = B_i$ for all i)

$$\frac{\partial E}{\partial \omega_{kl}} = - \frac{B}{A} \sum_j (t_j - x_{jo}) N_{jk}^{-1} f'(x_{ko}) x_{lo}, \qquad \ldots (29)$$

where N_{jk}^{-1} is the inverse of the matrix $N_{it} = \delta_{it} - \frac{B}{A} f'(x_{io}) \omega_{it}$.
The dynamical equations for the weights are therefore

$$\dot{\omega}_{kl} = \eta \frac{B}{A} \sum_j (t_j - x_{jo}) N_{jk}^{-1} f'(x_{ko}) x_{lo}. \qquad \ldots (30)$$

This learning rule can be difficult to implement as matrix inversion is computationally expensive. The inverse of N can be expanded as (in matrix notation)

$$N^{-1} = I + \sum_{n=1}^{\infty} (-1)^{n+1} (cF)^n, \qquad \ldots (31)$$

with $c = B/A$ and $F_{ij} = f'(x_{io}) \omega_{ij}$. In the case $|cF| \ll 1$ the expansion can be truncated without introducing too much error.

Pineda [11] has demonstrated how the weight updating can be made simpler but his method involves the introduction of an associated dynamical system. Here we only give a brief description of Pineda's method and refer to [12] for details. Pineda introduces a new variable z_j defined by

$$z_j \equiv \sum_n J_n N_{jn}^{-1}, \qquad \ldots (32)$$

with $J_n = (t_n - x_{o,n})$. It is a matter of simple calculation to show that these variables satisfy the evolution equation

$$\frac{dz_m}{dt} = J_m - \sum_j z_j N_{jm}, \qquad \ldots (33)$$

and that the learning rule associated with this system is given by

$$\frac{d\omega_{kl}}{dt} = \eta \sum_i \Lambda_{ki} z_i^o x_l^o. \qquad \ldots (34)$$

This learning rule does not include matrix inversion. At first glance Pineda's method appears to be rather obscure and it is not clear how the dynamics of the associated system relates to the dynamics of the system described by equation (14). But it can be shown that the learning rule in equation (34) is indeed identical to a learning rule derived from the first order approximation of the system equation (14). This has been pointed out by Almeida [11].

6. ATTRACTORS

So far we have briefly discussed the condition for a dynamical system to settle in an equilibrium. An equilibrium state is a special case of the more general concept of an attractor. An attractor is a set of states A in the system's configuration space so that all orbits close enough to the attractor converge towards it.

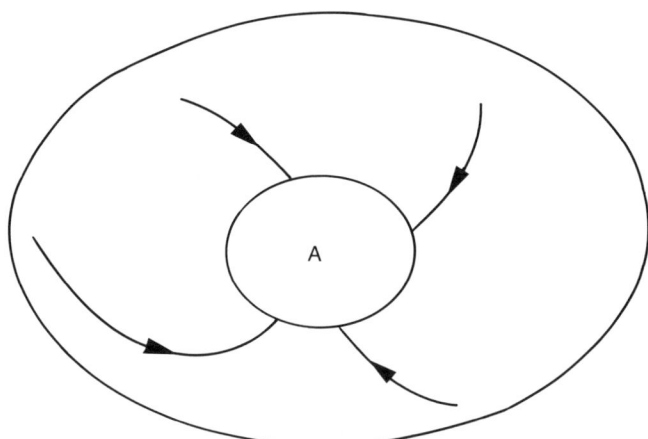

Fig. 2   Attractor.

In fact a whole variety of attractors with various different topologies can appear in dynamical systems. Some of these are:

(i) Point attractors. These are points towards which the system's trajectories converge given that they come close enough to the attracting point, Fig 3.

(ii) Cyclic or periodic attractors. After the system has reached the attractor set it can oscillate between two or more stable states. A formal presentation of this phenomenon is given by (35) and Fig 4.

(iii) Strange attractors. These attractor sets are typical for chaos, i.e. when the system has gone through a whole series of bifurcations. They will not be considered any further in this work.

$$\begin{aligned} x_i &= x(t_i) \\ x_i &= x_{i+n} \end{aligned} \qquad \ldots (35)$$

where n is the periodicity of the attractor.

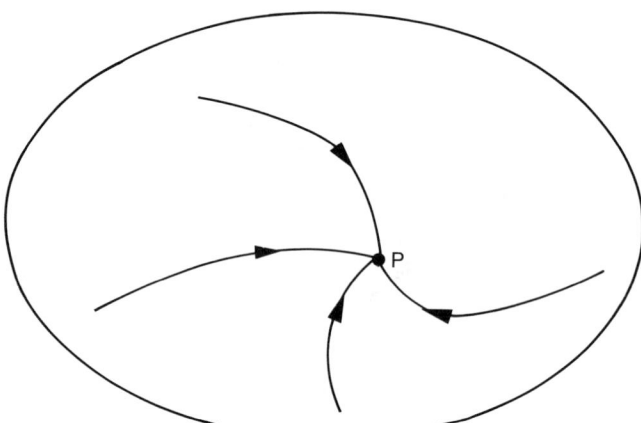

Fig. 3   Point attractor.

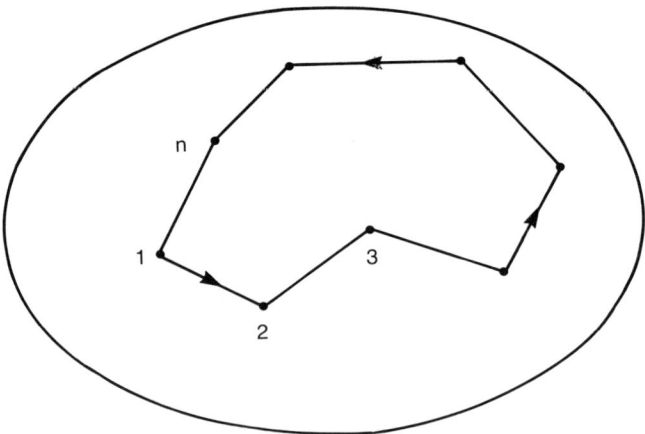

Fig. 4   Cyclic attractor.

For the training procedure adapted in this work only point attractors are of interest. This is not to say that periodic or even strange attractors are of no interest for neural networks. On the contrary, there is some evidence that chaotic processes could be of fundamental importance in the study of some psychological phenomena [18]. Whether the same is true for a deeper understanding and the application of neural network systems remains to be seen.

When dealing with differential equations the questions of the existence and uniqueness of their solution is of fundamental importance. An important condition for the existence and uniqueness of solutions is given by the Lipschitz condition.

A function $f(x)$ is said to satisfy the Lipschitz condition (LC) in a neighbourhood $U(x_o)$ of x_o if $|f(x)-f(x_o)| < L|x-x_o|$ where L is some finite constant, the Lipschitz constant.

One can prove the following statement. If the equations

$$\dot{x}_i = f_i(x_1, x_2, \ldots x_n), \qquad \ldots (36)$$

satisfy the LC in a neighbourhood $U(x_o)$ then these equations have unique, local solutions that for some t_o satisfy

$$x_i(t_o) = x_{i,o}. \qquad \ldots (37)$$

Here **local** means that the solutions cannot be extended to the whole state space and **uniqueness** means that two or more solution curves do not intersect. Solutions of this kind are termed ordinary solutions.

It is easy to see that the LC is always satisfied if the partial derivatives of $f_i(x_1, x_2, \ldots)$ with respect to x_j ($i,j = 1, \ldots, n$) are bounded on $U(x_o)$ i.e.

$$\Omega_{ij} \equiv |\partial f_i / \partial x_j| \le N < \infty, \qquad \ldots (38)$$

N positive constant. Let x_c be a critical point for the system (1), i.e. $f_i(x_c) = 0$. An important question in dynamical systems theory is: Let $U(x_c)$ be a surrounding (basin) that contains x_c. How long does it take the system, when it starts in $x_o \in U(x_c)$ to settle in x_c? The following statement can be proved. If equation (36) satisfies the LC in $U(x_c)$ then x_c can be reached from $x_o \ne x_c$ only for $t \to \pm\infty$, i.e. in its own time it takes the system infinitely long to settle in equilibrium.

7. TERMINAL ATTRACTORS

In 1988 Zak [13] demonstrated the existence of a different kind of attractors which he called 'terminal attractors' for reasons soon to become obvious. The origin of these peculiar attractors lies in the failure of the system's differential equations to satisfy the Lipschitz condition. In the presence of a terminal attractor the system's relaxation time becomes finite. As terminal attractors come about by the violation of the Lipschitz condition they can be built into the system by modifying its differential equations. Even though the concept of terminal attractors is new in the theory of neural networks they have been known to occur in various physical systems and have been described in the literature [19]. Usually they are associated with energy culmination effects, i.e. the culmination of energy density within a very small region of space. Here we would like to describe this effect in the case of waves propagating through some media. Let the speed of wave propagation be given by

$$v(x) = \frac{dx}{dt} = (x_s - x)^k, \qquad \ldots (39)$$

where k is some positive real number and x_s is a point in the medium where the speed is zero. The time T it takes for the wave to reach the 'stationary' point x_s from a starting point $x=0$ at $t=0$ is given by

$$T = \lim_{X \leftarrow x_s} \int_{x=0}^{X} \frac{dx}{(x_s - x)^k}. \qquad \ldots (40)$$

For $0 < k < 1$ we find that T is finite; that is the wave takes a finite time to reach the stationary point. For $k \geq 1$ however, the time taken to reach the stationary point is infinite. By examining equation (39) we see that $\frac{\partial v}{\partial x} = -k(x_s - x)^{k-1}$ which for $0 < k < 1$ converges towards $-\infty$ as x approaches x_s. Because of the results of the previous section this amounts to a violation of the Lipschitz condition in $U(x_s)$. Furthermore as discussed in section 2 the value of $\frac{\partial v}{\partial x}$ determines the stability of the system in x_s and if $\frac{\partial v}{\partial x} \to -\infty$, as $x \to x_s$, x_s is a point of infinite stability. The attractor becomes terminal.

The fact that terminal attractors are approached in a finite time is due to the violation of the Lipschitz condition which allows solution curves to intersect. This is demonstrated in the two pictures below. If $x_0 = 0$ is an equilibrium solution towards which the solution x_1 converges, Fig. 5 presents the case for ordinary solutions and Fig. 6 solutions that violate the Lipschitz condition. This violation allows the solution x_1 to intersect the solution $x_0 = 0$ which is necessary for the convergence time to be finite.

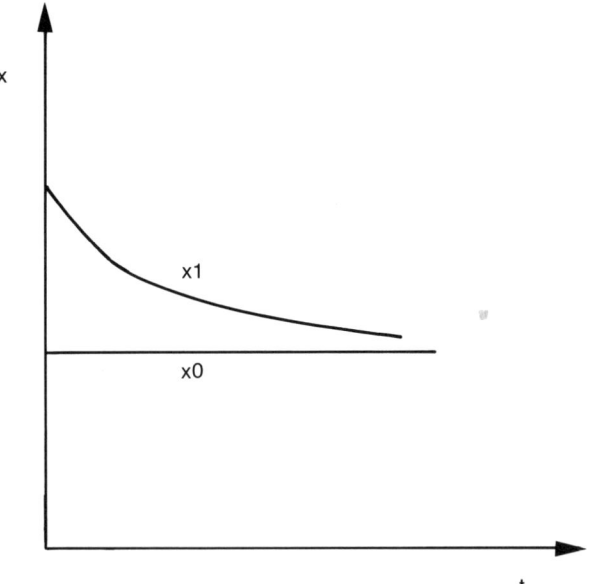

Fig. 5 Ordinary solutions.

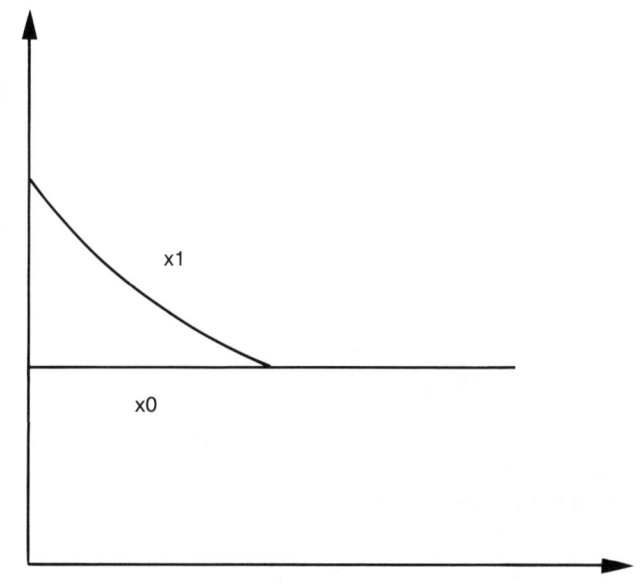

Fig. 6 Solutions that violate the Lipschitz condition.

8. TERMINAL ATTRACTORS IN NEURAL NETWORKS

We describe briefly the simplest neural model considered in [13]. It is a one neuron model described by the dynamical equation

$$\dot{x} + x = \omega f(x) - (x - x_0)^{\frac{1}{3}}. \qquad \ldots (41)$$

x is a variable that describes the neurons activation, ω is a constant and x_0 is the terminal attractor state we want the neuron to end in after a finite period of time. To this purpose the terminal attractor term $(x-x_0)^{\frac{1}{3}}$ is incorporated in the equation of motion. The activation function is of the sigmoid type, either $f(x) = \tanh(x)$ or $f(x) = 1/(1 + \exp(-x))$. Clearly to make x_0 a static state the coefficient has to satisfy the condition

$$\omega = x_0 / f(x_0). \qquad \ldots (42)$$

One easily calculates

$$\frac{d\dot{x}}{dx} = -1 + \omega \frac{\partial f(x)}{\partial x} - \frac{1}{3}(x - x_0)^{-\frac{2}{3}}, \qquad \ldots (43)$$

which implies $\frac{d\dot{x}}{dx} \to -\infty$ for $x \to x_0$, the system has infinite stability at $x = x_0$.

This neural model is deprived of all reality and is therefore only considered for pedagogical reasons. Now a generalisation of this model to more realistic neural networks will be considered.

The neural system we want to consider is governed by the dynamical equation

$$\dot{x}^a_i = -A_i x^a_i + B_i f(\sum_j \omega_{ij} x_j) + S^a_i. \qquad \ldots (44)$$

S^a_i is a source term put in to influence the network to develop towards one of its attractors. Let $x_{i,o}$ be an equilibrium point for this equation, i.e.

$$A_i x^a_{i,o} = B_i f(x^a_{i,o}) + S^a_i. \qquad \ldots (45)$$

To assess the system's stability in this point we expand equation (44) around $x_{o,i}$, $x_i = x_{o,i} + y_i$. (To avoid messy notation we drop the pattern index a.) We end up with the matrix equation

$$\dot{y}_i = \sum_{j=1}^{n} \Phi_{ij} y_j, \qquad \ldots (46)$$

where

$$\Phi_{ij} = -A_i\delta_{ij} + B_i f'(x_{i,o})\omega_{ij} + \frac{\partial S_i}{\partial x_j}. \qquad \ldots (47)$$

As discussed in section 2 the stability of the equilibrium point $x_{i,o}$ depends on the eigenvalues of the matrix Φ. To guarantee the existence of terminal attractors for the system described by equation (44) S_i has to be chosen so that the eigenvalues of Φ_{ij} approach $-\infty$ as x approaches x_o. This condition would give the equilibrium state x_o an infinite stability. We want all the equilibrium points of equation (44) to be equilibrium points of the initial equation (14) as well. To guarantee this S has to satisfy the condition $S(x,x_o) \to 0$ as $x \to x_o$. Choosing $S_i(x,x_o) = a_i(x_i - x_{i,o})^k$ will suffice. A simple calculation gives for Φ

$$\Phi_{ij} = (a_i k (x_i - x_{i,o})^k - A_i)\delta_{ij} + B_i f'(x_{i,o})\omega_{ij}. \qquad \ldots (48)$$

By assuming small values for the nondiagonal elements of Φ its diagonal elements can be taken as zeroth order eigenvalues. For $0 < k < 1$ they approach $-\infty$ as $x \to x_o$. The calculation can be extended without any difficulty to include a number of different patterns.

9. MLPs AS SPECIAL CASES OF GENERAL NETWORKS

As mentioned earlier, one reason for studying the dynamical models of the type given in equation (14) is that their static limit can, when certain restrictions have been put on the weights, be identified with feed forward networks. When the dynamical system shown in equation (14) has reached an equilibrium it is described by the equation

$$A_i x_{i,o} = B_i f_i \left(\sum_{j=1}^{n} \omega_{ij} x_{jo}\right) + I_i. \qquad \ldots (49)$$

Without restricting the generality of the arguments we put $A_i = B_i = 1$. To cast this equation into a feed forward equation of MLP type we start by arranging the neurons in layers $L_1,\ldots L_k$ where the number of neurons in the jth layer is given by n_j. The total number of neurons is $N = \sum_{j=1}^{k} n_j$. The next step is to put some rather strong limitations on the matrix entries ω_{ij} which initially is an arbitrary $N \times N$ matrix. First we put all the diagonal and upper diagonal elements in ω equal to zero. Then we arrange the nonzero elements into k-1 submatrices $\omega_1, \omega_2, \ldots, \omega_{k-1}$ of the dimensions $n_2 \times n_1$, $n_3 \times n_2, \ldots n_k \times n_{k-1}$ respectively so that the top right elements of all the submatrices lie in the first line below the diagonal of the main matrix ω. We end up with the following arrangement

$$\Omega = \begin{pmatrix} \omega_1 & & & \\ & \omega_2 & & \\ & & \ddots & \\ & & & \omega_{k-1} \end{pmatrix} \qquad \ldots (50)$$

With this new weight matrix it is easy to see that the system presents a network of the feed forward type. Initially the state vector of the neural network is given by a N-component vector $X = (x_1,\ldots,x_N)$ which describes the activation levels of the neurons. Split this vector into k ($=$ number of layers) vectors with $n_1, n_2, \ldots, n_k$ components each. We assume that only the first n_1 components have nonzero values $Y_1 = (y_1, 0, \ldots, 0)$. By applying Ω on this vector we receive a new vector $Y_2 = (0, y_2, 0, \ldots, 0)$ which has n_2 nonvanishing component values. This procedure can be repeated until we receive the vector $Y_k = (0, \ldots, y_k)$ with only n_k nonvanishing components. Here Y_1 represents the input vector to the MLP and Y_2 the input vector to the first hidden layer and so on. If a nonlinear activation function is applied on the input vectors, between the matrix multiplications this gives the well known 'repeated matrix multiplication' picture of an MLP.

10. SHORT REVIEW OF SELECTED LITERATURE

The first work we are aware of that studies the dynamical properties of neural networks formulated as Ising type related systems is that of M Y Choi and B A Huberman [20]. These authors studied the global dynamical properties of neural networks. They found an expression for the time dependence of the neural activity in terms of the system's master equation. The master equation gives the probability for the network being at the time t in some state $\alpha = (S_1, \ldots, S_N)$, where the neural variables S_i take on the discrete values $+1$ (for active) and -1 (for not active). The authors proved that the network displays a collective behaviour which can be either multiperiodic or deterministic chaotic.

In 1985 D J Amit, H Gutfreund and H Sompolinsky [21] developed further the spin glass models of neural networks. In their approach each neuron is assigned a potential $V_i = \sum_j J_{ij} S_j$ where $S_i \epsilon \{-1, +1\}$ and J_{ij} is the weight coupling, $J_{ij} = J_{ji}$ and $J_{ii} = 0$. The time evolution of the network is given by the simple equation $S_i(t+1) = \text{sign}(V_i(t))$. These models are able to store many patterns $\eta^\nu = (\eta_1^\nu, \ldots, \eta_N^\nu)$, $\nu = 1, \ldots, p$, as attractors in the two state neural system, if the weight couplings are chosen as $J_{ij} = \frac{1}{N} \sum_{\nu} \eta_i^{\nu} \eta_j^{\nu}$. The storage capacity was analysed by the authors and they proved that previous models developed by Hopfield [16] and Little [22] where indeed equivalent below the network's transition temperature. For details see [21].

The work of Amit et al. has been continued and improved by several authors. For example Sompolinsky and I Kanter [23] extended it to include asymmetric weight coefficients and proved that neurons connected asymmetrically had a slow dynamic response.

It appears somewhat strange that so much more emphasis has been put on the study of discrete models rather than their analog counterparts. The main explanation for this is probably due to the fact that most of these models can be studied in terms of well established physical theories such as statistical mechanics. Consequently these studies have mainly been done by theoretical physicists. As our work only considers neural networks as continuous dynamical systems we will not comment further on the development of neural networks as Ising spin type models.

Even though the theory of dynamical systems has been developed over the last 100 years its application to neural networks is rather new. Cohen and Grossberg [1] were the first to prove that dynamical neural networks can store stable content addressable memories. The underlying idea was to store the memory states as static attractors of the networks dynamics. These authors studied the dynamical system which describes the neuron's activation levels by the differential equations

$$\frac{dx_i}{dt} = a_i(x_i)(b_i(x_i) - \sum_j c_{ij} d_j(x_j)), \qquad \ldots (51)$$

$a_i \geq 0$ and $d'_j \geq 0$. For this system it can be assumed that $c_{ii} = 0$ since the term $c_{ii} d_i(x_i)$ can be absorbed into $b_i(x_i)$. These authors studied, by using the theorem of Lyapunov, the stability of this network and found that if the weights where symmetric, $c_{ij} = c_{ji}$, this system possesses the following Lyapunov function

$$V(x) = -\sum_{i=1}^{n} \int_0^{x_i} b_i(\eta) d'_i(\eta) d\eta + \frac{1}{2} \sum_{j,k} c_{jk} d_j(x_j) d_k(x_k). \qquad \ldots (52)$$

The Cohen and Grossberg model contains as a special case the Hopfield model

$$\frac{dx_i}{dt} = -\frac{x_i}{R_i} + \sum_j T_{ij} f(x_j) + I_i, \qquad \ldots (53)$$

and the Lyapunov function reduces to the one reported by Hopfield in [16]

Cohen [24] studied the so called 'shunting' networks which in their most general form are described by

$$\frac{dz_i}{dt} = -A_i x_i + (B_i - C_i x_i)\{I_i - f_i(x_i)\} - (E_i x_i + F_i)\{J_i + \sum_k G_{ik} g_k(x_k)\}, \quad \dots (54)$$

and proved that under certain conditions these models can engage in persistent oscillations. For details see [24,25]. This result disproved a conjecture made earlier by Cohen and Grossberg that shunting type networks could serve as content addressable memories.

Oscillations and stability in general are very important issues in the dynamical approach to neural networks. This question is not an issue in the usual MLP-implementation. The existence of a Lyapunov function always guarantees stability and so far a Lyapunov function has been found for a number of dynamical models. Almeida [11] has shown that a system of the type given in equation (14) has a Lyapunov function given that the activation function is strictly increasing and bounded and that the weights satisfy the condition $\alpha_j \omega_{ij} = \alpha_i \omega_{ji}$. For $\alpha_i = 1$, for all i, this is just the symmetry condition of Hopfield [16].

Hirsch [14] has derived mathematical results which allow him to prove the convergence of some interesting nets without making use of a Lyapunov function. He uses a theorem that goes back to Gerschgorin [26]. Unfortunately his results only apply to the neural dynamics where the weights are kept at constant values. Hirsch considers the system

$$\frac{dx_i}{dt} = -c_i x_i + \sum_j W_{ij} s_j(x) + I_i, \quad \dots (55)$$

and proves the following:

The system described by equation (55) is globally asymptotically stable, for any inputs I_i, provided there is a constant $g \geq 0$ such that for all i

$$0 \leq s'_i \leq g \text{ and } g(W_{ij} + \frac{1}{2}\sum_{ij}\{|W_{ij}| + |W_{ji}|\}) < c_i. \quad \dots (56)$$

But stability is not everything. As discussed in section 6 it takes a normal system a very long time to settle in equilibrium. Keeping in mind that the training procedure discussed in section 3 assumes that the network has reached equilibrium before the weight updating can be done it appears that training can take very long time. Furthermore neither the existence of a Lyapunov function nor the approach of Hirsch makes any statements about the stability of the degree of equilibrium states. These problems have been addressed by M Zak et al. [13].

Back in 1970 M Zak [19] introduced the concept of terminal attractor when studying the formation of supersonic snap at a free end of a filament suspended in a gravity and a centrifugal force field. The basic idea is to modify the dynamical equations, without shifting the position of the equilibrium states, so that the Lipschitz condition is violated in their vicinity. This makes the system's relaxation time finite and gives the equilibrium states infinite stability. Zak's motivation is mainly the possible construction of intelligent robots for industrial and military applications and other real time tasks. It is likely that terminal attractors could play an important role in the construction of trainable recognition systems.

Oscillatory and chaotic networks have been studied by many authors [27]. The treatment of Skarda and Freeman [18] is particularly interesting as these authors discuss how chaotic dynamics might be useful or even necessary in the neural system of some mammals.

Recurrent networks have been studied notably by Almeida [11] and Pineda [12], but there are other interesting studies of learning in recurrent networks by Rohwer and Forrest [17] and Jordan [28].

11. EXPERIMENTS

So far we have performed some initial experiments on a real world two-class classification problem. In this section we give a brief description of the data used, some of the implementation details and the results.

11.1 The data

The data consists of single utterances of the words 'yes' and 'no'. Part of the data is used for training and part for testing the network after it has been trained. The 'yes' training data contains 318 utterances and the 'no' training data contains 417 utterances. The 'yes' and the 'no' test data contain 301 and 319 utterances respectively. The data was collected by BT from national calls across the public switched telephone network. It consists of utterances from more than 700 people of different ages and sex. The same talker was never used for both training and testing data. Each utterance is represented by a 15 component feature vector derived from a segmentation of the utterance followed by a low order linear prediction analysis [29,30]. The values of the vector components lie in the interval ± 3.0.

11.2 Implementation

For the purpose of computer simulation we write the dynamical equations in a discrete form as follows

$$x_i(t+1) = (1-A_i)x_i(t) + B_i f(\sum_{j=1}^{n} \omega_{ij} x_j + I_i), \quad \ldots (57)$$

$$\omega_{ij}(k+1) = \omega_{ij}(k) - \eta \frac{\partial E}{\partial \omega_{ij}}. \quad \ldots (58)$$

Here we put the time step $\delta t = 1$. As mentioned earlier the time scale associated with the weight dynamics is nested within the time scale of the activation dynamics. To indicate this fact we use different letters, t and k, for the time variables in each equation. Only after the iteration in the activation leads to equilibrium states for the output nodes, do we update the weights according to the second equation.

After training, the weights and the activation values are stored for use in the testing phase. During testing the weights will not change but the activations will be updated according to the activation dynamics equation (57). The first test token is fed into the trained network and iterated until the activation values of the output nodes reach equilibrium. Then the performance is measured by recording the values of the output nodes. Before the second test token is fed into the net the activation values are reset to the values they had at the end of training. Now we iterate the second test token until the output neurons reach an equilibrium state and so on. In effect the neural activation levels only 'develop' as the net tries to recognize one particular test token.

11.3 Results

So far we have only run a few experiments and the best results were obtained for a fully connected network comprising 15 input nodes, a single hidden node and two output nodes. We randomised the weights in the interval $[-0.25, 0.25]$ and the activation levels in the positive interval $[0, 0.125]$. The equation parameters were set to the values $A_i = 1$ and $B_i = 0.5$ for all i. The updating was done after each input for a training period of 150 epochs. No momentum term was used and the learning rate had the value of 0.3.

For these parameter values and netsize we found the performance on the 'yes — no' data to be 91.7 % on the training set and 91.5% on the test set.

The best results for an MLP trained using conventional backpropagation so far reported on the 'yes-no' data, 95.2% occured with two nodes in the hidden layer [29]. This is better than the results achieved by the use of other classification techniques such as nearest neighbour (91.3%), Kohonen networks (92.0%) and Gaussian mixtures (93.2%) [28], but not as good as the results reported by the use of weight limited MLP (96.3%) [30].

12. DISCUSSION

This chapter has considered some basic properties of neural networks formulated as dynamical systems. We have worked towards the definition of neural networks as dynamical systems and deduced the behaviour of some neural models by analysing the equations used to describe them. A distinction was made between the activation dynamics that describe the activation levels of the neurons by fixed weights, and the weight dynamics that analyse the time evolution of the weights by fixed activation levels.

A realistic but more difficult model is the one that considers a synthesis of both models, i.e. a time dependent activation dynamics by varying weights. In this case the neural system is in principle described by a coupled dynamics of activation levels and weight connections. This leads to highly nonlinear equations that cannot be solved analytically.

The stability of this mixed dynamical system was discussed and we pointed out that the weight dynamics is always stable as it is described by a gradient dynamical system. The problems associated with the stability analysis of the activation dynamics were discussed. We derived a stability matrix whose eigenvalues determine the stability behaviour of the system in equilibrium points. The matrix's characteristic equation could either be solved by using numerical methods or by the use of perturbation theory. The latter is an easy option if some restriction is put on the possible weight values or the activation functions gain parameter (temperature).

We derived a learning rule for dynamical nets with a feedback, i.e. a total weight connection. The learning rule is difficult to implement in its generality as it requires a matrix inversion which is computationally very expensive. We therefore truncated the expansion of the inverse matrix which gave a good approximation for proper parameter values.

Terminal attractors were discussed, first in the general context but then within the framework of neural networks. We gave hints as to how terminal attractors can be incorporated into systems of the type given in equation (14) and how the resulting system, at least in first order approximation, leads to infinite stabilities in the equilibrium states.

In section 9 we showed how some of the dynamical models discussed lead to the well known feed forward networks in the static limit where some additional constraints are put on the weight connections.

In section 10 we gave a short review of recent literature on the dynamical theory of neural networks.

Section 11 discussed the implementation of dynamical networks, described the data used so far and gave the preliminary results on that data. The performance of the dynamical net is not as good as that of weight limited MLP, i.e. 91.5% as opposed to 96.3% on the test set, although there is potential for improvement.

To be able to improve the performance of dynamical networks it is essential to gain a better understanding of their dynamics and in particular their stability. This can only be done by performing extensive simulation experiments so that the stability of the net, as a function of the various parameters, can be assessed.

REFERENCES

1. Cohen M and Grossberg S: 'Absolute stability of global pattern formation and parallel memory storage by competitive neural network', IEEE Transactions on Systems, Man and Cybernetics, SMC-13, 815-826 (1983).

2. Grossberg S: 'Some nonlinear networks capable of learning a spatial pattern of arbitrary complexity', Proceedings of the National Academy of Sciences, 59 , 368—372 (1986).

3. Hirsch M W: 'Convergence almost everywhere', SIAM Journal of Mathematical Analysis, 16 , 423—439 (1985).

4. Hirsch M W and Smale S: 'Differential equations, dynamical systems, and linear algebra' New York, Academic Press (1974).

5. Sompolinsky H: 'Statistical mechanics of neural networks', Physics Today, December (1988).

6. Campbell C, Sherrington D and Wong K Y M: 'Statistical mechanics and neural networks', in Neural Computing Architectures, ed I Aleksander, North Oxford Academic (1989).

7. Shiino M and Fukai T: 'Replica-symmetric theory of nonlinear analogue neural networks', J Phys A: Math Gen 23 L1009—L1017 (1990).

8. Toulouse G: 'J Phys A:Math Gen 22, 1959 (1989).

9. Marcus C M, Waugh F R and Westervelt R M: 'Associative memory in an analog iterated-map neural network', Phys Rev A 41, 3355 (1990)

10. Rumelhart D E, Hinton G E and Williams R J: 'Parallel Distributed Processing', MIT Press, Cambridge, Ma (1986).

11. Almeida L B: 'A learning rule for asynchronous perceptrons with feedback in a combinatorial environment', IEEE First International Conference on Neural Networks, San Diego, California June 21-24 (1987).

REFERENCES 437

12. Pineda F J: 'Generalization of Backpropagation to Recurrent Neural Networks', Phys Rev Lett 59, 2229 (1987).

13. Zak M: 'Terminal attractors for addressable memory in neural networks', Phys Lett A 133, 18, 1988 and 'The least constraint principle for learning in neurodynamics', Phys Lett A 135, 25 (1989).

14. Hirsch M W: 'Convergent Activation Dynamics in Continuous Time Networks', Neural Networks 2, 331—349 (1989).

15. Barhen J, Gulati S and Zak M: 'Neural Learning of Constrained Nonlinear Transformations', Computer-IEEE, June, 67—76 (1989).

16. Hopfield J J: 'Neurons with graded response have collective computational properties like those of two-state neurons', Proc Natl Acad Sci, USA, 81, 3088 (1984).

17. Rohwer R and Forrest B: 'Training Time-Dependence in Neural Networks', IEEE First International Conference on Neural Networks, San Diego, California, June 21-24, Vol II, p 701 (1987).

18. Skarda C A and Freeman W: 'How brains make chaos in order to make sense of the world', Behavioral and Brain Sciences, 10, 161—195 (1987).

19. Zak M: 'Uniqueness and Stability of the Solution to a Filament With a Free End', Applied Math and Mech, 34 (6) 1048—1054, (1970).

20. Choi M Y and Hubermann B A: 'Dynamic Behaviour of Nonlinear Networks', Phys Rev A 28, 2, 1204—1206 (1983).

21. Amit D J, Gutfreund H and Sompolinsky H: 'Spin-glass models of neural networks', Phys Rev A, 32, 1007 (1985).

22. Little W A: 'The existence of persistent states in the brain', Math Biosci 19, 101—120.

23. Sompolinsky H and Kanter I: 'Temporal Association in Asymmetric Neural Networks', Phys Rev Lett 157, 22, 2861—2864 (1986).

24. Cohen M A: 'The Stability of Sustained Oscillations in a Symmetric Cooperative-Competitive Neural Networks', Neural Networks, 1, 217—221 (1988).

25. Cohen M A: 'The stability of Sustained Oscillations in Symmetric Cooperative-Competitive Networks', Neural Networks, 3, 609—612 (1990).

26. Noble B and Daniel J: 'Applied Linear Algebra', Englewood Cliffs, NJ: Prentice Hall (1988).

27. Elias S A and Grossberg S: 'Pattern formation, contrast control, and oscillation in the short term memory of shunting on-center of-surround networks', Biological Cybernetics, 56, 139—150 (1975).

28. Jordan M J: 'Attractor dynamics and parallelism in a connectionist sequential machine', Proceedings of the Eighth Annual Conference of the Cognitive Science Society, 531—546 (1987).

29. Woodland P C and Smyth S G: 'An experimental comparision of connectionist and conventional classification systems on natural data', Speech Communication, 9, 73—82 (1990).

30. Woodland P C: 'Weight Limiting, Weight Quantisation and Generalisation in Multi-Layer Perceptrons', First IEE International Conference on Artificial Neural Networks, p 297, London 16-18 October (1989).

Index

A-set   132, 135, 179
Activation function   41, 54–6, 69, 82, 137, 236, 250, 300, 304, 314–29, 354–7, 416–32
ADU   373–8
Ainsworth, W A   256
Alphabet   132, 135–46, 161–74, 178–90, 290
Amorphous silicon   291
Analogue technology   291
Analogue weight   291
Andrews, E C J   160
Architecture(s)   289–92, 293–300, 312–29, 331–46, 349, 350, 383
Associative memory   6, 205, 313, 389, 399, 400, 402
Associative net   100
Atomic data units, see ADU
Attractors   415, 420, 423, 430
  periodic   424
  point   425
  static   431
  strange   424, 425
  terminal   410, 412, 426, 428, 429, 433
Auto-scaling   301, 304, 310, 324

Backpropagation, backprop   14, 22–3, 50, 68, 94, 108, 138, 148–9, 158, 180, 205, 290–1, 293–4, 297–8, 303, 312–7, 321–3, 328, 353, 410–12, 419–21, 434
Bar coder   308, 309
Barnes, N   330
Bishop, J M   370
Boltzmann machine   50, 194, 315
Breath group   279, 286
Broadcast parameters   361, 362
Brown corpus   232

Central pattern generator   390

Centre-surround   98, 108
CFG   199, 203–5, 213–18, 366
Character recognition   303, 306, 307
Chi-Square test   79, 90
CNLP   193, 194, 195, 198, 199, 235
Computer vision   8, 112, 113
Confusion matrix   172, 179, 188
Connected speech   162, 177, 190
Connectionist natural language processing, see CNLP
Connectionist project   3
Constraint satisfaction   194, 197, 370, 373
Content addressable memory   399, 431
Context free grammar, see CFG

DCG   218–20
Debenham, R M   50
Definite clause grammar, see DCG
Delta-rule   96, 97, 106–8
Dendogram   247–9
Difference of Gaussians (DOG)   94
Directory access demonstrator   145
Distributed representation   149, 155, 158, 194, 195, 205
Dithering   301, 310
Double-sided epitaxy (DSE)   335
DTN   204, 350–67
DTW   131, 135, 143, 144, 189
Dynamic range   289–91, 293–304, 310, 324
Dynamical properties   410, 430
Dynamic time warping, see DTW
Dynamic topology net, see DTN

E-set   132, 135, 162, 165, 171–3, 179, 180
Early vision   9, 353
Ellacott, S W   65

INDEX

Endpoints, endpointing 140, 144–6, 177, 179, 180, 186, 189, 191
Entropy coder 309, 310
ERCE 55, 56, 63
Error backpropagation *see* Backpropagation, backprop
Euclidean distance 88, 152, 153, 156, 237, 241–3, 252, 253, 258
Evans, M R 65
Excitatory synpase 392, 396, 404
EXOR (exclusive-or) 336, 337, 345
Extended restricted Coulomb energy, *see* ERCE
Eye-location 9

Facial features 11, 30, 65
Fast Fourier Transform, *see* FFT
Feature detectors 13, 14, 19, 21, 23, 27, 28, 65, 106, 371, 372
Feature vector 23, 141, 164, 307, 433
FFT 107, 109, 131, 140, 145
Finite wordlength 293, 294, 304, 310, 323–5
Fixed point arithmetic 293
Formants 129, 130, 148
Fourier holograms 335, 341
Functional compositionality 199, 235, 326, 250

Gabor function 106, 112, 117
Ganglion 389, 390
Garth, S C J 50
Gated filtering 108, 110
Gaussian pyramid 102
Grammar 190, 194–9, 204–32, 366
Grammaticality determination 204–32

Hand, C C 65
HANNIBAL 293, 311–28
Hardware implementation 290, 291, 294, 298, 315, 346
Healey, P 330
Heteroassociative net 97, 98
Hidden Markov model, *see* HMM
Hierarchical perceptron feature locator, *see* HPFL
Hierarchical training 85
Higher order nets 21, 199, 203–8, 365
HMM 131, 144, 162, 178, 181, 185, 189, 191

HODYNE 205–32
HPFL 13, 20–9
Hutchinson, R A 13
Hyperplane fitting 34

Image analysis 2, 7, 9, 10
Image classification 112, 113, 117, 121, 125
Image coding 6
Image compression 5, 6, 10
Image enhancement 7
Image feature location 13
Image processing 5, 7, 10, 58, 63, 93, 121, 351
Image replication 342, 343, 345
Image test problems, *see* Test problems
Incremental training 44, 209, 210, 230
Indium phosphide 334
Inhibitory 356, 389, 390, 392
Inhibitory network 397
Inhibitory synapses, inhibitory weights 394, 396, 404
Integer arithmetic 293
Intonation 279, 286, 287
Irregular words 264–67

Kohonen 6, 14, 16, 51, 101, 102, 104, 105, 108, 109, 158, 435

Laplacian pyramid 94, 95, 106, 107
LBG 6, 7
Learning rate 38–41, 57, 689–91, 102, 139, 151, 157, 239, 257, 298, 317, 327, 419, 434
Least squares fitting 45
LED, light emitting diode 331, 333, 335
Linear predictive coding *see* LPC
Linggard, R 129, 388
Lipschitz condition 425–7, 433
Liquid crystal 333, 335, 342
Lisboa, P J G 112
London-Lund corpus of spoken English 232
LPC 129–34

Machine vision 8, 10, 381
Mason, J S 160
Matrix-vector product 331, 332
McKee, P 330
Median filtering 66, 121, 122
MFCC 132, 140, 141, 143, 145, 184, 186

Minchinton cells   383, 384
Minimum energy   389, 398
Miss America   15, 16, 93
MLP training, see Backpropagation
MLP training times   30
Model head   10
Momentum   91, 139, 140, 151, 157, 239, 257, 281, 298, 317, 419, 434
Morphological pre-processing   272
MQW (multiple-quantum-well)   331, 334, 335, 337, 338, 339
Multilayer perceptron, see MLP
Multi-resolution   13, 19, 20, 29, 65, 66, 67, 77, 78, 85, 94
Myers, D J   1, 13, 289, 312

Natural language processing
Natural language test problems, see Test problems
Nightingale, C   1, 5, 203, 349, 353
NLP   1–3, 134, 193–9, 203–32, 235–354, 369
Node creation   360
Node processor   315, 316, 317, 318, 323, 326
Node sequence network   388–409
Noise removal   94, 96, 106, 107, 109
NPA   238–53

O'Neill, A W   330
Olafsson, S   410
Optical emitter   331
Opto-electronic   290, 292, 330–46
Order sensitivity   352, 364
Orrey, D A   312
Oxford Alvey Vowel Database   158

Parse, parsers, parsing   185, 190, 193, 195, 204–31, 237
Pattern completion   196
Perceptually based linear prediction, see PLP
Periodic Attractor   424
Perturbation theory   435
Phoneme   130, 131, 257–61, 263, 267–71, 274, 285
Phoneme string   257
Phonemic representation   256, 276, 287
Pipeline communication, pipeline processing   318, 321, 322, 328

Pixel expansion   24, 26, 27, 28
PLP   162, 163, 167, 170, 172, 174
Point attractor   425
PRBS   303
Principal components, analysis   30, 34, 38, 40, 43, 44, 45, 47
Projected weights   72, 73, 75, 76
Pronunciation of clock times   276
Psuedo-random binary sequence, see PRBS
Psychological modelling   198

Quad tree   66, 86, 87
Quantization error   295

RBF   14, 50, 51
RCE   51, 53, 54, 55, 56
Receptive field   97, 98, 99, 100, 103, 150, 151, 152, 154, 156
Recursive structure   194
Refractory period   390
Rejman-Greene, M A Z   330
Residual, LPC residual   130, 132, 133, 134
Retinocentric, retinocentric cell, retinocentric feature   371, 372, 373

Scott, E G   330
Segmentation   113, 178–91, 286, 307, 433
Sequential firing   396, 402, 403
Sharkey, N E   235
Sigmoid   41, 51, 69, 82, 145, 244, 250, 296–9, 308, 325, 421, 428
Simulated annealing   194, 205, 292, 340, 349
Singular point   413
Smith, L S   148
Smyth, S G   177
Soft preference rules   199, 235–51
Spatial frequency   94, 101, 105, 106, 117
Spatial pruning   24, 25, 26, 27
Spatiotemporal filter   7, 93, 100
Spatiotemporal image   93
Speaker independent speech recognition   136–46, 148, 155, 163–71, 178, 191
Speaker recognition   160, 163, 165, 174, 175

Speech coding   133
Speech processing   129, 130, 132
Speech processing test problems   132
Speech recognition   131–4, 135–46, 153, 162–6, 171, 204, 364, 410
Speech synthesis   130, 134, 146, 272
Speech test problems, *see* Test problems
Spin glass   411, 430
Stability criteria   376, 410, 414
Static attractor   431
Stochastic diffusion   377–81
Stochastic net   351, 370–87
Stochastic search   351, 370–7, 382–7
Stochastic search network   381
Strange attractor   424, 425
Sub-word unit   131, 178–88, 191
Surveillance   2, 8
Syllable boundary   257, 267–71
Synapse   158, 291, 294–300, 308, 310, 318, 340, 389, 390–96, 403–5
Syntactic category   214, 2225, 279–86
Syntactic constraints   193, 239
Syntax   190, 191, 194, 203

Tang, C   148
TDNN   161, 162
Temporal pruning   24, 26, 27, 28, 29
Terminal attractor   410, 412, 426, 428, 429, 433
Test problems
  natural language
    grammaticality recognition 203–34
    preference rules   235–5
    text-to-phoneme   256–88
  speech
    alphabet recognition   135–47, 160–76
    speaker recognition   160–76

vowel recognition   148–59
syllable boundary detection   256–88
vision
  eye-location   13–92, 112–28
  mouth-location   13–29
  noisy image sequence   93–111
Text-to-speech   130, 199, 256, 257, 272, 279, 280, 285, 286
Thermometer coding   382
Time delay neural network, *see* TDNN
Torr, P   370

Vector quantisation   6
Very large scale integration, *see* VLSI
Videophone   8
Vincent, J M   13, 293, 312
Vision test problems, *see* Test problems
Visual cortex   117
Visual nervous system   116, 117
Viterbi algorithm   183, 184, 185, 190
VLSI   290–3, 312, 318, 331
Vocoder   129, 130, 148
Vowel quadrilateral   148–152, 155–7
Vowel recognition   148
VPA, verb-phrase attachment   238, 242–50, 253

Waite, J B   30
Warren, N P   256
Webb, R P   330
Weight analysis   82
Weight storage   291, 310, 321, 323
Wood, D C   330
Woodland, P C   135
Wright, M J   93
Wyard, P J   193, 203

Yes/no test problem   133, 213, 307